The Motorcycle Yearbook

2001

CHRONOSPORTS

GSN

A more powerful energy
An invisible energy
An inexhaustible energy

THE TELEFÓNICA MOVISTAR TEAM HAS TRANSFORMED THE WORLD CHAMPIONSHIP.

Toni Elías, Daniel Pedrosa and Joan Olivé have given us the best in 125cc motorcycling. They've demonstrated a new way of racing full of youth, daring and bravery. And they've shown they're united by the same spirit.

Telefónica

The Motorcycle Yearbook

2001

PHOTOS
Stan Perec

∞

TEXTS
Jean-Claude Schertenleib

CHRONOSPORTS

GSN

Contents

Contributors :

GSN Publishing Manager Diane Michiels

English version Sheona Dorson-King
Mark Dorson-King

Marketing Judith Tomaselli

● ISBN 2-940125-91-0
"The Motorcycle Yearbook 2001" is also published in French under the title "L 'Année Grands Prix Moto 2001" (ISBN 2-940125-78-3)

● © 2001, Chronosports GSN Publishing :
GSN : Bldv. Louis Schmidt 119, B-1040 Brussels, Belgium. Tel (+32 2) 743 26 46 - Fax (+32 2) 743 26 41
Chronosports : Jordils Park, Chemin des Jordils 40, CH-1025 St-Sulpice, Suisse. Tel (+41 21) 697 14 14 - Fax (+41 21) 697 14 16

● Photoengraving : Snel Graphics, Liège

● Layout: Bruno Senny – NIG, Brussels

Foreword

A Euro-friendly product

The "Motorcycle Grand Prix Yearbook 2001-2002" which you have in your hands is published in two languages: French and English. Its price is now fixed in Euros. And its contents, thanks to a few champions and extraordinary technicians, are very Euro-friendly.

The 125cc World Champion is Manuel Poggiali, a rider from the Republic of San Marino, riding a bike – the Italian Gilera, like its twin sister, the Spanish Derbi – created by an Austrian engineer, Harald Bartol.

The 250cc World Champion is Japanese. Riding a Japanese Honda. Oops, that takes us a long way out of Europe. But not really, because behind this triumph and Daijiro Katoh's total domination is an Italian team – managed by double World Champion, Fausto Gresini – and Spanish sponsorship. And don't forget that Katoh lives for half the year on the Adriatic coast.

The 500cc World Champion is Italian. And what an Italian: Mr Valentino Rossi, the second Mr 875 in history (like Phil Read, Rossi has won world titles in 125cc, 250cc and 500cc), a world phenomenon who lives in London and who attracts crowds in the four corners of the earth. And in each port of call on the European continent.

We could go on with this list ad infinitum: the Italian make Ducati dominated world superbike, the Kawasaki team that is based in Germany won the Supersport title, etc.

The history of Grand Prix racing, created on the Old Continent after the War (in 1949), a direct descendant of an international competition that went by the name of "European Championship" is marked by important periods. From the Italian/British domination to the appearance of the Japanese makes, from the Japanese withdrawal to its triumphant return, from the Agostini era to that of the American riders, started by a certain Kenny Roberts, the modern GPs are the absolute internationalisation of the show, with ever increasing races overseas.

At the start of the third millenium and as Valentino Rossi has just won the last ever 500cc world crown – from next year onwards, the main category will be open to machines powered by four-stroke engines and will be known as MotoGP – road racing is more than ever a Euro-friendly product. You just need to leaf through the next 200 pages to discover that in addition to the Japanese giants of Honda and Yamaha, there are numerous European projects for the future. A glance at the sixteen races and the thousands of exploits and a study of the results in the secondary championship, go to show that for many years to come, European riders and teams seem set to hold centre stage.

Which is by no means unwelcome to the team at "The Motorcycle Yearbook", the only annual on the market printed in two essential languages. Totally Euro-friendly, as we've just explained!

Jean-Claude Schertenleib

The Champions

500^{CC}

A born showman, the World Champion was a veritable phenomenon.

Alone in front out on his own, all the rest could do was to follow in his wake: Valentino Rossi's 2001 season in one image.

Life after GP ? Maybe rally car racing.

Rossi,
the triumph of a phenomenon

Rossi in his Hawaiian colours. This was taken at the Mugello circuit before the Italian GP.

Graziano Rossi, Valentino's father. "Sometimes I have the impression that I am older than him" said Valentino "when I hear about some of the things he gets up to."

Thanks to him, motorcycle racing has broken out of its specialist niche. Thanks to him, his talent, the quality of his races, but especially his way of life, of playing with the others, of inventing a particular scenario for each occasion, of permanently smiling to the camera, GP broadcasts now reach audiences close to Formula One and football. In all the countries in Europe and overseas where motorcycling exists, the Rossi phenomenon marches on. Rossi is the favourite in Italy, of course, but also in Germany, Great Britain, France and even Spain. Not to mention Japan and Australia and the yellow caps and T-shirts that appear in the grandstands in Malaysia, Brazil and South Africa. Rossi is a phenomenon who at the age of just 22 has joined Phil Read in the history books with three world titles in 125, 250 and 500cc. Valentino Rossi is a genius who never seems to take himself seriously, but who works tirelessly. He is a perfectionist, a Champion with a capital C. In the great history of motorcycle racing, there will be the before and after Rossi!

- One year to learn, then one year to win. What is the Rossi recipe?

> - I don't have one. If I could have avoided the mistakes I made in 1996, 1998 and 2000, I would have tried to win straight away. My first season in 125 was also my first in GP racing and I had lots of things to learn. Then afterwards, in 250 in 1998 and then 500 in 2000 I finished second in the championship in my first year in the category. There wasn't much lacking for me to achieve success immediately, just a little experience with the bike and the team.

- And what if you hadn't won the title in the second year?

> - I would have come back for another season. At the end of 1996, Aprilia offered me a works 250. I refused, because I first wanted to win the 125 title. Even my father thought I was crazy. It was the same in 1999. I waited to win the 250 title before giving my reply to Honda for the 500. If I had changed category without winning the title, I would have felt there was unfinished business.

- Three titles – do they bring the same enjoyment?

- *The same satisfaction of having reached my goal. There are of course differences in terms of the emotions. 500cc remains the ultimate challenge for a motorcycle racer. It requires a lot of work to master all the components and the pressure is very intense. In 125, it's more of a game. The settings are not too important, what matters is opening the throttle. 250 is more similar to 500, because set-up becomes important as does tyre management.*

"THE MONTH OF JULY WAS DIFFICULT"

- What was the most difficult thing during the 2001 season?

- *After the first three grand prix, everyone was already considering me the World Champion and that was fairly disruptive. I had difficulties concentrating even though I knew the season had only just begun. The month of July was difficult. We had three races close together and I had to take part in the Eight Hours of Suzuka after problems in Germany. Problems that gave Biaggi the edge..*

- The best memories?

- *I won two very important victories. In Brno I got back on track after a disastrous outing in Germany. This victory also allowed me to open up a strong lead over Biaggi who had closed right in. But my finest win was in Donington. I had big problems in practice and I started from the third row. That race was one of the best of my career.*

The horsebreaker in action.

- What about the pressure with Max and Capirossi?

- *You have to live with it. Three Italians, several times World Champion, who are battling for the same goal. It's bound to arouse excitement. Not to mention the stories fabricated by Italian journalists who are more interested about what happens on Sunday evening than during the race. And who invent a large proportion of what they write.*

- Before the Catalunyan GP, Rossi was the goodie and Biaggi the baddie. Afterwards the roles seemed to have been reversed. True or false?

- *Outside of Italy, I'm the goodie and he's the baddie. But at home you have to remember that it was always the opposite. In Barcelona, Biaggi was very clever with the journalists again. I won the race after being fifteenth on the first corner. So who was the most tense at the finish, him or me? Personally, I was calm and happy...*

- In Suzuka, Biaggi committed a flagrant foul. In 1998, Capirossi torpedoed Harada in Argentina to take the 250 title. Out of the three top riders in 500, is Rossi the only one to act as a gentleman in the race?

- *I don't know. In order to win, you need to be aggressive. The question is knowing the limits. I always forced myself to do it. Sometimes I get angry with the riders that stick in the middle of the track, but I have never made any suspect manoeuvres like Biaggi or Capirossi. But although it's true there are things that you shouldn't do, when he closes his visor on the starting grid, a rider is no longer the same person.*

- Was the Honda better than the Yamaha this season?

- *In 2000, we had a major handicap in terms of top speed. In the second half of the season, I couldn't even stay in the slipstream of the Yamaha. The HRC engineers took note and worked throughout the winter. This year, I think the bikes were more equal. Biaggi raced some fine races and claimed several pole positions.*

- What is the team's role in your success?

- *A larger role than that of the bike. On a technical and human level, I have great support. The most important thing is to work with people who stay calm whatever happens. Even if we have some problems, no-one gets irate. That's fundamental. Since the German GP, the level of collaboration is even better than ever. We have modified our working methods which were too close to those that worked for Doohan, who was a fairly conservative rider. I need to try more things out than he does.*

"DOOHAN WORKS FOR HONDA."

- Let's talk about Doohan's role.

- *Mick works for Honda, not for Valentino Rossi. He spends more time in my garage than the other Honda riders because my team is his old one. In any case, our riding styles are very different and what worked for him doesn't necessarily do so for me.*

- Is Valentino Rossi capable of winning five titles in a row like him?

- I'm not sure I have enough motivation. I need to fix myself new challenges every time. After my 125 title, I went into 250, then 500. I took part in the Eight Hours of Suzuka because I wanted to win it and now that I have done, I know I won't do it again. Next year is a new story with four-strokes. Afterwards we'll see what happens. I might do some car rallies. To be honest, I don't know at the moment.

- Is 2002 RCV for Valentino Rossi?

- I talked with the HRC bosses for a long time in Motegi and they made me understand how important this new machine is for them. They are convinced it will be competitive in its very first GP. At present, I've only completed a few laps in Suzuka with it on a track that was partially damp. So I haven't had time to form a real opinion. What worries me most, is that some very good riders will still be riding two-stroke 500s next year. If the bike is not up to scratch it will be difficult to mount an offensive.

- How do you explain the phenomenon of Rossimania that has become international?

- I think a sportsman can only be popular if he gets good results. It's the basis. After that, if people like him and thinks he's approachable, it's even better. The fact that I'm only 22 also appeals to a lot of young people too because they can identify with me. One thing is certain, I try to stay how I am and not to take myself too seriously!

- Is Valentino Rossi the same today as he was in 1997 when he won his first title?

- No of course not. Life changes so do people. When I won the 125 title, racing was only a game for me. Today, the stakes are different, and the pressure is higher. I have also grown up. I have learnt about jealousy, rancour and that my exuberance could be misunderstood. Nowadays when I win a race, I prefer to celebrate more discreetly on the Sunday evening in a restaurant with my team.

Identity Card

NAME: ROSSI.

FIRST NAME: VALENTINO.

BORN ON 16 FEBRUARY 1979.

IN URBINO (PESARO/ITALY).

FIRST RACE: 1992.

FIRST GP: MALAYSIAN GP, 1996 (125).

CAREER

1992: ITALIAN MINIBIKE ENDURANCE CHAMPION.

1993: 12TH IN ITALIAN 125 SPORT PRODUCTION CHAMPIONSHIP (CAGIVA).

1994: ITALIAN 125 SPORT PRODUCTION CHAMPION (CAGIVA).

1995: 3RD IN EUROPEAN 125 CHAMPIONSHIP, ITALIAN 125 CHAMPION, 11TH IN SPANISH 125 OPEN CHAMPIONSHIP (APRILIA).

1996: 9TH IN 125 WORLD CHAMPIONSHIP, 10TH IN EUROPEAN 125 CHAMPIONSHIP (APRILIA).

1997: 125 WORLD CHAMPION (APRILIA).

1998: 2ND 250 WORLD CHAMPIONSHIP (APRILIA).

1999: 250 WORLD CHAMPION (APRILIA).

2000: 2ND 500 WORLD CHAMPIONSHIP (HONDA).

2001: 500 WORLD CHAMPION (HONDA).

NUMBER OF GP VICTORIES: 38 (12/125; 14/250; 12/500).

FIRST GP VICTORY: CZECH REPUBLIC GP, 1996 (125).

WORLD TITLES: 3 (125/1997; 250/1999; 500/2001).

Going flat out. On this day during the British GP, Rossi came from eleventh to claim first place.

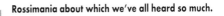
Rossimania about which we've all heard so much.

E.T. exists, we have seen him!

It was the eve of the French GP. At the start of the season, Daijiro Katoh had won the first four GPs, a feat only previously matched by Mike Hailwood. Little less than six months later, the Japanese rider was crowned 250 World Champion in Malaysia. An encounter with an unusual individual...

"We will meet him in a small group of around ten journalists. An interpreter will be on hand". Ian McKay Honda GP spokesman could almost have suggested first passing though a decontamination chamber. But on the other hand, we were going to have an interview with a kind of extra-terrestrial: Daijiro Katoh!

A staircase, the plush meeting room in the management truck of the biggest constructor in the world and there he is, leaning against a panel. No big blue eyes, more like little slits and you ask yourself how they can assimilate so much information when E.T. is flying at 200 km/h astride his Honda NSR250. Then a full head of hair, which still retains the traces of a dye job that went wrong!

Here he is, like a startled rabbit, looking for reassurance in the eyes of his interpreter. "Where are the other Honda riders?", he asks. "They're not coming today. These men are all here for you", she replies. Daijiro Katoh sinks even lower into his cushion, E.T. is ready to reply to the questions from these strange people, also ill-at-ease by the presence of this bizarre individual... Well it's not every day you get to talk to an extra-terrestrial.

- Daijiro, we only know about you from your remarkable sporting achievements. Do you never talk?

  - *Even with your Japanese colleagues, I have always been reticent. I don't talk much, it's my nature, a part of my personality.*

- And with your crew (note: all Italian!)?

  - *Since I live with my wife and child in Misano, I'm trying to learn Dante's language. I can already say pizza and pasta...*

It was in Suzuka that Katoh had his first ever victory. At this circuit which is a fetish for all of the Japanese riders, right from the start he was the pace setter.

- Do you miss Japan?

- Yes. The Adriatic is not really a top destination for the Japanese. However one day when I was taking a walk in Cattolica, I noticed one of my fellow countrymen, but I didn't dare to speak to him.

- So you live completely isolated from daily life?

- No, not at all. Thanks to modern technology – e-mail – I am in daily contact with loads of friends in Japan. Even in the paddock we sometimes communicate in this way. It's funny to think that I'm in my motorhome just a few metres away from Noboru Ueda – the longest serving Japanese rider in GP, in 125 – and we are communicating via a satellite that's thousands of kilometres away.

- What do you do between races?

- I sleep.

- Sorry?

- I love sleeping. When I go back to Japan, I have to see lots of people: my family, my friends, etc. When I'm in Europe, I sleep. You know with the sun in Italy it's quite easy. I sit on the balcony and doze.

- And in the paddock?

- I sleep...

- I see...

- On Sunday, they have to come and wake me up for the race. The same goes for practice. Once during qualifying, when I was stuck in the pits for a few minutes because of mechanical work, I dozed off on a chair. Everyone thought I was concentrating.

A blue and yellow arrow against a green backdrop. Daijiro Katoh on his way to another victory at the Phillip Island circuit.

DAIJIRO KATOH AND...

...the secret of his success. "My bike has been perfect since the beginning of the season. We haven't made any major changes in comparison with last year, but the balance was ideal".

...his strengths. "I don't know. However, I know I'm not a good braker, I need to work on that. And as for rain..."

...his worries during the race. "When I'm alone up front, I worry about losing my concentration. Because I know that if I make a mistake due to lack of attention, my team will tell me off!"

...his experience in other categories. "I tried out 500 once two years ago. In 2000, I won the 8 Hours of Suzuka on a VTR superbike. But for the moment I prefer 250 because I'm too small for the 1000 four-stroke. My feet don't touch the ground!"

...his best memory. "My win in Portugal last year. It was the first time I had won outside Japan".

...his bad habits. "I'm crazy about shoes. I go into a shop and buy everything in my size. When I go home, my wife gets angry and throws everything away".

...his contact with Valentino Rossi. "I don't speak Italian well enough and I'm a little scared to speak to him. So we just make do with Ciao, Ciao".

Popping the cork on a magnum of champagne. This was the first of eleven times that he would do this.

THE MODEL STUDENT...

Flash back. We are in March 1997 at Suzuka. The racing world discovers a new winner, Daijiro Katoh. Even in Japanese, he responds in monosyllables reinforced by head movements. The winner of the Japanese GP left hospital the day before practice to participate in the event. "I had been in a very serious road accident just a month before. I got a bad bang on the head and didn't remember much".

Someone then asked him what he did before becoming a professional rider for HRC, Honda's racing department. "I studied. But don't ask me where or what because I can't remember".

Daijiro Katoh in civilian clothes, well nearly.
This quiet, timid man does not like to be disturbed.

Another place, another attitude. "During
one test session during which we had a
lot of work to do on the bike, Daijiro fell
asleep in the pits" said his team boss
Fausto Gresini.

Identity Card

NAME: KATOH.

FIRST NAME: DAIJIRO.

BORN ON 4 JULY 1976.

AT SAITAMA PREFECTURE (JAPAN).

FIRST RACE: 1984.

FIRST GP: JAPANESE GP 1996 (250).

CAREER

1985: JAPANESE POCKET BIKE CHAMPION.

1986: FIRST MINIBIKE RACES.

1988: JAPANESE MINIBIKE CHAMPION.

1989: JAPANESE MINIBIKE CHAMPION.

1990: JAPANESE MINIBIKE CHAMPION.

1991: JAPANESE MINIBIKE CHAMPION.

1992: FIRST ROAD RACES.

1993: DEBUT IN JAPANESE NATIONAL CHAMPIONSHIP (HONDA).

1994: 7TH IN JAPANESE 250 CHAMPIONSHIP (HONDA).

1995: 199TH IN ENDURANCE WORLD CHAMPIONSHIP, 5TH IN GERMAN 250
CHAMPIONSHIP (HONDA).

1996: 23RD IN 250 WORLD CHAMPIONSHIP, JAPANESE 250 VICE-CHAMPION
(HONDA).

1997: 19TH IN 250 WORLD CHAMPIONSHIP, JAPANESE 250 CHAMPION, 98TH
IN WORLD ENDURANCE CHAMPIONSHIP (HONDA).

1998: 20TH IN 250 WORLD CHAMPIONSHIP, 8TH IN JAPANESE 250
CHAMPIONSHIP (HONDA).

1999: 20TH IN 250 WORLD CHAMPIONSHIP, JAPANESE 250 VICE-CHAMPION,
111TH IN WORLD ENDURANCE CHAMPIONSHIP (HONDA).

2000: 3RD IN 250 WORLD CHAMPIONSHIP, 50TH IN WORLD ENDURANCE
CHAMPIONSHIP (HONDA).

2001: 250 WORLD CHAMPION (HONDA).

NUMBER OF GP VICTORIES: 16 (250).

FIRST GP VICTORY: JAPANESE GP, 1997 (250).

WORLD TITLES: 1 (250/2001).

He is yet another example of how efficient the Italian system of training riders has become. The line is complete, minibike racing to world championship level, enabling talented youngsters to make a niche for themselves. Is Manuel Poggiali talented? "As much natural talent as Valentino Rossi, " say some. His first GP at the age of barely 15, first title at 18, Manuel Poggiali has offered the Republic of San Marino its first ever motorcycle racing world title. And also to Gilera its first 125cc crown as a return to business for the make with a glorious past.

Who is Manuel Poggiali? Before the season started he was "one of" the favourites for the 125cc title, often the most hotly disputed. And 2001 was no exception since it was only after the last GP of the season in Rio that the name of the champion became known. Even though we had a fairly clear idea of the last few weeks, to be exact, since Toni Elias made his mistake in Motegi. With 23 points over his Japanese half-team-mate Youichi Ui before the carioca meeting, Manuel Poggiali only had to play safe: thirteenth place was still enough. But in this category of young furies, the gaps are sometimes minimal and "playing safe" doesn't really come into it. And in Rio amid difficult grip conditions, Poggiali went through all the emotions before dedicating his title to his father, taken from him so soon.

Poggiali:
"LONG LIVE THE REPUBLIC"

Maximum tension on the starting grid in Rio. The Gilera and Derbi father, Austrian Harald Bartol (left) and Giampiero Sacchi surround the future World Champion. The sky is menacing and any error is out of the question.

With his nose under the windshield in South Africa. At this moment in the season, Poggiali is just one of a number of favourites for the title.

"WITHOUT HIM I WOULDN'T BE HERE"

Zoom forward and it's interview time in the rooms at the Nelson Piquet circuit at Jacarepagua. "It's true, I would first like to thank the one who put me on a bike when I was still a kid. Without him I wouldn't be here now..." His young face hardens up a little, and Manuel Poggiali tries to contain the emotion, showing astonishing maturity and a kind of gentle strength that enabled him in the hardest moments of the season to make a minimum of errors. It's the only recipe to become World Champion.

- Manuel Poggiali, now you've won the title, do you not regret having signed another contract in 125cc with Gilera?

  - *Not at all. Of course I will have the number one plate on my bike, but I know that the task will not be easy. If I manage to defend my crown successfully it will be soon enough to think of the future.*

- Have you had other contacts in recent months?

  - *Yes, there were a few opportunities even in other categories. But for me the choice was soon clear: in this domain you must have material that enables you to race up front. With Gilera in 125, I am well served.*

- You must guess that some are already dreaming of seeing Rossi-Poggiali in the MotoGP?

   - *Well they'll have to carry on dreaming. Valentino is a great. But I still hope that someday we'll meet up on the track.*

- What would you say to those who say you are Valentino Rossi 2?

   - *Very simple – I just reply that I am Manuel Poggiali.*

- Why number 54?

   - *It's a number I had at the start and it's always brought me luck. In 1997, it was also the number for Miss Italy and in the same year, I won my first Championship in minibike with a Pasini.*

- Is it true that in the commune of Chiesanuova there's been a request to change the speed limit from 50 to 54 km/h?

   - *That's a joke that came about on the day of the Rio GP when everyone was gathered round to watch the race on TV. They also delayed the start of the local football match by fifteen minutes to let everyone get to the stadium after the race.*

- How does it feel to be World Champion at 18?

   - *It's a great emotion. But I think it 's better to win when you're young, because you have less other things to think about at our age. What's my dream? To win the championship in every category.*

- It you look back on the season, when was the deciding moment?

   - *Certainly the Grand Prix in Valencia when I won the race in Toni Elias' backyard. Personally my first every GP win in Le Mans lies close to my heart. And then, there were some brilliant battles: with Youichi Ui, my almost team-mate, and several times with Elias.*

A hair's breadth between them: each GP weekend, it's a lottery to pick the winners in order in 125cc.

ID CARD

Barely 18 and already World Champion: Manuel Poggiali.

Name: Poggiali.

First name: Manuel.

Born on 14 February 1983.

At: Chiesanuova (San Marino).

First race: 1994.

First GP: Imola GP 1998 (125).

CAREER

1994: 5th in Italian Junior Minibike Championship (Polini)

1995: 2nd in Italian Junior Minibike Championship (Pasini)

1996: 11th in Italian Junior Minibike Championship (Pasini)

1997: Italian Minibike Champion (Pasini)

1998: 5th in European 125 Championship, Italian 125 Champion, Winner of the Honda Italy Trophy (Honda)

1999: 17th in 125 World Championship (Aprilia)

2000: 16th in 125 World Championship (Derbi)

2001: 125 World Champion (Gilera)

Number of GP victories: 3 (125)

First GP Victory: French GP 2001 (125)

World titles: 1 (125/2001)

THE GILERA MYTH

- Make founded in 1909 by Giuseppe Gilera in Milan. In 1925, the headquarters moved to Arcore where production continued until 1993. The Piaggio bought the make in 1969 and the main factory was based near Pisa at Pontedera.

- Manuel Poggiali offered Gilera its seventh world title, after Umberto Masetti (500/1950 and 1952), Geoff Duke (500/1953, 1954 and 1955) and Libero Liberati (500/1957)

- Gilera has won 47 races in GP, 4 in 125cc, 2 in 350cc, 35 in 500cc and 6 in side-cars.

- After a long absence and a previous short lived attempt in 1992 and 1993 (in 250), Gilera made its GP comeback in 2001, with the Piaggio group taking advantage of the purchase of the Spanish make Derbi to revive the myth. With the success we all know.

A name to remember... With all the rest.

Suzuka

Grand Prix of JAPAN

A big wheel, a narrow chicane, non stop overtaking, Suzuka remains a magic place.

Masao Azuma: an ideal start to the season for the set up rider for the Belgian Olivier Liégeois.

He burns rubber after leaving his rivals out in the cold: Daijiro Katoh.

KIRIN

500cc GP of Japan

8 April
Suzuka - 5.859 m

STARTING GRID

1.	65	L. Capirossi	West Honda Pons	2'04.777
2.	56	S. Nakano	Gauloises Yamaha Tech 3	2'05.588
3.	3	M. Biaggi	Marlboro Yamaha Team	2'05.703
4.	5	G. McCoy	Red Bull Yamaha WCM	2'05.833
5.	11	T. Ukawa	Repsol YPF Honda Team	2'05.924
6.	6	N. Abe	Antena 3 Yamaha-d'Antin	2'05.927
7.	46	V. Rossi	Nastro Azzurro Honda	2'06.140
8.	4	A. Barros	West Honda Pons	2'06.295
9.	1	K. Roberts	Telefonica Movistar Suzuki	2'06.469
10.	41	N. Haga	Red Bull Yamaha WCM	2'06.597
11.	28	A. Crivillé	Repsol YPF Honda Team	2'06.714
12.	7	C. Checa	Marlboro Yamaha Team	2'06.858
13.	10	J.L. Cardoso	Antena 3 Yamaha-d'Antin	2'06.993
14.	15	S. Gibernau	Telefonica Movistar Suzuki	2'07.121
15.	33	A. Ryo	Telefonica Movistar Suzuki	2'07.580
16.	17	J. vd Goorbergh	Proton TEAM KR	2'08.419
17.	12	H. Aoki	Arie Molenaar Racing	2'08.906
18.	8	C. Walker	Shell Advance Honda	2'09.129
19.	19	O. Jacque	Gauloises Yamaha Tech 3	2'09.409
20.	9	L. Haslam	Shell Advance Honda	2'10.478
21.	24	J. Vincent	Pulse GP	2'11.232
22.	16	J. Stigefelt	Sabre Sport	2'11.282
23.	68	M. Willis	Pulse GP	2'12.791
24.	21	B. Veneman	Dee Cee Jeans Racing Team	2'13.133

RACE: 21 LAPS = 123.039 KM

1. Valentino Rossi -21 laps in 44'51.501 (164.570 km/h)
2. Garry McCoy   at 0.724
3. Max Biaggi   at 0.956
4. Norick Abe   at 1.176
5. Shinya Nakano   at 3.256
6. Alex Barros   at 14.515
7. Kenny Roberts   at 22.876
8. Loris Capirossi   at 28.732
9. Alex Crivillé   at 34.478
10. Carlos Checa   at 53.765
11. Jürgen vd Goorbergh at 58.688
12. Haruchika Aoki   at 1'17.338
13. Leon Haslam   at 1'17.681

RETIREMENTS

Jose Luis Cardoso	1st lap not finished
Chris Walker	1st lap not finished
Jason Vincent	at 2 laps
Tohru Ukawa	at 5 laps (fall)
Mark Willis	at 6 laps
Akira Ryo	at 9 laps (fall)
Olivier Jacque	at 10 laps
Noriyuki Haga	at 11 laps (fall)
Sete Gibernau	at 13 laps (fall)
Barry Veneman	at 16 laps
Johan Stigefelt	at 18 laps

RACE FACTS

Pole Position:	Loris Capirossi	2'04.777
Fastest lap:	Tohru Ukawa	2'06.805
Circuit record lap:	Max Biaggi	2'06.746 (1998)
Circuit best lap:	Loris Capirossi	2'04.777 (2001)

CHAMPIONSHIP

1. V. Rossi   25 (1 victory)
2. G. McCoy   20
3. M. Biaggi   16
4. N. Abe   13
5. S. Nakano   11
6. A. Barros   10
7. K. Roberts   9
8. L. Capirossi 8
9. A. Crivillé   7
10. C. Checa   6

PRACTICE:

Biaggi is the fastest on the first day but Rossi dominates free practice on Saturday morning. Haga falls twice (remaining KO for a few seconds after the second fall). But it's Capirossi who has the last laugh in practice setting a phenomenal time of 2'04"777 in the final seconds of qualifying. Nakano grabs the headlines (second for his very first 500cc GP). World Champion Kenny Roberts is only on the third row (9th overall).

START:

Biaggi and Capirossi are quickest off the mark with the pole man finishing the first lap 0"168 ahead of Nakano and Biaggi. Rossi is in eighth place and Spaniard Cardoso and 500 newcomer Chris Walker do not last very long.

5TH LAP:

McCoy takes the lead on the third lap with Nakano breathing down his neck. Just behind, the duel of the year begins between Biaggi and Rossi. Valentino tries to take his opponent by surprise on the outside on the pit straight but Biaggi sticks his elbow out and Rossi runs into the dirt at 260 km/h. On the next lap, Rossi goes past with a graphic gesture to Max.

7TH LAP:

For the first time in the season (but not the last), Rossi takes the lead of a 500 GP.

9TH LAP:

Gibernau crashes out.

10TH LAP (MID-RACE):

Rossi has a lead of 0"529 over the chasing group made up of Biaggi, Ukawa, McCoy and Haga who will soon crash.

12TH LAP:

Overcome by the pain – a

Garry McCoy lives up to expectations. It was the beginning of the season...

fractured scaphoid during private testing in Sepang on 30 January – Olivier Jacque, the 250 reigning champion, promoted to 500, pulls up.

15TH LAP:

Rossi now has a lead of 2"951 and seems in control.

17TH LAP:

Ukawa crashes out in spectacular fashion coming out of the chicane. Biaggi just manages to avoid him.

FINISH (20 LAPS):

Defending Champion Kenny Roberts is well and truly beaten. Sportingly he shakes Valentino Rossi's hand who provides Honda with their 500th GP victory.

CHAMPIONSHIP:

"Tino" Rossi is already in the lead. But until when?

True love in real life, success on the track: Loris Capirossi and Ingrid.

Jostling at the chicane: Rossi on the attack, McCoy lies low, Biaggi resists.

Sauber: from F1 to motorcycling

Heijiro Yoshimura can hardly contain himself. The presentation of the new four-stroke engine developed by Sauber-Petronas Engineering has just begun on the terrace overlooking the pits in Suzuka. And the boss of the HRC four-stroke department is worried he'll learn nothing. "I hope the Swiss will not settle just for a film. Are you sure a new four-stroke engine will be on show?"

We are witnessing a new war of words and secrets. Everyone knows that Honda are developing a new V5 engine for future GPs. The pictures of the engine went round the world twice before the start of the season. Will there be a public announcement to confuse people further? To satisfy the curious and allow engineers to pursue other projects? "Each time that HRC embarks on a new project, our specialists work on various approaches. In our case, we have considered single cylinder possibilities as well as six cylinder options", explains Yoshimura-San.

The film has just finished. The curtain goes up on the engine created in Hinwil in Switzerland. Mr Yoshimura is one of the first to take a closer look. Is he surprised by the engineer Goto's choice? (Formerley of Honda and Ferrari in F1, having moved to Sauber after the Swiss team acquired the rights for the Maranello 10 cylinder engine). "Not really," says the Japanese specialist. "What struck me most was the size of the engine".

Honda and Yamaha (four cylinders in a row on the future OW-M1) have played open book but Kawasaki and Suzuki are working in secret (on the eve of the Japanese GP, Garry Taylor's team press service announced that Suzuki was not even in a position to give details of any four stroke projects). With MZ, the Piaggio group (with Swissauto?), Aprilia and Roberts Senior (with Cosworth?) also working on four stroke projects (not to mention the expected arrival of Ducati and BMW), the blue riband category seems full of promise for tomorrow.

But it remains to be seen at what price. And this is the sticking point. "If a team wants exclusivity for our engine, the price will certainly not be the same as supplying several teams", explained Jost Capito, the general manager for Sauber Petronas Engineering. How much? At Suzuka, the sum of 10 million dollars was bandied about for the first engine to be derived from Formula One. "We know there's a long way to go," said Capito. "I hope that between now and the middle of the season we'll be able to determine the exact costs and thus determine a little more precisely our future direction".

Will the Sauber Petronas team come with a completely new official bike? What price will the Japanese constructors charge for the future dominant supreme machines? "At the moment everyone's talking a lot. But that's a long way from having concrete responses and we shall have to be patient", explains the boss of the new project.

So just a few hours from the start of the new season the trends were showing two distinct leanings. On the track with a more balanced 500 line-up than ever before reinforced by the arrival of three of the best 250 riders. But also behind the scenes with all eyes looking to future development.

Looking to the future: Sauber Engineering presents its first engine in Suzuka. At the end of the season, on the occasion of the Malaysian GP, a prototype will complete two laps in the hands of Niall McKenzie.

250cc
GP
of Japan

8 April
Suzuka - 5.859m

Daijiro Katoh triumphs: an image that would repeat itself...

STARTING GRID

1.	74	D. Katoh	Telefonica Movistar Honda	2'07.414
2.	5	M. Melandri	MS Aprilia Racing	2'08.546
3.	15	R. Locatelli	MS Eros Ramazotti Racing	2'08.633
4.	6	A. Debon	Valencia Circuit Aspar Team	2'09.295
5.	99	J. McWilliams	Aprilia Grand Prix	2'09.363
6.	21	F. Battaini	MS Eros Ramazotti Racing	2'09.450
7.	8	N. Matsudo	Petronas Sprinta Yamaha T	2'09.563
8.	31	T. Harada	MS Aprilia Racing	2'09.683
9.	44	R. Rolfo	Safilo Oxydo Race	2'09.741
10.	81	R. de Puniet	Equipe de France – Scrab G	2'10.013
11.	9	S. Porto	Yamaha Cruz	2'10.046
12.	10	F. Nieto	Valencia Circuit Aspar Team	2'10.251
13.	12	K. Nöhles	MS Aprilia Racing	2'10.261
14.	87	H. Aoyama	Team Harc-Pro	2'10.264
15.	46	T. Sekiguchi	Club Ventis	2'10.473
16.	48	S. Nakatomi	Team Kotake Rsc	2'10.477
17.	37	L. Boscoscuro	Campetella Racing	2'10.497
18.	66	A. Hofmann	Dark Dog Racing Factory	2'10.528
19.	7	E. Alzamora	Telefonica Movistar Honda	2'10.594
20.	22	D. De Gea	Antena 3 Yamaha-d'Antin	2'10.598
21.	18	S. Yuzy	Petronas Sprinta Yamaha T	2'10.678
22.	19	J. Allemand	Antena 3 Yamaha-d'Antin	2'10.732
23.	20	J. Vidal	PR2 Metrored	2'11.775
24.	42	D. Checa	Team Fomma	2'11.787
25.	50	S. Guintoli	Equipe de France – Scrab G	2'11.816
26.	57	L. Lanzi	Campetella Racing	2'11.887
27.	47	T. Kayoh	FCC-TSR	2'12.344
28.	55	D. Giugovaz	Edo Racing	2'12.952
29.	11	R. Chiarello	Aprilia Grand Prix	2'14.376
30.	98	K. Poensgen	Dark Dog Racing Factory	2'15.821
31.	45	S. Edwards	FCC-TSR	2'15.957

RACE: 19 LAPS = 111.321 KM

1. Daijiro Katoh - 19 laps in 41'03.596 (162.670 km/h)
2. Tetsuya Harada — at 18.763
3. Roberto Locatelli — at 18.835
4. Naoki Matsudo — at 23.135
5. Roberto Rolfo — at 24.423
6. Marco Melandri — at 26.595
7. Franco Battaini — at 31.142
8. Jeremy Mc Williams — at 43.953
9. Sebastian Porto — at 45.887
10. Taro Sekiguchi — at 48.496
11. Fonsi Nieto — at 53.583
12. Alex Hofmann — at 1'05.172
13. Hiroshi Aoyama — at 1'05.267
14. Klaus Nöhles — at 1'17.422
15. Sylvain Guintoli — at 1'18.183
16. David Checa — at 1'18.602
17. Lorenzo Lanzi — at 1'26.040
18. Jeronimo Vidal — at 1'35.868
19. Shinichi Nakatomi — at 1'41.647
20. Tekkyu Kayoh — at 1'43.891
21. Diego Giugovaz — at 1'49.324
22. Katja Poensgen — at 1 lap

RETIREMENTS

Julien Allemand	1st lap not finished
Luca Boscoscuro	at 3 laps
Shahrol Yuzy	at 4 laps (fall)
David De Gea	at 5 laps (fall)
Alex Debon	at 13 laps (fall)
Riccardo Chiarello	at 13 laps
Stuart Edwards	at 14 laps
Randy de Puniet	at 15 laps
Emilio Alzamora	at 18 laps (fall)

RACE FACTS

Pole Position:	Daijiro Katoh	2'07.414
Fastest lap:	Daijiro Katoh	2'08.658
Circuit record lap:	Shinya Nakano	2'08.581 (2000)
Circuit best lap:	Daijiro Katoh	2'07.414 (2001)

CHAMPIONSHIP

1. D. Katoh — 25 (1 victory)
2. T. Harada — 20
3. R. Locatelli — 16
4. N. Matsudo — 13
5. R. Rolfo — 11

PRACTICE:

He is the definite favourite after dominating winter testing : Daijiro Katoh (Honda) leaves no-one else a chance to occupy the top spot on the starting grid for "his" grand prix.

His major rival Marco Melandri is more than a second adrift and the Italian's participation in the race remains in doubt for a long time after a heavy crash on Saturday afternoon during which "Macio" dislocated his shoulder. With the major stars (Nakano, Jacque and Ukawa) having moved up to 500, there are some new faces on the front row (World Champion Roberto Locatelli is third, Alex Debon fourth). German rider Katja Poensgen achieves a major feat by qualifying.

START:

Melandri is quickest off the mark but Tetsuya Harada soon takes control to be quickly joined by Katoh who takes the lead at the end of the first lap and surges ahead.

3RD LAP:

Emilio Alzamora crashes out meaning he has no time to complete the stop and go inflicted for a jump start.

5TH LAP:

Katoh racks up fastest lap after fastest lap. He now has a lead of 3"003 over Harada, Locatelli and Melandri who grits his teeth and manages to hold off Matsudo.

9TH LAP (MID-RACE):

Katoh's lead is now 8"365. With second place at stake, Locatelli takes Harada by surprise. Behind them Melandri plays the role of injured hero and battles for this honour with Gonzales, Battaini and McWilliams.

15TH LAP:

Nothing to report except a lead of 15"010 for Katoh.

FINISH (19 LAPS):

Victory number 499 for Honda in GP with the first historic gap: 18"763. Harada takes Locatelli by surprise on the line. Melandri (6th) can thank Doctor Costa. Katja Poensgen finishes her first GP in 22nd place.

CHAMPIONSHIP:

Katoh is (already) the leader with Harada winning the internal war at Aprilia but way behind the Honda victor.

Marco Melandri is still holding out. The 250 season will belong to one man (Katoh) in the face of an armada (Aprilia).

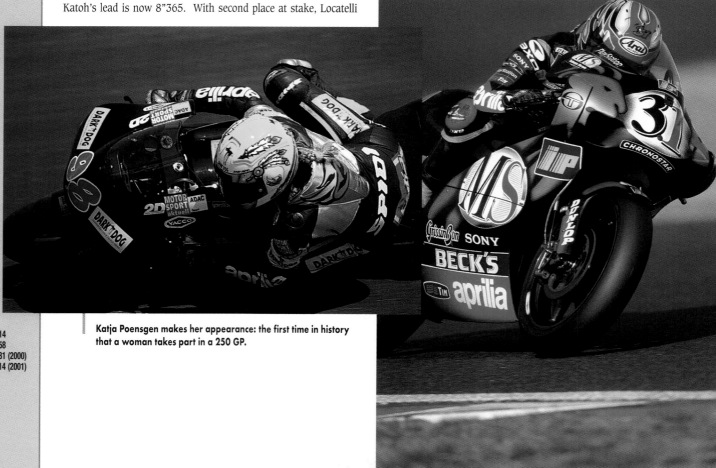

Katja Poensgen makes her appearance: the first time in history that a woman takes part in a 250 GP.

Future World Champion, Manuel Poggiali, leads the game from the first 125 GP of the season. But on the line, Japanese Masao Azuma takes the honours.

8 April
Suzuka – 5.859m

STARTING GRID

1.	41	Y. Ui	L & M Derbi Team	2'14.686
2.	54	M. Poggiali	Gilera Racing Team	2'14.832
3.	9	L. Cecchinello	MS Aprilia LCR	2'14.941
4.	4	M. Azuma	Liegeois competition	2'14.986
5.	17	S. Jenker	LAE – UGT 3000	2'15.253
6.	.23	G. Borsoi	LAE – UGT 3000	2'15.292
7.	5	N. Ueda	FCC – TSR	2'15.614
8.	7	S. Perugini	Italjet Racing Team	2'15.899
9.	11	M. Sabbatini	Bossini Fontana Racing	2'16.265
10.	55	H. Nakajoh	JHA Racing	2'16.293
11.	29	A. Nieto Jr	Viceroy Team	2'16.414
12.	8	G. Scalvini	Italjet Racing Team	2'16.537
13.	39	J. Hules	Matteoni Racing	2'16.602
14.	15	A. de Angelis	Matteoni Racing	2'16.648
15.	57	H. Kikuchi	Wanpapa – Team Wheely	2'16.713
16.	6	M. Giansanti	Axo Racing Team	2'16.765
17.	24	A. Elias	Telefonica Movistar jnr Team	2'16.827
18.	21	A. Vincent	Team Fomma	2'16.976
19.	16	S. Sanna	Safilo Oxydo Race	2'17.078
20.	20	G. Caffiero	Bossini Fontana Racing	2'17.291
21.	10	J. Müller	PEV-Spalt-ADAC-Sachsen	2'17.401
22.	22	P. Nieto	L & M Derbi Team	2'17.465
23.	26	D. Pedrosa	Telefonica Movistar jnr Team	2'17.476
24.	34	E. Bataille	Axo Racing Team	2'17.730
25.	98	M. Ono	Team Harc-Pro	2'17.771
26.	18	J. Smrz	Budweiser Budvar Hanusch	2'17.898
27.	27	M. Petrini	Racing Service	2'17.898
28.	56	Y. Fujioka	Team Plus One	2'18.247
29.	31	A. Rodriguez	Valencia Circuit Aspar Team	2'18.487
30.	19	A. Brannetti	Du Martel S.A.	2'18.795
31.	28	G. Talmacsi	Racing Service	2'18.851
32.	14	P. Hafeneger	Liegeois Competition	2'19.127
33.	97	N. Katoh	JHA Racing	2'19.319
34.	25	J. Olive	Telefonica Movistar jnr Team	2'19.347
35.	12	R. Jara	MS Aprilia LCR	2'20.001

RACE : 18 TOURS = 105.462 KM

1.	Masao Azuma - 18 laps in 40'59.192 (154.385 km/h)	
2.	Youichi Ui	at 0.067
3.	Simone Sanna	at 0.604
4.	Gino Borsoi	at 0.898
5.	Manuel Poggiali	at 1.151
6.	Lucio Cecchinello	at 1.376
7.	Steve Jenker	at 14.173
8.	Mirko Giansanti	at 14.632
9.	Arnaud Vincent	at 15.735
10.	Pablo Nieto	at 16.333
11.	Angel Nieto Jr	at 17.384
12.	Max Sabbatini	at 17.992
13.	Gianluigi Scalvini	at 18.621
14.	Alex De Angelis	at 18.628
15.	Hiroyuki Kikuchi	at 23.655
16.	Antonio Elias	at 34.401
17.	Jaroslav Hules	at 34.521
18.	Daniel Pedrosa	at 46.838
19.	Joan Olive	at 47.378
20.	Masafumi Ono	at 48.164
21.	Jakub Smrz	at 58.746
22.	Yuzo Fujioka	at 1'00.982
23.	Gabor Talmacsi	at 1'01.962
24.	Jarno Müller	at 1'21.581
25.	Phillipp Hafeneger	at 1'49.589

RETIREMENTS

Raul Jara	1st lap not finished
Marco Petrini	1st lap not finished
Naoki Katoh	1st lap not finished
Hideyuki Nadkajoh	at 3 laps
Noboru Ueda	at 4 laps
Angel Rodriguez	at 4 laps
Alessandro Brannetti	at 5 laps
Gaspare Caffiero	at 6 laps
Eric Bataille	at 7 laps
Stefano Perugini	at 13 laps

RACE FACTS

Pole Position:	Youichi Ui	2'14.686
Fastest lap:	Masao Azuma	2'15.353
Circuit record lap:	Roberto Locatelli	2'15.406 (2000)
Circuit best lap:	Youichi Ui	2'14.597 (2001)

CHAMPIONSHIP

1.	M. Azuma	25 (1 victory)
2.	Y. Ui	20
3.	S.Sanna	16
4.	G. Borsoi	13
5.	M. Poggiali	11
6.	L. Cecchinello	10
7.	S. Jenker	9
8.	M.Giansanti	8
9.	A. Vincent	7
10.	P. Nieto	6

PRACTICE:

The close season has been fairly animated behind the scenes with the Piaggio group purchasing Spanish constructor Derbi. It was made from an economical standpoint but it had consequences on the World Championship. From now on the little 125s manufactured by Austrian engineer Harald Bartol are entered in GP under two different names (Derbi for Youichi Ui on pole position for this first GP and Pablo Nieto; Gilera for Manuel Poggiali, 2nd fastest time in qualifying). Four different makes are therefore represented on the front row. And the Italjet created by Jörg Möller (with Perugini and Scalvini the German can make some real development) is not far behind.

START:

Gino Borsoi (test rider for Aprilia in the category) surges through from the second row. He has a lead of 0"442 over Ui and Masao Azuma at the end of the first lap.

5TH LAP:

Lucio Cecchinello has taken the lead on the preceding lap. Aprilia's new recruit leads Azuma and Borsoi.

6TH LAP:

Stefano Perugini crashes out on the Italjet while running in sixth place.

9TH LAP (MID-RACE):

There are now seven riders within 1.7 seconds. Cecchinello leads ahead of Poggiali and Azuma. The big favourite Youichi Ui is last in this leading group.

14TH LAP:

Noboru Ueda (TSR-Honda) has taken matters in hand and Ui, who senses the danger, is now in fourth place.

15TH LAP:

Ueda crashes out heavily (but fortunately without serious consequences).

FINISH (18 LAPS):

Six riders are on course for victory. Cecchinello leads going into the last lap with Ui the first to offer a threat. But Azuma with his Honda belonging to Belgian team Olivier Liégeois is the fastest in the leading group and has the last laugh.

CHAMPIONSHIP:

A favourite – Ueda – loses a few feathers. A sign of the times: the time where the Japanese dominated at Suzuka with wild card riders has long gone. The first guest rider (Hideyuki Kikuchi) could only score the single point for fifteenth place.

Azuma and his crew chief, Belgian Olivier Liégeois: an ideal start to the season.

Team-mates but sporting different colours: Angel Nieto Junior and Frenchman Arnaud Vincent.

27

Welkom

Grand Prix of
SOUTH AFRICA

Daijiro Katoh (74) and Tetsuya Harada (31): this will be the duel of the year. Which rapidly leads to total domination by the Honda rider.

In the land of gold mines, Valentino Rossi harvests diamonds: another victory for the future world champion in Welkom.

One Japanese rider chasing another. After Azuma in Suzuka, it is the turn of Youichi Ui and Derbi to win their first victory of the season in South Africa.

500cc
GP
of South Africa

22 April
Welkom - 4.242 m

STARTING GRID

1.	46 V. Rossi	Nastro Azzurro Honda	1'34.629
2.	65 L. Capirossi	West Honda Pons	1'34.872
3.	56 S. Nakano	Gauloises Yamaha Tech 3	1'35.216
4.	5 G. McCoy	Red Bull Yamaha WCM	1'35.434
5.	1 K. Roberts	Telefonica Movistar Suzuki	1'35.476
6.	11 T. Ukawa	Repsol YPF Honda Team	1'35.537
7.	6 N. Abe	Antena 3 Yamaha-d'Antin	1'35.692
8.	3 M. Biaggi	Marlboro Yamaha Team	1'35.921
9.	28 A. Crivillé	Repsol YPF Honda Team	1'35.996
10.	41 N. Haga	Red Bull Yamaha WCM	1'36.125
11.	15 S. Gibernau	Telefonica Movistar Suzuki	1'36.138
12.	4 A. Barros	West Honda Pons	1'36.149
13.	17 J. vd Goorbergh	Proton TEAM KR	1'36.169
14.	12 H. Aoki	Arie Molenaar Racing	1'36.694
15.	19 O. Jacque	Gauloises Yamaha Tech 3	1'37.038
16.	8 C. Walker	Shell Advance Honda	1'37.410
17.	10 J.L. Cardoso	Antena 3 Yamaha-d'Antin	1'37.471
18.	9 L. Haslam	Shell Advance Honda	1'37.921
19.	14 A. West	Dee Cee Jeans Racing Team	1'38.287
20.	16 J. Stigefelt	Sabre Sport	1'38.743
21.	24 J. Vincent	Pulse GP	1'39.222
22.	21 B. Veneman	Dee Cee Jeans Racing Team	1'39.564
23.	68 M. Willis	Pulse GP	1'40.412

RACE: 28 LAPS = 118.776 KM

1. Valentino Rossi - 18 laps in 45'03.414 (158.168 km/h)		
2. Loris Capirossi	at 0.660	
3. Tohru Ukawa	at 7.530	
4. Shinya Nakano	at 8.653	
5. Norick Abe	at 9.224	
6. Alex Crivillé	at 13.211	
7. Kenny Roberts	at 13.305	
8. Max Biaggi	at 13.663	
9. Alex Barros	at 17.357	
10. Sete Gibernau	at 21.697	
11. Jurgen vd Goorbergh	at 37.649	
12. Haruchika Aoki	at 48.587	
13. Jose Luis Cardoso	at 1'01.110	
14. Anthony West	at 1'06.173	
15. Chris Walker	at 1'08.255	
16. Olivier Jacque	at 1'10.262	
17. Leon Haslam	at 1'15.130	
18. Johan Stigefelt	at 1 lap	
19. Barry Veneman	at 1 lap	
20. Mark Willis	at 1 lap	

RACE FACTS

Pole Position:	Valentino Rossi	1'34.629
Fastest lap:	Valentino Rossi	1'35.508
Circuit record lap:	Sete Gibernau	1'36.554 (1999)
Circuit best lap:	Valentino Rossi	1'34.629 (2001)

RETIREMENTS

Jason Vincent	1st lap not finished
Garry McCoy	at 11 laps (fall)
Noriyuki Haga	at 24 laps (fall)

CHAMPIONSHIP

1. V. Rossi	50 (2 victories)
2. L. Capirossi	28
3. M. Biaggi	24
4. N. Abe	24
5. S. Nakano	24
6. G. McCoy	20
7. K. Roberts	18
8. A. Barros	17
9. A. Crivillé	17
10. T. Ukawa	16

Jurgen van den Goorbergh brings a lift to Proton.

PRACTICE:

A new duel between Rossi-Capirossi. This time Valentino has the last word, with his first pole position in 500. To celebrate the occasion Jeremy Burgess' whole team hides at the back of the stand so Rossi returns to a totally empty garage.

START:

Capirossi gets the perfect start, but Roberts tries a suicidal manoeuvre on the first corner. He almost causes Rossi to crash and Capirossi has to run wide to avoid disaster. Rossi takes advantage of this and moves into the lead (0"213 ahead at the end of the first lap).

5TH LAP:

Haga is the first major runner to be eliminated (crash).

7TH LAP:

Rossi's dreams of pulling away are thwarted. First Roberts is

Kenny Roberts at the front in the first few laps. The World Champion will not be able to resist Rossi's assault for very long.

ahead and McCoy, Abe and Ukawa are not far behind. Biaggi is already beaten.

9TH LAP:

The race is being run at a deceptive pace which enables the defending World Champion Roberts to create an illusion. Roberts leads Rossi, McCoy and Abe.

14TH LAP (MID RACE):

A new leader in the shape of Japanese Norifume Abe. The race takes on a new rhythm. Rossi is already assuming the role of master. He clings to Abe's rear wheel biding his time.

18TH LAP:

He was a favourite for many, but this time he goes too far: last year's winner, Garry McCoy crashes out. At the same time, the final act begins. The duel for victory is now between Rossi and Capirossi.

21ST LAP:

The two Italians are wheel for wheel. Valentino records fastest lap after fastest lap but Loris holds fast.

FINISH (28 LAPS):

Rossi has to pull out all the stops to guarantee another win. He

who is now known as the "Doctor" has to improve on the fastest time five times during the last seven laps.

CHAMPIONSHIP:

A perfect start to the season for Rossi. Two races, two victories and 50 points. Even better, his fellow podium finishers in Suzuka (McCoy and Biaggi) were not to be found in Welkom – the Australian crashed out and the Roman Emperor could only manage 8th. Tino already has a lead of 20 points over Capirossi his closest rival.

Valentino Rossi communicates: on the starting grid, a message for the fight against AIDS.

HELP AFRICA
GIVE FREE ANTI AIDS DRUGS
AND USE CONDOMS!
The Doctor

Grand Prix of South Africa

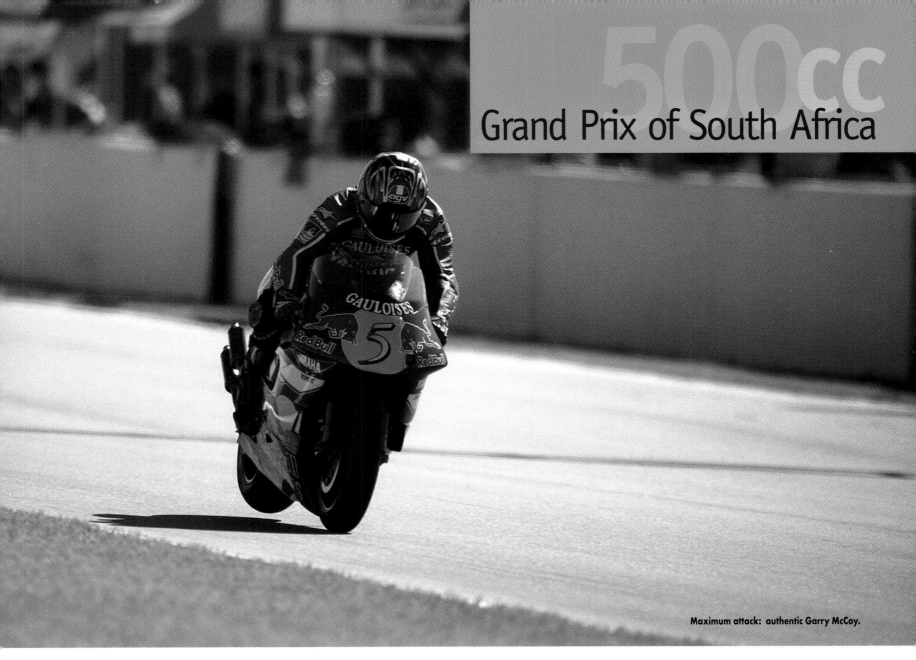

Maximum attack: authentic Garry McCoy.

THE REVOLUTION ONE YEAR ON...

Flash back. It's March 19 2000 and after 28 laps around the track in Welkom, Garry McCoy has just entered the history books. The general public have just discovered his face. The paddock veterans can remember his first escapades in 125cc, his first victories. The specialists in riding techniques cannot believe their eyes; it's almost like rediscovering the great racing talents of ten years ago: Wayne Gardner, Wayne Rainey, Kevin Schwantz or Michael Doohan, all those artists whose speciality was to slide the back wheel to be able to take corners at top speed. It was the time when the engine characteristics combined with the limits of the chassis and the tyres demanded a sliding riding style.

Garry McCoy was the first to take a renewed interest in Michelin's 16.5" rear tyre but at this stage in the 2000 season, he didn't realise that he had just set a revolution in motion. Twelve months on, even though the South African GP finished early for the little Australian, the whole pack of favourites had followed his lead. And the show is the better for it. The race rhythm is once again on the up in 500cc.

"The 16.5" tyre offers more grip at the maximum angle in the middle of the corner, precisely at the point when the rider has to open the throttle. The 17" that we used until then was flatter, so there was less rubber in contact with the track when the bike was at an angle", explained Garry McCoy. Is he a revolutionary? "It's surprising but everyone seems to have forgotten that seven years ago, all the good riders were using this

technique. Of course there will always be a few purists who maintain that I would be more effective if I slid less, but that's how I feel comfortable, so why should I change? You know there are some surprising moments when I put my Yamaha at an angle going into a corner and even before I bring it straight again, I've already accelerated and gone through the whole corner with the back sliding. It's a fantastic feeling".

So is 16.5 the new lucky number in 500? It's thanks to tiny Garry McCoy that Valentino Rossi and all the others, after some hesitation – notably from Massimiliano Biaggi, who made numerous tests throughout the season with two types of tyre – joined the clan and forced Michelin from one grand prix to the next to work on two levels: "In spite of the little Australian's sliding style, we often notice that Garry heats up his tyres less than other riders. On a purely physical level, the temperature of the rubber has a direct influence on the speed at which the wheel rotates and the pressure applied, ie the weight. Therefore since Garry McCoy is very light – 56 kilos – he has a distinct advantage in this respect. Also even though the rear wheel of his Yamaha slides a lot, the rubber only heats up at the surface whereas it only gets worn if the inside of the tyre heats up. So Garry often finishes a race with his tyres in better condition than his rivals even though it looks like he uses up much more rubber", explains Nicolas Goubert, of Michelin's motorcycle racing department. In 2001, the context was not quite the same for the little acrobat (crash).

250cc
GP South Africa

22 April
Welkom - 4.242 m

STARTING GRID

1. 74	D. Katoh	Telefonica Movistar Honda	1'36.937
2. 31	T. Harada	MS Aprilia Racing	1'36.998
3. 5	M. Melandri	MS Aprilia Racing	1'37.221
4. 15	R. Locatelli	MS Eros Ramazotti Racing	1'37.579
5. 10	F. Nieto	Valencia Circuit Aspar Team	1'37.925
6. 37	L. Boscoscuro	Campetella Racing	1'37.930
7. 21	F. Battaini	MS Eros Ramazotti Racing	1'37.998
8. 9	S. Porto	Yamaha Kruz	1'38.052
9. 20	J. Vidal	PR2 Metrored	1'38.142
10. 6	A. Debon	Valencia Circuit Aspar Team	1'38.188
11. 99	J. McWilliams	Aprilia Grand Prix	1'38.213
12. 44	R. Rolfo	Safilo Oxydo Race	1'38.251
13. 8	N. Matsudo	Petronas Sprinta Yamaha T	1'38.311
14. 81	R. de Puniet	Equipe de France - Scrab G	1'38.450
15. 50	S. Guintoli	Equipe de France - Scrab G	1'38.507
16. 42	D. Checa	Team Fomma	1'38.540
17. 12	K. Nöhles	MS Aprilia Racing	1'38.773
18. 7	E. Alzamora	Telefonica Movistar Honda	1'38.938
19. 18	S. Yuzy	Petronas Sprinta Yamaha T	1'39.193
20. 22	D. De Gea	Antena 3 Yamaha-d 'Antin	1'39.240
21. 19	J. Allemand	Antena 3 Yamaha-d 'Antin	1'39.507
22. 57	L. Lanzi	Campetella Racing	1'39.556
23. 66	A. Hofmann	Dark Dog Racing Factory	1'39.568
24. 23	C. Barros	Yamaha Kruz	1'40.107
25. 55	D. Giugovaz	Edo Racing	1'40.430
26. 51	J. Van Vuuren	Privest Yamaha d'Antin	1'41.131
27. 26	I. Silva	Queroseno Racing Team	1'41.442
28. 98	K. Poensgen	Dark Dog Racing Factory	1'41.517
29. 45	S. Edwards	FCC-TSR	1'42.374
30. 11	R. Chiarello	Aprilia Grand Prix	1'42.958

RACE: 26 LAPS = 110.292 KM

1. Daijiro Katoh - 26 laps in 42'31.371 (155.622 km/h)

2.	Marco Melandri	at 0.083
3.	Tetsuya Harada	at 15.806
4.	Roberto Locatelli	at 17.666
5.	Fonsi Nieto	at 34.031
6.	Jeremy Mc Williams	at 34.233
7.	Sebastian Porto	at 34.312
8.	Roberto Rolfo	at 35.074
9.	Naoki Matsudo	at 35.185
10.	Alex Hofmann	at 51.599
11.	Shahrol Yuzy	at 53.805
12.	Sylvain Guintoli	at 54.066
13.	David Checa	at 54.475
14.	Klaus Nöhles	at 55.285
15.	Alex Debon	at 57.738
16.	Jeronimo Vidal	at 1'09.396
17.	Lorenzo Lanzi	at 1'19.289
18.	Julien Allemand	at 1'19.734
19.	Emilio Alzamora	at 1'20.139
20.	Franco Battaini	at 1'20.329
21.	Cesar Barros	at 1 lap
22.	Diego Giugovaz	at 1 lap
23.	Jonathan Van Vuuren	at 1 lap
24.	Katja Poensgen	at 1 lap

RETIREMENTS

Randy de Puniet	at 2 laps
David De Gea	at 14 laps
Ivan Silva	at 14 laps (black flag)
Stuart Edwards	at 17 laps
Luca Boscoscuro	at 20 laps (fall)
Riccardo Chiarello	at 24 laps

RACE FACTS

Pole Position:	Daijiro Katoh	1'36.937
Fastest lap:	Marco Melandri	1'36.828
Circuit record lap:	Daijiro Katoh	1'37.440 (2000)
Circuit best lap:	Marco Melandri	1'36.828 (2001)

CHAMPIONSHIP

1.	D. Katoh	50 (2 victories)
2.	T. Harada	36
3.	M. Melandri	30
4.	R. Locatelli	29
5.	N. Matsudo	20
6.	R. Rolfo	19
7.	J. Mc Williams	18
8.	F. Nieto	16
9.	S. Porto	16
10.	A. Hofmann	10
11.	F. Battaini	9
12.	T. Sekiguchi	6
13.	S. Yuzy	5
14.	S. Guintoli	5
15.	K. Nöhles	4
16.	H. Aoyama	3
17.	D. Checa	3
18.	A. Debon	1

Melandri looks back. His wake-up call comes a little late.

PRACTICE:

The Aprilia patrol headed on the first day by Marco Melandri puts Daijiro Katoh in more trouble than in Suzuka. However on Saturday, the little Japanese rider records the fastest time but not by much (61 thousandths ahead of Harada).

START:

Melandri surprises everyone and takes the lead ahead of Harada and Katoh. Together with Locatelli there are four of them neck and neck.

3RD LAP:

Katoh takes command and increases the pace. In just one lap he opens up a lead of 1"298. The race would seem to be over, but it's not the case.

6TH LAP:

The Japanese Honda rider has a lead of 2"780 over the Aprilia trio (in order Harada, Melandri and Locatelli). Behind them, Argentinian Sebastian Porto is holding off Jeremy McWilliams (who didn't train throughout the winter since his team had major financial headaches).

13TH LAP (MID-RACE):

Katoh is still up front. Melandri and Harada are around 5 seconds adrift, and Locatelli is slightly further back.

18TH LAP:

Melandri is the fastest man on the track and has come back to within 2"814 of Katoh.

20TH LAP:

The Young Italian records the fastest race lap on the previous lap but is 2"621 behind Katoh who looks to have the situation under control. Behind them Harada and Locatelli are riding in tandem.

22ND LAP:

Another lap record with the gap between Katoh and Melandri reduced to 1"712.

FINISH (26 LAPS):

With 1"106 between the two at the start of the last lap, Loris Reggiani's protégé's best efforts (another record in the last few kilometres) are still not enough. Katoh wins again but only by 83 thousandths of a second.

CHAMPIONSHIP:

An ideal result for Katoh (50 points from 2 races) which also makes him a firm favourite for the title. But the Aprilias are not out of the picture. In spite of his injured shoulder sustained during practice for the Japanese GP, Melandri (3rd in the provisional table with 20 points) magnificently limited the damage in South Africa.

Daijiro Katoh on a high – it's already two out of two.

R. de Puniet: pain and more pain.

Hot-headed Latinos: Nieto Junior ahead of Elias and Caffiero (20), Japanese Ueda keeps in contact.

PRACTICE:

Suzuka winner Masao Azuma is not at the party (some of the parts prepared by his team manager, Olivier Liégeois, only arrived very late in Welkom after a luggage problem at Zurich airport). Youichi Ui (Derbi) records another pole position but a first pretender is already on the floor. Suffering from serious concussion after a heavy fall during free practice on Saturday morning, Simone Sanna (Aprilia) withdraws from the race.

START:

Ui is the fastest ahead of the revelation in practice, young Spaniard Toni Elias, who clings to the Derbi's rear wheel. The two riders have eight tenths of a second's advantage over the rest of the pack at the end of the first lap. Cecchinello and Müller jump the start and are penalised with a stop and go.

6TH LAP:

Ui clocks up fastest lap upon fastest lap. He now has a lead of 3"059 over another pretender, Manuel Poggiali (the Gilera rider passed Elias on the preceding lap). Behind them, Elias is now battling with Nieto Junior and Caffiero for third place.

10TH LAP:

Caffiero battles in the chasing group but makes contact with Elias (who seems to be everywhere) and finishes up on the floor.

12TH LAP (MID-RACE):

The situation at the front is settled (Ui has a 5"018 lead over Poggiali). Three seconds behind, there's a tough battle ensuing between Nieto Junior, Ueda, Sabbatani and Borsoi with last year's winner Arnaud Vincent catching the group.

18TH LAP:

Nothing has changed at the front except that Nieto Junior has opened up a gap in third place. Azuma is ill at ease in 12th position after an excursion into the grass.

FINISH (24 LAPS):

Ui wins ahead of Poggiali. Ueda settles the score with Borsoi, Nieto Junior and Vincent for third place. Azuma takes the six points from tenth place.

CHAMPIONSHIP:

Ui takes over the lead with 45 out of a possible 50 points. Azuma and Poggiali share second place 14 points behind. The shape of things to come is already apparent with no real surprises.

A veteran on the podium. For the penultimate time this season, Ueda gets to taste champagne.

South Africa

22 April
Welkom – 4.242 m

STARTING GRID

1.	41	Y. Ui	L & M Derbi Team	1'42.059
2.	5	N. Ueda	FCC – TSR	1'42.365
3.	54	M. Poggiali	Gilera Racing Team	1'42.691
4.	9	L. Cecchinello	MS Aprilia LR	1'42.803
5.	29	A. Nieto Jr	Viceroy Team	1'42.920
6.	24	T. Elias	Telefonica Movistar Jnr Team	1'43.119
7.	23	G. Borsoi	LAE – UGT 3000	1'43.120
8.	8	G. Scalvini	Italjet Racing Team	1'43.148
9.	4	M. Azuma	Liegeois Competition	1'43.185
10.	20	G. Caffiero	Bossini Fontana Racing	1'43.376
11.	21	A. Vincent	Team Fomma	1'43.395
12.	22	P. Nieto	L & M Derbi Team	1'43.428
13.	7	S. Perugini	Italjet Racing Team	1'43.556
14.	15	A. de Angelis	Matteoni Racing	1'43.594
15.	26	D. Pedrosa	Telefonica Movistar Jnr Team	1'43.658
16.	11	M. Sabbatani	Bossini Fontana Racing	1'43.664
17.	6	M. Giansanti	Axo Racing Team	1'43.895
18.	17	S. Jenkner	LAE – UGT 3000	1'43.945
19.	10	J. Müller	PEV – Spalt-ADAC Sachsen	1'44.296
20.	39	J. Hules	Matteoni Racing	1'44.398
21.	31	A. Rogriguez	Valencia Circuit Aspar Team	1'44.455
22.	19	A. Brannetti	Team Crae	1'44.472
23.	18	J. Smrz	Budweiser Budvar Hanusch	1'44.533
24.	28	G. Talmacsi	Racing Service	1'44.699
25.	27	M. Petrini	Racing Service	1'44.867
26.	25	J. Olive	Telefonica Movistar Jnr Team	1'44.931
27.	34	E. Bataille	Axo Racing Team	1'45.702
28.	14	P. Hafeneger	Liegeois Competition	1'46.046
29.	12	R. Jara	MS Aprilia LCR	1'46.283

RACE: 24 LAPS = 101.808 KM

1.	Youichi Ui - 24 laps in 41'27.323 (147.350 km/h)	
2.	Manuel Poggiali	at 1.288
3.	Noburu Ueda	at 7.149
4.	Gino Borsoi	at 7.365
5.	Angel Nieto Jr	at 7.731
6.	Arnaud Vincent	at 7.989
7.	Max Sabbatani	at 8.114
8.	Steve Jenkner	at 15.140
9.	Alex de Angelis	at 24.741
10.	Masao Azuma	at 30.750
11.	Stefano Perugini	at 30.833
12.	Mirko Giansanti	at 31.005
13.	Daniel Pedrosa	at 321.190
14.	Gianluigi Scalvini	at 31.818
15.	Pablo Nieto	at 32.198
16.	Joan Olive	at 35.977
17.	Alessandro Branetti	at 36.383
18.	Toni Elias	at 37.833
19.	Lucio Cecchinello	at 58.806
20.	Eric Bataille	at 1'01.405
21.	Gabor Talmacsi	at 1'12.989
22.	Jaroslav Hules	at 1'25.036
23.	Jarno Müller	at 1 lap
24.	Raul Jara	at 1 lap

RETIREMENTS

Jakub Smrz	1st lap not finished
Philipp Hafeneger	at 11 laps
Marco Petrini	at 13 laps (fall)
Gaspare Caffiero	at 15 laps (fall)
Angel Rodriguez	at 16 laps

RACE FACTS

Pole Position:	Youichi Ui	1'42.059
Fastest lap:	Youichi Ui	1'42.611
Circuit record lap:	Arnaud Vincent	1'42.782 (2000)
Circuit best lap:	Youichi Ui	1'42.059 (2001)

CHAMPIONSHIP

1.	Y. Ui	45 (1 victory)
2.	M. Azuma	31 (1 victory)
3.	M. Poggiali	31
4.	G. Borsoi	26
5.	A. Vincent	17
6.	S. Jenkner	17
7.	S. Sanna	16
8.	N. Ueda	16
9.	A. Nieto Jr	16
10.	M. Sabbatani	13

A red Gilera behind a white wall: Poggiali in Welkom.

Jerez 🇪🇸
Grand Prix
of
SPAIN

Noriyuki Haga grimaces, the Japanese star of world superbike is having a difficult apprenticeship in Grand Prix racing.

Stefano Perugini unseated from his Italjet...

The youngster and the old pro, Marco Melandri riding against a man old enough to be his father, Marcellino Lucchi.

500cc
GP
of Spain

6 May
Jerez - 4.423 m

Rossi on the outside, or shake-down on the first lap.

Race: 27 laps = 119.421 km

1.	Valentino Rossi - 27 laps in 47'15.126 (151.638 km/h)	
2.	Norick Abe	at 2.307
3.	Alex Crivillé	at 2.845
4.	Shinya Nakano	at 4.157
5.	Tohru Ukawa	at 5.932
6.	Alex Barros	at 7.577
7.	Kenny Roberts	at 14.459
8.	Loris Capirossi	at 18.970
9.	Garry McCoy	at 19.725
10.	Sete Gibernau	at 20.239
11.	Max Biaggi	at 20.621
12.	Noriyuki Haga	at 29.891
13.	Jurgen vd Goorbergh	at 42.838
14.	Carlos Checa	at 45.530
15.	Anthony West	at 45.848
16.	Leon Haslam	at 1'02.358
17.	Johan Stigefelt	at 1'13.081
18.	Jason Vincent	at 1'23.194
19.	Mark Willis	at 1 lap

Retirements

Chris Walker	at 22 laps (fall)
Jose Luis Cardoso	at 23 laps
Barry Veneman	at 24 laps (fall)

Race facts

Pole Position:	Valentino Rossi	1'42.739
Fastest lap:	Valentino Rossi	1'43.779 (non official)
Circuit record lap:	Kenny Roberts	1'44.127 (2000)
Circuit best lap:	Valentino Rossi	1'42.421 (2001)

Championship

1. V. Rossi	75 (3 victories)
2. N. Abe	44
3. S. Nakano	37
4. L. Capirossi	36
5. A. Crivillé	33
6. M. Biaggi	29
7. G. McCoy	27
8. T. Ukawa	27
9. A. Barros	27
10. K. Roberts	27

PRACTICE:

Rossi is at the front again with everyone else behind. Best time on Friday, pole on Saturday, Valentino nonetheless gives himself a fright with both wheels on the grass going onto the straight. Capirossi is once again his strongest rival. The Japanese contingent are out in force with Abe and Nakano completing the front row. However, the Spanish challenge goes from bad to worse (the best of them Crivillé is twelfth and Checa falls twice). Olivier Jacque only completes three laps on Saturday afternoon and withdraws from the race after a final attempt during warm-up. The Frenchman decides to return to Paris to consult Professor Saillant. To be continued...

START:

Abe is the fastest off the mark, but Rossi takes control halfway through the first lap. Like in Welkom, Roberts battles with Capirossi.

Chris Walker: it's a steep learning curve in the blue ribbon category.

3RD LAP:

Capirossi breaks the lap record for the first time and is already fourth.

7TH LAP:

Walker has crashed and Cardoso is in the pits. Rossi has a lead of 0"409 over Abe. Capirossi makes a slight error and ends up more than 4.5 seconds behind the leading duo.

14TH LAP (MID-RACE):

Rossi makes his first mistake of the season allowing Abe to take advantage and he crosses the line just 325 thousandths ahead. Biaggi takes a turn in the sand trap, soon to be copied by Capirossi who finds himself in ninth place. One lap later, Crivillé moves into third place to the delight of the crowd.

21ST LAP:

Rossi decides that his game of cat and mouse with Abe has lasted long enough. He retakes control and in just one lap his lead goes from 222 thousandths to 1"559 breaking a new record in the process.

FINISH (27 LAPS):

He stands up, pretends to meditate before collecting as pillion one of his fans disguised as a doctor, Rossi's new nickname.

CHAMPIONSHIP:

Maximum points for Rossi. With a 31 point lead over Abe, and nearly 40 over Nakano and Capirossi, Valentino is on the right track.

Choice of the right tyre: Shinya Nakano hesitates.

It's Ducati's turn

Smiling for the occasion, with a pause as relaxed as possible for an historic handshake: Friday 4 May 2001 at 12h30. The President of the American controlled holding company that includes the make Ducati, Federico Minoli and the President of the FIM, Francesco Zerbi, look like parents about to announce a happy event. Ducati the superbike specialist has begun work on a four-stroke prototype in keeping with the new regulations that will come into force in GP next year. "This announcement confirms that the revolution planned by the Federation with the constructors' support is the right one", declares President Zerbi.

So exactly a month after the Sauber engine was unveiled at the Japanese GP, Ducati has entered the ring. "There are three main reasons," explains Federico Minoli. "Firstly, Ducati and racing are one and the same thing. Racing is in our blood and forms part of our history, but also our future. Secondly, the excellent economic results from 2000 – an increase in income of 28.9% with 588 million Swiss Francs, an operating profit of 14.7% at 47 million – has enabled us to launch the project while still maintaining our activities in world superbike. Finally, and especially, for a very long time we have subscribed to the dictum "racing is for pleasure". And to design all the parts that make up a prototype from the drawing board to the track is the finest and greatest challenge a team of engineers can undertake".

After Sauber's personalised F1 technology, Ducati will bring its knowledge of 2 cylinder four-strokes. "We have made computer generated assessments of all the technical possibilities allowed in the new regulations, ranging from 2 to 6 cylinders. And none of them emerge above the rest. Since Ducati is a specialist in two cylinders , we will pursue that route although high technology will also be adopted. Perhaps using oval pistons or multi-valve distribution", explains Claudio Domenicali, the boss of Ducati Corsica. "Our racing department currently has 70 people and it will be increased to around 110".

As a footnote and as proof that Ducati will not just settle for entering a "super-superbike", Alan Jenkins the engineer who has worked in Formula 1 for McLaren, Prost

GP and Jaguar is involved in this ambitious ...and costly project. For the return of four-stroke technology to GP racing coincides with a marked rise in the budgets required. Claudio Domenicali estimates the development costs for the bike of the future to be around 50 million Swiss Francs. "Then come the costs for operating the official team which for one season will total a further 15 million".

After dominating world superbike - here Ruben Xaus leads World Champion Troy Bayliss in Valencia - Ducati is coming into GP.

So what's the point? "Such a project is not an extraordinary expense, it's an investment", explains the big boss, Federico Minoli. "Both for our product image as well as the technological application on the machines we market".

Another factor is the current popularity of motorcycle racing in Italy: the figures released by RAI after showing the South African 500 GP show a record audience of 7 million viewers for a market share of 34%.

250cc

GP of Spain

6 May

Jerez - 4.423 m

"My name is Alzamora. Emilio Alzamora..."

STARTING GRID

1. 74	D. Katoh	Telefonica Movistar Honda	1'43.959
2. 34	M. Lucchi	MS Aprilia Racing	1'44.090
3. 15	R. Locatelli	MS Eros Ramazotti Racing	1'44.488
4. 10	F. Nieto	Valencia Circuit Aspar Team	1'44.489
5. 31	T. Harada	MS Aprilia Racing	1'44.635
6. 5	M. Melandri	MS Aprilia Racing	1'44.688
7. 8	N. Matsudo	Petronas Sprinta Yamaha T	1'44.795
8. 99	J. McWilliams	Aprilia Grand Prix	1'44.878
9. 21	F. Battaini	MS Eros Ramazotti Racing	1'45.123
10. 7	E. Alzamora	Telefonica Movistar Honda	1'45.131
11. 6	A. Debon	Valencia Circuit Aspar Team	1'45.238
12. 44	R. Rolfo	Safilo Oxydo Race	1'45.550
13. 81	R. de Puniet	Equipe de France - Scrab G	1'45.627
14. 12	K. Nöhles	MS Aprilia Racing	1'45.675
15. 18	S. Yuzy	Petronas Sprinta Yamaha T	1'45.711
16. 42	D. Checa	Team Fomma	1'45.801
17. 9	S. Porto	Yamaha Kruz	1'45.821
18. 66	A. Hofmann	Dark Dog Racing Factory	1'46.114
19. 20	J. Vidal	PR2 Metrored	1'46.228
20. 37	L. Boscoscuro	Campetella Racing	1'46.303
21. 50	S. Guintoli	Equipe de France - Scrab G	1'46.487
22. 22	D. De Gea	Antena 3 Yamaha-d 'Antin	1'46.622
23. 19	J. Allemand	Antena 3 Yamaha-d 'Antin	1'47.059
24. 57	L. Lanzi	Campetella Racing	1'47.173
25. 55	D. Giugovaz	Edo Racing	1'48.239
26. 38	A. Molina	Kolmer Racing Team	1'48.461
27. 39	I. Bonilla	BRT Ismael Bonilla	1'48.520
28. 23	C. Barros	Yamaha Kruz	1'48.571
29. 98	K. Poensgen	Dark Dog Racing Factory	1'48.828
30. 16	D. Tomas	By Queroseno Racing Team	1'49.050
31. 45	S. Edwards	FCC-TSR	1'49.688
32. 41	D. Nacher	PR2 Metrored	1'51.038

RACE: 25 LAPS = 110.575 KM

1. Daijiro Katoh - 25 laps in 43'49.748 (151.371 km/h)
2. Tetsuya Harada — at 11.789
3. Marco Melandri — at 17.335
4. Marcellino Lucchi — at 17.870
5. Fonsi Nieto — at 23.696
6. Emilio Alzamora — at 24.979
7. Roberto Rolfo — at 25.757
8. Roberto Locatelli — at 32.201
9. Franco Battaini — at 39.404
10. Jeremy Mc Williams — at 39.510
11. Alex Hofmann — at 53.435
12. Naoki Matsudo — at 53.471
13. Alex Debon — at 1'02.113
14. Klaus Nöhles — at 1'02.437
15. Lorenzo Lanzi — at 1'07.791
16. David Checa — at 1'12.964
17. Jeronimo Vidal — at 1'16.192
18. Randy de Puniet — at 1'35.023
19. Julien Allemand — at 1'35.337
20. Diego Giugovaz — at 1'37.041
21. Ismael Bonilla — at 1 lap
22. Alvaro Molina — at 1 lap
23. Katja Poensgen — at 1 lap
24. Cesar Barros — at 1 lap
25. David Tomas — at 1 lap
26. Stuart Edwards — at 1 lap
27. Damaso Nacher — at 1 lap

RETIREMENTS

David De Gea	at 1 lap (fall)
Shahrol Yuzy	at 7 laps (fall)
Luca Boscoscuro	at 13 laps
Sebastian Porto	at 18 laps
Sylvain Guintoli	at 20 laps (fall)

RACE FACTS

Pole Position:	Daijiro Katoh	1'43.959
Fastest lap:	Daijiro Katoh	1'44.444
Circuit record lap:	Shinya Nakano	1'44.875 (1999)
Circuit best lap:	Daijiro Katoh	1'43.959 (2001)

CHAMPIONSHIP

1. D. Katoh	75	(3 victories)
2. T. Harada	56	
3. M. Melandri	46	
4. R. Locatelli	37	
5. R. Rolfo	28	
6. F. Nieto	27	
7. N. Matsudo	24	
8. J. Mc Williams	24	
9. F. Battaini	16	
10. S. Porto	16	

PRACTICE:

It has become a tradition in Jerez: the race veteran (44 since 13 March) and test rider for Aprilia, Marcellino Lucchi, is astride a rolling laboratory. And it shows! Locatelli records the fastest time on Friday, but Daijiro Katoh sets the record straight during the deciding session, with Lucchi the only one capable of staying with him (131 thousandths). Alfonso Gonzales-Nieto achieves his first ever qualification on the front row in front of his home crowd.

START:

Sensation already after the warm-up lap, since the riders are requested to stop their engines. Everyone on the grid wonders what's happened and we soon find out. One of the safety cars – a BMW M3 – has finished up in the wall! Everything starts again a quarter of an hour later: Katoh takes control ahead of Harada, Lucchi, Gonzales and Melandri.

3RD LAP:

De Puniet crashes while in 11th position but rejoins the race.

4TH LAP:

Harada takes Katoh by surprise on the inside, the two Japanese bikes touch but stay upright.

7TH LAP:

Katoh retakes the lead but Harada is still right behind. Lucchi has lost touch and Melandri and Alzamora are a second behind the veteran.

One Honda – Katoh – and three Aprilias on the front row: the image of the 2001 250 season.

13TH LAP (MID-RACE):

Katoh is piling on the pressure. He has just broken the track record and has a lead of 674 thousandths over Harada.

19TH LAP:

Yuzy falls. Debon just manages to avoid him. Katoh's lead is now 5"975.

FINISH (25 LAPS):

With a lead of 11"789 there's no catching Katoh. In Harada's camp there are smiles all round because they know that second place behind the little Japanese Honda rider is as good as a win this year. De Gea takes a massive fall on the last corner.

CHAMPIONSHIP:

A full house for Katoh with 75 points gained from a possible 75. Harada (19 points behind) and Melandri (29) confirm themselves as the Aprilia ring leaders but are way behind the Katoh-Honda combination.

The most populated paddock of the season: welcome to the crowd at Jerez de la Frontera.

6 May
Jerez - 4.423m

Ole...

PRACTICE:

Ui (Derbi) confirms his status as big favourite, smashing the record for fastest 125cc ever at Jerez. On provisional pole on Friday, the lightweight jockey – 38 kilos, 1m40 – Max Sabbatani celebrates his feat in Doctor Costa's clinic after a fall caused by Toni Elias. On Saturday he is the only one of the leading riders not to improve on his time. Poggiali (riding for Gilera) is second but 7 tenths behind.

START:

Poggiali and Ui are on the ball, but it's Toni Elias who gets a flying start from the second row. Cecchinello is left standing. After the first lap, Ui goes through into the lead.

6TH LAP:

Azuma is the fastest man on the track. The Japanese rider from Olivier Liégeois' team has closed right in on Ui. Poggiali and Perugini are chasing hard and Azuma soon takes the lead.

8TH LAP:

Giansanti and Jenkner fall while battling for 11th place.

9TH LAP:

Azuma and Ui are endangering the pace, so Poggiali takes things in hand.

12TH LAP (MID-RACE):

There are four riders within 491 thousandths. In order: Ui, Poggiali, Azuma and Perugini riding an Italjet in perpetual progress.

Manuel Poggiali in the lead until the last lap: he will not make many more errors.

18TH LAP:

There are still four riders at the front with Poggiali leading ahead of Perugini. Behind them, Cecchinello is the fastest on the track and has come back to fifth place after his disastrous start.

20TH LAP:

It's a bleak day for Derbi: Pablo Nieto runs off the track and Youichi Ui falls. Azuma and Poggiali make a slight break.

FINISH (23 LAPS):

After taking the lead one lap from the end, Azuma increases the pace and Poggiali makes a mistake falling in spectacular fashion. Perugini's Italjet doesn't stand the distance (the Italian crawls home), so Cecchinello and Borsoi find themselves on the podium.

CHAMPIONSHIP:

Azuma takes the lead overall taking full advantage from the fall of his main rival, Youichi Ui. After two fourth places, Borsoi wins the second podium of his career.

Lucio Cecchinello: rider, team boss, press officer, sponsors contact, the Italian wears many racing hats.

STARTING GRID

1.	41	Y. Ui	L & M Derbi Team	1'48.002
2.	54	M. Poggiali	Gilera Racing Team	1'48.762
3.	9	L. Cecchinello	MS Aprilia LCR	1'48.838
4.	7	S. Perugini	Italjet Racing Team	1'49.070
5.	16	S. Sanna	Safilo Oxydo Race	1'49.071
6.	24	T. Elias	Telefonica Movistar Jr Team	1'49.158
7.	11	M. Sabbatani	Bossini Fontana Racing	1'49.170
8.	5	N. Ueda	FCC – TSR	1'49.236
9.	4	M. Azuma	Liegeois Competition	1'49.262
10.	23	G. Borsoi	LAE – UGT 3000	1'49.264
11.	20	G. Caffiero	Bossini Fontana Racing	1'49.328
12.	17	S. Jenkner	LAE – UGT 3000	1'49.331
13.	26	D. Pedrosa	Telefonica Movistar Jr Team	1'49.483
14.	28	G. Talmacsi	Racing Service	1'49.525
15.	31	A. Rodriguez	Valencia Circuit Aspar Team	1'49.621
16.	15	A. de Angelis	Matteoni Racing	1'49.639
17.	22	P. Nieto	L & M Derbi Team	1'49.654
18.	21	A. Vincent	Team Fomma	1'49.694
19.	6	M. Giansanti	Axo Racing Team	1'49.742
20.	29	A. Nieto Jr	Viceroy Team	1'49.817
21.	8	G. Scalvini	Italjet Racing Team	1'49.979
22.	10	J. Müller	PEV-Spalt-ADAC Sachsen	1'50.210
23.	39	J. Hules	Matteoni Racing	1'50.368
24.	44	H. Faubel	Valencia Circuit – Aspar	1'50.374
25.	25	J. Olive	Telefonica Movistar Jr Team	1'50.506
26.	18	J. Smrz	Budweiser Budvar Hanusch	1'50.580
27.	12	R. Jara	MS Aprilia LCR	1'50.675
28.	34	E. Bataille	Axo Racing Team	1'50.783
29.	19	A. Brannetti	Team Crae	1'51.011
30.	27	M. Petrini	Racing Service	1'51.265
31.	43	D. Pinera	By Queroseno Racing Team	1'51.990
32.	14	P. Hafeneger	Liegeois Competition	1'52.391

RACE: 23 LAPS = 101.729 KM

1. Masao Azuma -23 laps in 42'09.849 (144.761 km/h)
2. Lucio Cecchinello — at 4.623
3. Gino Borsoi — at 5.753
4. Noburu Ueda — at 10.197
5. Angel Nieto Jr — at 10.384
6. Angel Rodriguez — at 10.604
7. Alex de Angelis — at 10.747
8. Max Sabbatani — at 15.231
9. Jaroslav Hules — at 15.798
10. Daniel Pedrosa — at 19.497
11. Arnaud Vincent — at 24.705
12. Stefanu Perugini — at 27.712
13. Toni Elias — at 28.109
14. Joan Olive — at 28.221
15. Jakub Smrz — at 28.969
16. Hector Faubel — at 33.743
17. Gabor Talmacsi — at 33.905
18. Jarno Müller — at 38.247
19. Raul Jara — at 58.393
20. Eric Bataille — at 1'13.859

RACE FACTS

Pole Position:	Youichi Ui	1'48.002
Fastest lap:	Masao Azuma	1'48.385
Circuit record lap:	Tomomi Manako	1'49.360 (1998)
Circuit best lap:	Youichi Ui	1'48.002 (2001)

RETIREMENTS

Manuel Poggiali	at 1 lap (fall)
Daniel Pinera	at 2 laps
Youichi Ui	at 4 laps (fall)
Pablo Nieto	at 5 laps
Phillipp Hafeneger	at 5 laps
Gaspare Caffiero	at 13 laps
Gianluigi Scalvini	at 14 laps
Alessandro Brannetti	at 16 laps
Marco Petrini	at 16 laps
Mirko Giansanti	at 17 laps (fall)
Steve Jenkner	at 17 laps
Simone Sanna	at 19 laps

CHAMPIONSHIP

1. M. Azuma — 56 (2 victories)
2. Y. Ui — 45 (1 victory)
3. G. Borsoi — 42
4. M. Poggiali — 31
5. L. Cecchinello — 30
6. N. Ueda — 29
7. A. Nieto Jr — 27
8. A. Vincent — 22
9. M. Sabbatani — 21
10. A. de Angelis — 18

Le Mans.

Grand Prix of FRANCE

A highly promising sight on the Bugatti circuit. Two ex-world champions, Alex Crivillé and Kenny Roberts leading Norifumi Abe.

Toni Elias, a new face for the race-going public to discover.

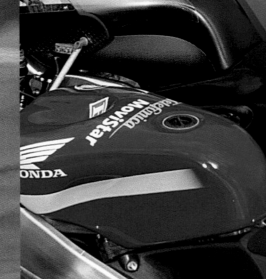

All lined up ready to go.

500cc GP of France

Max Biaggi... as we know him.

20 May
Le Mans - 4.305m

Starting grid

1.	3	M. Biaggi	Marlboro Yamaha Team	1'38.421
2.	1	K. Roberts	Telefonica Movistar Suzuki	1'38.668
3.	46	V. Rossi	Nastro Azzurro Honda	1'38.852
4.	56	S. Nakano	Gauloises Yamaha Tech 3	1'38.891
5.	7	C. Checa	Marlboro Yamaha Team	1'39.093
6.	41	N. Haga	Red Bull Yamaha WCM	1'39.115
7.	6	N. Abe	Antena 3 Yamaha-d'Antin	1'39.132
8.	65	L. Capirossi	West Honda Pons	1'39.247
9.	28	A. Crivillé	Repsol YPF Honda Team	1'39.275
10.	17	J. vd Goorbergh	Proton TEAM KR	1'39.651
11.	11	T. Ukawa	Repsol YPF Honda Team	1'39.973
12.	4	A. Barros	West Honda Pons	1'40.062
13.	15	S. Gibernau	Telefonica Movistar Suzuki	1'40.312
14.	10	J.L. Cardoso	Antena 3 Yamaha-d'Antin	1'40.509
15.	8	C. Walker	Shell Advance Honda	1'40.869
16.	24	J. Vincent	Pulse GP	1'41.475
17.	16	J. Stigefelt	Sabre Sport	1'42.463
18.	68	M. Willis	Pulse GP	1'43.625
19.	21	B. Veneman	Dee Cee Jeans Racing Team	1'43.684
20.	32	J. Janssen	Arie Molenaar Racing	1'43.872

Race: 28 laps = 120.54 km

1.	Max Biaggi - 27 laps in 46'59.346 (153.916 km/h)	
2.	Carlos Checa	at 3.266
3.	Valentino Rossi	at 4.830
4.	Norick Abe	at 14.561
5.	Alex Crivillé	at 14.977
6.	Kenny Roberts	at 23.180
7.	Loris Capirossi	at 29.597
8.	Alex Barros	at 31.205
9.	Sete Gibernau	at 32.499
10.	Jurgen vd Goorbergh	at 33.019
11.	Shinya Nakano	at 36.476
12.	Chris Walker	at 1'15.798
13.	Jose Luis Cardoso	at 1'19.446
14.	Barry Veneman	at 1 lap
15.	Jarno Janssen	at 1 lap

Retirements

Jason Vincent	at 12 laps
Mark Willis	at 13 laps
Tohru Ukawa	at 18 laps (fall)
Noriyuki Haga	at 18 laps (fall)
Johan Stigefelt	at 26 laps

Race facts

Pole Position:	Max Biaggi	1'38.421
Fastest lap:	Valentino Rossi	1'39.954 (non official)
Circuit record lap:	Max Biaggi	1'40.089 (2000)
Circuit best lap:	Max Biaggi	1'38.421 (2001)

Championship

1. V. Rossi	91 (3 victories)
2. N. Abe	57
3. M. Biaggi	54 (1 victory)
4. L. Capirossi	45
5. A. Crivillé	44
6. S. Nakano	42
7. K. Roberts	37
8. A. Barros	35
9. C. Checa	28
10. G. McCoy	27

Practice:

"It's difficult to find the right rhythm on the Bugatti. Braking and accelerating is brusque and so there are a lot of crashes and often serious ones". 1984 250 World Champion Christian Sarron knows what he's talking about. From the very first free practice on Friday, there is already one forfeit – Jacque still suffering from a blocked bone on his right radius, following his free practice crash in Jerez (collision with Checa). McCoy is the fastest on Friday but doesn't finish free practice on Saturday: crying forfeit with a fractured scaphoid and an operation pending. Haslam and West are also out. On the track it's the comeback for those beaten in the first few races. Biaggi is on pole next to reigning World Champion Kenny Roberts with Rossi and Nakano completing the front row.

Start:

Biaggi and Roberts take control with Rossi getting an appalling start. After the first lap, the World Champion leads ahead of Max and the second Marlboro-Yamaha rider Carlos Checa. Rossi is only eighth.

7th lap:

Biaggi goes on the attack and runs into the sand. But he keeps the throttle open and rejoins the track right under Roberts' nose. Rossi has just recorded the fastest lap in seventh position.

11th lap:

Haga and Ukawa crash out.

14th lap (mid-race):

The two Yamahas are still in control, with Checa leading Biaggi (who smashes the record for the first time). Rossi is in fourth place.

21st lap:

Biaggi has retaken control and has a lead of 3"569 over Checa. Rossi is third and Roberts has just been passed by Crivillé.

Finish (28 laps):

The first win of the season for Massimiliano Biaggi. Rossi has closed in on Checa but would have needed a few more laps to snatch second place.

Kenny Roberts once again at the front. But only at the start of the race.

Rossimania in full swing. In France like elsewhere.

Championship:

In spite of being beaten, Rossi consolidates his position by finishing ahead of Abe and Capirossi. With just two weeks to go until the Italian GP, Biaggi stakes a claim ... but is 37 points behind the leader.

Olivier Jacque, 250 World Champion is suffering from his wrist, after an operation following his crash in winter testing in Malaysia. Forced to withdraw, he still remains at the track all weekend to encourage the French contingent.

THE HERO'S TORMENT

"Two days either way don't make any difference. It's the French GP and I owe it to my fans to make an appearance. Unfortunately they won't see me race, perhaps just a slow lap just to say hello". Olivier Jacque 250 World Champion who has moved to 500 this season is keeping a low profile. It's Friday afternoon in the Bugatti paddock in Le Mans, France. In French motorcycling terms it's "the" race of the year. And it will take place without its hero. The bombshell came a few hours earlier after around fifteen laps of free practice: "I consulted Professor Gérard Saillant ten days ago, and he prescribed special treatment in the form of injections. Although I was able to lift fifty kilos and do push-ups in the morning and evening, I knew I would have to wait until I was on the bike to find out my real possiblities. And..." And? "After ten laps I knew. I couldn't control my bike, I had big problems just manipulating the throttle. In these circumstances..."

In these circumstances... the French GP would take place without its World Champion. It's another episode in the tale "Olivier Jacque in 2000", the story of a strange journey punctuated by often conflicting information:

- End January 2001: during private testing in Sepang in Malaysia, the 250 World Champion suffers two falls. Nothing serious on Monday 29, a little more serious on Tuesday 30. "After a brief visit to hospital, Olivier Jacque returned to his hotel. He is suffering from a clean fracture to the right forearm (radius). No surgery is necessary".

- Early February: first (unpleasant) surprise. On his return home, OJ consulted his own doctor. X-rays showed another additional fracture: in the right scaphoid, a small bone in the wrist. "The specialists all agree that a fractured scaphoid requires three months to

recover. But the first GP will take place exactly two months after the operation", warns Hervé Poncharal, Tech 3 Team boss, the team that lines up Jacque and the Japanese rider Nakano.

- 8 April, Japanese GP: the Frenchman grits his teeth and starts the race in Suzuka before retiring.

- 22 April, South African GP: "I was feeling better. It was now two and a half months after the operation and if I hadn't got a penalty for a jumped start I would have scored my first points in 500". In Welkom OJ finished the race.

- 4 May, first practice for the Spanish GP: the famous threshold of three months has passed. And the scaphoid? "It's just a bad memory". Yet... "During the first lap of free practice, Checa literally threw himself under my wheels. I fell and at that moment, the pain came back in my forearm. The bone was not fully matted where the radius had fractured. We tried everything, but in vain".

- 18 May, the famous Friday in Le Mans. "I have an appointment on Monday for an operation. They will put a plate in my arm. I will have to stay in hospital for a few days".

Two days later, Yamaha scored a one-two (Biaggi ahead of Checa). As for Jacque he had to settle for a lap of honour as a man injured physically and morally in a luxury car. And two weeks later, OJ cried forfeit for the Italian GP...

250cc
GP of France

20 May

Le Mans - 4.305m

STARTING GRID
1.	74	D. Katoh	Telefonica Movistar Honda	1'41.065
2.	31	T. Harada	MS Aprilia Racing	1'41.108
3.	5	M. Melandri	MS Aprilia Racing	1'41.328
4.	10	F. Nieto	Valencia Circuit Aspar Team	1'41.595
5.	7	E. Alzamora	Telefonica Movistar Honda	1'41.840
6.	81	R. de Puniet	Equipe de France - Scrab G	1'41.895
7.	99	J. McWilliams	Aprilia Grand Prix	1'42.117
8.	8	N. Matsudo	Petronas Sprinta Yamaha T	1'42.181
9.	9	S. Porto	Yamaha Kruz	1'42.184
10.	15	R. Locatelli	MS Eros Ramazotti Racing	1'42.225
11.	6	A. Debon	Valencia Circuit Aspar Team	1'42.487
12.	44	R. Rolfo	Safilo Oxydo Race	1'42.559
13.	21	F. Battaini	MS Eros Ramazotti Racing	1'42.659
14.	12	K. Nöhles	MS Aprilia Racing	1'42.920
15.	66	A. Hofmann	Dark Dog Racing Factory	1'43.054
16.	22	D. De Gea	Antena 3 Yamaha-d 'Antin	1'43.301
17.	42	D. Checa	Team Fomma	1'43.583
18.	18	S. Yuzy	Petronas Sprinta Yamaha T	1'43.747
19.	57	L. Lanzi	Campetella Racing	1'43.818
20.	37	L. Boscoscuro	Campetella Racing	1'44.127
21.	50	S. Guintoli	Equipe de France - Scrab G	1'44.173
22.	20	J. Vidal	PR2 Metrored	1'44.188
23.	55	D. Giugovaz	Edo Racing	1'45.316
24.	11	R. Chiarello	Aprilia Grand Prix	1'45.513
25.	23	C. Barros	Yamaha Kruz	1'46.005
26.	54	H. Mora	Bentin Motorsport	1'46.107
27.	64	H. Marchand	Equipe de France	1'46.310
28.	45	S. Edwards	FCC-TSR	1'46.489
29.	16	D. Tomas	By Queroseno Racing Team	1'46.862
30.	56	D. Fouloi	Fouloi Racing Team	1'47.442
31.	52	G. Dietrich	Equipe de France	1'47.526
32.	53	T. Ouvrard	Ouvrard Racing Team	1'48.050

RACE: 26 RACE = 111.93 KM
1. Daijiro Katoh - 26 laps in 44'29.546 (150.942 km/h)		
2. Tetsuya Harada	at 0.204	
3. Marco Melandri	at 13.599	
4. Emilio Alzamora	at 16.813	
5. Fonsi Nieto	at 18.428	
6. Roberto Locatelli	at 29.025	
7. Jeremy Mc Williams	at 42.813	
8. Sebastian Porto	at 44.429	
9. Roberto Rolfo	at 45.077	
10. Alex Debon	at 45.351	
11. Alex Hofmann	at 47.253	
12. Klaus Nöhles	at 55.500	
13. Franco Battaini	at 56.474	
14. Sylvain Guintoli	at 57.653	
15. Shahrol Yuzy	at 1'04.735	
16. David Checa	at 1'19.767	
17. Luca Boscoscura	at 1'31.159	
18. David De Gea	at 1'31.496	
19. David Tomas	at 1'37.808	
20. Riccardo Chiarello	at 1 lap	
21. Herve Mora	at 1 lap	
22. Stuart Edwards	at 1 lap	
23. Guillaume Dietrich	at 1 lap	
24. David Fouloi	at 1 lap	
25. Cesar Barros	at 1 lap	
26. Tom Ouvrard	at 2 laps	

RETIREMENTS
Jeronimo Vidal	at 15 laps
Naoki Matsudo	at 19 laps
Diego Guigovaz	at 23 laps
Randy de Puniet	at 24 laps (fall)
Lorenzo Lanzi	at 24 laps
Hugo Marchand	at 25 laps (fall)

RACE FACTS
Pole Position:	Daijiro Katoh	1'41.065
Fastest lap:	Daijiro Katoh	1'41.473
Circuit record lap:	Tohru Ukawa	1'42.312 (2000)
Circuit best lap:	Daijiro Katoh	1'41.065 (2001)

CHAMPIONSHIP
1. D. Katoh	100 (4 victories)
2. T. Harada	76
3. M. Melandri	62
4. R. Locatelli	47
5. F. Nieto	38
6. R. Rolfo	35
7. J. Mc Williams	33
8. N. Matsudo	24
9. S. Porto	24
10. E. Alzamora	23

PRACTICE:

Still Katoh and his Honda ("Winning every grand prix will be very difficult", he confided on the Saturday morning of the French GP), but the Aprilia threat remains very real. On the first day of qualifying, Melandri is the fastest, but the young Italian makes a mistake on Saturday with painful consequences: a discolated left shoulder and severe bruising to his left foot. "Macio" visits a Le Mans hospital before returning to the track to take part in the Sunday morning warm-up and the race. Truly inspired by his home crowd, Randy de Puniet qualifies on the second row (6th place). But trouble in store for Julien Allemand whose divorce from Luis D'Antin's team has turned nasty. And all this in front of the French fans...

START:

Harada, Katoh and Melandri are already the fastest with the undisputed Championship leader taking the lead in the middle of the first lap and crossing the line with more than 5 seconds advantage.

4TH LAP:

The hero of practice, Randy de Puniet suffers a spectacular crash at the Raccordement corner.

8TH LAP:

Harada passes Katoh. Melandri stays with the two Japanese riders, but McWilliams is already four seconds adrift.

13TH LAP (MID-RACE):

Katoh takes the lead again over Harada's and Melandri's Aprilias.

20TH LAP:

Katoh and Harada are talking exactly the same language. Japanese, of course, but also the panache and lap records smashed lap after lap. Melandri can't match the pace, so the victory will be between the two of them.

FINISH (26 LAPS):

Harada retakes control on the 22nd lap. The gap between the two Japanese riders is a mere thousandths of a second. Katoh plans a perfect final attack and improves on the lap record again on the last lap. Harada has no response and Melandri is a courageous third and congratulated by Dr Costa.

CHAMPIONSHIP:

Four pole positions, four victories, one hundred points, Dajiro Katoh continues his march.

Another tumble, another victim over the weekend: German Katja Poensgen.

Marco Melandri, third only twenty four hours after a terrible crash.

125cc GP
of France

Poggiali in action: the dye is cast.

STARTING GRID

1. 41	Y. Ui	L & M Derbi Team	1'47.494
2. 54	M. Poggiali	Gilera Racing Team	1'47.582
3. 9	L. Cecchinello	MS Aprilia LCR	1'47.949
4. 39	J. Hules	Matteoni Racing	1'48.097
5. 5	N. Ueda	FCC – TSR	1'48.104
6. 24	T. Elias	Telefonica Movistar Jr Team	1'48.155
7. 6	M. Giansanti	Axo Racing Team	1'48.283
8. 23	G. Borsoi	LAE – UGT 3000	1'48.344
9. 29	A. Nieto Jr	Viceroy Team	1'48.451
10. 21	A. Vincent	Team Fomma	1'48.624
11. 7	S. Perugini	Italjet Racing Team	1'48.707
12. 11	M. Sabbatani	Bossini Fontana Racing	1'48.790
13. 16	S. Sanna	Safilo Oxydo Race	1'48.817
14. 15	A. de Angelis	Matteoni Racing	1'49.025
15. 26	D. Pedrosa	Telefonica Movistar Jr Team	1'49.033
16. 28	G. Talmacsi	Racing Service	1'49.103
17. 4	M. Azuma	Liegeois Competition	1'49.288
18. 17	S. Jenkner	LAE – UGT 3000	1'49.311
19. 10	J. Müller	PEV-Spalt-ADAC Sachsen	1'49.335
20. 22	P. Nieto	L & M Derbi Team	1'49.443
21. 25	J. Olive	Telefonica Movistar Jr Team	1'49.922
22. 34	E. Bataille	Axo Racing Team	1'50.085
23. 20	G. Caffiero	Bossini Fontana Racing	1'50.265
24. 12	R. Jara	MS Aprilia LCR	1'50.349
25. 27	M. Petrini	Racing Service	1'50.429
26. 18	J. Smrz	Budweiser Budvar Hanusch	1'50.821
27. 63	J. Petit	Racing Moto Sport	1'50.934
28. 61	G. Lefort	Provence Moto Sport	1'51.214
29. 62	E. Nigon	AJP Team	1'52.632
30. 60	X. Herouin	MOB 77	1'52.785
31. 59	J. Enjolras	Tati Team Beaujolais Racing	1'52.818
32. 14	P. Hafeneger	Liegeois Competition	1'53.269

RACE: 24 LAPS = 103.32 KM

1.	Manuel Poggiali – 24 laps in 43'33.372 (142.326km/h)	
2.	Mirko Giansanti	at 0.218
3.	Toni Elias	at 0.298
4.	Gino Borsoi	at 0.515
5.	Lucio Cecchinello	at 0.969
6.	Arnaud Vincent	at 7.357
7.	Noburu Ueda	at 7.940
8.	Masao Azuma	at 8.464
9.	Jaroslav Hules	at 8.751
10.	Angel Nieto Jr	at 11.523
11.	Youichi Ui	at 11.962
12.	Steve Jenkner	at 12.496
13.	Simone Sanna	at 12.514
14.	Alex de Angelis	at 20.667
15.	Max Sabbatani	at 35.012
16.	Gabor Talmacsi	at 36.143
17.	Daniel Pedrosa	at 37.580
18.	Jajub Smrz	at 42.565
19.	Jakub Müller	at 45.597
20.	Eric Bataille	at 59.597
21.	Marco Petrini	at 1'16.293
22.	Jimmy Petit	at 1'22.325
23.	Gaspare Caffiero	at 1'35.945
24.	Erwan Nigon	at 1'58.711
25.	Xavier Herouin	at 1 lap
26.	Phillipp Hafeneger	at 1 lap
27.	Julien Enjolras	at 1 lap

RETIREMENTS

Pablo Nieto	did not start
Joan Olive	at 4 laps
Raul Jara	at 6 laps
Stefano Perugini	at 5 laps
Gregory Lefort	at 18 laps

RACE FACTS

Pole Position:	Youichi Ui	1'47.494
Fastest lap:	Lucio Cecchinello	1'47.766
Circuit record lap:	Noboru Ueda	1'48.011 (2000)
Circuit best lap:	Youichi Ui	1'47.494 (2001)

CHAMPIONSHIP

1.	M. Azuma	64
2.	M. Poggiali	56
3.	G. Borsoi	55
4.	Y. Ui	50
5.	L. Cecchinello	41
6.	N. Ueda	38
7.	A. Nieto Jr	33
8.	M. Giansanti	32
9.	A. Vincent	32
10.	M. Sabbatani	22

PRACTICE:

Harald Bartol's bikes are still dominating proceedings. Ui takes another pole for Derbi by just 88 thousandths of a second from his "team-mate" at Gilera, Manuel Poggiali. This logical conclusion taking into account previous races, cannot obscure the events and emotions of practice: Ui makes a mistake on Saturday afternoon taking Gianluigi Scalvini (Italjet) with him. Scalvini is forced to retire (fractured right collarbone).

START:

Poggiali is the fastest starter from the front row, but Toni Elias, the revelation of the early season, does even better from the second row of the grid. On the first lap, the Gilera leads the young Spaniard's Honda, veteran Noboru Ueda's TSR and Ui's Derbi.

6TH LAP:

Giansanti takes the lead for the first time on the preceding lap, but Poggiali is again in control at the end of the sixth lap. There are ten riders separated by just 2"187 – Giansanti, Elias, Ueda, Borsoi, Jaroslav Hules, Cecchinello, Vincent, Ui and Azuma.

12TH LAP (MID-RACE):

The leading pack has disbanded. A first group of five riders has formed: Poggiali, Borsoi, Giansanti, Ueda and Cecchinello..

18TH LAP:

Nothing to report except that the difference between this group of five and the chasing pack has increased to 3"274.

FINISH (24 LAPS):

Alberto Puig's protégé (boss of the Junior Movistar team) Toni Elias, tries everything he can, but Poggiali counters and resists. He offers Gilera its first 125cc GP success since the German GP in 1956, its first solo GP success since the Dutch 500 GP in 1963 (John Hartle) and the first win in all categories since the Swiss sidecar rider Florian Camathias. This was during the Spanish GP in 1964.

CHAMPIONSHIP:

With Azuma (only eighth) and Ui (eleventh) not on form, there is a general regrouping of the main contenders and only 14 points now separate the first four including the consistent Aprilia test rider, Gino Borsoi.

History in the making: the San Marino national anthem accompanies Manuel Poggiali's first GP victory.

Arnaud Vincent pulls a face – it's only the continuation of a difficult season for the Frenchman.

Mugello ▪

Grand Prix of ITALY

This is known as
Rossimania.

FEBBRE

46

OFFICIAL FANS CLUB VALENTINO ROSSI TAVULLIA

REPSOL
YPF

NO FEAR

Devils and Tigers,
Italy has its own
special appeal.

500cc GP of Italy

3 June
Mugello - 5.245 m

Starting grid

1.	46	V. Rossi	Nastro Azzurro Honda	1'52.554
2.	1	K. Roberts	Telefonica Movistar Suzuki	1'52.688
3.	65	L. Capirossi	West Honda Pons	1'52.834
4.	3	M. Biaggi	Marlboro Yamaha Team	1'52.942
5.	4	A. Barros	West Honda Pons	1'53.021
6.	28	A. Crivillé	Repsol YPF Honda Team	1'53.142
7.	17	J. vd Goorbergh	Proton TEAM KR	1'53.241
8.	7	C. Checa	Marlboro Yamaha Team	1'53.253
9.	11	T. Ukawa	Repsol YPF Honda Team	1'53.335
10.	56	S. Nakano	Gauloises Yamaha Tech 3	1'53.406
11.	6	N. Abe	Antena 3 Yamaha-d'Antin	1'53.589
12.	15	S. Gibernau	Telefonica Movistar Suzuki	1'54.036
13.	41	N. Haga	Red Bull Yamaha WCM	1'54.091
14.	10	J.L. Cardoso	Antena 3 Yamaha-d'Antin	1'54.384
15.	8	C. Walker	Shell Advance Honda	1'54.827
16.	24	J. Vincent	Pulse GP	1'55.780
17.	12	H. Aoki	Arie Molenaar Racing	1'56.390
18.	14	A. West	Dee Cee Jeans Racing Team	1'57.119
19.	16	J. Stigefelt	Sabre Sport	1'57.765
20.	21	B. Veneman	Dee Cee Jeans Racing Team	1'58.009
21.	68	M. Willis	Pulse GP	1'58.365

Race: 23 laps = 120.635 km

1. Alex Barros - 23 laps in 49'26.006 (146.421 km/h)
2. Loris Capirossi — at 8.359
3. Max Biaggi — at 8.509
4. Alex Crivillé — at 8.996
5. Haruchika Aoki — at 20.651
6. Sete Gibernau — at 24.723
7. Tohru Ukawa — at 27.745
8. Shinya Nakano — at 32.768
9. Norick Abe — at 51.357
10. Noriyuki Haga — at 1'08.505
11. Jose Luis Cardoso — at 1'18.026
12. Jurgen vd Goorbergh — at 1'49.333
13. Mark Willis — at 1 lap

Retirements

Valentino Rossi	at 1 lap (fall)
Kenny Roberts	at 3 laps (fall)
Jason Vincent	at 3 laps (fall)
Chris Walker	at 12 laps
Anthony West	at 13 laps (fall)
Carlos Checa	at 16 laps
Johan Stigefelt	at 21 laps (fall)
Barry Veneman	Excluded (black flag)

Race facts

Pole Position:	Valentino Rossi	1'52.554
Fastest lap:	Valentino Rossi	1'54.994
Circuit record lap:	Mick Doohan	1'53.342 (1998)
Circuit best lap:	Tetsuya Harada	1'52.454 (1999)

Championship

1. V. Rossi — 91 (3 victories)
2. M. Biaggi — 70 (1 victory)
3. L. Capirossi — 65
4. N. Abe — 64
5. A. Barros — 60 (1 victory)
6. A. Crivillé — 57
7. S. Nakano — 50
8. K. Roberts — 37
9. T. Ukawa — 36
10. S. Gibernau — 29

Visibility nil, uncertain grip – the elements hit back in Tuscany.

Practice:

We expected the Battle of Italy, we got the Rossi Extravaganza. Valentino arrives on Saturday with a Hawaiian coloured bike. Biaggi is in trouble on the first day (two crashes). Jacque (operated on in Paris) and McCoy (in hospital in Clermont-Ferrand) are not there.

Start:

Roberts and Capirossi are the quickest off the mark ahead of Biaggi and Rossi. At the end of the first lap, the Suzuki Number One and the Honda 65 have a few tenths lead.

6th lap:

Biaggi takes control on the third lap. Max currently counts a lead of 0"650 on the trio formed by Barros, Capirossi and Rossi.

9th lap:

Umbrellas are making an appearance. Barros who has taken the lead raises his arm .. but gets no support. He repeats the same gesture a little further on. This time the three leading men (Barros, Biaggi and Rossi) are in agreement. So a second start is given for a further 16 laps.

Second start:

A cause for excitement with Rossi falling on the formation lap. He comes back to his pit as a passenger on a scooter driven by former rider Gianni Rolando and climbs onto his second bike. Barros and Biaggi take command ahead of a spectacular Haruchika Aoki (Honda V2).

An experienced Barros will make no mistakes.

8th lap (mid-heat):

On the track, Roberts leads ahead of Barros, but the Brazilian is ahead of Biaggi and the World Champion on aggregate times.

13th lap:

Abe falls. Barros is now keeping a firm eye on his team-mate Capirossi's comeback.

Finish (16th lap, 23 overall):

Aoki wins the second heat (Barros the GP), but Rossi provides the show on the last laps completely forgetting that the track is slippery. With 300 metres to go, and running in second on aggregate times while closing in on Barros, the championship leader crashes out. Capirossi just manages to avoid the crash.

Championship:

With Rossi at fault, Biaggi moves to within a race victory of his rival (21 points). Capirossi is 26 points behind.

Opposing fans... but still friends: a Roman from Biaggi's following meets a Rossi fan who chose hippy flowers for the occasion.

BARROS, THE BRAVE BRAZILIAN

A bad day for the traditional image of Brazil with its often exaggerated jokey, party-loving image. On the track at Mugello, a child of the country of contrasts used his wisdom and vast experience to find the arms to triumph in the most difficult 500 GP for the last ten years in terms of the weather. His name? Barros. Alexandre Barros. A young hothead who had a habit of kicking his bike when it wouldn't work properly in his early days in 80cc, he has become one of the calmest riders in the paddock. In Mugello, Barros started his 183rd GP and his 152nd in 500cc.

And on a track that had become a skating rink with every lap becoming more slippery, he had a ball. While others floundered...

Valentino Rossi? A crash in the formation lap preceding the second start, another one just 300m from the finish when he was surfing on the waves astride a Honda that had been decorated with Hawaiian blue flowers for the occasion. Loris Capirossi? Second. But what a second place! He burst into laughter on the podium because he was completely aware that

Barros could show his killer instinct able to stab his rivals in the back if the situation demanded. And his capability – even though he was aided and abetted by those around him – to open up a void around him. In Mugello his charming but invasive wife Patricia was absent and Alex was not able to talk to her all weekend due to the "mysterious" disappearance of his portable phone.

Alexandre Barros on the starting grid: the Brazilian will go on to ride a perfect race in cataclysmic conditions.

like Moses in other circumstances, he had just taken on the role of victim escaping the waters. Only minutes earlier, at the moment when Rossi's wheel was crossing through a torrent, Capirossi just behind miraculously and acrobatically managed to stay in the saddle.

Massimilano Biaggi? Third. But here again, what a third place! A haggard, Max lost for most of the race unable to figure anything out as he was passed by one rival after the other (Rossi, Crivillé). While he just sat there uneasily..

It was a fiery race with one serene winner. Astonishingly calm, terrible calculating and incontestable boss of a race where for the first time in a long time, everything seemed to be going right for the shy Brazilian. For little people know that behind the sometimes grizzly exterior hides a sensitive soul. He has trouble saying no and for a very long time he listened to too many people.

All this is a thing of the past. His capital which has increased other the years and just lay waiting to emerge in extreme conditions, was his ability for the meek and gentle

Up until Sunday evening. While Sito Pons' team celebrated a superb one-two, the Brazilian had already left the paddock by helicopter. He was on his way to Japan and the track at Suzuka where a Honda SP-1 was waiting for him for the first private test for the Eight Hours. And after a day's adaptation, a Brazilian specialising in 500 two strokes would teach the Japanese riders a lesson. In their own backyard. In difficult weather conditions which are good for experience.

Has a new Barros been born? To know the answer, just turn ahead a few pages.

250cc
GP of Italy

3 June

Mugello - 5.245 m

STARTING GRID

1.	31	T. Harada	MS Aprilia Racing	1'53.922
2.	14	M. Lucchi	MS Aprilia Racing	1'54.585
3.	99	J. McWilliams	Aprilia Grand Prix	1'54.691
4.	81	R. de Puniet	Equipe de France - Scrab G	1'54.915
5.	15	R. Locatelli	MS Eros Ramazotti Racing	1'55.018
6.	74	D. Katoh	Telefonica Movistar Honda	1'55.024
7.	21	F. Battaini	MS Eros Ramazotti Racing	1'55.248
8.	5	M. Melandri	MS Aprilia Racing	1'55.272
9.	6	A. Debon	Valencia Circuit Aspar Team	1'55.416
10.	44	R. Rolfo	Safilo Oxydo Race	1'55.426
11.	9	S. Porto	Yamaha Kruz	1'55.473
12.	10	F. Nieto	Valencia Circuit Aspar Team	1'55.492
13.	66	A. Hofmann	Dark Dog Racing Factory	1'55.709
14.	12	K. Nöhles	MS Aprilia Racing	1'55.774
15.	8	N. Matsudo	Petronas Sprinta Yamaha T	1'55.853
16.	50	S. Guintoli	Equipe de France - Scrab G	1'55.920
17.	7	E. Alzamora	Telefonica Movistar Honda	1'55.921
18.	18	S. Yuzy	Petronas Sprinta Yamaha T	1'56.375
19.	20	J. Vidal	PR2 Metrored	1'56.796
20.	42	D. Checa	Team Fomma	1'56.823
21.	57	L. Lanzi	Campetella Racing	1'57.266
22.	37	L. Boscoscuro	Campetella Racing	1'57.695
23.	22	D. De Gea	Antena 3 Yamaha-d 'Antin	1'57.957
24.	55	D. Giugovaz	Edo Racing	1'58.416
25.	16	D. Tomas	By Queroseno Racing Team	1'58.529
26.	11	R. Chiarello	Aprilia Grand Prix	1'59.361
27.	36	L. Costa	Antena 3 Yamaha-d 'Antin	1'59.831
28.	98	K. Poensgen	Dark Dog Racing Factory	2'00.698
29.	23	C. Barros	Yamaha Kruz	2'01.062

RACE: 21 LAPS = 110.145 KM

1.	Tetsuya Harada - 21 laps in 46'11.129 (143.090km/h)	
2.	Roberto Rolfo	at 12.729
3.	Marco Melandri	at 37.673
4.	Roberto Locatelli	at 43.860
5.	Fonsi Nieto	at 47.149
6.	Emilio Alzamora	at 54.884
7.	David Checa	at 57.903
8.	Alex Debon	at 59.092
9.	Shahrol Yuzy	at 1'00.763
10.	Daijiro Katoh	at 1'11.795
11.	Lorenzo Lanzi	at 1'13.110
12.	Naoki Matsudo	at 1'40.274
13.	David De Gea	at 1'42.351
14.	Katja Poensgen	at 1'42.515
15.	Jeronimo Vidal	at 1'42.911
16.	Klaus Nöhles	at 1'43.602
17.	David Tomas	at 1'45.253
18.	Alex Hofmann	at 1'51.411
19.	Luis Costa	at 1 lap

RETIREMENTS

Diego Giugovaz	Excluded (black flag)
Luca Boscoscuro	at 5 laps
Riccardo Chiarello	at 6 laps (fall)
Sylvain Guintoli	at 12 laps
Sebastian Porto	at 16 laps (fall)
Franco Battaini	at 16 laps
Marcellino Lucchi	at 17 laps (fall)
Jeremy Mc Williams	at 17 laps (fall)
Randy de Puniet	at 18 laps (fall)
Cesar Barros	at 20 laps (fall)

RACE FACTS

Pole Position:	Tetsuya Harada	1'53.922
Fastest lap:	Roberto Locatelli	2'07.403
Circuit record lap:	Shinya Nakano	1'54.462 (2000)
Circuit best lap:	Tetsuya Harada	1'53.922 (2001)

CHAMPIONSHIP

1.	D. Katoh	106 (4 victories)
2.	T. Harada	101 (1 victory)
3.	M. Melandri	78
4.	R. Locatelli	60
5.	R. Rolfo	55
6.	F. Nieto	49
7.	E. Alzamora	33
8.	J. Mc Williams	33
9.	N. Matsudo	28
10.	S. Porto	24

Harada alone on the track, in Aprilia's backyard.

PRACTICE:

On the Aprilia test track, the Noale lions perform miracles especially veteran test rider, Marcellino Lucchi (44). After dominating the first day of practice, Lucchi has a dreadful Saturday, crashing during free practice (bruising to the hip and lombar muscle) and then falling heavily in the afternoon (quadruple fracture to the left foot). Harada claims pole ahead of Lucchi, McWilliams and a fantastic Randy de Puniet who at just 20 qualifies on the front row for the first time. Championship dominator, Daijiro Katoh is "only" sixth.

Marcellino Lucchi could have given his team-mate a run for his money. Alas....

START:

Lucchi gets the best start ahead of McWilliams and Matsudo while Battaini crashes on the line having accelerated too abruptly. Katoh doesn't like the rain and ends the first lap in 18th place.

4TH LAP:

Practice hero de Puniet falls.

5TH LAP:

The situation is degenerating: Lucchi and McWilliams become victims of the conditions just one lap apart.

11TH LAP (MID-RACE):

Harada is comfortably in the lead (more than 6 seconds). Second place is now Rolfo with Matsudo (Yamaha) in third place. Katoh is back in the points (14th), Katja Poensgen is sixteenth.

14TH LAP:

Matsudo crashes but rejoins the race in ninth place.

16TH LAP:

The track is drying and Harada is still in the lead; Rolfo is a solid second ahead of Melandri.

19TH LAP:

For the first time this season, Katja Poensgen is in the points in 14th place.

FINISH (21 LAPS):

Harada completes a perfect race with a win for Aprilia (five RSWs in the first five places). Katoh saves tenth position. The race will go down in history after Katja Poensgen in 14th place becomes the first woman ever to score points in the category.

CHAMPIONSHIP:

After Katoh's absolute domination at the beginning of the season, (four races, four victories), the championship is wide open again since Harada is now within five points of his fellow countryman.

The waltz of the semi-works riders: Roberto Rolfo leads Randy de Puniet and Shahrol Yuzy.

The new wave: Poggiali leads Angel Nieto Junior.
N° 24 Elias is not far away on the outside.

3 June
Mugello - 5.245m

1.	41	Y. Ui	L & M Derbi Team	1'59.246
2.	24	T. Elias	Telefonica Movistar Jr Team	1'59.656
3.	9	L. Cecchinello	MS Aprilia LCR	1'59.878
4.	50	A. Ballerini	Team Ciaron	1'59.881
5.	7	S. Perugini	Italjet Racing Team	2'00.165
6.	5	N. Ueda	FCC – TSR	2'00.231
7.	4	M. Azuma	Liegeois Competition	2'00.291
8.	23	G. Borsoi	LAE – UGT 3000	2'00.305
9.	17	S. Jenkner	LAE – UGT 3000	2'00.309
10.	29	A. Nieto Jr	Viceroy Team	2'00.420
11.	16	S. Sanna	Safilo Oxydo Race	2'00.507
12.	54	M. Poggiali	Gilera Racing Team	2'00.619
13.	8	G. Scalvini	Italjet Racing Team	2'00.835
14.	39	J. Hules	Matteoni Racing	2'00.878
15.	10	J. Müller	PEV-Spalt-ADAC Sachsen	2'01.011
16.	22	P. Nieto	L & M Derbi Team	2'01.091
17.	31	A. Rodriguez	Valencia Circuit Aspar Team	2'01.562
18.	15	A. de Angelis	Matteoni Racing	2'01.612
19.	11	M. Sabbatani	Bossini Fontana Racing	2'01.647
20.	21	A. Vincent	Team Fomma	2'01.905
21.	18	J. Smrz	Budweiser Budvar Hanusch	2'01.927
22.	25	J. Olive	Telefonica Movistar Jr Team	2'01.998
23.	51	A. Dovizioso	RCGM Rubincone Corse	2'02.124
24.	28	G. Talmacsi	Racing Service	2'02.420
25.	34	E. Bataille	Axo Racing Team	2'02.425
26.	27	M. Petrini	Racing Service	2'02.933
27.	19	A. Branetti	Team Crae	2'02.941
28.	26	D. Pedrosa	Telefonica Movistar Jr Team	2'02.984
29.	12	R. Jara	MS Aprilia LCR	2'03.054
30.	52	M. Conti	BNY Racing	2'03.192
31.	20	G. Caffiero	Bossini Fontana Racing	2'03.761

RACE: 20 LAPS = 104.9 KM

1. Noboru Ueda - 20 laps in 45'15.046
2. Gino Borsoi — at 3.810
3. Manuel Poggiali — at 6.917
4. Toni Elias — at 12.917
5. Simone Sanna — at 13.280
6. Angel Nieto Jr — at 14.127
7. Arnaud Vincent — at 21.103
8. Masao Azuma — at 21.250
9. Jarno Müller — at 21.263
10. Alex de Angelis — at 25.424
11. Andrea Ballerini — at 27.084
12. Steve Jenkner — at 34.483
13. Alessandro Branetti — at 1'01.136
14. Gabor Talmacsi — at 1'01.892
15. Jaroslav Hules — at 1'38.445
16. Joan Olive — at 1'50.790
17. Raul Jara — at 2'00.237
18. Youichi Ui — at 1 lap
19. Gaspare Caffiero — at 1 lap
20. Angel Rogriguez — at 1 lap
21. Marco Petrini — at 1 lap
22. Michele Conti — at 1 lap
23. Daniel Pedrosa — at 1 lap

RACE FACTS

Pole Position:	Youichi Ui	1'59.246
Fastest lap:	Noboru Ueda	2'12.363
Circuit record lap:	Roberto Locatelli	2'00.029
Circuit best lap:	Roberto Locatelli	1'58.923

RETIREMENTS

Jakub Smrz	at 5 laps (fall)
Gianluigi Scalvini	at 6 laps
Pablo Nieto	at 7 laps
Andrea Dovizioso	at 8 laps
Max Sabbatani	at 13 laps
Eric Bataille	at 16 laps
Lucio Cecchinello	at 17 laps (fall)
Stefano Perugini	at 18 laps (fall)

CHAMPIONSHIP

1. G. Borsoi — 75
2. M. Azuma — 72 (2 victories)
3. M. Poggiali — 72 (1 victory)
4. N. Ueda — 63 (1 victory)
5. Y. Ui — 50 (1 victory)
6. A. Nieto jr — 43
7. L. Cecchinello — 41
8. A. Vincent — 41
9. M. Giansanti — 32
10. T. Elias — 32

PRACTICE:

Ui dominates practice again. Wild Card rider Ballerini qualifies on the front row. One high profile absentee is Giansanti. On Saturday morning the Italian was unable to avoid Pablo Nieto's Derbi sliding in the middle of the track (heavy bruising).

START:

Ui is the fastest off the mark ahead of Elias and Perugini who takes Poggiali by surprise before the end of the first lap.

2ND LAP:

The sky is growing ever darker and soon it can't contain itself. The leading riders raise their arms. Since the race is interrupted before the end of the third lap, the whole distance will be rerun under the banner of a "wet race". The race can therefore not be stopped a second time. In the second formation lap, the rain gets even harder. Pablo Nieto is the only one to appear on the starting grid with three riders going into the pits to change tyres. All the others take a short cut and normally should be disqualified. The clerks of the course turn a blind eye to avoid giving the start to just four bikes.

SECOND START:

Elias gets a dream start, but Perugini soon takes control and ends the first lap with a lead of 1"428 over Azuma.

3RD LAP:

Perugini falls. Sanna is in the lead ahead of Azuma and Borsoi.

4TH LAP:

Cecchinello falls. Azuma is in the lead.

5TH LAP:

There are three riders in the lead, in order, Azuma, Sanna and Borsoi.

10TH LAP (MID-RACE):

Borsoi is all alone up front (0"750 ahead of Sanna) but Ueda in third place is the fastest man on the track.

15TH LAP:

Ueda doesn't beat about the bush. He takes the lead deposing Borsoi.

FINISH (20 LAPS):

Ueda's experience pays off in the difficult conditions. Ui (poor tyre choice) finishes one lap behind. Borsoi and Poggliani complete the podium (Sanna crawls home).

CHAMPIONSHIP:

Gino Borsoi's consistency pays off. The Italian finds himself leading a World Championship for the first time in his career, three points ahead of Azuma and Poggliani. Youichi Ui is 25 points behind.

A little ray of sunshine in Tuscany. Unfortunately on race day...

Gino Borsoi's lap of honour: for the first time in his career, the Italian leads the Championship.

Catalunya

Grand of Prix
CATALUNYA

Pablo Nieto: home, sweet home...

46

Emilio Alzamora, a Spaniard riding for an Italian team comes back to Catalunya.

A one man burn out: another imperial demonstration by the king, Valentino Rossi.

500cc
GP
of Catalunya

17 June
Circuit de Catalunya - 4.727 m

... Rossi wins...

STARTING GRID

1.	46	V. Rossi	Nastro Azzurro Honda	1'45.507
2.	56	S. Nakano	Gauloises Yamaha Tech 3	1'45.518
3.	65	L. Capirossi	West Honda Pons	1'45.587
4.	3	M. Biaggi	Marlboro Yamaha Team	1'45.682
5.	4	A. Barros	West Honda Pons	1'45.761
6.	17	J. vd Goorbergh	Proton TEAM KR	1'45.833
7.	1	K. Roberts	Telefonica Movistar Suzuki	1'45.952
8.	6	N. Abe	Antena 3 Yamaha-d'Antin	1'46.067
9.	11	T. Ukawa	Repsol YPF Honda Team	1'46.159
10.	15	S. Gibernau	Telefonica Movistar Suzuki	1'46.601
11.	28	A. Crivillé	Repsol YPF Honda Team	1'46.650
12.	7	C. Checa	Marlboro Yamaha Team	1'46.760
13.	41	N. Haga	Red Bull Yamaha WCM	1'46.834
14.	10	J.L. Cardoso	Antena 3 Yamaha-d'Antin	1'47.066
15.	19	O. Jacque	Gauloises Yamaha Tech 3	1'47.618
16.	8	C. Walker	Shell Advance Honda	1'47.860
17.	12	H. Aoki	Arie Molenaar Racing	1'48.110
18.	14	A. West	Dee Cee Jeans Racing Team	1'48.958
19.	24	J. Vincent	Pulse GP	1'49.528
20.	68	M. Willis	Pulse GP	1'49.902
21.	16	J. Stigefelt	Sabre Sport	1'49.960

RACE: 25 LAPS = 118.175 KM

1.	Valentino Rossi -25 laps in 44'57.142 (157.733 km/h)	
2.	Max Biaggi	at 2.579
3.	Loris Capirossi	at 3.216
4.	Shinya Nakano	at 3.257
5.	Sete Gibernau	at 3.989
6.	Norick Abe	at 4.705
7.	Tohru Ukawa	at 4.769
8.	Carlos Checa	at 13.459
9.	Jurgen vd Goorbergh	at 13.903
10.	Noriyuki Haga	at 19.616
11.	Alex Crivillé	at 26.378
12.	Olivier Jacque	at 37.301
13.	Chris Walker	at 1'01.010
14.	Jose Luis Cardoso	at 1'13.371
15.	Haruchika Aoki	at 1'19.363
16.	Jason Vincent	at 1'19.756
17.	Johan Stigefelt	at 1'24.089
18.	Mark Willis	at 2 laps

RACE FACTS

Pole Position:	Valentino Rossi 1'45.507
Fastest lap:	Valentino Rossi 1'46.619 (non official)
Circuit record lap:	Alex Barros 1'46.810 (1998)
Circuit best lap:	Valentino Rossi 1'45.507 (2001)

RETIREMENTS

Anthony West	at 19 laps
Alex Barros	at 19 laps
Kenny Roberts	at 22 laps (fall)

CHAMPIONSHIP

1. V. Rossi	116 (4 victories)
2. M. Biaggi	90 (1 victory)
3. L. Capirossi	81
4. N. Abe	74
5. S. Nakano	63
6. A. Crivillé	62
7. A. Barros	60 (1 victory)
8. T. Ukawa	45
9. S. Gibernau	40
10. K. Roberts	37

PRACTICE:

The question that everyone is asking is can Valentino Rossi overcome his fall in Mugello? "When you have worked throughout the whole race and all the benefit disappears just 300m from the finish, you've a right to be angry", he explains upon arrival in Catalunya. What's worse: on Friday afternoon, he pulverises his NSR at top speed but with no injury to himself. Yet on Saturday, Rossi still claims pole position, eleven thousandths ahead of Nakano. Loris Capirossi is kicking himself: just when he had the pole in the bag, he left his pit for the final attack a few seconds too late. When he passed the finish line, the flag had already been shown. Jacque and McCoy are both back after surgery, but the Australian doesn't start the race. Haslam also cries forfeit.

19TH LAP:

Rossi has the race in the bag, Biaggi is back in second place.

FINISH (25 LAPS):

An Italian treble, but the show has only just begun with Biaggi and Rossi turning into boxers on the steps leading to the podium.

Three Italians on the front row.

START:

It's a Japanese party with Abe and Nakano – Hervé Poncharal's protege – leading at the end of the first lap. Things are a lot harder for Rossi, blocked on the first corner by Gibernau; the Italian will begin an astonishing comeback.

4TH LAP:

Roberts crashes after setting the fastest time.

6TH LAP:

Capirossi has been leading the dance since the second lap, but a very aggressive Gibernau is breathing down his neck. Rossi has already come back into third place, even though he is 860 thousands adrift from the leading pair.

13TH LAP (MID-RACE):

He passed Gibernau on the preceding lap, he takes Capirossi by surprise at the end of the straight. Rossi is in the lead and forgets all his rivals.

CHAMPIONSHIP:

Even more important than the results on paper, Rossi has just made a psychological point, proving he can emerge triumphant from the pressure of scoring his first zero of the year.

... and Biaggi licks his wounds...

Rossi - Biaggi at war

The tension is at its height. The staircase leading to the podium at Catalunya is fairly narrow. And Valentino Rossi's entourage includes a large number of people. Probably too many. Ranging from the adviser for this, the specialist in that, the representative for them both or the delegate for someone else, the whole paddock seems invaded by yellow.

On Sunday 17 June after a rather particular race – first Rossi played tag with Barros before running into the dirt, forced out by Criville, who in turn was touched by Gibernau – which saw the Italian come back from fifteenth place to claim victory, emotions overflowed. And well before the champagne!

The background for the curious scene was the inside corridors of the circuit of Catalunya with its limited access through which the heroes of the hour – three Italians, the same ones who are dominating 500 cc this year – rejoin their fans: 84,844 spectators and millions of TV viewers. And there...

No-one really saw what happened but everyone is talking about it. "Biaggi was in a hurry to get things over because he wanted to watch an important football match on TV that his favourite team AS Roma were playing. He apparently jostled Rossi's personal manager, Gibo Badioli. Tensions mounted and Rossi came back down a few steps to tell his rival what he thought of him. And then the fight started". Started by whom? "Not me, I was immediately surrounded by security", explained Valentino via his press officer, Carlo Florenzano. So it must have been Max then, even though the Roman's entourage claims that Rossi launched himself at him and scratched him! An incriminating factor: "Since one of the special envoys from Italian TV was following the group with his mike in his hand, millions of Italians could hear Rossi's voice saying "But what are you doing, idiot?"

On the podium and during interviews, Rossi and Capirossi spoke, Capirossi shook Biaggi's hand but there was nothing between Rossi and Biaggi. They ignored each other completely. And Rossi's outburst? And the little drops of blood on Biaggi's face? "What happened?" The question was no sooner asked than Biaggi replied, "I didn't see anything". "Yes, but what about the blood?" "It's nothing, it's just a mosquito bite". At his side there appeared to be a sardonic smile on Valentino Rossi's face. For a double victory: in terms of points, he now has 26 ahead. And in terms of fisticuffs?

The race, the funny race ("because of the strong wind, the pace was not fast, we all had grip problems", claimed Rossi) was immediately relegated to a secondary level. The paddock had its own story. And privileged witnesses such as Carlo Pernat, the man who put both champions on a racing bike for the first time and who now ironically takes care of the business affairs of the third member of the Italian tribe, Loris Capirossi: "Max and Valentino ressemble each other in just one aspect, they both have the same burning desire to win. In every other respect they are different: Biaggi is an introvert, calculating, meticulous but sneaky, Rossi is a complete extrovert and is also more honest. When he does something stupid, he says so and forgets it. But it's difficult to say who puts the most oil on the fire in their feud. One thing is sure, if you shut them away in a room, I think they would fight to the death".

On that particular day, everything finished with a warning from the race director to each of them. Until the next round?

The scandal-soaked podium: a forced smile from Rossi, a scowl from Biaggi and Loris Capirossi looks on in indifference.

250cc
GP of Catalunya

17 June

Circuit de Catalunya - 4.727 m

STARTING GRID

1. 74	D. Katoh	Telefonica Movistar Honda	1'47.261
2. 31	T. Harada	MS Aprilia Racing	1'47.626
3. 10	F. Nieto	Valencia Circuit Aspar Team	1'47.800
4. 5	M. Melandri	MS Aprilia Racing	1'47.882
5. 99	J. McWilliams	Aprilia Grand Prix	1'47.944
6. 44	R. Rolfo	Safilo Oxydo Race	1'48.092
7. 7	E. Alzamora	Telefonica Movistar Honda	1'48.136
8. 15	R. Locatelli	MS Eros Ramazotti Racing	1'48.225
9. 81	R. de Puniet	Equipe de France - Scrab G	1'48.245
10. 6	A. Debon	Valencia Circuit Aspar Team	1'48.405
11. 8	N. Matsudo	Petronas Sprinta Yamaha T	1'48.761
12. 12	K. Nöhles	MS Aprilia Racing	1'48.785
13. 21	F. Battaini	MS Eros Ramazotti Racing	1'48.985
14. 66	A. Hofmann	Dark Dog Racing Factory	1'49.117
15. 9	S. Porto	Yamaha Kruz	1'49.167
16. 50	S. Guintoli	Equipe de France - Scrab G	1'49.373
17. 42	D. Checa	Team Fomma	1'49.415
18. 46	T. Sekiguchi	Edo Racing	1'49.693
19. 57	L. Lanzi	Campetella Racing	1'49.748
20. 37	L. Boscoscuro	Campetella Racing	1'49.891
21. 18	S. Yuzy	Petronas Sprinta Yamaha T	1'50.078
22. 20	J. Vidal	PR2 Metrored	1'50.229
23. 22	D. De Gea	Antena 3 Yamaha-d 'Antin	1'50.845
24. 16	D. Tomas	By Queroseno Racing Team	1'50.910
25. 98	K. Poensgen	Dark Dog Racing Factory	1'51.468
26. 11	R. Chiarello	Aprilia Grand Prix	1'51.569
27. 38	A. Molina	Kolmer Racing Team	1'51.814
28. 36	L. Costa	Antena 3 Yamaha-d 'Antin	1'53.294
29. 45	S. Edwards	FCC-TSR	1'53.325

RACE: 23 LAPS = 108.721 KM

1.	Daijiro Katoh - 23 laps in 41'40.347 (156.536km/h)	
2.	Tetsuya Harada	at 0.114
3.	Roberto Rolfo	at 12.573
4.	Roberto Locatelli	at 19.077
5.	Fonsi Nieto	at 22.776
6.	Jeremy McWilliams	at 22.853
7.	Emilio Alzamora	at 22.876
8.	Randy de Puniet	at 31.224
9.	Alex Hofmann	at 33.567
10.	Naoki Matsudo	at 37.754
11.	Alex Debon	at 38.039
12.	Shahrol Yuzy	at 38.100
13.	Taro Sekiguchi	at 38.182
14.	Sebastian Porto	at 38.312
15.	Klaus Nöhles	at 38.701
16.	David Checa	at 42.643
17.	Luca Boscoscuro	at 42.647
18.	Sylvain Guintoli	at 49.236
19.	Lorenzo Lanzi	at 50.798
20.	Franco Battaini	at 56.073
21.	David De Gea	at 1'30.364
22.	David Tomas	at 1'30.432
23.	Riccardo Chiarello	at 1'53.441
24.	Alvaro Molina	at 1'53.584
25.	Luis Costa	at 1 lap
26.	Katja Poensgen	at 1 lap

RETIREMENTS

Marco Melandri	at 13 laps (fall)
Jeronimo Vidal	at 17 laps
Stuart Edwards	at 18 laps

RACE FACTS

Pole Position:	Daijiro Katoh	1'47.261
Fastest lap:	Daijiro Katoh	1'48.014
Circuit record lap:	Valentino Rossi	1'47.585 (1998)
Circuit best lap:	Daijiro Katoh	1'47.261 (2001)

CHAMPIONSHIP

1. D. Katoh	131 (5 victories)
2. T. Harada	121 (1 victory)
3. M. Melandri	78
4. R. Locatelli	73
5. R. Rolfo	71
6. F. Nieto	60
7. J. Mc Williams	43
8. E. Alzamora	42
9. N. Matsudo	34
10. A. Hofmann	27

The Japanese duel continues: Katoh will once again triumph over Harada.

PRACTICE:

Katoh is back on form after his difficult weekend in Mugello. Everyone including the Aprilia riders realised that on the very first day. Harada remains in the fight with Gonzales-Nieto and Melandri completing the front row. Practice is dominated by the collision between Alzamora and Debon with the former 125 World Champion losing control of his Honda as he took his fellow countryman on the inside. A change at Aprilia: Jeremy McWilliams has joined the team managed by Dieter Stappert in a move to relieve Klaus Nöhles from the task of setting up the bike which doesn't appear to be the young German's cup of tea.

START:

Harada, Melandri and Katoh immediately take control ahead of Alzamora and de Puniet. Katja Poensgen falls on the first lap, but rejoins the track. Harada ends the first lap with a 456 thousandths lead over his team-mate Melandri.

6TH LAP:

Katoh takes the lead on the fourth lap. Harada is 136 thousandths behind. Melandri has just recorded the fastest race lap and is reeling in the leading pair. Rolfo and Alzamora are a little further back.

Jeremy McWilliams, GP veteran.

9TH LAP:

Katoh makes a small mistake and Harada goes through, but the Honda rider soon regains the upper hand.

11TH LAP:

Melandri crashes.

12TH (MID-RACE):

Katoh and Harada are still inseparable (142 thousandths). Robert Rolfo is now a lonely third.

18TH LAP:

The two Japanese riders are neck and neck – 118 thousandths between them.

FINISH (23 LAPS):

79, 113, 115 and 95 – Harada plays with thousandths of a second right up to the line, but to no avail. Apparently there is no stopping Daijiro Katoh.

CHAMPIONSHIP:

Katoh doubles his advantage that now stands at ten points. All the others are way behind. This year the championship is being run at two speeds: Katoh and Harada at the front, then all the others further back. The promotion of Jacque, Nakano and Ukawa to 500 is being keenly felt.

The little brother of... Cesar Barros learns the hard way! Ouch.

The old and the new: in the final pecking order, Lucio Cecchinello's experience will get the better of Toni Elias' flair.

125cc GP of Catalunya

17 June
Circuit de Catalunya - 4.727 m

STARTING GRID

1.	9	L. Cecchinello	MS Aprilia LCR	1'51.368
2.	5	N. Ueda	FCC – TSR	1'52.090
3.	41	Y. Ui	L & M Derbi Team	1'52.146
4.	7	S. Perugini	Italjet Racing Team	1'52.410
5.	24	T. Elias	Telefonica Movistar Jr Team	1'52.560
6.	17	S. Jenkner	LAE – UGT 3000	1'52.682
7.	54	M. Poggiali	Gilera Racing Team	1'52.705
8.	31	A. Rodriguez	Valencia Circuit Aspar Team	1'52.787
9.	10	J. Müller	PEV-Spalt-ADAC Sachsen	1'52.803
10.	39	J. Hules	Matteoni Racing	1'52.938
11.	11	M. Sabbatani	Bossini Fontana Racing	1'53.001
12.	16	S. Sanna	Safilo Oxydo Race	1'53.019
13.	26	D. Pedrosa	Telefonica Movistar Jr Team	1'53.050
14.	23	G. Borsoi	LAE – UGT 3000	1'53.160
15.	22	P. Nieto	L & M Derbi Team	1'53.196
16.	8	G. Scalvini	Italjet Racing Team	1'53.369
17.	6	M. Giansanti	Axo Racing Team	1'53.481
18.	4	M. Azuma	Liegeois Competition	1'53.519
19.	25	J. Olive	Telefonica Movistar Jr Team	1'53.553
20.	15	A. de Angelis	Matteoni Racing	1'53.624
21.	21	A. Vincent	Team Fomma	1'53.990
22.	18	J. Smrz	Budweiser Budvar Hanusch	1'53.998
23.	29	A. Nieto Jr	Viceroy Team	1'54.186
24.	28	G. Talmacsi	Racing Service	1'54.558
25.	27	M. Petrini	Racing Service	1'54.604
26.	19	A. Branetti	Team Crae	1'54.915
27.	12	R. Jara	MS Aprilia LCR	1'55.812
28.	43	D. Pinera	By Queroseno Racing Team	1'55.959
29.	20	G. Caffiero	Bossini Fontana Racing	1'56.529
30.	77	A. Araujo	Liegeois Competition	1'57.621

RACE: 22 LAPS = 103.994 KM

1. Lucio Cecchinello - 22 laps in 41'31.696 (150.250 km/h)

2. Toni Elias	at 0.573
3. Manuel Poggiali	at 6.764
4. Steve Jenkner	at 6.854
5. Youichi Ui	at 7.029
6. Pablo Nieto	at 7.558
7. Daniel Pedrosa	at 7.788
8. Joan Olive	at 18.438
9. Alex De Angelis	at 18.602
10. Simone Sanna	at 23.109
11. Stefano Perugini	at 23.232
12. Angel Nieto jr	at 23.291
13. Gianluigi Scalvini	at 23.652
14. Arnaud Vincent	at 24.308
15. Jarno Müller	at 24.465
16. Mirko Giansanti	at 31.927
17. Gabor Talmacsi	at 31.955
18. Gino Borsoi	at 33.274
19. Jakub Smrz	at 42.904
20. Alessandro Brannetti	at 53.226
21. Max Sabbatani	at 1'09.855
22. Gaspare Caffiero	at 1'30.468
23. Raul Jara	at 1 lap
24. Adrian Araujo	at 1 lap

RACE FACTS

Pole Position:	Lucio Cecchinello	1'51.368
Fastest lap:	Stefano Perugini	1'51.811
Circuit record lap:	Noboru Ueda	1'52.813 (1999)
Circuit best lap:	Lucio Cecchinello	1'51.368 (2001)

RETIREMENTS

Angel Rodriguez	1st lap (fall)
Masao Azuma	at 1 lap (fall)
Marco Petrini	at 10 laps
Noboru Ueda	at 13 laps
Jaroslav Hules	at 14 laps
Daniel Pinera	at 20 laps

CHAMPIONSHIP

1. M. Poggiali	88	(1 victory)
2. G. Borsoi	75	
3. M. Azuma	72	(2 victories)
4. L. Cecchinello	66	(1 victory)
5. N. Ueda	63	(1 victory)
6. Y. Ui	61	(1 victory)

PRACTICE:

For the first time this season, Ui is beaten in the battle for pole position. The Japanese rider falls on Friday morning sustaining a fracture to his little finger and a cracked bone in his right foot. Cecchinello becomes the fastest 125cc rider ever on the Catalunya track. Ueda is second and Perugini (not fully fit) puts the Italjet in fourth position.

START:

Elias surges through from the second row to take the lead ahead of Ueda and Perugini. Championship leader Borsoi falls on the first lap, but rejoins the race. Cecchinello's start is average.

5TH LAP:

Still Elias up front but Cecchinello is right behind him (72 thousandths). He passes on the straight and Elias is also taken by surprise by Ueda and Perugini.

10TH LAP:

Ueda falls and Perugini goes into the sand to avoid him. Hules is missing after a very good start. So there are now only two battling for victory: Cecchinello and Elias.

Lucio of Italy: a well known character in the paddock. And a winner!

He has the Spanish crowd at his feet: Toni Elias, the revelation of the 2001 season.

11TH LAP (MID-RACE):

Cecchinello and Elias are within a whisker (273 thousandths). The chasing group led by Poggiali is six seconds adrift.

16TH LAP:

Nothing to report at the front except the minuscule difference: 65 thousandths in favour of Cecchinello. The battle for third place is a different story with Poggiali, Pedrosa, Pablo Nieto, Azuma, Jenkner and Ui all jostling for position..

18TH LAP:

Elias takes Cecchinello by surprise.

FINISH (22 LAPS):

The veteran Italian retook the lead on the 20th lap, but the young Spaniard is not deterred. He goes on the attack on the last lap (Azuma crashes out) but the veteran holds firm. The two bikes touch but don't fall. Cecchinello wins, but Elias confirms his role as the new Spanish hero.

CHAMPIONSHIP:

Borsoi's fall on the first lap, then Ueda on the tenth and Azuma on the last lap, together with Ui's "lowly" fourth place mean that Poggiali (Gilera) is the day's winner – third in the race but on top of the championship.

2001

Assen—
Grand Prix
of
HOLLAND

The colour orange is on show. In his own country Jurgen van den Goorgbergh is a national hero. And the nation salutes him.

Raul Jara: an
involuntary
summersault.

The highlight of 250 cc GP: the French "rookie"
Sylvain Guintoli just fails to make it onto the podium.

500cc
GP
of Holland

30 June

Assen - 6.049 m

STARTING GRID

1.	65	L. Capirossi	West Honda Pons	2'00.743
2.	3	M. Biaggi	Marlboro Yamaha Team	2'00.876
3.	46	V. Rossi	Nastro Azzurro Honda	2'01.185
4.	4	A. Barros	West Honda Pons	2'01.492
5.	56	S. Nakano	Gauloises Yamaha Tech 3	2'01.646
6.	1	K. Roberts	Telefonica Movistar Suzuki	2'01.773
7.	7	C. Checa	Marlboro Yamaha Team	2'01.897
8.	6	N. Abe	Antena 3 Yamaha-d'Antin	2'02.218
9.	15	S. Gibernau	Telefonica Movistar Suzuki	2'02.440
10.	28	A. Crivillé	Repsol YPF Honda Team	2'02.521
11.	11	T. Ukawa	Repsol YPF Honda Team	2'02.913
12.	19	O. Jacque	Gauloises Yamaha Tech 3	2'03.264
13.	41	N. Haga	Red Bull Yamaha WCM	2'03.116
14.	17	J. vd Goorbergh	Proton TEAM KR	2'03.134
15.	9	L. Haslam	Shell Advance Honda	2'04.589
16.	12	H. Aoki	Arie Molenaar Racing	2'04.607
17.	10	J.L. Cardoso	Antena 3 Yamaha-d'Antin	2'04.609
18.	14	A. West	Dee Cee Jeans Racing Team	2'05.042
19.	16	J. Stigefelt	Sabre Sport	2'06.146
20.	24	J. Vincent	Pulse GP	2'07.008
21.	21	B. Veneman	Dee Cee Jeans Racing Team	2'07.190
22.	68	M. Willis	Pulse GP	2'07.574

RACE: 15 LAPS = 90.735 KM

1. Max Biaggi - 15 laps in 30'56.346 (175.961 km/h)
2. Valentino Rossi — at 0.126
3. Loris Capirossi — at 0.732
4. Alex Barros — at 1.231
5. Shinya Nakano — at 9.844
6. Kenny Roberts — at 10.622
7. Sete Gibernau — at 14.259
8. Tohru Ukawa — at 18.620
9. Jurgen vd Goorbergh — at 18.857
10. Noriyuki Haga — at 22.557
11. Olivier Jacque — at 32.629
12. Jose Luis Cardoso — at 1'00.316
13. Leon Haslam — at 1'00.461
14. Haruchika Aoki — at 1'00.686
15. Anthony West — at 1'07.276
16. Mark Willis — at 1'19.375
17. Barry Veneman — at 1'27.921
18. Johan Stigefelt — at 2 laps

RETIREMENTS

Alex Crivillé	at 12 laps (fall)
Norick Abe	at 13 laps (fall)
Carlos Checa	at 13 laps (fall)
Jason Vincent	at 14 laps

RACE FACTS

Pole Position:	Loris Capirossi	2'00.743
Fastest lap:	Valentino Rossi	2'02.662
Circuit record lap:	Kevin Schwantz	2'02.443 (1991)
Circuit best lap:	Loris Capirossi	2'00.743 (2001)

CHAMPIONSHIP

1. V. Rossi	136 (4 victories)
2. M. Biaggi	115 (2 victories)
3. L. Capirossi	97
4. N. Abe	74
5. S. Nakano	74
6. A. Barros	73 (1 victory)
7. A. Crivillé	62
8. T. Ukawa	53
9. S. Gibernau	49
10. K. Roberts	47

Valentino Rossi is the fastest on the track. Alas, a black cloud looms.

A Dutchman and a Frenchman: a local supporter for Olivier Jacque.

PRACTICE:

Capirossi loves Assen. Last year he qualified on pole then fractured a bone in his hand during warm-up before finishing a heroic third in the race. This time, Sito Pons' rider dominates qualifying and becomes the first man to lap below 2'01 (2'00"743). Biaggi and Rossi are not far behind and Barros completes the front row. McCoy withdraws after the first day of practice. Walker suffers a serious accident on Friday morning and is taken to hospital where he remains under observation for 24 hours (serious concussion).

START:

Biaggi is the fastest off the mark, but Barros soon takes control. He finishes the first lap with a lead of 0"283 over Biaggi, who has a second over Abe, Capirossi and Rossi.

3RD LAP:

Abe and Checa both crash out. Barros leads Capirossi, Biaggi, Rossi and Roberts.

4TH LAP:

Crivillé falls at the chicane while in 6th position. Capirossi takes the lead.

5TH LAP:

Capirossi appears to have some problems. First he's passed by his team-mate Barros and then by Biaggi. The top five are running within a second of each other.

10TH LAP (MID-RACE):

Roberts loses contact on the 8th lap and now Biaggi is leading ahead of Capirossi who has taken Barros by surprise. Rossi, is the last in the leading group.

11TH LAP:

Rossi passes Barros and so the three Italians are leading this tremendous Dutch GP.

15TH LAP:

The show is fast and furious. Biaggi has a lead of 0"126 over Rossi who soon goes through only for Max to retake the upper hand before the end of the lap.

16TH LAP:

The Clerks of the Course show the red flag (it has started to rain). Since two thirds race distance has been covered – the positions on the preceding lap, the 15th out of 20 are the ones that count – the full quota of points is attributed.

CHAMPIONSHIP:

Rossi has still 21 points over the day's winner Biaggi. On the podium, the two enemies shake hands.

Max Biaggi comes into the pits. Saved by the water, like Moses?

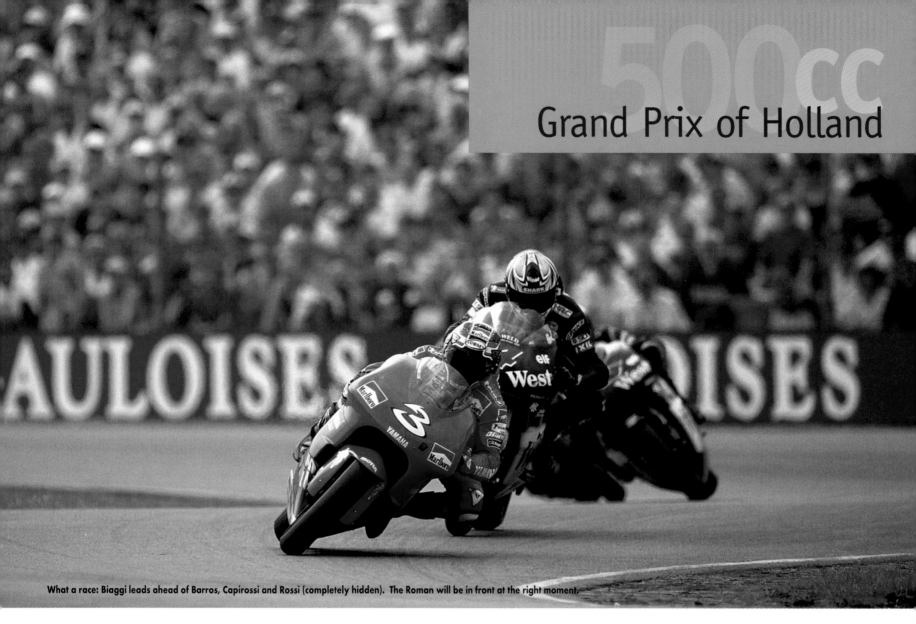

What a race: Biaggi leads ahead of Barros, Capirossi and Rossi (completely hidden). The Roman will be in front at the right moment.

THE SKY PUTS A DAMPER ON PROCEEDINGS

On the right, Loris Capirossi. He speaks in a choked monotone, his disappointment evident. "I knew exactly where to mount an attack on the last lap. There was a place where I was faster than Rossi and Biaggi. I don't like this situation at all".

On the far left, Valentino Rossi tries to look relaxed but he's obviously angry. "I was ready for a race of twenty laps not sixteen. On the fifteenth lap, I got past Biaggi and then I saw the first drops of rain. It was in a really fast section and I didn't want to go crazy when the race was far from over. So I eased off the throttle a little and that was enough for Max to go through. And then..."

And then? The Clerks of the Course showed the red flag because it was raining on the other side of the track. The ranking on the preceding lap was taken as the final one (15th out of the 20 laps scheduled): 1st Biaggi, 2nd Rossi and 3rd Capirossi. Since two thirds of the race had been completed the full quota of points was attributed meaning twenty-five for Max. Valentino Rossi again: "In Mugello the red flag came too late for me..they didn't show it and I fell 300m from the finish. Here it maybe came a bit too early." Really? "But that's racing. It's normal to give priority to safety. I like to gamble, this time I didn't win."

Finally in the centre, Massimiliano Biaggi, the Roman Emperor. Or if you prefer, Max the Great. Biaggi enjoys his second win of the season licking the last traces of champagne from his goatee. A few moments earlier, Valentino Rossi had spontaneously shaken his hand in congratulations in an effort to show the world that the hatchet was now well and truly buried. (On the eve of practice, the World Championship organisers had arranged a conciliatory handshake between the two boxers from Catalunya). The battle would now be strictly fought on the race track. "Perhaps I was lucky today but the Clerks of the Course made the right decision. You know I think Biaggi is currently at the height of his form".

Max spoke of himself in the third person, a sign that doesn't deceive. In fact at this moment in time, the 2001 Championship is not exclusively reserved for Valentino Rossi.

In Assen Biaggi played his cards to perfection furiously withstanding – in extremely difficult conditions – the first assault from his opponents. It was the infamous fifteenth lap that would prove so important. The sky opened its doors and wanted its share of the spoils while the crowd pulled a face. Max didn't know at the time that he was offering Yamaha its first win on Dutch soil since Wayne Rainey in 1989.

The hundreds of thousands of spectators left the track on bicycles, motorbikes or in the flood of cars imprisoned for hours until liberated onto the Dutch highways! The Dutch TT 2001 was the last in history on the current configuration in the Drenthe.

250cc
GP of Holland

With Jeremy McWilliams winning his first GP, Emilio Alzamora claiming his first 250 podium and David De Gea making the right choice of tyres, the Assen 250 GP will be one full of surprises.

30 June
Assen - 6.049 m

STARTING GRID

1.	31	T. Harada	MS Aprilia Racing	2'04.363
2.	74	D. Katoh	Telefonica Movistar Honda	2'04.549
3.	5	M. Melandri	MS Aprilia Racing	2'04.644
4.	99	J. McWilliams	Aprilia Grand Prix	2'04.911
5.	44	R. Rolfo	Safilo Oxydo Race	2'05.492
6.	81	R. de Puniet	Equipe de France - Scrab G	2'05.763
7.	8	N. Matsudo	Petronas Sprinta Yamaha T	2'05.874
8.	9	S. Porto	Yamaha Kruz	2'06.139
9.	15	R. Locatelli	MS Eros Ramazotti Racing	2'06.287
10.	18	S. Yuzy	Petronas Sprinta Yamaha T	2'06.318
11.	6	A. Debon	Valencia Circuit Aspar Team	2'06.340
12.	66	A. Hofmann	Dark Dog Racing Factory	2'06.388
13.	50	S. Guintoli	Equipe de France - Scrab G	2'06.739
14.	37	L. Boscoscuro	Campetella Racing	2'06.825
15.	57	L. Lanzi	Campetella Racing	2'06.866
16.	12	K. Nöhles	MS Aprilia Racing	2'06.931
17.	7	E. Alzamora	Telefonica Movistar Honda	2'06.938
18.	42	D. Checa	Team Fomma	2'07.248
19.	22	D. De Gea	Antena 3 Yamaha-d 'Antin	2'07.498
20.	20	J. Vidal	PR2 Metrored	2'07.826
21.	21	F. Battaini	MS Eros Ramazotti Racing	2'07.882
22.	16	D. Tomas	By Queroseno Racing Team	2'09.152
23.	11	R. Chiarello	Aprilia Grand Prix	2'09.378
24.	62	J. Di Salvo	Cruise America Gr. Prix Raci	2'10.288
25.	36	L. Costa	Antena 3 Yamaha-d 'Antin	2'10.948
26.	55	D. Giugovaz	Edo Racing	2'11.229
27.	98	K. Poensgen	Dark Dog Racing Factory	2'11.725
28.	23	C. Barros	Yamaha Kruz	2'12.164
29.	61	J. Boesveld	Performance Racing	2'12.324
30.	63	A. Litjens	M.R.T.T. Hugen Racing	2'12.377
31.	60	G. Pieper	Car Centre Nijmwegen	2'12.816
32.	45	S. Edwards	FCC-TSR	2'12.832

RACE: 18 LAPS = 108.882 KM

1. Jeremy McWilliams - 18 laps in 39'28.516 (165.494km/h)
2. Emilio Alzamora — at 16.371
3. David De Gea — at 38.409
4. Sylvain Guintoli — at 39.214
5. Franco Battaini — at 1'09.461
6. Marco Melandri — at 1'29.468
7. Luca Boscoscuro — at 1'37.463
8. Riccardo Chiarello — at 1'41.959
9. Jeronimo Vidal — at 1'42.287
10. David Tomas — at 1'44.715
11. Daijiro Katoh — at 2'08.641
12. Alex Hofmann — at 1 lap
13. Randy de Puniet — at 1 lap
14. Sebastian Porto — at 1 lap
15. Jonathan Boesveld — at 1 lap
16. Lorenzo Lanzi — at 1 lap
17. Roberto Locatelli — at 1 lap
18. Klaus Nöhles — at 1 lap
19. Naoki Matsudo — at 1 lap
20. Alex Debon — at 1 lap
21. Gert Pieper — at 1 lap
22. Luis Costa — at 1 lap
23. Arnold Lintjens — at 1 lap
24. Tetsuya Harada — at 1 lap
25. Cesar Barros — at 2 laps
26. Shahrol Yuzy — at 3 laps

RETIREMENTS

Katja Poensgen — at 3 laps (fall)
Diego Giugovaz — at 6 laps (fall)
Jason Di Salvo — at 10 laps
Roberto Rolfo — at 12 laps
Stuart Edwards — at 13 laps (fall)
David Checa — at 17 laps (fall)

RACE FACTS

Pole Position:	Tetsuya Harada	2'04.363
Fastest lap:	Tetsuya Harada	2'06.988
Circuit record lap:	Valentino Rossi	2'05.696 (1999)
Circuit best lap:	Tetsuya Harada	2'04.363 (2001)

CHAMPIONSHIP

1. D. Katoh — 136 (5 victories)
2. T. Harada — 121 (1 victory)
3. M. Melandri — 88
4. R. Locatelli — 73
5. R. Rolfo — 71
6. J. Mc Williams — 68 (1 victory)
7. E. Alzamora — 62
8. F. Nieto — 60
9. N. Matsudo — 34
10. A. Hofmann — 31

PRACTICE:

Aprilia or Katoh? The bikes from Noale dominate the first day with Katoh leading the dance on the second. So another pole position? No, because in the dying seconds, Harada puts in a perfect lap. Fonsi Gonzales-Nieto withdraws (fall, two fractured malleoles).

START:

The racing line is dry in several places. The race is declared "wet", so it won't be stopped. Katoh gets the best start ahead of Melandri, McWilliams and the two Yamahas belonging to Matsudo and Yuzy. At the end of the first lap, McWilliams has a lead of 0"213 over the young Italian and 1"380 over Katoh. Harada completely misses the boat running in 14th position.

Sylvain Guintoli is in a state of grace: he has just taken Roberto Locatelli by surprise. Two laps later and the young Frenchman will find himself with a magnum of champagne in his hands.

2ND LAP:

David Checa falls. The Spaniard touches Rolfo who retrieves the situation by running onto the grass.

3RD LAP:

Locatelli stops in his pits to change tyres.

5TH LAP:

McWilliams is charging away. He has a lead of 13"307 over Alzamora and De Gea who have just passed Melandri.

6TH LAP:

Yuzo and Rolfo return to the pits.

8TH LAP:

Harada also comes in to change wheels, but his team isn't ready for him.

9TH LAP (MID-RACE):

Those who started on rain tyres are in trouble while those who took the risk are reaping the benefits. McWilliams has a lead of 13"680 over Alzamora; the young Frenchman Guintoli is fifth and reeling in Melandri.

14TH LAP:

Still McWilliams ahead of Alzamora (18 seconds between the two). Guintoli is fourth, Katja Poensgen is in the points for the second time in her career (she falls on the last lap).

FINISH (18 LAPS):

At the age of 37, Jeremy McWilliams has just won his first GP. It's a surprising podium with Alzamora (best result in 250) and especially David De Gea who claims an advance of 805 thousandths on the line from Guintoli.

CHAMPIONSHIP:

Katoh is eleventh, Harada way out of the points after stopping in the pits and Marco Melandri limits the damage in 6th place. In the championship Katoh's lead over Harada is now 15 points.

Local colour...

He's been hovering on the brink all season. Now he wins: Toni Elias tastes the victory champagne.

125cc
GP
of Holland

30 June
Assen – 6.049 m

STARTING GRID

1.	23 G. Borsoi	LAE – UGT 3000	2'12.212
2.	9 L. Cecchinello	MS Aprilia LCR	2'12.373
3.	41 Y. Ui	L & M Derbi Team	2'12.393
4.	17 S. Jenkner	LAE – UGT 3000	2'12.461
5.	24 T. Elias	Telefonica Movistar Jr Team	2'12.673
6.	54 M. Poggiali	Gilera Racing Team	2'13.464
7.	39 J. Hules	Matteoni Racing	2'13.781
8.	22 P. Nieto	L & M Derbi Team	2'13.782
9.	15 A. de Angelis	Matteoni Racing	2'13.824
10.	26 D. Pedrosa	Telefonica Movistar Jr Team	2'13.918
11.	10 J. Müller	PEV – Spalt ADAC Sachsen	2'13.997
12.	18 J. Smrz	Budweiser Budvar Hanusch	2'14.567
13.	21 A. Vincent	Team Fomma	2'14.579
14.	29 A. Nieto Jr	Viceroy Team	2'14.596
15.	8 G. Scalvini	Italjet Racing Team	2'14.632
16.	31 A. Rodriguez	Valencia Circuit Aspar Team	2'14.677
17.	4 M. Azuma	Liegeois Competition	2'14.726
18.	16 S. Sanna	Safilo Oxydo Race	2'14.738
19.	7 S. Perugini	Italjet Racing Team	2'14.769
20.	5 N. Ueda	FCC – TSR	2'14.800
21.	11 M. Sabbatani	Bossini Fontana Racing	2'14.854
22.	20 G. Caffiero	Bossini Fontana Racing	2'14.855
23.	25 J. Olive	Telefonica Movistar Jr Team	2'14.979
24.	28 G. Talmacsi	Racing Service	2'15.142
25.	19 A.Brannetti	Team Crae	2'15.321
26.	6 M. Giansanti	Axo Racing Team	2'15.784
27.	27 M. Petrini	Racing Service	2'16.727
28.	12 R. Jara	MS Aprilia LCR	2'16.959
29.	34 E. Bataille	Axo Racing Team	2'17.348
30.	68 W. Van Leeuwen	Luvro/Tennen V.Leeuwen Team	2'18.224
31.	77 A. Araujo	Liegeois Competition	2'18.419
32.	70 P. Lakerveld	D.S.A	2'19.143
33.	67 A. Den Bekker	Admin. Kant Harkens/Vts Snelt	2'20.905
34.	69 R. Timmer	Spijkse Metaalhandel Racing	2'21.425

RACE: 26 LAPS = 104.598 KM

1.	Toni Elias - 17 laps in 41'34.738	
2.	Arnaud Vincent	at 0.607
3.	Steven Jenkner	at 23.253
4.	Noboru Ueda	at 33.979
5.	Jakub Smrz	at 40.196
6.	Gino Borsoi	at 48.556
7.	Mirko Giansanti	at 48.892
8.	Jaroslav Hules	at 57.998
9.	Alessandro Brannetti	at 1'14.063
10.	Jarno Müller	at 1'15.060
11.	Simone Sanna	at 1'26.168
12.	Stefano Perugini	at 1'44.150
13.	Adrian Araujo	at 1'49.270
14.	Raul Jara	at 1'51.773
15.	Max Sabbatani	at 1'52.151
16.	Marco Petrini	at 1'52.504
17.	Eric Bataille	at 2'23.022
18.	Wilhem Van Leeuwen	at 1 lap
19.	Ronnie Timmer	at 1 lap

RETIREMENTS

Alex de Angelis	1st lap not finished (fall)
Gaspare Caffiero	1st lap not finished (fall)
Pablo Nieto	1st lap not finished (fall)
Gianluigi Scalvini	1st lap not finished (fall)
Youichi Ui	at 5 laps (fall)
Manuel Poggiali	at 6 laps (fall)
Daniel Pedrosa	at 7 laps (fall)
Patrick Lakerveld	at 7 laps (fall)
Agel Rodriguez	at 8 laps (fall)
Angel Nieto jr	at 9 laps (fall)
Lucio Cecchinello	at 11 laps
Joan Olive	at 12 laps (fall)
Adri Den Bekker	at 14 laps (fall)
Gabor Talmacsi	at 15 laps (fall)
Masao Azuma	at 15 laps (fall)

RACE FACTS

Pole Position:	Gino Borsoi	2'12.212
Fastest lap:	Toni Elias	2'23.889
Circuit record lap:	Noboru Ueda	2'13.225 (1999)
Circuit best lap:	Gino Borsoi	2'12.212 (2001)

CHAMPIONSHIP

1.	M. Poggiali	88 (1 victory)
2.	G. Borsoi	85
3.	T. Elias	77 (1 victory)
4.	N. Ueda	76 (1 victory)
5.	M. Azuma	72 (2 victories)
6.	L. Cecchinello	66 (1 victory)
7.	A. Vincent	63
8.	Y. Ui	61 (1 victory)
9.	S. Jenkner	54
10.	A. Nieto jr	47

PRACTICE:

After his mistake in Catalunya, Borsoi who had temporarily led the championship takes matters in hand again and records the first pole position of his career. Troubles are rife among the top men: Azuma is only 17th and Ueda 20th.

START:

It has been raining since 5 o'clock in the morning. Elias storms through from the second row and takes the lead ahead of Borsoi and Poggiali. Vincent (13th in practice) is fourth. Alex de Angelis falls taking Scalvini with him. Pablo Nieto doesn't finish the first lap.

2ND LAP:

Poggiali the championship leader falls (he rejoins in 20th place). Vincent is second fighting with Jenkner..

3RD LAP:

Azuma falls.

4TH LAP:

Borsoi has a lead of 1"843 over Vincent, who has shaken off the Elias-Jenkner duo. Poggiali is 18th.

6TH LAP:

Cecchinello retires (plugs). Borsoi's lead over Vincent is now only 788 thousandths.

7TH LAP:

Borsoi falls after leading the race from the first lap.

8TH LAP (MID-RACE):

Vincent leads ahead of Elias (a lead of 1"364) and Jenkner (3"176 behind the Spaniard). Poggiali has come back into 9th place.

10TH LAP:

Elias records the fastest lap in the race and takes the lead.

12TH LAP:

Vincent retakes control. Poggiali falls for the second time in the race while running in 8th place. Borsoi has come back into 7th place.

13TH LAP:

Ui falls.

FINISH (17 LAPS):

Elias retakes control one lap from the end and holds off Vincent. It's a great day for Spanish racing with the reward for the hard work put in by Alberto Puig over the past few years (creation of the Honda cup which selects a Junior team to compete in GPs).

CHAMPIONSHIP:

Poggiali, Azuma, Cecchinello and Ui score no points and there is a general regrouping at the top of the provisional rankings. Poggiali retains the lead, but just three points ahead of Borsoi. Elias is now third.

Poggiali doesn't like the rain. At Gilera however, they have a fine appetite.

Under very difficult conditions, Arnaud Vincent races at the front with Toni Elias.

British

BRITISH
OTORCYCLE
AND PRIX
AY 8th JULY
GTON PARK

CINZANO CINZ

Jaroslav Hules, a Czech at the Day of Champions which is organised to raise money for the association Riders For Health.

Donington Park

Grand Prix of GREAT BRITAIN

Typical British weather and scenery for the British GP.

Barry Sheene: the British myth alive and well in Donnington. Sheene retook the handlebars to ride in the classic bike race.

500cc
GP
of Great Britain

8 July
Donington Park - 4.023m

STARTING GRID

1.	3	M. Biaggi	Marlboro Yamaha Team	1'31.964
2.	65	L. Capirossi	West Honda Pons	1'32.077
3.	4	A. Barros	West Honda Pons	1'32.384
4.	56	S. Nakano	Gauloises Yamaha Tech 3	1'32.515
5.	17	J. vd Goorbergh	Proton TEAM KR	1'32.593
6.	1	K. Roberts	Telefonica Movistar Suzuki	1'32.866
7.	15	S. Gibernau	Telefonica Movistar Suzuki	1'32.988
8.	19	O. Jacque	Gauloises Yamaha Tech 3	1'33.059
9.	7	C. Checa	Marlboro Yamaha Team	1'33.066
10.	10	J.L. Cardoso	Antena 3 Yamaha-d'Antin	1'33.204
11.	46	V. Rossi	Nastro Azzurro Honda	1'33.266
12.	41	N. Haga	Red Bull Yamaha WCM	1'33.487
13.	28	A. Crivillé	Repsol YPF Honda Team	1'33.495
14.	8	C. Walker	Shell Advance Honda	1'33.501
15.	6	N. Abe	Antena 3 Yamaha-d'Antin	1'33.619
16.	11	T. Ukawa	Repsol YPF Honda Team	1'33.654
17.	12	H. Aoki	Arie Molenaar Racing	1'33.707
18.	14	A. West	Dee Cee Jeans Racing Team	1'33.752
19.	24	J. Vincent	Pulse GP	1'34.731
20.	9	L. Haslam	Shell Advance Honda	1'34.732
21.	68	M. Willis	Pulse GP	1'35.996
22.	16	J. Stigefelt	Sabre Sport	1'36.083
23.	21	B. Veneman	Dee Cee Jeans Racing Team	1'36.354

RACE: 30 LAPS= 120.69 KM

1. Valentino Rossi - 30 laps in 46'53.349 (154.436 km/h)
2. Max Biaggi — at 1.794
3. Alex Barros — at 2.011
4. Noriyuki Haga — at 7.610
5. Carlos Checa — at 12.526
6. Shinya Nakano — at 12.766
7. Alex Crivillé — at 16.225
8. Kenny Roberts — at 16.699
9. Olivier Jacque — at 16.780
10. Loris Capirossi — at 24.781
11. Sete Gibernau — at 29.205
12. Jurgen vd Goorbergh — at 44.984
13. Jason Vincent — at 49.907
14. Anthony West — at 50.033
15. Chris Walker — at 59.116
16. Tohru Ukawa — at 1'04.876
17. Leon Haslam — at 1'10.748
18. Johan Stigefelt — at 1 lap
19. Mark Willis — at 1 lap

RETIREMENTS

Haruchika Aoki — at 9 laps
Barry Veneman — at 9 laps
Norick Abe — at 12 laps
Jose Luis Cardoso — at 16 laps

RACE FACTS

Pole Position:	Max Biaggi	1'31.964
Fastest lap:	Valentino Rossi	1'33.056
Circuit record lap:	Simon Crafar	1'32.661 (1998)
Circuit best lap:	Max Biaggi	1'31.964 (2001)

CHAMPIONSHIP

1. V. Rossi — 161 (5 victories)
2. M. Biaggi — 135 (2 victories)
3. L. Capirossi — 103
4. A. Barros — 89 (1 victory)
5. S. Nakano — 84
6. N. Abe — 74
7. A. Crivillé — 71
8. K. Roberts — 55
9. S. Gibernau — 54
10. T. Ukawa — 53

Noriyuki Haga knows Donington very well. For the first time this season, the Japanese rider is going to race with the big boys.

Valentino Rossi, 11th on the grid after his practice tumble makes an extraordinary comeback. In Donington he was at the front and all the rest were behind.

PRACTICE:

Things move fast from the very first practice session. Frenchman Sébastien Gimbert riding the Paton breaks his ankle. There are falls also for Capirossi and Rossi who totally destoys his NSR and ends the session in 11th place. Since the track only dries out in the dying minutes of Saturday qualifying – only Nakano improves on his time – the championship leader will start from the third row. Biaggi is giving a demonstration beating Crafar's

Alexandre Barros in discussion with Jacques Morelli, Michelin GP boss.

time set in 1998. However on Saturday morning, Max is also the victim of a slippery track.

START:

Biaggi, Roberts and Capirossi get the best start with the reigning world champion ending the first lap in the lead. Abe (100th GP), Cardoso and Ukawa have all jumped the start and are punished with a stop and go penalty. Rossi is eleventh at the end of the first lap.

7TH LAP:

Rossi has reeled in Olivier Jacque (what a start to the race!) in sixth place. He tries to go by on the outside but has to widen his racing line to avoid the 250 World Champion. Roberts is still ahead.

15TH LAP (MID-RACE):

Biaggi takes control on the eleventh lap, but it's Rossi who steals the show. He has clawed back the Roman and Brazilian Alexandre Barros with the three riders separated by just 695 thousandths.

18TH LAP:

From eleventh place on the grid, Rossi finds himself in the lead.

22ND LAP:

The crowd's favourite increases the pace, the others follow. The lead is now 583 thousandths over Biaggi.

FINISH (30 LAPS):

After clocking up fastest lap after fastest lap he can now kiss the fairing on his yellow Honda. Rossi has won the British 500 GP for the second time in two years.

CHAMPIONSHIP:

Twenty six points – ie one GP – lead for Rossi over Biaggi. Capirossi is adrift (58 points behind).

ROSSI, THE PREDATOR

They say that perfection doesn't exist. That's certainly true especially when you try to integrate it into the ephemeral world of racing, where champions come and go and rarely resemble each other, often disappearing as rapidly as they have arrived. And yet...

Where others ride, he races. When others are just trying to stay on two wheels, he slides, controls, throws his yellow and blue machine with his lucky number into the next obstacle. Then he turns himself into a rubber man to hide his 182 cc frame behind the fairing, giving only minimum resistance to the curtain of air his bike creates. The others? All those who against their will find themselves every fortnight in another motorcycling version of "Mission Impossible". And he is? Valentino Rossi, who has just won his fifth race of the season and the most important victory in his 500cc career.

What was Valentino Rossi's task on this grey Sunday in Albion? On paper apparently impossible, since he would first have to get himself out of an awkward situation: a place on the third row of the grid (terrible crash on the first day of practice). So around ten riders ahead of him. Did we say impossible? We know that this word doesn't exist when applied to Rossi.

In eleventh place at the end of the first lap and already sixth five laps later, third on the twelfth of thirty laps and in the lead on the 24th before setting the fastest laps to protect his position: the Italian chooses strong-arm tactics. To the extent that he can disillusion even the most motivated opponent. "Sometimes, you feel like you're racing in two different championships. He starts in 11th place and still wins!" The tribute comes from his main rival Massimiliano Biaggi. Who lost more than a race in Great Britain. He realised that in normal circumstances, Rossi is quite simply unbeatable this season!

Rossi? In spite of the apparent ease, the winner of the day had to pull out the stops to meet this new challenge: "It wasn't just that damned 11th place on the grid, but there were also big set-up problems. After morning warm-up we made a mixture of all the data recorded by the computer all weekend. By a miracle (or rather by experience, his team being the best in the world for the last ten years) my bike became more efficient over the laps than that of my rivals. After the problems suffered in practice, it's definitely the most important win of my 500 career".

It's a victory which also sees the triumph of an amazing phenomenon: whether the race is in the heart of Andalusia, in the French Sarthe or the Derbyshire countryside, the crowd only gathers now around this young man with his seemingly limitless talent and whose courage never fails him. A gambler but a perfectionist. He adores the challenges but is also calculating.

In the annals of racing history, Valentino Rossi will most certainly leave an indelible trace. His career is only in its beginnings, but it has already been marked as the one that got GP motorcycling really noticed. In Italy where the RAI – national television – is breaking all records. But also elsewhere where the crowd completely identifies with this exceptional rider.

Valentino Rossi still unbeatable: "Donington was one of the best races of my career", he said after he won the title.

250cc
GP of Great Britain

STARTING GRID

1.	31	T. Harada	MS Aprilia Racing	1'33.651
2.	74	D. Katoh	Telefonica Movistar Honda	1'34.002
3.	5	M. Melandri	MS Aprilia Racing	1'34.108
4.	7	E. Alzamora	Telefonica Movistar Honda	1'34.519
5.	99	J. McWilliams	Aprilia Grand Prix	1'34.551
6.	8	N. Matsudo	Petronas Sprinta Yamaha T	1'34.727
7.	44	R. Rolfo	Safilo Oxydo Race	1'34.843
8.	81	R. de Puniet	Equipe de France - Scrab G	1'35.365
9.	10	F. Nieto	Valencia Circuit Aspar Team	1'35.533
10.	9	S. Porto	Yamaha Kruz	1'35.678
11.	6	A. Debon	Valencia Circuit Aspar Team	1'35.726
12.	66	A. Hofmann	Dark Dog Racing Factory	1'35.831
13.	50	S. Guintoli	Equipe de France - Scrab G	1'36.165
14.	18	S. Yuzy	Petronas Sprinta Yamaha T	1'36.190
15.	42	D. Checa	Team Fomma	1'36.297
16.	12	K. Nöhles	MS Aprilia Racing	1'36.459
17.	22	D. De Gea	Antena 3 Yamaha-d 'Antin	1'36.587
18.	21	F. Battaini	MS Eros Ramazotti Racing	1'36.784
19.	37	L. Boscoscuro	Campetella Racing	1'36.968
20.	57	L. Lanzi	Campetella Racing	1'37.032
21.	58	S. Norval	Right Track Racing	1'37.299
22.	20	J. Vidal	PR2 Metrored	1'37.503
23.	16	D. Tomas	By Queroseno Racing Team	1'37.543
24.	11	R. Chiarello	Aprilia Grand Prix	1'37.608
25.	59	G. Jackson	Team Jackson	1'38.258
26.	68	S. Easton	Monster-Mob	1'38.484
27.	45	S. Edwards	FCC-TSR	1'38.576
28.	62	J. Di Salvo	Cruise America Gr. Prix Raci	1'39.022
29.	36	L. Costa	Antena 3 Yamaha-d 'Antin	1'39.189
30.	55	D. Giugovaz	Edo Racing	1'39.269
31.	23	C. Barros	Yamaha Kruz	1'39.446
32.	98	K. Poensgen	Dark Dog Racing Factory	1'39.503
33.	67	M. Herzberg	EPS Racing	1'39.752

RACE: 27 LAPS = 108.621 KM

1.	Daijiro Katoh - 27 laps in 42'46.466 (152.363km/h)	
2.	Roberto Rolfo	at 10.173
3.	Marco Melandri	at 10.401
4.	Emilio Alzamora	at 25.100
5.	Naoki Matsudo	at 46.668
6.	Franco Nieto	at 51.130
7.	Sylvain Guintoli	at 51.926
8.	Alex Debon	at 52.491
9.	Alex Hofmann	at 53.797
10.	Shahrol Yuzy	at 57.984
11.	David Checa	at 58.117
12.	Klaus Nöhles	at 1'02.663
13.	Franco Battaini	at 1'06.628
14.	Lorenzo Lanzi	at 1'14.493
15.	Luca Boscoscuro	at 1'16.335
16.	David Tomas	at 1'21.487
17.	David De Gea	at 1'25.057
18.	Tetsuya Harada	at 1'26.254
19.	Stuart Edwards	at 1 lap
20.	Diego Giugovaz	at 1 lap
21.	Luis Costa	at 1 lap
22.	Jason Di Salvo	at 1 lap
23.	Katja Poensgen	at 1 lap
24.	Michale Herzberg	at 1 lap
25.	Cesar Barros	at 2 laps

RETIREMENTS

Shane Norval	did not start
Stuart Easton	at 3 laps
Sebastian Porto	at 4 laps
Riccardo Chiarello	at 6 laps
Jeronimo Vidal	at 10 laps
Jeremy McWilliams	at 12 laps (fall)
Gary Jackson	at 20 laps
Randy de Puniet	at 25 laps (fall)

RACE FACTS

Pole Position:	Kitoh Tetsuya Harada	1'33.651
Fastest lap:	Daijiro Katoh	1'34.096
Circuit record lap:	Tetsuya Harada	1'34.137 (1997)
Circuit best lap:	Tetsuya Harada	1'33.651 (2001)

CHAMPIONSHIP

1.	D. Katoh	161 (6 victories)
2.	T. Harada	121 (1 victory)
3.	M. Melandri	104
4.	R. Rolfo	91
5.	E. Alzamora	75
6.	R. Locatelli	73 (1 victory)
7.	F. Nieto	70
8.	J. Mc Williams	68
9.	N. Matsudo	45
10.	A. Hofmann	38

Tetsuya Harada has reason to look glum: his direct rival has taken 25 points off him in one fell swoop.

PRACTICE:

Continuation of the duel Harada – Katoh. McWilliams is the fastest on the first day, but the two Japanese riders take centre stage on Saturday. Melandri and Alzamora complete the front row. Bad luck for Locatelli: the reigning 125cc World Champion suffers a high speed crash and breaks his right shoulder. He takes to the track for the warm-up before withdrawing from the race..

START:

Harada charges ahead on Redgate Corner and finishes the first lap with a lead of 510 thousandths over Katoh who is followed by Melandri.

3RD LAP:

Randy de Puniet falls while running in eighth place.

5TH LAP:

Katoh leaves his position as privileged observer to Harada. On the line the Honda rider has a lead of 0"507 and is beginning to increase the pace.

7TH LAP:

Still Katoh and Harada (0"537 between the two men). McWilliams is third more than 3.5 seconds down and is battling with Melandri and Alzamora.

10TH LAP:

Another fastest lap for Katoh who now has a lead of 3"109 over Harada (a plug on the Aprilia is letting him down).

Katoh yet again.

14TH LAP (MID-RACE):

Katoh has a lead of more than ten seconds, but makes a mistake under braking on the last corner and runs into the grass. He crosses the line with a lead of 5"507 over Melandri, McWilliams, Rolfo and Alzamora. Harada is losing 2.5 seconds a lap (he is sixth).

16TH LAP:

McWilliams falls (collarbone).

21ST LAP:

Still Katoh with a lead of 7"967 on the duo Melandri-Rolfo (what a race for the luxury privateer!). Harada is still resisting Gonzales-Nieto who is heroic in spite of his physical shape (fractured malleoles in Assen, the Spaniard moves around the paddock on crutches).

FINISH (27 LAPS):

Still Katoh, while Tetsuya Harada finishes out of the points. Rolfo is on the podium again ahead of Melandri. The talent of the Frenchman Sylvain Guintoli is confirmed by a seventh position.

CHAMPIONSHIP:

A slap in the face for Aprilia with Harada now 40 points behind Katoh at the mid-season stage. Melandri is 57 points behind representing a chasm to overcome.

Marco Melandri finishes on the podium. But way behind Daijiro Katoh...

Practice:

We should no longer be talking about surprises: just a week after his first win, Spaniard Toni Elias records the first pole position of his GP career during practice which only takes place on the first day (rain on Saturday). Cecchinello crashes (fracture and abrasion of the little finger on his left hand), but grits his teeth to make the start. However Jarno Müller withdraws (collarbone). Borsoi (10th on the grid) is the fastest in the rain on Saturday.

Start:

Poggiali and Elias show the best reflexes, Youichi Ui moves into second position in the steep drop on the Donington track. At the end of the first lap, Poggiali has a lead of 137 thousandths over Elias.

2nd lap:

Hules falls and, a few hundred metres further on, Ueda also falls but rejoins the race. Elias and Ui are opening up a lead.

Youichi Ui dominates the weekend in 125.

Neck and neck on the track: Ui and Elias, fairing against fairing.

7th lap:

Ui takes the lead on the fourth lap. Azuma is now second (0"597 behind) ahead of Elias, Poggiali, Perugini and Cecchinello.

13th lap (mid-race):

Ui is riding a lonely race with a lead of 4"692 over Azuma. The main focus of the race is now on the battle for third position between Elias and Poggiali. Angel Nieto Junior and Alex de Angelis have just fallen.

19th lap:

Everyone is fighting ... to stay awake. Ui is way ahead, with Azuma in second. Elias and Poggiali are battling for third place.

23rd lap:

Elias and Poggiali have reeled in Azuma. The young Spaniard is now second.

Finish (26 laps):

Ui has no worries. Elias definitely has no fear and touches Poggiali's fairing under braking on the penultimate corner. He finishes second with Azuma only fourth after making a mistake under braking on the last hairpin. Poggiali indicates his unhappiness to Elias on the line.

Championship:

Poggiali is still in the lead, but Elias is now second, seven points behind. Borsoi finishes in eighth place and is eleven points behind the leader.

The pupil and the master: Toni Elias listens attentively to Alberto Puig.

Starting grid

1.	24	T. Elias	Telefonica Movistar Jr Team	1'38.844
2.	41	Y. Ui	L & M Derbi Team	1'38.854
3.	54	M. Poggiali	Gilera Racing Team	1'39.124
4.	4	M. Azuma	Liegeois Competition	1'39.268
5.	7	S. Perugini	Italjet Racing Team	1'39.481
6.	39	J. Hules	Matteoni Racing	1'39.618
7.	22	P. Nieto	L & M Derbi Team	1'39.636
8.	5	N. Ueda	FCC – TSR	1'39.643
9.	9	L. Cecchinello	MS Aprilia LCR	1'39.824
10.	23	G. Borsoi	LAE – UGT 3000	1'39.828
11.	8	G. Scalvini	Italjet Racing Team	1'39.843
12.	29	A. Nieto Jr	Viceroy Team	1'39.878
13.	15	A. de Angelis	Matteoni Racing	1'39.990
14.	17	S. Jenkner	LAE – UGT 3000	1'39.996
15.	16	S. Sanna	Safilo Oxydo Race	1'40.113
16.	6	M. Giansanti	Axo Racing Team	1'40.274
17.	21	A. Vincent	Team Fomma	1'40.436
18.	73	C. Stoner	Movistar Team	1'40.589
19.	11	M. Sabbatani	Bossini Fontana Racing	1'40.609
20.	18	J. Smrz	Budweiser Budvar Hanusch	1'40.621
21.	34	E. Bataille	Axo Racing Team	1'40.905
22.	28	G. Talmacsi	Racing Service	1'40.946
23.	20	G. Caffiero	Bossini Fontana Racing	1'41.039
24.	25	J. Olive	Telefonica Movistar Jr Team	1'41.103
25.	27	M. Petrini	Racing Service	1'41.159
26.	26	D. Pedrosa	Telefonica Movistar Jr Team	1'41.369
27.	19	A. Branetti	Team Crae	1'41.387
28.	31	A. Rodriguez	Valencia Circuit Aspar Team	1'41.850
29.	72	C. Martin	Wilson Racing	1'42.519
30.	12	R. Jara	MS Aprilia LCR	1'42.655
31.	31	P. Robinson	Valencia Circuit Aspar Team	1'42.705
32.	77	A. Araujo	Liegeois Competition	1'46.172

Race: 26 laps = 104.598 km

1.	Youichi Ui - 26 laps in 43'17.675(144.957km/h)	
2.	Toni Elias	at 3.129
3.	Manuel Poggiali	at 3.869
4.	Masao Azuma	at 3.966
5.	Lucio Cecchinello	at 17.386
6.	Simone Sanna	at 23.647
7.	Steve Jenkner	at 24.201
8.	Gino Borsoi	at 24.422
9.	Angel Rodriguez	at 28.039
10.	Gabor Talmacsi	at 28.612
11.	Mirko Giansanti	at 28.620
12.	Daniel Pedrosa	at 33.089
13.	Jakub Smrz	at 36.125
14.	Joan Olive	at 36.583
15.	Max Sabbatani	at 36.948
16.	Gaspare Caffiero	at 43.849
17.	Casey Stoner	at 50.842
18.	Arnaud Vincent	at 1'01.114
19.	Eric Bataille	at 1'06.140
20.	Marco Petrini	at 1'11.505
21.	Adrian Araujo	at 1'32.712
22.	Raul Jara	at 1'33.146
23.	Nobru Ueda	at 1 lap

Retirements

Stephano Perugini	at 10 laps
Christopher Martin	at 13 laps
Alex de Angelis	at 15 laps (laps)
Angel Nieto jr	at 15 laps (laps)
Paul Robinson	at 16 laps
Gianluigi Scalvini	at 17 laps
Alessandro Brannetti	at 20 laps (laps)
Pablo Nieto	at 21 laps (laps)
Jaroslav Hules	at 25 laps (laps)

Race facts

Pole Position:	Toni Elias	1'38.844
Fastest lap:	Youichi Ui	1'38.626
Circuit record lap:	Masao Azuma	1'39.077 (2000)
Circuit best lap:	Youichi Ui	1'38.413

Championship

1.	M. Poggiali	104 (1 victory)
2.	T. Elias	97 (1 victory)
3.	G. Borsoi	93
4.	Y. Ui	86 (2 victories)
5.	M. Azuma	85 (2 victories)
6.	L. Cecchinello	77 (1 victory)
7.	N. Ueda	76 (1 victory)
8.	A. Vincent	63
9.	S. Jenkner	63
10.	S. Sanna	51

Sachsenring
Grand Prix of GERMANY

Emilio Alzamora: now that's what we call a slide.

Olivier Jacque behind the branches: welcome to the Sachsenring.

Simone Sanna: V...
is for victory.

500cc

GP of Germany

22 July
Sachsenring – 3.704 m

STARTING GRID

1.	3	M. Biaggi	Marlboro Yamaha Team	1'26.097
2.	56	S. Nakano	Gauloises Yamaha Tech 3	1'26.250
3.	4	A. Barros	West Honda Pons	1'26.262
4.	7	C. Checa	Marlboro Yamaha Team	1'26.313
5.	19	O. Jacque	Gauloises Yamaha Tech 3	1'26.506
6.	5	G. McCoy	Red Bull Yamaha WCM	1'26.638
7.	65	L. Capirossi	West Honda Pons	1'26.654
8.	6	N. Abe	Antena 3 Yamaha-d'Antin	1'26.765
9.	1	K. Roberts	Telefonica Movistar Suzuki	1'26.784
10.	15	S. Gibernau	Telefonica Movistar Suzuki	1'26.942
11.	46	V. Rossi	Nastro Azzurro Honda	1'26.955
12.	10	J.L. Cardoso	Antena 3 Yamaha-d'Antin	1'27.119
13.	17	J. vd Goorbergh	Proton TEAM KR	1'27.294
14.	11	T. Ukawa	Repsol YPF Honda Team	1'27.455
15.	14	A. West	Dee Cee Jeans Racing Team	1'28.230
16.	41	N. Haga	Red Bull Yamaha WCM	1'28.248
17.	12	H. Aoki	Arie Molenaar Racing	1'28.323
18.	9	L. Haslam	Shell Advance Honda	1'28.326
19.	16	J. Stigefelt	Sabre Sport	1'28.589
20.	18	B. Clarke	Shell Advance Honda	1'29.613
21.	24	J. Vincent	Pulse GP	1'29.930
22.	21	B. Veneman	Dee Cee Jeans Racing Team	1'30.238

RACE: 30 LAPS = 111.12 KM

1. Max Biaggi - 30 laps in 43'36.983 (152.859 km/h)
2. Carlos Checa — at 3.249
3. Shinya Nakano — at 3.642
4. Norick Abe — at 4.784
5. Alex Barros — at 21.164
6. Olivier Jacque — at 21.385
7. Valentino Rossi — at 21.945
8. Loris Capirossi — at 22.485
9. Kenny Roberts — at 23.331
10. Sete Gibernau — at 24.404
11. Garry McCoy — at 24.410
12. Noriyuki Haga — at 43.996
13. Jose Luis Cardoso — at 44.216
14. Jurgen vd Goorbergh — at 44.329
15. Anthony West — at 1'22.533
16. Jason Vincent — at 1 lap

RETIREMENTS

Haruchika Aoki	1st lap not finished
Leon Haslam	1st lap not finished
Tohru Ukawa	at 3 laps (fall)
Brendan Clarke	at 12 laps (fall)
Barry Veneman	at 17 laps
Johan Stigefelt	at 21 laps

RACE FACTS

Pole Position:	Max Biaggi	1'26.097
Fastest lap:	Shinya Nakano	1'26.808
Circuit record lap:	New circuit	
Circuit best lap:	Max Biaggi	1'26.097 (2001)

CHAMPIONSHIP

1. V. Rossi — 170 (5 victories)
2. M. Biaggi — 160 (3 victories)
3. L. Capirossi — 111
4. A. Barros — 100 (1 victory)
5. S. Nakano — 100
6. N. Abe — 87
7. A. Crivillé — 71
8. C. Checa — 67
9. K. Roberts — 62
10. S. Gibernau — 60

Best race lap for Shinya Nakano: the Tech3 rider has got totally to grips with 500.

PRACTICE:

Max Biaggi places the bar very high on the first day. Rossi is having problems finding a balanced set-up. "Tino" admits he doesn't feel on form after three days testing for the Eight Hour in Suzuka. All these events on the track are overshadowed on Saturday at the end of the session with a second crash in less than 40 minutes for Alex Crivillé. Suffering from serious concussion, the former World Champion withdraws from the race. In the Shell Advance team, Walker has been relieved of his services and Haslam has inherited the NSR V4 with his V2 given to the young 18-year-old Australian Brendan Clarke.

START:

Biaggi, Checa, Abe: the only colour on view at the Sachsenring is red. No black (Capirossi is eleventh), nor yellow (Rossi is twelfth on the first corner).

4TH LAP:

Biaggi has a lead of 0"833 over his team-mate. Rossi has climbed back into 8th place.

8TH LAP:

Three Yamahas at the front – Biaggi, Checa (0"567 behind) and Abe. Barros is holding on and Nakano is reeling in the Brazilian.

15TH LAP (MID-RACE):

Yamaha's domination is total. Biaggi has built up a cushion (1"358 ahead of Abe/Checa), Nakano is now fourth. Rossi continues his comeback and is running in sixth.

18TH LAP:

The crowd is rejoicing – their favourite, Rossi, is now fifth.

Valentino Rossi's fans turned out in force...

23RD LAP:

Biaggi is alone up front but there is a superb battle for second place between Checa, Abe and Nakano; and the fight for fifth place is even tougher between Capirossi, Rossi, Barros, Roberts and Jacque.

25TH LAP:

Barros and Jacque pass Rossi.

29TH LAP:

Ukawa falls while in a discreet 12th position.

FINISH (30 LAPS):

Biaggi has had a ball. Like in Le Mans, there's a one-two for the "reds". Nakano claims his first 500cc podium and Jacque is a brilliant sixth after a spectacular final duel with Barros. Rossi finishes seventh.

CHAMPIONSHIP:

Whatever happened at the Sachsenring, we knew that Rossi would spend his holidays first overall. But his lead over Biaggi is now only ten points.

... but it's Max Biaggi who steals the day.

Alex Crivillé remounts his NSR N° 28. A few minutes later, there's another painful fall.

THE DAY WHEN ALEX CRIVILLÉ...

Anna Nogué, his fiancée, sits on a small concrete wall with her head in her hands. Her whole body is shaken by her sobs. She sits and waits, alone in the world. Alex Crivillé, who became a living myth in Spain when he gave it its first ever 500 world title, has just arrived at the Sachsenring medical centre. The rider's face shows no emotion; just perhaps total incomprehension. For the second time in forty minutes, he has crashed on the same corner. The first time was without injury following contact with Loris Capirossi. But this time the images are dreadful: the accident happened flat out in fifth gear at 198 km/h according to the telemetry.

The shock was terrible, the verdict painful: "Massive concussion. Alex doesn't even remember that he crashed twice today. A finger on his left hand is perhaps broken. It's..." It's what? Jesus Benitez, the special correspondent for the huge Spanish daily Marca, has more and more difficulty finding the right words: "Of course, it's..." Perhaps the end of his career, even if no-one dares say it for the moment. As if the whole Spanish racing family which each day has grown in numbers around "its" champion refuses to see the truth. Refuses to accept the obvious: Alex Crivillé is a sensitive soul and never came to terms with his 500 title. Too kind, too well brought up, he paid the price in the very first races of last year for his inability to say no to requests that followed his title.

Physically worn out: "after I won the title, I didn't get a break and only ten days rest in total away from the massive celebrations in Spain". Psychologically disturbed, his 2000 season was a total disaster (only one win). Was it just a glitch or an irreversible and definitive descent towards retirement? This year has was even totally displaced in the HRC hierarchy (Honda Racing Department) in favour of Valentino Rossi. Criville only emerged ahead on one occasion during "his" GP in Jerez de la Frontera.

As for the rest, it was the same terrible, repetitive scenario: each time the former number one upped the tempo, he would find himself on the floor. And the questions and doubts would come into his mind. One day it would be: "I need a change of scene, a new team, new start, different people at my side". The next day – the day before his accident in the Sachsenring, there would be renewed hope: "Michael Doohan watched me from the side of the track and gave me some good advice; he confirmed some things I had been seeking to resolve for some time". On Saturday 21 July 2001 at 14h59, Alex Crivillé was on his best lap when for the second time in just forty minutes, he found himself on the ground.

The next day, the Iberian press barely mentioned anything else, not even the talent of young Toni Elias in 125cc. Not even Carlos Checa's newly found form who would go on to finish second in the race. Not even the next episode in the Rossi/Biaggi saga, which would take a new twist that day. No, the only topic of conversation was Alex. And the question on everybody's lips: would we once again see him leading a race or would this fall be the one fall too many? Would it be a Crivillé comeback or farewell?

250cc

GP of Germany

22 July
Sachsenring - 3.704 m

STARTING GRID

1. 31	T. Harada	MS Aprilia Racing	1'26.906
2. 5	M. Melandri	MS Aprilia Racing	1'27.064
3. 74	D. Katoh	Telefonica Movistar Honda	1'27.374
4. 99	J. McWilliams	Aprilia Grand Prix	1'27.593
5. 10	F. Nieto	Valencia Circuit Aspar Team	1'27.642
6. 9	S. Porto	Yamaha Kruz	1'27.868
7. 44	R. Rolfo	Safilo Oxydo Race	1'27.882
8. 81	R. de Puniet	Equipe de France - Scrab G	1'27.943
9. 7	E. Alzamora	Telefonica Movistar Honda	1'27.982
10. 6	A. Debon	Valencia Circuit Aspar Team	1'28.079
11. 15	R. Locatelli	MS Eros Ramazzotti Racing	1'28.215
12. 66	A. Hofmann	Dark Dog Racing Factory	1'28.300
13. 8	N. Matsudo	Petronas Sprinta Yamaha T	1'28.371
14. 21	F. Battaini	MS Eros Ramazzotti Racing	1'28.491
15. 42	D. Checa	Team Fomma	1'28.520
16. 22	D. De Gea	Antena 3 Yamaha-d 'Antin	1'29.087
17. 18	S. Yuzy	Petronas Sprinta Yamaha T	1'29.185
18. 37	L. Boscoscuro	Campetella Racing	1'29.209
19. 12	K. Nöhles	MS Aprilia Racing	1'29.216
20. 57	L. Lanzi	Campetella Racing	1'29.274
21. 50	S. Guintoli	Equipe de France - Scrab G	1'29.498
22. 16	D. Tomas	By Queroseno Racing Team	1'29.562
23. 20	J. Vidal	PR2 Metrored	1'29.778
24. 11	R. Chiarello	Aprilia Grand Prix	1'30.256
25. 75	D. Heidolf	Freudenberg Racing Team	1'30.424
26. 25	V. Philippe	Tecmas Racing	1'30.776
27. 55	D. Giugovaz	Edo Racing	1'31.037
28. 76	C. Gemmel	Kiefer Castrol Honda Racing	1'31.442
29. 23	C. Barros	Yamaha Kruz	1'31.502
30. 36	L. Costa	Antena 3 Yamaha-d 'Antin	1'31.787
31. 45	S. Edwards	FCC-TSR	1'31.966
32. 78	M. Neukirchner	Adac sachsen	1'31.977
33. 98	K. Poensgen	Dark Dog Racing Factory	1'31.998
34. 77	M. Schneider	Kiefer Castrol Honda Racing	1'32.496

RACE: 29 LAPS = 107.416 KM

1. Marco Melandri - 29 laps in 42'37.696 (151.189km/h)
2. Daijiro Katoh — at 0.052
3. Tetsuya Harada — at 0.203
4. Roberto Rolfo — at 18.310
5. Randy de Puniet — at 28.108
6. Alex Debon — at 36.566
7. Alex Hofmann — at 36.764
8. Naoki Matsudo — at 36.918
9. Franco Battaini — at 40.466
10. Fonsi Nieto — at 43.174
11. Shahrol Yuzy — at 43.256
12. Lorenzo Lanzi — at 57.398
13. Jeronimo Vidal — at 1'11.662
14. Riccardo Chiarello — at 1'25.007
15. David Tomas — at 1'25.614
16. Dirk Heidolf — at 1 lap
17. Christian Gemmel — at 1 lap
18. Max Neukirchner — at 1 lap
19. Luis Costa — at 1 lap
20. Katja Poensgen — at 1 lap

RETIREMENTS

Vincent Philippe	did not start
Klaus Nöhles	at 2 laps (fall)
Sylvain Guintoli	at 2 laps (fall)
Cesar Barros	at 16 laps
Stuart Edwards	at 18 laps (fall)
Diego Giugovaz	at 21 laps (fall)
Jeremy McWilliams	at 22 laps (fall)
Emilio Alzamora	at 22 laps (fall)
Marcel Schneider	at 23 laps (fall)
David Checa	at 24 laps (fall)
Sebastian Porto	at 27 laps (fall)
David De Gea	at 27 laps (fall)
Roberto Locatelli	at 28 laps (fall)
Luca Boscoscuro	at 28 laps (fall)

RACE FACTS

Pole Position:	Tetsuya Harada	1'26.906
Fastest lap:	Marco Melandri	1'27.233
Circuit record lap:	New Circuit	
Circuit best lap:	Tetsuya Harada	1'26.906 (2001)

CHAMPIONSHIP

1. D. Katoh — 181 (6 victories)
2. T. Harada — 137 (1 victory)
3. M. Melandri — 129 (1 victory)
4. R. Rolfo — 104
5. F. Nieto — 76
6. E. Alzamora — 75 (1 victory)
7. R. Locatelli — 73
8. J. Mc Williams — 68
9. N. Matsudo — 53
10. A. Hofmann — 47

PRACTICE:

There was a lot of talk of Katja Poensgen, and the problems within her team. On Friday, the German fell heavily in free practice before encountering mechanical problems in the afternoon. So she did not qualify on the first day, but set the record straight on Saturday. On Sunday a few hours before the race, Dieter Theis, the Darg Dog Racing Factory team manager, announced that there would be a parting of the ways after the German GP. Harada set pole position followed by Melandri and Katoh.

START:

Katoh, Melandri and McWilliams are fastest off the blocks. Katoh is in the lead at the end of the first lap followed by Melandri and Harada who doesn't wait long to make an attack.

2ND LAP:

Boscoscuro falls. Locatelli doesn't manage to avoid the Aprilia which he involuntarily uses as a trampoline. The 125 champion gets away without serious injury.

4TH LAP:

Porto and De Gea crash.

7TH LAP:

Five riders are neck and neck at the start finish line. Alzamora makes a mistake in the next corner. Harada has a lead of 0"392 over McWilliams and Melandri, Katoh is fourth.

8TH LAP:

McWilliams falls.

15TH LAP (MID-RACE):

Melandri had taken control on the previous lap, and leads from Harada and Katoh. Rolfo and de Puniet are battling for fourth place.

A trap for Vincent Philippe. Who dreams of finding a ride in GP next year.

22ND LAP:

The men at the front have caught the back-markers. Melandri has a lead of 341 thousandths over Katoh who leads Harada by half a second. On the next lap, Katoh records the fastest lap and takes the lead.

FINISH (29 LAPS):

Melandri pulls out all the stops and the last two laps of his duel with Katoh are breathtaking. He wins his first victory in 250cc. So Katoh is no longer invincible and Aprilia has understood that there is no question of giving priority to one rider over another.

CHAMPIONSHIP:

Katoh takes four points back from Harada, who is now threatened by his young team-mate Marco Melandri. It looks like it will go right down to the wire!

Marco Melandri at the stove...

... the same with the champagne!

Sanna wins, Elias second, Manual Poggiali places the Gilera once again on the podium.

22 July
Sachsenring – 3.704 m

STARTING GRID

1.	11	M. Sabbatani	Bossini Fontana Racing	1'30.186
2.	16	S. Sanna	Safilo Oxydo Race	1'30.217
3.	9	L. Cecchinello	MS Aprilia LCR	1'30.314
4.	54	M. Poggiali	Gilera Racing Team	1'30.504
5.	24	T. Elias	Telefonica Movistar Jr Team	1'30.628
6.	17	S. Jenkner	LAE – UGT 3000	1'30.636
7.	23	G. Borsoi	LAE – UGT 3000	1'30.732
8.	41	Y. Ui	L & M Derbi Team	1'30.775
9.	18	J. Smrz	Budweiser Budvar Hanusch	1'30.865
10.	26	D. Pedrosa	Telefonica Movistar Jr Team	1'30.884
11.	4	M. Azuma	Liegeois Competition	1'30.890
12.	22	P. Nieto	L & M Derbi Team	1'30.978
13.	29	A. Nieto Jr	Viceroy Team	1'30.982
14.	31	A. Rodriguez	Valencia Circuit Aspar Team	1'31.184
15.	15	A. de Angelis	Matteoni Racing	1'31.231
16.	39	J. Hules	Matteoni Racing	1'31.331
17.	27	M. Petrini	Racing Service	1'31.430
18.	6	M. Giansanti	Axo Racing Team	1'31.433
19.	8	G. Scalvini	Italjet Racing Team	1'31.456
20.	34	E. Bataille	Axo Racing Team	1'31.502
21.	7	S. Perugini	Italjet Racing Team	1'31.621
22.	19	A. Branetti	Team Crae	1'31.930
23.	25	J. Olive	Telefonica Movistar Jr Team	1'31.941
24.	21	A. Vincent	Team Fomma	1'32.169
25.	12	M. Kallio	Team Red Devil Honda	1'32.381
26.	28	G. Talmacsi	Racing Service	1'33.060
27.	80	T. Kirmeier	Ivetra-Seel Racing	1'33.166
28.	78	C. Klein	ADAC jr Team German	1'33.235
29.	12	R. Jara	MS Aprilia LCR	1'33.262
30.	79	A. Hahn	Team Hahn	1'33.386
31.	81	R. Knoefler	HKS Racing Team Moto Mei	1'34.155
32.	77	A. Araujo	Liegeois Competition	1'34.995

RACE: 27 LAPS= 100.008 KM

1.	Simone Sanna - 27 laps in 41'09.327	
2.	Toni Elias	at 0.247
3.	Manuel Poggiali	at 0.701
4.	Masao Azuma	at 0.734
5.	Lucio Cecchinello	at 1.370
6.	Jaroslav Hules	at 2.202
7.	Max Sabbatani	at 2.326
8.	Angel Rodriguez	at 5.877
9.	Jakub Smrz	at 6.132
10.	Steve Jenkner	at 10.071
11.	Daniel Pedrosa	at 23.066
12.	Alex de Angelis	at 23.089
13.	Angel Nieto jr	at 23.309
14.	Mirko Giansanti	at 27.801
15.	Joan Olive	at 28.065
16.	Stefano Perugini	at 28.139
17.	Alessandro Brannetti	at 28.948
18.	Gabor Talmacsi	at 32.317
19.	Youichi Ui	at 35.643
20.	Eric Bataille	at 40.978
21.	Marco Petrini	at 44.624
22.	Gianluigi Scalvini	at 1'06.673
23.	Raul Jara	at 1'07.108
24.	Andreas Kahn	at 1'08.085
25.	Claudius Klein	at 1'08.383
26.	Tobias Kirmeier	at 1'08.632
27.	Rene Koefler	at 1 lap

RETIREMENTS

Mika Kallio	1st lap not finished
Adrian Araujo	at 12 laps
Pablo Nieto	at 19 laps (fall)
Arnaud Vincent	at 19 laps (fall)
Gino Borsoi	at 21 laps

RACE FACTS

Pole Position:	Max Sabbatani 1'30.186
Fastest lap:	Lucio Cecchinello 1'30.371
Circuit record lap:	New Circuit
Circuit best lap:	Max Sabbatani 1'30.186 (2001)

CHAMPIONSHIP

1.	M. Poggiali	120 (1 victory)
2.	T. Elias	117 (1 victory)
3.	M. Azuma	98 (2 victories)
4.	G. Borsoi	93
5.	L. Cecchinello	88 (1 victory)
6.	Y. Ui	86 (2 victories)
7.	N. Ueda	76 (1 victory)
8.	S. Sanna	76 (1 victory)
9.	S. Jenkner	69
10.	A. Vincent	63

PRACTICE:

Toni Elias dominated the first day of practice and Aprilia the second. Paddock jockey Sabbatani – 1m50, 39 kg – wins the first pole position of his career ahead of Sanna and Cecchinello. Jenkner, lives close to the circuit and for a moment was on pole (you can imagine the crowd!) before falling in the last few minutes. Ueda withdraws from the race with a fractured left ankle. The proof of a close battle is in the times: less than a second covers the first fifteen riders. A warning for Elias during the warm-up: the on-form man suffers a fall but without serious consequences.

START:

Elias, Sabbatani and Sanna get the perfect start. In contrast to last year, everything goes well on the first corner. Borsoi and Scalvini are penalised with a stop and go for jumping the start.

The pack at the start. This time, everything goes fine at the first corner.

2ND LAP:

Ui falls but rejoins the race. The three men at the front have already opened up a gap of 1"587 on the rest of the pack.

5TH LAP:

Sanna has taken control, but Poggiali and Cecchinello are closing in together with a second pack comprising Jenkner, Azuma, Smrz, Pablo Nieto and Vincent.

7TH LAP:

Poggiali now leads ahead of Elias, Cecchinello and Sanna. Borsoi stops even before completing his stop and go.

Simone Sanna: "Victory is this way"

9TH LAP:

Bumps and crashes for Pablo Nieto and Arnaud Vincent.

14TH LAP (MID-RACE):

Cecchinello heads a group of nine furies. Positions are changing at every corner.

21ST LAP:

Still Cecchinello ahead of Sanna and Azuma. The three men look like they are pulling away but nothing is ever final in this category.

FINISH (27 LAPS):

Sanna has a lead of 6 tenths going into the last lap and it proves to be enough in spite of Elias and Poggiali's comeback. The Italian approaches the crowd to start a strip-tease.

CHAMPIONSHIP:

Poggiali will go on holiday still leading the championship, but he has only a three point lead over Elias. Azuma and Borsoi are more than twenty points behind.

Marco Melandri,
a born acrobat.

Brno
Grand Prix
of CZECH REPUBLIC

The sky is blue, the leaves are green, the bikes are orange (Jurgen van den Goorbergh) and ocean blue (Olivier Jacque): a postcard from Brno.

Toni Elias, the Spanish phenomenon is in the form of his life.

500cc

GP
of Czech Republic

26 August
Brno – 5.403 m

STARTING GRID

1.	3	M. Biaggi	Marlboro Yamaha Team	2'00.347
2.	46	V. Rossi	Nastro Azzurro Honda	2'00.503
3.	65	L. Capirossi	West Honda Pons	2'00.675
4.	17	J. vd Goorbergh	Proton TEAM KR	2'00.949
5.	5	G. McCoy	Red Bull Yamaha WCM	2'01.142
6.	1	K. Roberts	Telefonica Movistar Suzuki	2'01.142
7.	7	C. Checa	Marlboro Yamaha Team	2'01.265
8.	28	A. Crivillé	Repsol YPF Honda Team	2'01.421
9.	4	A. Barros	West Honda Pons	2'01.452
10.	15	S. Gibernau	Telefonica Movistar Suzuki	2'01.486
11.	6	N. Abe	Antena 3 Yamaha-d'Antin	2'01.755
12.	19	O. Jacque	Gauloises Yamaha Tech 3	2'01.764
13.	11	T. Ukawa	Repsol YPF Honda Team	2'02.109
14.	10	J.L. Cardoso	Antena 3 Yamaha-d'Antin	2'02.802
15.	41	N. Haga	Red Bull Yamaha WCM	2'02.823
16.	9	L. Haslam	Shell Advance Honda	2'03.410
17.	12	H. Aoki	Arie Molenaar Racing	2'04.068
18.	14	A. West	Dee Cee Jeans Racing Team	2'04.147
19.	16	J. Stigefelt	Sabre Sport	2'06.105
20.	18	B. Clarke	Shell Advance Honda	2'06.231
21.	21	B. Veneman	Dee Cee Jeans Racing Team	2'06.426
22.	25	S. Geronimi	Paton Grand Prix	2'07.824

RACE: 22 LAPS = 118.866 KM

1. Valentino Rossi - 22 laps in 45'01.044 (158.426 km/h)	
2. Alex Crivillé	at 3.374
3. Loris Capirossi	at 3.767
4. Norick Abe	at 4.057
5. Tohru Ukawa	at 6.574
6. Garry McCoy	at 7.344
7. Carlos Checa	at 10.689
8. Sete Gibernau	at 15.201
9. Alex Barros	at 24.732
10. Max Biaggi	at 29.758
11. Noriyuki Haga	at 42.667
12. Olivier Jacque	at 43.063
13. Jose Luis Cardoso	at 56.432
14. Haruchika Aoki	at 1'13.315
15. Johan Stigefelt	at 2'03.200
16. Barry Veneman	at 2'07.065

RETIREMENTS

Kenny Roberts	at 7 laps
Anthony West	at 8 laps
Leon Haslam	at 13 laps (fall)
Jurgen vd Goorbergh	at 14 laps
Brendan Clarke	at 17 laps
Shaun Geronimi	at 17 laps

RACE FACTS

Pole Position:	Max Biaggi	2'00.347
Fastest lap:	Valentino Rossi	2'01.461
Circuit record lap:	Alex Crivillé	2'02.335 (1998)
Circuit best lap:	Max Biaggi	2'00.347 (2001)

CHAMPIONSHIP

1. V. Rossi	195 (6 victories)
2. M. Biaggi	166 (3 victories)
3. L. Capirossi	127
4. A. Barros	107 (1 victory)
5. N. Abe	100
6. S. Nakano	100
7. A. Crivillé	91
8. C. Checa	76
9. S. Gibernau	68
10. T. Ukawa	64

Biaggi on pole, Rossi alongside: nobody could guess at this stage, that the Championship would take a decisive turn today.

The hunter Rossi, observes Biaggi, his prey, who will soon commit a fatal mistake.

PRACTICE:

The tension is palpable after the summer break. On "his own" circuit where he has shone so much in the past and where just a few weeks ago he completed testing, Max Biaggi sets the standards high from Friday onwards, setting the fastest time ever recorded on the Czech track. Rossi is still not completely on form following his triumphant return from Suzuka – he won the 8 hours – and seems completely out of touch on Friday. On Saturday he restakes his claim. van den Goorbergh qualifies the Proton on the front row. Nakano suffers a heavy fall on Friday morning (fractured right hand); he takes to the track on Saturday afternoon only to cry forfeit from the race.

START:

Roberts surges through ahead of Biaggi. Rossi gets a bad start, but manages to finish the first lap just behind Max' Yamaha. There then follows Abe, van den Goorbergh, Capirossi, Crivillé and Checa.

3RD LAP:

After a first failed attempt, Biaggi takes the lead.

5TH LAP:

Rossi overcomes Roberts. Biaggi has an eight tenths lead over the two men. It will be the best advantage he will get all race.

8TH LAP:

Rossi puts the pressure on Biaggi. van den Goorbergh comes into the pits. Abe is leading Roberts who has lost five seconds and is now being threatened by Crivillé, Capirossi, McCoy and Ukawa.

11TH LAP (MID-RACE):

Crivillé has just passed Roberts whose descent into hell continues.

13TH LAP:

Biaggi falls but rejoins in eleventh position. So Abe takes over second place while Capirossi battles with Crivillé.

16TH LAP:

A furious Roberts comes into the pits and the iron curtain closes very rapidly.

21ST LAP:

Crivillé and Capirossi overtake Abe.

FINISH (22 LAPS):

Rossi wins ahead of Criville and Capirossi. Biaggi finishes tenth.

CHAMPIONSHIP:

Rossi's "difficult" period only lasted one GP in Germany. Valentino retakes the initiative and now has a lead of 39 points over Biaggi. Beaten in his own backyard, Max has just taken a severe blow to his morale.

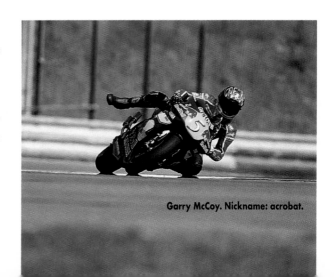

Garry McCoy. Nickname: acrobat.

Grand Prix of Czech Republic

THE THIRTEENTH LAP...

The rumours were growing in the "yellow" camp. But the reds were keeping silent. Open mouthed with terrified with incredulous expressions on their faces, this was the team's joint reaction to the fact that on the downhill part of the Mazarik circuit at Brno, Massimiliano Biaggi had just committed a huge mistake. The great favourite for this Czech GP, the man with all the aces in his hand to set the 500 championship alight again was now sliding along on his back. He picked himself up and remounted his Yamaha to save a few points. We could not guess at this stage of the championship that the scene would be repeated several times before the final curtain.

He's quietly rejoicing, but for the cameras Valentino Rossi plays things down. And even pretends to share his rival's pain. With just a hint of a smile, in Italian he emphasised the difference of just one little letter between "fortunato" (fortunately) and "sfortunato" (unfortunately) as he described the moment when Biaggi fell in front of him. "A typical Max crash", explains Carlo Pernat, the manager for the two best riders in the world at the start of their careers. "Biaggi thinks he's god and is convinced that nothing can happen to him. On Friday when he set his amazing qualifying time, his confidence grew even stronger. Then.." Then? "Well we moved into the second phase of the weekend with Rossi's comeback on Saturday. And then on Sunday morning during warm-up when the riders use their race set-ups, it was a slap in the face for the "reds". Rossi was clocking up fast laps. It's a bit like a game of poker with Biaggi's opponent taking the hand. At exactly the right time".

There followed a duel that lasted thirteen laps until around mid-distance of the Czech Republic GP. Biaggi looked back several times to see if his opponent was still there. "Typical Max," continues Carlo Pernat. "When things don't go the way he expects, he gets nervous". And nerves are the last thing you need in a sport that combines speed and balance.

Rossi makes his move. Biaggi – on the 13th lap – can resist no longer.

Valentino Rossi could now begin to savour a dessert he hadn't even ordered and one he thought he would not have at this race: a new victory, a huge bonus, perhaps decisive for the championship outcome. "Of course 29 points ahead is better than ten. But we mustn't just focus on this race. I have to keep my concentration right up to the end and convince myself that it's not over yet". It's wise words coming from a guy who still knows very well that something important has just happened on this Sunday 26 August 2001. From now on, in an attempt to reverse the course of events, Biaggi will have to take even more risks.

Everyone was expecting a Yamaha demonstration race – the works teams came to test in the Czech Republic the day after the German GP, setting fast times and perfect race simulations. But it turned into a Honda treble in spite of Rossi's fatigue after using the summer break to win the Eight Hours of Suzuka. We thought the points difference would be marginal, when in fact what we have is Rossi more than a race ahead again. There are six to go...

250cc
GP of Czech Republic

STARTING GRID

1. 31	T. Harada	MS Aprilia Racing	2'02.953
2. 74	D. Katoh	Telefonica Movistar Honda	2'03.724
3. 99	J. McWilliams	Aprilia Grand Prix	2'04.119
4. 5	M. Melandri	MS Aprilia Racing	2'04.225
5. 10	F. Nieto	Valencia Circuit Aspar Team	2'04.258
6. 7	E. Alzamora	Telefonica Movistar Honda	2'04.531
7. 6	A. Debon	Valencia Circuit Aspar Team	2'04.623
8. 9	S. Porto	Yamaha Kruz	2'04.625
9. 15	R. Locatelli	MS Eros Ramazzotti Racing	2'04.747
10. 81	R. De Puniet	Equipe de France - Scrab G	2'04.785
11. 44	R. Rolfo	Safilo Oxydo Race	2'04.827
12. 21	F. Battaini	MS Eros Ramazzotti Racing	2'05.040
13. 8	N. Matsudo	Petronas Sprinta Yamaha T	2'05.193
14. 37	L. Boscoscuro	Campetella Racing	2'05.320
15. 46	T. Sekiguchi	Edo Racing	2'05.569
16. 42	D. Checa	Team Fomma	2'05.698
17. 66	A. Hofmann	Dark Dog Racing Factory	2'05.902
18. 12	K. Nöhles	MS Aprilia Racing	2'06.012
19. 50	S. Guintoli	Equipe de France - Scrab G	2'06.225
20. 24	J. Vincent	QUB Team Optimum	2'06.304
21. 18	S. Yuzy	Petronas Sprinta Yamaha T	2'06.410
22. 57	L. Lanzi	Campetella Racing	2'06.421
23. 20	J. Vidal	PR2 Metrored	2'06.424
24. 22	D. De Gea	Antena 3 Yamaha-d 'Antin	2'06.637
25. 16	D. Tomas	By Queroseno Racing Team	2'07.572
26. 11	R. Chiarello	Aprilia Grand Prix	2'07.696
27. 36	L. Costa	Antena 3 Yamaha-d 'Antin	2'08.254
28. 83	G. Rizmayer	Biro Racing Team	2'08.701
29. 23	C. Barros	Yamaha Kruz	2'08.883
30. 80	V. Castka	Edo Racing	2'09.102
31. 62	J. Di Salvo	Cruise America GP Racing	2'09.619
32. 45	S. Edwards	FCC-TSR	2'10.256
33. 79	N. Rank	MSC Schleizer Dreieck	2'11.282

RACE: 20 LAPS = 107.416 KM

1. Tetsuya Harada	- 29 laps in 41'32.599 (156.068km/h)	
2. Marco Melandri	at 2.743	
3. Daijiro Katoh	at 2.797	
4. Fonsi Nieto	at 31.115	
5. Roberto Rolfo	at 32.569	
6. Randy Du Puniet	at 33.823	
7. Emilio Alzamora	at 35.171	
8. Sebastian Porto	at 35.386	
9. Naoki Matsudo	at 35.663	
10. Alex Debon	at 41.559	
11. Klaus Nöhles	at 46.303	
12. Roberto Locatelli	at 46.613	
13. Sylvain Guintoli	at 49.736	
14. Franco Battaini	at 50.375	
15. Lorenzo Lanzi	at 51.492	
16. Taro Sekiguchi	at 56.553	
17. Luca Boscoscuro	at 56.605	
18. David Checa	at 1'02.337	
19. David De Gea	at 1'17.395	
20. Riccardo Chiarello	at 1'17.512	
21. David Tomas	at 1'17.734	
22. Jeronimo Vidal	at 1'17.840	
23. Jay Vincent	at 1'18.157	
24. Luis Costa	at 1'34.555	
25. Gabor Rizmayer	at 1'59.296	
26. Jason Di Salvo	at 1 lap	
27. Norman Rank	at 1 lap	
28. Cesar Barros	at 1 lap	

RETIREMENTS

Alex Hofmann	did not start
Shahrol Yuzy	at 6 laps (fall)
Jeremy McWilliams	at 7 laps
Vladimir Castka	at 13 laps (fall)
Stuart Edwards	at 15 laps

RACE FACTS

Pole Position:	Tetsuya Harada	2'02.953
Fastest lap:	Marco Melandri	2'03.836
Circuit record lap:	Shinya Nakano	2'04.113 (2000)
Circuit best lap:	Tetsuya Harada	2'02.953 (2001)

CHAMPIONSHIP

1. D. Katoh	197 (6 victories)
2. T. Harada	162 (2 victories)
3. M. Melandri	149 (1 victory)
4. R. Rolfo	115
5. F. Nieto	89
6. E. Alzamora	84 (1 victory)
7. R. Locatelli	77
8. J. Mc Williams	68
9. N. Matsudo	60
10. A. Debon	47

"Fonsi" Gonzales-Nieto just misses the podium.

PRACTICE:

Harada spent the break in Japan where the weather was bad. Also, the former world champion has not ridden a bike at all, just played a few video simulation games. And this break has done him the world of good, because he totally dominates practice, leaving Katoh more than 7 tenths behind (0"771 to be exact). McWilliams and Melandri complete the front row. Pretty German Katja Poensgen was not at the track, but there was talk of her with the official announcement of her contract with the Shell Advance team. She should be back for the Portuguese GP.

START:

Daijiro Katoh has the best reflexes ahead of Harada, Marco Melandri, Alfonso "Fonsi" Gonzales-Nieto and the veteran Jeremy McWilliams.

2ND LAP:

Harada takes the lead ahead of Katoh. McWilliams falls again having already crashed heavily in practice.

4TH LAP:

Harada ups the tempo and opens up a gap. In this quarter litre category he is definitely the strongest on the track at Brno.

5TH LAP:

Melandri overtakes Katoh. He will go on to claim a one-two for Aprilia at the end of a fine demonstration.

7TH LAP:

A superb comeback from the Frenchman de Puniet who at this stage is in sixth place, behind Emilio Alzamora.

10TH LAP (MID-RACE):

Harada has a two second advantage over Melandri and Katoh. de Puniet has just overtaken Alzamora.

11TH LAP:

Katoh passes Melandri again with second place at stake. The Italian takes the advantage back a little further on.

14TH LAP:

Rolfo mounts an unstoppable attack on de Puniet.

FINISH (20 LAPS):

Harada wins ahead of Melandri who heroically holds off Katoh to the end. Gonzales-Nieto just misses the podium after winning the battle of the semi-works Aprilias (Rolfo is fifth and de Puniet is sixth).

Marco Melandri at the service of Tetsuya Harada.

Sylvain Guintoli: "I'm on a roll"

CHAMPIONSHIP:

Thanks to Marco Melandri's support, Harada has taken back nine points from Katoh who still has a 35 point lead. In the overall rankings Melandri remains in his team-mate Harada's slipstream.

The first row live, the formation lap slightly delayed on the giant screen.

Jakob Smrz: a difficult name to pronounce, but a talent in the making.

Toni Elias wins again. The Championship is hotting up.

PRACTICE:

Elias has the wind in his sails and although dominated on Friday by Ui's Derbi, the young Spaniard claims a new pole position with the best time ever recorded by a 125 on the track at Brno. In the grandstands the crowd go crazy on Saturday afternoon as new local hero Jakub Smrz provisionally heads the leader board (the Czech rider falls off on the next lap). Ui, Cecchinello and Sanna complete the front row.

START:

Elias gets away quickly. Ui, Sanna, Hules, Cecchinello, Jenkner and Hungarian Gabor Talmacsi, taking advantage of his brilliant time – 8th on the grid, pleading a strong case for the return of the world championship to his country – all give chase.

4TH LAP:

Sanna has come back into Elias' slipstream with Ui, Jenkner, Cecchinello and Sabbatani.

7TH LAP:

Ui moves into second place. Seven riders are now out in the lead.

8TH LAP:

Ui takes the lead. Cecchinello and Sanna take advantage by also getting past Elias.

10TH LAP (MID-RACE):

Cecchinello takes advantage of a mistake by Ui to move into the lead. Elias comes to his senses and passes Ui and Sanna.

12TH LAP:

Poggiali crashes in "only" tenth place. It's the end of a miserable weekend for the San Marino rider. Frenchman Arnaud Vincent also ends up on the floor.

13TH LAP:

Elias takes first place for a few moments, but as proof of the intensity of the battle, is in fifth place two laps later.

17TH LAP:

Now it's German Steve Jenkner's turn to take control ahead of Sanna and Ui.

FINISH (19 LAPS):

The last lap is fast and furious: Sanna falls just a few yards from the chequered flag and Elias wins ahead of two Aprilias belonging to Cecchinello and Jenkner.

CHAMPIONSHIP:

Poggiali had trouble from the very first day and is the weekend's loser. Elias takes a cushion with a 22 point lead in the Championship.

125cc GP
of Czech Republic

26 August
Brno – 5.403 m

STARTING GRID

1.	24	T. Elias	Telefonica Movistar Jr Team	2'09.062
2.	41	Y. Ui	L & M Derbi Team	2'09.174
3.	9	L. Cecchinello	MS Aprilia LCR	2'09.245
4.	16	S. Sanna	Safilo Oxydo Race	2'09.314
5.	18	J. Smrz	Budweiser Budvar Hanusch	2'09.487
6.	17	S. Jenker	LAE – UGT 3000	2'09.831
7.	5	N.Ueda	FCC – TSR	2'09.877
8.	28	G. Talmacsi	Racing Service	2'09.952
9.	11	M. Sabbatani	Bossini Fontana Racing	2'09.971
10.	39	J. Hules	Matteoni Racing	2'10.006
11.	54	M. Poggiali	Gilera Racing Team	2'10.107
12.	4	M. Azuma	Liegeois Competition	2'10.307
13.	26	D. Pedrosa	Telefonica Movistar Jr Team	2'10.405
14.	7	S. Perugini	Italjet Racing Team	2'10.475
15.	22	P. Nieto	L & M Derbi Team	2'10.545
16.	19	A. Branetti	Team Crae	2'10.626
17.	15	A. de Angelis	Matteoni Racing	2'10.816
18.	25	J. Olive	Telefonica Movistar Jr Team	2'10.840
19.	34	E. Bataille	Axo Racing Team	2'11.078
20.	27	M. Petrini	Racing Service	2'11.323
21.	12	R. Jara	MS Aprilia LCR	2'12.375
22.	8	G. Scalvini	Italjet Racing Team	2'12.393
23.	20	G. Caffiero	Bossini Fontana Racing	2'12.590
24.	23	G. Borsoi	LAE – UGT 3000	2'12.755
25.	96	M. Smrz	Sonax Racing Aprilia	2'12.879
26.	30	J. Buch	PEV-Spalt-ADAC Sachsen	2'13.185
27.	80	T. Kirmeier	Ivetra-Seel Racing	2'13.452
28.	84	I. Kalab	Elf Revena Team	2'13.875
29.	77	A. Araujo	Liegeois Competition	2'13.967
30.	83	V. Bittman	BRC Racing Team	2'14.414
31.	85	T. Miksovsky	KLUB R.J.T	2'16.564

RACE: 19 LAPS = 102.657 KM

1.	Toni Elias - 19 laps in 41'27.703	
2.	Lucio Cecchinello	at 0.689
3.	Steve Jenkner	at 1.086
4.	Youichi Ui	at 1.156
5.	Max Sabbatani	at 3.668
6.	Jakub Smrz	at 7.804
7.	Jaroslav Hules	at 7.817
8.	Daniel Pedrosa	at 7.985
9.	Gabor Talmacsi	at 8.528
10.	Simone Sanna	at 13.875
11.	Noburu Ueda	at 20.490
12.	Alex de Angelis	at 25.982
13.	Masao Azuma	at 26.127
14.	Joan Olive	at 30.135
15.	Eric Bataille	at 30.593
16.	Mirko Giansanti	at 30.738
17.	Angel Rodriguez	at 30.954
18.	Pablo Nieto	at 31.290
19.	Angel Nieto jr	at 32.111
20.	Alessandro Brannetti	at 45.231
21.	Gaspare Caffiero	at 58.341
22.	Adrian Araujo	at 1'10.907
23.	Gino Borsoi	at 1'10.918
24.	Jascha Buch	at 1'11.480
25.	Tobias Kirmeier	at 1'11.692
26.	Igor Kalab	at 1'11.984
27.	Matej Smrz	at 1'12.105
28.	Vaclav Bittman	at 1'12.660
29.	Tomas Miksosky	at 1'12.749

RETIREMENTS

Stefano Perugini	at 2 laps (fall)
Marco Petrini	at 6 laps
Manuel Poggiali	at 8 laps (fall)
Arnaud Vincent	at 8 laps (fall)
Raul Jara	at 11 laps
Gianluigi Scalivini	at 15 laps

RACE FACTS

Pole Position:	Toni Elias	2'09.062
Fastest lap	Jaroslav Hules	2'09.648
Circuit record lap:	Youichi Ui	2'09.416 (2000)
Circuit best lap:	Toni Elias	2'09.062 (2001)

CHAMPIONSHIP

1.	T. Elias	142 (2 victories)
2.	M. Poggiali	120 (1 victory)
3.	L. Cecchinello	108 (1 victory)
4.	M. Azuma	101 (2 victories)
5.	Y. Ui	99 (1 victories)
6.	G. Borsoi	93
7.	S. Jenkner	85
8.	S. Sanna	82 (1 victory)
9.	N. Ueda	81 (1 victory)
10.	A. Vincent	63

Estoril

Grand Prix of PORTUGAL

Kenny Roberts: the rise and fall of the current World Champion.

Katoh the king and Harada, his prince.

The rocky hills that surround the Estoril circuit, a fine coating of sand blown in on the sea breeze, it's the second GP in Portuguese history.

9 September
Estoril – 4.182 m

STARTING GRID

1.	3	M. Biaggi	Marlboro Yamaha Team	1'40.076
2.	65	L. Capirossi	West Honda Pons	1'40.258
3.	46	V. Rossi	Nastro Azzurro Honda	1'40.324
4.	11	T. Ukawa	Repsol YPF Honda Team	1'40.531
5.	17	J. vd Goorbergh	Proton TEAM KR	1'40.540
6.	4	A. Barros	West Honda Pons	1'40.670
7.	15	S. Gibernau	Telefonica Movistar Suzuki	1'40.713
8.	7	C. Checa	Marlboro Yamaha Team	1'40.752
9.	5	G. McCoy	Red Bull Yamaha WCM	1'40.894
10.	6	N. Abe	Antena 3 Yamaha-d'Antin	1'40.901
11.	1	K. Roberts	Telefonica Movistar Suzuki	1'40.969
12.	28	A. Crivillé	Repsol YPF Honda Team	1'41.037
13.	41	N. Haga	Red Bull Yamaha WCM	1'41.139
14	56	S. Nakano	Gauloises Yamaha Tech 3	1'41.520
15.	19	O. Jacque	Gauloises Yamaha Tech 3	1'41.586
16.	10	J.L. Cardoso	Antena 3 Yamaha-d'Antin	1'41.887
17.	12	H. Aoki	Arie Molenaar Racing	1'42.130
18.	14	A. West	Dee Cee Jeans Racing Team	1'43.173
19.	9	L. Haslam	Shell Advance Honda	1'43.645
20.	16	J. Stigefelt	Sabre Sport	1'43.715
21.	21	B. Veneman	Dee Cee Jeans Racing Team	1'44.446
20.	18	B. Clarke	Shell Advance Honda	1'45.593

RACE: 28 LAPS = 117.096 KM

1.	Valentino Rossi - 28 laps in 47'25.357 (148.152 km/h)	
2.	Loris Capirossi	at 1.756
3.	Garry McCoy	at 14.030
4.	Carlos Checa	at 24.337
5.	Max Biaggi	at 31.348
6.	Kenny Roberts	at 31.925
7.	Jurgen vd Goorbergh	at 37.140
8.	Olivier Jacque	at 41.043
9.	Shinya Nakano	at 50.273
10.	Jose Luis Cardoso	at 58.227
11.	Haruchika Aoki	at 1'27.139
12.	Anthony West	at 1'27.459
13.	Johan Stigefelt	at 1 lap
14.	Brendan Clarke	at 1 lap
15.	Barry Veneman	at 1 lap

RETIREMENTS

Tohru Ukawa	1st lap not finished
Alex Barros	1st lap not finished
Norick Abe	1st lap not finished
Noriyuki Haga	at 3 laps (fall)
Leon Haslam	at 10 laps (fall)
Alex Crivillé	at 16 laps
Sete Gibernau	at 26 laps

RACE FACTS

Pole Position:	Max Biaggi	1'40.076
Fastest lap:	Loris Capirossi	1'40.683
Circuit record la:	Valentino Rossi	1'42.200 (2000)
Circuit best lap:	Max Biaggi	1'40.076 (2001)

CHAMPIONSHIP

1.	V. Rossi	220 (7 victories)
2.	M. Biaggi	177 (3 victories)
3.	L. Capirossi	147
4.	A. Barros	107 (1 victory)
5.	S. Nakano	107
6.	N. Abe	100
7.	A. Crivillé	91
8.	C. Checa	89
9.	K. Roberts	72
10.	S. Gibernau	68

Biaggi cries, Rossi applauds. McCoy and Capirossi are at his side on the podium.

PRACTICE:

Everyone was waiting for Biaggi, now forced to show his claws in his role as pursuer. But on Friday, it's Valentino Rossi who sets the pace on a day marked by a dreadful crash for Norifumi Abe. After being transformed into a rag doll, the Japanese rider gets away with just two small fractures to his hand and multiple bruising. On Saturday, the three Italians are at the forefront including Capirossi who has received the latest Honda improvements after putting pressure on the Japanese. But Biaggi claims his fourth pole in a row so on paper it looks set to be a promising race.

START:

Biaggi and Capirossi are quickest off the blocks but Ukawa causes a "strike" on the first corner. Abe (whose bike catches fire), Barros and Criville on the ground, Haga in the grass and Gibernau hit by Ukawa's bike and forced to return to the pits.

7TH LAP:

Rossi makes his first attack (3rd lap) and has a lead of 0"556 over his two fellow countrymen (in order Capirossi then Biaggi).

14TH LAP (MID-RACE):

Crivillé who has spent a poor night and didn't come out for the warm-up stops as a consequence of the first corner pile-up. Rossi now has almost a second's advantage (0"815).

22ND LAP:

There's consternation again in the Yamaha-Marlboro pit. Just like in Brno two weeks earlier, without any cause or provocation, Biaggi loses the front end. The championship has been decided even though Max retakes to the track in sixth place.

FINISH (28 LAPS):

Valentino Rossi has run the perfect race, Loris Capirossi is helpless to repost. McCoy rejoins the podium for the first time since his accident at the French GP. Biaggi finishes fifth ahead of a fairly demotivated Kenny Roberts.

CHAMPIONSHIP:

43! Those who dreamt of a grande finale on 3 November at Jacarepagua de Rio are sadly disappointed. Rossi has made another surge ahead.

The same image, the same outcome: Max Biaggi has just lost the front end of the Yamaha.

The Yamaha duel: Nakano ahead of McCoy.

WHEN THE DOCTOR CALLS...

Under the auspices of "Dottore" Rossi, the 500 Championship has turned into a one-man show. From now on there is this phenomenal Italian who racks up perfect race after perfect race and there are the rest. The ones who count the points lost when they didn't try to quench the sparks from an attack too direct and too precise. GP weekends follow each other and they all look the same.

- 13h40: on a scorching Sunday afternoon in Portugal, Rossi, helmeted and armoured like a knight, repeats the movements he knows by heart. After a loosening up exercise behind his bike, he folds his hands around the footpegs of his NSR 500. Valentino wants to be in complete communion with his steed.

- 13h50: on the starting grid, he takes the time to take care of his image, offering F1 boss Bernie Ecclestone his racing helmet. "A unique gesture", says one of his entourage, "because Valentino is a bit of a hoarder".

- 13h52: zoom ahead to another facet of his character. His gaze is fixed ahead on the goal he will soon achieve: the supreme title.

- 14h35: the race was filled with premature emotions (massive first-corner pile-up caused by the Japanese Tohru Ukawa). The championship is decided as Biaggi loses the front end of his Yamaha. Just like in Brno. Rossi's reaction "I learnt what happened at the finish but I knew he wasn't there anymore because I watched the giant screen on every lap". So Mr Rossi has time to watch TV as well!!

- 14h47: Rossi makes his bike rear up, kisses the nose on his fairing before performing a fine "burn-out". At the same time, Biaggi skulks round on his slow-down lap.

- 14h58: he hears the Italian national anthem, he holds the trophy, the champagne flows. It's a Sunday like any other for him. But not for his opponents.

- Once again, the Doctor has struck, pointing his little syringes at his favourite rival Massimiliano Biaggi. And the injection has been effective. Apart from a few physical set-backs (forearms) that have hampered him since the Eight Hours of Suzuka, Rossi remains the absolute master in the category. The proof is threefold:

- The talk: beaten in the pursuit of pole position on the Saturday, he takes great delight in playing himself down. "Oh, you know, our aim was the front row. So everything's fine... But I still don't know which tyre to use for the race. The twenty minutes of warm-up will be important for me. And the race will be hard: it's very hot in Portugal, the track is demanding physically with some heavy braking. And there are lots of bumps". Anymore and you would almost be in tears through pity for this poor soul lacking in confidence.

- The technique: Rossi knows he's got the best bike on the grid. And especially the best team capable of finding the best solutions for every event, except minor "faux pas" like the Sachsenring.

- The tactics: Valentino excels in every situation. He can take on the role of attacking pursuer biding his time for his rival to make a mistake (like in Brno), or he can play the part of the prey that goes too fast for his rival to keep him in view (like in Estoril).

Quite simply, Valentino Rossi is just too good.

Rossi is merciless with his opponents. When the doctor goes through, the patients just step aside.

250cc
GP of Portugal

9 September
Estoril - 4.182 m

STARTING GRID

1.	31	T. Harada	MS Aprilia Racing	1'41.993
2.	74	D. Katoh	Telefonica Movistar Honda	1'42.205
3.	99	J. McWilliams	Aprilia Grand Prix	1'42.451
4.	10	F. Nieto	Valencia Circuit Aspar Team	1'42.588
5.	5	M. Melandri	MS Aprilia Racing	1'42.706
6.	7	E. Alzamora	Telefonica Movistar Honda	1'42.775
7.	8	N. Matsudo	Petronas Sprinta Yamaha T	1'42.836
8.	15	R. Locatelli	MS Eros Ramazzotti Racing	1'43.019
9.	6	A. Debon	Valencia Circuit Aspar Team	1'43.273
10.	44	R. Rolfo	Safilo Oxydo Race	1'43.298
11.	81	R. de Puniet	Equipe de France - Scrab G	1'43.495
12.	57	L. Lanzi	Campetella Racing	1'43.544
13.	46	T. Sekiguchi	Edo Racing	1'43.751
14.	66	A. Hofmann	Dark Dog Racing Factory	1'43.949
15.	22	D. De Gea	Antena 3 Yamaha-d 'Antin	1'43.981
16.	21	F. Battaini	MS Eros Ramazzotti Racing	1'43.984
17.	12	K. Nöhles	MS Aprilia Racing	1'44.013
18.	18	S. Yuzu	Petronas Sprinta Yamaha T	1'44.018
19.	50	S. Guintoli	Equipe de France - Scrab G	1'44.025
20.	9	S. Porto	Yamaha Kruz	1'44.173
21.	20	J. Vidal	PR2 Metrored	1'44.237
22.	16	D. Tomas	By Queroseno Racing Team	1'44.793
23.	37	L. Boscoscuro	Campetella Racing	1'45.106
24.	24	J. Vincent	QUB Team Optimum	1'45.315
25.	11	R. Chiarello	Aprilia Grand Prix	1'45.566
26.	36	L. Costa	Antena 3 Yamaha-d 'Antin	1'47.001
27.	45	S. Edwards	FCC-TSR	1'47.777
28.	14	K. Poensgen	Shell Advance Honda	1'47.808
29.	23	C. Barros	Yamaha Kruz	1'47.836
30.	71	J. Diaz	Team Motorsport Racing	1'48.293
31.	72	M. Garcia	PS Racing	1'49.040

RACE: 26 LAPS = 108.732 KM

1. Daijiro Katoh - 26 laps in 44'38.464 (146.141km/h)
2. Marco Melandri — at 16.993
3. Tetsuya Harada — at 27.360
4. Roberto Rolfo — at 34.207
5. Jeremy McWilliams — at 36.916
6. Naoki Matsudo — at 37.101
7. Fonsi Nieto — at 44.441
8. David Checa — at 45.404
9. Franco Battaini — at 49.202
10. Shahrol Yuzu — at 51.072
11. Klaus Nöhles — at 55.776
12. Alex Debon — at 59.663
13. David De Gea — at 1'19.420
14. Jay Vincent — at 1'19.835
15. Jeronimo Vidal — at 1'20.435
16. David Tomas — at 1'20.795
17. Randy du Puniet — at 1'23.776
18. Luca Boscoscuro — at 1'27.354
19. Luis Costa — at 1 lap
20. Katja Poensgen — at 1 lap
21. Javier Diaz — at 1 lap
22. Michel Garcia — at 1 lap

RETIREMENTS

Stuart Edwards	did not start
Cesar Barros	at 6 laps
Alex Hofmann	at 14 laps (fall)
Taro Sekiguchi	at 14 laps
Riccardo Chiarello	at 16 laps
Lorenzo Lanzi	at 17 laps
Emilio Alzamora	at 21 laps (fall)
Roberto Locatelli	at 22 laps
Sebastian Porto	at 22 laps
Sylvain Guintoli	at 24 laps (fall)

RACE FACTS

Pole Position:	Tetsuya Harada	1'41.993
Fastest lap:	Daijiro Katoh	1'42.285
Circuit record lap:	Olivier Jacque	1'42.985 (2000)
Circuit best lap:	Tetsuya Harada	1'41.993 (2001)

CHAMPIONSHIP

1. D. Katoh — 222 (7 victories)
2. T. Harada — 178 (2 victories)
3. M. Melandri — 169 (1 victory)
4. R. Rolfo — 128
5. F. Nieto — 98
6. E. Alzamora — 84 (1 victory)
7. J. Mc Williams — 79
8. R. Locatelli — 77
9. N. Matsudo — 70
10. A. Debon — 51

PRACTICE:

Qualifying was promising (for the championship at any rate), since Tetsuya Harada was ahead both on Friday and Saturday of category strongman Daijiro Katoh. McWilliams and Gonzales-Nieto make up the front row. David Checa – Carlos' younger brother had already made his mark twelve months previously in Portugal – creates the surprise in practice with eighth place.

For a large part of the race, Katoh battles with the Aprilia riders. Before taking control of the situation.

Fonsi Gonzales-Nieto's team-mate Alex Debon.

FINISH (26 LAPS):

Another victory for Katoh who has opened up a mammoth lead (16"993). Melandri now seems determined to stake his own claim for the title....of vice-champion.

START:

Melandri (5th on the grid) is fastest off the mark, ahead of Harada, Katoh and Gonzales-Nieto. But Harada finishes the first lap in the lead although his young Italian team-mate takes him by surprise on the following lap. Frenchman Randy de Puniet falls but rejoins the track.

6TH LAP:

Melandri is still in the lead, but Katoh has signalled his charge. For the first time in the race, the Honda rider sets the fastest race lap. He soon takes the lead but his team-mate Emilio Alzamora crashes out while making a strong comeback.

13TH LAP (MID-RACE):

It's boring. Melandri looked like he might hold on, but Katoh is now setting times that his rivals can't hope to match. The gap is already 1"915 over "Macio" who has shaken off Harada.

19TH LAP:

One figure: 7"886. Katoh has the race in the bag and the places are fixed. So attention focuses on the impressive comeback of Roberto Rolfo (from 18th to fourth place) and the cameras record for posterity Fonsi Gonzales-Nieto's acrobatics when thrown off his bike as he does a "Mamola" running alongside his bike before jumping on again.

Katja Poensgen: a new bike, a new look.

CHAMPIONSHIP:

44 points advantage for Daijiro (there are still 125 to play for), Honda (thanks to Katoh) has a one-point lead in the constructors' championship in the face of the Noale armada.

Two reds and a blue:
Ui and Poggiali ahead of Elias.

Poggiali: celebration of a second victory.

STARTING GRID

1.	54	M. Poggiali	Gilera Racing Team	1'45.932
2.	41	Y. Ui	L & M Derbi Team	1'46.045
3.	16	S. Sanna	Safilo Oxydo Race	1'46.439
4.	9	L. Cecchinello	MS Aprilia LCR	1'46.651
5.	24	T. Elias	Telefonica Movistar Jr Team	1'46.676
6.	31	A. Rodriguez	Valencia Circuit Aspar Team	1'47.095
7.	18	J. Smrz	Budweiser Budvar Hanusch	1'47.153
8.	26	D. Pedrosa	Telefonica Movistar Jr Team	1'47.246
9.	15	A. de Angelis	Matteoni Racing	1'47.293
10.	39	J. Hules	Matteoni Racing	1'47.301
11.	11	M. Sabbatani	Bossini Fontana Racing	1'47.315
12.	17	S. Jenkner	LAE – UGT 3000	1'47.360
13.	25	J. Olive	Telefonica Movistar Jr Team	1'47.467
14.	21	A. Vincent	Team Fomma	1'47.660
15.	20	G. Caffiero	Bossini Fontana Racing	1'47.704
16.	28	G. Talmacsi	Racing Service	1'47.715
17.	6	M.Giansanti	Axo Racing Team	1'47.743
18.	19	A. Branetti	Team Crae	1'47.752
19.	34	E. Bataille	Axo Racing Team	1'47.796
20.	22	P. Nieto	L & M Derbi Team	1'47.823
21.	7	S. Perugini	Italjet Racing Team	1'47.979
22.	23	G. Borsoi	LAE – UGT 3000	1'48.072
23.	5	N.Ueda	FCC – TSR	1'48.136
24.	4	M. Azuma	Liegeois Competition	1'48.272
25.	29	A. Nieto jr	Viceroy Team	1'48.457
26.	12	R. Jara	MS Aprilia LCR	1'48.939
27.	8	G. Scalvini	Italjet Racing Team	1'49.076
28.	27	M. Petrini	Racing Service	1'49.319
29.	77	A. Araujo	Liegeois Competition	1'50.274
30.	30	J. Buch	PEV-Spalt-ADAC Sachsen	1'51.053
31.	90	J.L. Nion	By Queroseno Racing	1'51.334
32.	86	J. Leite	AFL Racing Team	1'52.063

RACE: 24 LAPS = 100.368 KM

1.	Manuel Poggiali - 24 laps in 42'55.454	
2.	Youichi Ui	at 0.011
3.	Toni Elias	at 8.306
4.	Simone Sanna	at 8.473
5.	Daniel Pedrosa	at 26.230
6.	Jakub Smrz	at 30.439
7.	Jaroslav Hules	at 30.513
8.	Mirko Giansanti	at 31.500
9.	Max Sabbatani	at 33.982
10.	Arnaud Vincent	at 35.553
11.	Alessandro Brannetti	at 36.820
12.	Gabor Talmacsi	at 37.344
13.	Gaspare Caffiero	at 50.138
14.	Raul Jara	at 57.302
15.	Gino Borsoi	at 57.409
16.	Lucio Cecchinello	at 1'10.035
17.	Adrian Araujo	at 1'12.889
18.	Gianluigi Scalvini	at 1'24.889
19.	Jascha Buch	at 1'40.128
20.	José Leite	at 1 lap

RETIREMENTS

Eric Bataille	1st lap not finished
José L. Nion	at 7 laps
Angel Nieto jr	at 12 laps
Stefano Perugini	at 12 laps
Marco Petrini	at 13 laps
Pablo Nieto	at 15 laps
Noburu Ueda	at 16 laps (fall)
Steve Jenkner	at 19 laps
Angel Rodriguez	at 19 laps
Masao Azuma	at 20 laps
Alex de Angelis	at 22 laps (fall)
Joan Olive	at 23 laps (fall)

RACE FACTS

Pole Position:	Manuel Poggiali	1'49.923
Fastest lap:	Youichi Ui	1'46.329
Circuit record lap:	Roberto Locatelli	1'47.279 (2000)
Circuit best lap:	Manuel Poggiali	1'45.923 (2001)

CHAMPIONSHIP

1.	T. Elias	158 (2 victories)
2.	M. Poggiali	145 (2 victories)
3.	Y. Ui	119 (2 victories)
4.	L. Cecchinello	108 (1 victory)
5.	M. Azuma	101 (2 victories)
6.	S. Sanna	95 (1 victory)
7.	G. Borsoi	94
8.	S. Jenkner	85
9.	N. Ueda	81 (1 victory)
10.	A. Vincent	69

PRACTICE:

The two red cousins (Poggiali's Gilera and Ui's Derbi) dominate qualifying which is marked by the talents of two youngsters from Spain: Olive (provisional front row place on Friday, fall on Saturday) and Rodriguez (sixth time).

START:

Elias is the master of the fast starts and surprises everyone surging through from the second row. He takes the lead ahead of Sanna and Ui, who soon takes control. Olive and Cecchinello (crashes) don't finish the second lap.

6TH LAP:

The red dye is cast since Poggiali catches Ui and the two Gilera bikes leave behind the competition led by Sanna and championship leader Elias.

12TH LAP (MID-RACE):

Elias has begun his challenge. Ueda is no longer there (crash) and there are three men with a slight lead, in order, Ui, Poggiali and Elias; Sanna is a few lengths behind, but then there is a huge gap: the pack is already ten seconds adrift.

18TH LAP:

Ui increases the pace, Poggialia stays calm and continues to bide his time. Behind, things are calm between Elias and Sanna.

FINISH (24 LAPS):

The final laps are ferocious. Between Ui and Poggiali (59 thousandths with two laps to go) but more still between Sanna and Elias, with his spectacular and measured attacks. Podium places are within thousandths of a second at the chequered flag: 11 in Poggiali's favour for victory; 167 for Elias against Sanna. Behind them Pedrosa, Smrz (getting better all the time) and Hules finally had no right to the spoils.

CHAMPIONSHIP:

Cecchinello's fall, Azuma's technical worries, three of the four heroes of the day (Sanna is already way back in the standings) are in the top three places. Poggiali has clawed back nine points from Elias who still has a 13 point advantage over the San Marino Republic's representative. And although "veteran" Ui is still around, it is definitely the new (and very young) brigade that's taking over.

Guiseppe Caffiero: a sparkle on Portuguese soil.

Comunitat
Grand Prix of VALENCIA

The look of determination on the face of Manuel "Sete" Gibernau showing in adverse conditions that the Spaniard would reign imperial on the day.

Valenciana

Shahrol Yuzy, one of the victims of a crash at the start of the 250 cc race, which hastily required the red flag to be shown.

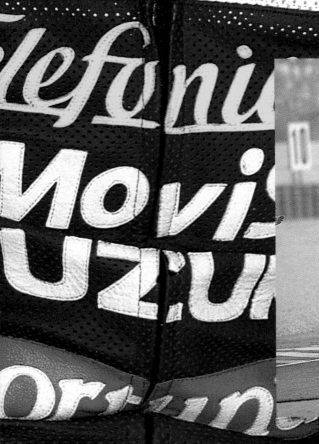

Toni Elias before a spellbound crowd. However, on the day, it was Manuel Poggiali who took the decisive steps to becoming world champion.

500cc
GP
of Valencia

23 September
Comunitat Valenciana –
4.005 m

STARTING GRID

1.	3	M. Biaggi	Marlboro Yamaha Team	1'34.496
2.	46	V. Rossi	Nastro Azzurro Honda	1'34.703
3.	56	S. Nakano	Gauloises Yamaha Tech 3	1'34.959
4.	65	L. Capirossi	West Honda Pons	1'35.234
5.	5	G. McCoy	Red Bull Yamaha WCM	1'35.305
6.	28	A. Crivillé	Repsol YPF Honda Team	1'35.319
7.	1	K. Roberts	Telefonica Movistar Suzuki	1'35.326
8.	7	C. Checa	Marlboro Yamaha Team	1'35.390
9.	17	J. vd Goorbergh	Proton TEAM KR	1'35.433
10.	11	T. Ukawa	Repsol YPF Honda Team	1'35.452
11.	4	A. Barros	West Honda Pons	1'35.556
12.	15	S. Gibernau	Telefonica Movistar Suzuki	1'35.634
13.	6	N. Abe	Antena 3 Yamaha-d'Antin	1'35.839
14.	19	O. Jacque	Gauloises Yamaha Tech 3	1'35.863
15.	41	N. Haga	Red Bull Yamaha WCM	1'35.906
16.	10	J.L. Cardoso	Antena 3 Yamaha-d'Antin	1'36.299
17.	12	H. Aoki	Arie Molenaar Racing	1'37.066
18.	14	A. West	Dee Cee Jeans Racing Team	1'37.117
19.	9	L. Haslam	Shell Advance Honda	1'37.488
20.	21	B. Veneman	Dee Cee Jeans Racing Team	1'38.524
21.	16	J. Stigefelt	Sabre Sport	1'38.605
22.	18	B. Clarke	Shell Advance Honda	1'38.830

RACE: 30 LAPS = 120.15 KM

1. Sete Gibernau - 30 laps in 54'39.391 (131.896 km/h)
2. Alex Barros   at 0.293
3. Kenny Roberts   at 1.241
4. Carlos Checa   at 7.052
5. Olivier Jacque   at 29.809
6. Tohru Ukawa   at 29.863
7. Shinya Nakano   at 31.093
8. Norick Abe   at 31.609
9. Jurgen vd Goorbergh at 32.783
10. Max Biaggi   at 37.774
11. Valentino Rossi   at 40.512
12. Garry McCoy   at 1'36.743
13. Anthony West   at 1 lap
14. Johan Stigefelt   at 1 lap
15. Barry Veneman   at 2 laps
16. Leon Haslam   at 2 laps
17. Jose Luis Cardoso   at 4 laps

RETIREMENTS

Haruchika Aoki   1st lap (fall)
Loris Capirossi   1st lap (fall)
Brendan Clarke   at 16 laps
Alex Crivillé   at 23 laps (fall)
Noriyuki Haga   at 29 laps (fall)

RACE FACTS

Pole Position:	Max Biaggi	1'34.496
Fastest lap:	Sete Gibernau	1'36.792
Circuit record lap:	Alex Crivillé	1'36.085 (2000)
Circuit best lap:	Max Biaggi	1'34.496 (2001)

CHAMPIONSHIP

1. V. Rossi   225 (7 victories)
2. M. Biaggi   183 (3 victories)
3. L. Capirossi   147
4. A. Barros   127 (1 victory)
5. S. Nakano   116
6. N. Abe   108
7. C. Checa   102
8. S. Gibernau   93 (1 victory)
9. A. Crivillé   91
10. K. Roberts   88

PRACTICE:

There have already been two GPs on the Cheste track but a Honda has never finished on the podium in 500cc. Last year's winner McCoy seems a safe bet but Rossi puts everyone in their place on Friday. He came testing here at Valencia at the beginning of August. Since Biaggi is way adrift and in a black mood, it looks like the trend will continue. However on Saturday, Max pulls out the stops: he sets a time so fast that we can hardly believe it. Just as he crosses the finish line, a short, heavy shower begins at the track! It's Biaggi's fifth pole position in a row.

START:

The race is to become a gamble with the tyres. Capirossi and Checa both fall on the warm-up lap and both come back to their pits to change bikes. Barros, Nakano and Rossi are the fastest off the mark but proceed tentatively in the conditions. Capirossi falls for the second time! At the end of the first lap, Rossi – racing with an intermediate at the front - has a lead of 3"059 over Gibernau and Barros.

4TH LAP:

Haga and Cardoso are no longer there and Rossi's lead is now 4"845. But the track is starting to dry out.

The start of the race. Everyone is racing on tenterhooks; Rossi is still matching Gibernau's pace.

22ND LAP:

Barros takes command.

FINISH (30 LAPS):

Gibernau mounts a last attack on the penultimate lap and Barros is powerless to resist. Behind them, Biaggi passes Rossi with tenth place at stake. It's the first victory of his career for Manuel "Sete" Gibernau.

CHAMPIONSHIP:

A slight glitch for the two favourites, with Biaggi taking back a point from Rossi who shows signs of nervousness, attacking the clerks of the course for starting the race in precarious slippery conditions.

Biaggi takes a point back from Rossi. The two men were only battling for tenth spot in Valencia.

8TH LAP:

Crivillé crashes out after racing extremely rashly taking into account the conditions. Gibernau has taken the lead.

15TH LAP (MID-RACE):

There are three riders neck and neck at the front (Gibernau, Barros and Roberts). Rossi is still fourth, but already seven seconds adrift.

Loris Capirossi's war cabinet. Far left, Carlo Pernat, his personal manager, will soon be tearing out his hair.

GLORY FOR THE PADDOCK LAUGHING STOCK!

There are some who make fun of his sunglasses that are a permanent fixture. But he really appreciates them now because the dark glass covers his tears at the sound of the national anthem played in his honour. The emotion of the moment is palpable.

Others say that he has had good rides since the start of his GP career (with Wayne Rainey in 250cc, then with HRC in 500 before joining World Champion Kenny Roberts at Suzuki), only because of his passport – Spanish, his good looks and a grandfather with a mythical name in the world of motorcycling, Don Paco Bulto, the founder of the make Bultaco.

"I always say the same thing to the people who peddle these stories. First of all I try not to pay too much attention to them. I know my own level of riding, I know that I'll win a grand prix one day and perhaps even more. And it's also a great honour for me to have a relative as respected as Don Paco. I hope that he's looking down on me now and is pleased that he passed the passion onto me".

That was a flashback to Manuel "Sete" Gibernau two months before this last European race (in Valencia, his home country). The meeting took place in Châtel-Saint-Denis, a little country hideaway nestling in the Swiss hills. We enjoyed the local delicacy of cheese fondue together while outside the heavens opened on the starting line for a national hillclimb race. "Sete" had come to spend the day at his flat that he has occupied officially for a year now. For some peace and quiet. Far away from the maddening crowd. "In Spain, it's often difficult to lead a normal life, if you're a public figure. Here, I'm scarcely recognised. And when winter comes, I can ski in peace."

Brought up in a good family, this is Manuel Gibernau. A World Championship rider since 10 May 1992 (first GP, Jerez de la Frontera, in 250cc) and now a winner since 23 September 2001 nine years and four months later. "I've had some hard times. I didn't find the way to the top of the podium until today, but those close to me know I've always held my head up high. People often refer to a clan when talking about my family: but the fact that we are fairly influential is the direct result of our solidarity".

"Sete" won on the Riccardo Tormo track at Cheste, near Valencia. By making a bold tyre choice ("It was Russian Roulette. It came to the time to make a decision and I said, s..t, let's put a slick at the front. So from then on in, it depended on when the track would dry out").

And the rider mocked by a large proportion of the paddock was right. He was right when Rossi got it wrong and lost his temper. He was right, when Biaggi was scared. "When you're at the centre of attention, you know that you won't remain there forever. But it's good to make the most of it". He replaces his dark glasses with a huge smile on his face. Then he gets up and says thank you. For an aristocrat – even a GP winner – has a good education. And never misses an occasion to show it.

"On that day, I was thinking of my grandad. I said to myself that he wouldn't be too upset with me up there".

250cc
GP of Valencia

23 September
Comunitat Valenciana -
4.005 m

STARTING GRID

1.	10	F. Nieto	Valencia Circuit Aspar Team	1'36.379
2.	6	A. Debon	Valencia Circuit Aspar Team	1'36.782
3.	15	R. Locatelli	MS Eros Ramazzotti Racing	1'36.946
4.	31	T. Harada	MS Aprilia Racing	1'37.033
5.	74	D. Katoh	Telefonica Movistar Honda	1'37.064
6.	5	M. Melandri	MS Aprilia Racing	1'37.071
7.	99	J. McWilliams	Aprilia Grand Prix	1'37.094
8.	8	N. Matsudo	Petronas Sprinta Yamaha T	1'37.152
9.	7	E. Alzamora	Telefonica Movistar Honda	1'37.264
10.	44	R. Rolfo	Safilo Oxydo Race	1'37.553
11.	21	F. Battaini	MS Eros Ramazzotti Racing	1'37.653
12.	66	A. Hofmann	Dark Dog Racing Factory	1'37.738
13.	42	D. Checa	Team Fomma	1'37.756
14.	81	R. De Puniet	Equipe de France - Scrab G	1'37.783
15.	50	S. Guintoli	Equipe de France - Scrab G	1'37.957
16.	22	D. De Gea	Antena 3 Yamaha-d 'Antin	1'38.010
17.	57	L. Lanzi	Campetella Racing	1'38.222
18.	9	S. Porto	Yamaha Kruz	1'38.321
19.	18	S. Yuzy	Petronas Sprinta Yamaha T	1'38.339
20.	37	L. Boscoscuro	Campetella Racing	1'38.397
21.	46	T. Sekiguchi	Edo Racing	1'38.635
22.	11	R. Chiarello	Aprilia Grand Prix	1'38.681
23.	16	D. Tomas	By Queroseno Racing Team	1'38.812
24.	20	J. Vidal	PR2 Metrored	1'38.947
25.	24	J. Vincent	QUB Team Optimum	1'39.288
26.	36	L. Costa	Antena 3 Yamaha-d 'Antin	1'39.797
27.	38	A. Molina	Kolmer Racing Team	1'40.084
28.	23	C. Barros	Yamaha Kruz	1'40.586
29.	14	K. Poensgen	Shell Advance Honda	1'41.560
30.	45	S. Edwards	FCC-TSR	1'42.018
31.	83	G. Rizmayer	Biro Racing Team	1'42.222

RACE: 27 LAPS = 108.135 KM

1. Daijiro Katoh - 27 laps in 44'01.853 (147.353km/h)
2. Tetsuya Harada — at 4.943
3. Fonsi Nieto — at 12.371
4. Emilio Alzamora — at 14.972
5. Jeremy McWilliams — at 21.045
6. Naoki Matsudo — at 25.817
7. Roberto Locatelli — at 26.623
8. Roberto Rolfo — at 26.776
9. Alex Debon — at 35.372
10. Randy de Puniet — at 46.273
11. David Checa — at 47.766
12. Shahrol Yuzy — at 47.887
13. Sebastian Porto — at 49.132
14. Franco Battaini — at 51.582
15. David De Gea — at 52.052
16. Sylvain Guintoli — at 53.057
17. Taro Sekiguchi — at 53.108
18. Jeronimo Vidal — at 1'17.203
19. Riccardo Chiarello — at 1'42.393
20. Alvaro Molina — at 1'53.681
21. Cesar Barros — at 2'07.720
22. David Tomas — at 2'12.659
23. Stuart Edwards — at 2'14.370
24. Katja Poensgen — at 2'23.258

RETIREMENTS

Luis Costa	at 8 laps
Alex Hofmann	at 11 laps
Luca Boscoscuro	at 14 laps
Gabor Rizmayer	at 18 laps
Lorenzo Lanzi	at 21 laps
Jay Vincent	at 22 laps
Marco Melandri	at 24 laps

RACE FACTS

Pole Position:	Fonsi Nieto	1'36.379
Fastest lap:	Daijiro Katoh	1'36.701
Circuit record lap:	Shinya Nakano	1'36.398 (2000)
Circuit best lap:	Fonsi Nieto	1'36.379 (2001)

CHAMPIONSHIP

1. D. Katoh — 247 (8 victories)
2. T. Harada — 198 (2 victories)
3. M. Melandri — 169 (1 victory)
4. R. Rolfo — 136
5. F. Nieto — 114
6. E. Alzamora — 97 (1 victory)
7. J. Mc Williams — 90
8. R. Locatelli — 86
9. N. Matsudo — 80
10. A. Debon — 58

The same scenario yet again: Katoh ahead of Harada.

PRACTICE:

Aprilia leads the show on and off the track. In this respect, the sky falls in on German Klaus Nöhles, shown the door by the Noale management. On the track, Melandri and Harada lead the dance but the show is stolen on Saturday by Jorge Martinez' riders, Gonzales-Nieto and Debon who take the first two places on the grid. With four Aprilias ahead of him, Katoh is "only" fifth.

START:

Harada and Katoh surprise the Spaniards and take the lead.

4TH LAP:

Melandri falls. Katoh and Harada are already alone at the front.

7TH LAP:

Katoh and Harada are within 199 thousandths of a second, Gonzales-Nieto is 3"852 behind.

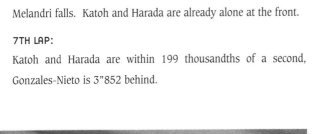

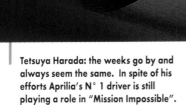

Tetsuya Harada: the weeks go by and always seem the same. In spite of his efforts Aprilia's N° 1 driver is still playing a role in "Mission Impossible".

11TH LAP:

A few drops of rain begin to fall and Katoh raises his arm. Things are going badly behind between Debon, Locatelli, de Puniet and Yuzy. Since it's the positions on the lap completed by the whole pack before the race is stopped, a restart is given thirty minutes later for a race lasting 18 laps.

SECOND START:

Still Harada and Katoh, this time ahead of McWilliams, "Fonsi" Nieto and Alzamora.

13TH LAP (MID-RACE):

As with every race run over two legs, you have to be on your toes since the real ranking isn't always the same as on the track. Harada is ahead on both counts, ahead of Katoh. On aggregate times, McWilliams is third; on the track Alzamora is closing in on his team leader, the World Championship leader.

20TH LAP:

The two Hondas have reeled in Harada and Katoh is ahead on aggregate times. In second place on the track, Alzamora is third in the ranking, nine seconds adrift and battling with Gonzales.

FINISH (27 LAPS):

Still and definitively, Katoh. Alzamora is third at the flag, but fourth on aggregate times.

CHAMPIONSHIP:

Katoh's (Honda) lead over Harada (Aprilia) is now 49 points. Remember a victory is worth 25 points and there are still 100 left.

The feat of the GP: a crash at the start of the race which is stopped under a red flag, Gonzales-Nieto takes out his second bike and ends up on the podium.

23 September
Communitat Valenciana -
4.005 m

STARTING GRID

1.	24	T. Elias	Telefonica Movistar Jr Team	1'40.481
2.	16	S. Sanna	Safilo Oxydo Race	1'40.497
3.	9	L. Cecchinello	MS Aprilia LCR	1'40.534
4.	11	M. Sabbatani	Bossini Fontana Racing	1'40.743
5.	17	S. Jenkner	LAE – UGT 3000	1'40.875
6.	23	G. Borsoi	LAE – UGT 3000	1'40.907
7.	5	N.Ueda	FCC – TSR	1'41.005
8.	26	D. Pedrosa	Telefonica Movistar Jr Team	1'41.040
9.	25	J. Olive	Telefonica Movistar Jr Team	1'41.203
10.	41	Y. Ui	L & M Derbi Team	1'41.209
11.	28	G. Talmacsi	Racing Service	1'41.331
12.	54	M. Poggiali	Gilera Racing Team	1'41.418
13.	34	E. Bataille	Axo Racing Team	1'41.437
14.	22	P. Nieto	L & M Derbi Team	1'41.520
15.	29	A. Nieto jr	Viceroy Team	1'41.538
16.	21	A. Vincent	Team Fomma	1'41.545
17.	44	H. Faubel	CC Valencia Aspar	1'41.634
18.	6	M.Giansanti	Axo Racing Team	1'41.699
19.	31	A. Rodriguez	Valencia Circuit Aspar Team	1'41.736
20.	4	M. Azuma	Liegeois Competition	1'41.796
21.	15	A. de Angelis	Matteoni Racing	1'41.893
22.	8	G. Scalvini	Italjet Racing Team	1'42.117
23.	18	J. Smrz	Budweiser Budvar Hanusch	1'42.130
24.	19	A. Branetti	Team Crae	1'42.173
25.	39	J. Hules	Matteoni Racing	1'42.238
26.	12	R. Jara	MS Aprilia LCR	1'42.239
27.	45	J. Fores	CC Valencia Aspar	1'42.337
28.	20	G. Caffiero	Bossini Fontana Racing	1'42.508
29.	7	S. Perugini	Italjet Racing Team	1'42.517
30.	30	J. Buch	PEV-Spalt-ADAC Sachsen	1'42.802
31.	75	F. Lai	Engines Engeneering	1'43.252
32.	82	M.Kallio	Team Red Devil Honda	1'43.343
33.	37	W. De Angelis	Racing Service	1'43.483
34.	77	A. Araujo	Liegeois Competition	1'43.688

RACE: 25 LAPS = 100.125 KM

1.	Manuel Poggiali - 24 laps in 42'55.454	
2.	Toni Elias	at 0.022
3.	Daniel Pedrosa	at 0.263
4.	Youichi Ui	at 0.305
5.	Gino Borsoi	at 0.561
6.	Simone Sanna	at 0.586
7.	Steve Jenkner	at 0.654
8.	Lucio Cecchinello	at 1.596
9.	Max Sabbatani	at 2.005
10.	Joan Olive	at 2.078
11.	Gabor Talmacsi	at 15.746
12.	Stefano Perugini	at 17.225
13.	Mirko Giansanti	at 17.369
14.	Pablo Nieto	at 17.456
15.	Angel Rodriguez	at 17.709
16.	Angel Nieto jr	at 18.686
17.	Eric Bataille	at 20.387
18.	Arnaud Vincent	at 20.537
19.	Gaspare Caffiero	at 21.800
20.	Alessandro Brannetti	at 24.857
21.	Jakub Smrz	at 24.946
22.	Gianluigi Scalvini	at 38.255
23.	Masao Azuma	at 38.692
24.	Adrian Araujo	at 42.858
25.	Raul Jara	at 43.450
26.	Jascha Buch	at 1'01.078

RETIREMENTS

Alex de Angelis	at 1 lap
Hector Faubel	at 7 laps
Jaroslav Hules	at 11 laps
Javier Fores	at 11 laps
Fabrizio Lai	at 14 laps (fall)
Noburu Ueda	at 18 laps (fall)
William de Angelis	at 19 laps
Mika Kallio	at 21 laps (fall)

RACE FACTS

Pole Position:	Toni Elias	1'40.481
Fastest lap:	Gino Borsoi	1'41.464
Circuit record lape:	Youichi Ui	1'40.631 (2000)
Circuit best lap:	Toni Elias	1'40.481 (2001)

CHAMPIONSHIP

1.	T. Elias	178 (2 victories)
2.	M. Poggiali	170 (3 victories)
3.	Y. Ui	132 (2 victories)
4.	L. Cecchinello	116 (1 victory)
5.	S. Sanna	105 (1 victory)
6.	G. Borsoi	105
7.	M. Azuma	101 (2 victories)
8.	S. Jenkner	94 (1 victory)
9.	N. Ueda	81
10.	A. Vincent	69

Jostling for position on the last corner,
Manuel Poggiali could have done without it.

Everyone has been talking about Toni Elias since the start of the
season (right alongside Alberto Puig). Now we've discovered his
two team-mates Daniel Pedrosa and Joan Olive.

PRACTICE:

Toni Elias is astonishing. He has become the darling of the
Spanish media following Alex Crivillé's repeated
misfortunes. There is enormous pressure on the youngster's
shoulders before this race "at home", but Alberto Puig's pupil
refuses to be affected. He claims pole ahead of five Aprilia riders.
Youichi Ui (Derbi) is only tenth and Manual Poggiali who has
extended his contract with Gilera for two additional years can only
manage twelfth place.

START:

Elias takes matters in hand immediately, ahead of team-mate
Pedrosa and the pint-sized Max Sabbatani. At the end of the first
lap he has a lead of 1"438 over the following pack.

5TH LAP:

Under Sabbatani's influence, the group reforms. The jockey even
takes the initiative for a few metres before going wide. Elias is still
leading, ahead of Sanna (0"506 behind), Sabbatani, Jenkner and
Pedrosa.

8TH LAP:

There used to be twelve in a pocket handkerchief of 2"072, now
there are only eleven (Ueda falls).

10TH LAP:

Jenkner takes control, and at the same time, Elias is taken by
surprise by Cecchinello, Sanna and Sabbatani.

12TH LAP (MID-RACE):

Jenker still leads, but Elias has just set the fastest race lap. The
Spaniard is in second place. His rivals for the title, Poggiali (7th)
and Ui (9th) are more than a second adrift.

15TH LAP:

Elias is definitely the strongest and retakes the lead.

18TH LAP:

Positions keep changing at every turn and now it's Cecchinello who
leads. Poggiali and Ui have regained contact with Elias.

FINISH (25 LAPS):

The race comes alive on the twentieth lap under Ui and Poggiali's
instigation. The last lap is ferocious with Elias, Sanna and Ui side
by side on the last corner; Poggiali takes advantage of the
situation to pass his rival on the line.

CHAMPIONSHIP:

Poggiali is within eight points of Elias. The title will be decided
between these two spectacular youngsters.

The big battle between veteran Lucio Cecchinello, Elias and
Simone Sanna.

Motegi

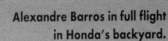

Grand Prix of THE PACIFIC

On an explosive day at the Motegi circuit, in 250 cc, Harada is on the top of the podium but Katoh is not there. At this point in the season one starts to think that just maybe...

Alexandre Barros in full flight in Honda's backyard.

PACIFIC GR

motogp

motograndprix.com
motograndprix.com
motograndprix.com

PA
GRA
OF M

Mote

Team Derbi fans in the land of the rising sun.
In the 125 cc category red reigns supreme.

500cc

GP
of the Pacific

7 October

Motegi - 4.801 m

Michael Doohan alongside Tohru Ukawa: the Motegi GP has particular significance for HRC.

STARTING GRID

1.	65	L. Capirossi	West Honda Pons	1'49.800
2.	3	M. Biaggi	Marlboro Yamaha Team	1'50.248
3.	4	A. Barros	West Honda Pons	1'50.511
4.	46	V. Rossi	Nastro Azzurro Honda	1'50.591
5.	56	S. Nakano	Gauloises Yamaha Tech 3	1'50.687
6.	1	K. Roberts	Telefonica Movistar Suzuki	1'50.944
7.	15	S. Gibernau	Telefonica Movistar Suzuki	1'51.108
8.	19	O. Jacque	Gauloises Yamaha Tech 3	1'51.210
9.	11	T. Ukawa	Repsol YPF Honda Team	1'51.246
10.	17	J. vd Goorbergh	Proton TEAM KR	1'51.370
11.	7	C. Checa	Marlboro Yamaha Team	1'51.602
12.	28	A. Crivillé	Repsol YPF Honda Team	1'51.622
13.	5	G. McCoy	Red Bull Yamaha WCM	1'51.630
14.	64	Y. Kagayama	Telefonica Movistar Suzuki	1'51.659
15.	41	N. Haga	Red Bull Yamaha WCM	1'51.664
16.	6	N. Abe	Antena 3 Yamaha-d'Antin	1'51.789
17.	10	J.L. Cardoso	Antena 3 Yamaha-d'Antin	1'52.248
18.	14	A. West	Dee Cee Jeans Racing Team	1'52.259
19.	12	H. Aoki	Arie Molenaar Racing	1'52.660
20.	9	L. Haslam	Shell Advance Honda	1'54.253
21.	16	J. Stigefelt	Sabre Sport	1'54.384
22.	21	B. Veneman	Dee Cee Jeans Racing Team	1'54.972
23.	18	B. Clarke	Shell Advance Honda	1'56.805

RACE: 25 LAPS = 120.025 KM

1. Valentino Rossi - 25 laps in 46'32.600 (154.726 km/h)
2. Alex Barros — at 2.607
3. Loris Capirossi — at 9.765
4. Norick Abe — at 13.951
5. Tohru Ukawa — at 21.994
6. Shinya Nakano — at 22.279
7. Carlos Checa — at 27.332
8. Kenny Roberts — at 27.607
9. Sete Gibernau — at 33.822
10. Yukio Kagayama — at 38.139
11. Alex Criville — at 41.866
12. Garry McCoy — at 50.419
13. Jose Luis Cardoso — at 56.204
14. Anthony West — at 1'05.286
15. Leon Haslam — at 1 lap
16. Barry Veneman — at 1 lap
17. Brendan Clarke — at 1 lap

RETIREMENTS

Olivier Jacque	at 7 laps
Jurgen vd Goorbergh	at 17 laps
Haruchika Aoki	at 18 laps (fall)
Noriyuki Haga	at 19 laps (fall)
Max Biaggi	at 20 laps (fall)
Johan Stigefelt	at 21 laps

RACE FACTS

Pole Position:	Loris Capirossi	1'49.800
Fastest lap:	Valentino Rossi	1'51.030
Circuit record lap:	Valentino Rossi	1'50.591 (2000)
Circuit best lap:	Loris Capirossi	1'49.800 (2001)

CHAMPIONSHIP

1. V. Rossi — 250 (8 victories)
2. M. Biaggi — 183 (3 victories)
3. L. Capirossi — 163
4. A. Barros — 147 (1 victory)
5. S. Nakano — 126
6. N. Abe — 121
7. C. Checa — 111
8. S. Gibernau — 100 (1 victory)
9. A. Crivillé — 96
10. K. Roberts — 96

PRACTICE:

Take the same players and start again: Rossi, Biaggi, Capirossi and Barros are definitely the fastest riders in the 2001 championship and, in terms of setting the perfect lap in final qualifying, Capirossi has only a few equals. He confirms this by putting half a second over Biaggi.

START:

Roberts gets the best start ahead of Biaggi who soon takes control. Rossi allows his title rival no leeway whatsoever and settles into his slipstream. Sito Pons' two riders are behind Roberts with Barros ahead of Capirossi.

6TH LAP:

Yet again, yet again.... The images are becoming ever the same. Tailed by Rossi since the start of the race, Biaggi loses the front end and falls at high speed. With no damage to himself, which is more than can be said of his Yamaha or of his championship hopes.

7TH LAP:

Haga crashes out.

13TH LAP (MID-RACE):

Abe passed Roberts on the preceding lap with fourth place at stake. At the front, Barros is 1"630 behind Rossi who has just set the fastest race lap.

17TH LAP:

The only interest is in the battle for fifth place. Gibernau is hounding his World Champion team-mate Kenny Roberts. Ukawa and Nakano are not far behind and go through on the next lap. Rossi now has a lead of two seconds over Barros.

20TH LAP:

Jacque returns to the pits (brake problems).

FINISH (25 LAPS):

It was a really boring race in 500cc for the first time in a long time. Gibernau loses the benefit from a superb race when he runs out of fuel on the last lap (he still saves seven points from ninth place).

CHAMPIONSHIP:

Rossi has a lead of 67 points so he can lose a maximum of 17 to Biaggi in Australia to win the title at Phillip Island. If Biaggi wins, Rossi has to finish in the top eight; if Max is second, Valentino can settle for thirteenth place.

Max Biaggi at the start. He still couldn't know...

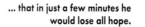

... that in just a few minutes he would lose all hope.

Valentino Rossi was stronger than the bad luck that struck Katoh (74) and Elias (24).

Grand Prix of the Pacific

to the future 500 champion: "Everything is settled, the contract with Subaru is signed". The journalist had just omitted to mention that Rossi was talking about his participation in a winter rally in Italy. An event he does every year just for fun.

The reaction provoked by this announcement was astonishing and shows how much the public are attached to him, whether it be racing enthusiasts or ordinary people attracted by his personality. And by winning another K.O. contest with his

ROSSI STRONGER THAN BAD LUCK

For the first time in the season in normal weather conditions, we detected signs of nerves in Valentino Rossi's preparation. It was a few minutes to two in Motegi, Japan. Valentino knew that bad luck had already struck two 2001 championship leaders – the Spaniard Toni Elias in 125cc and the Japanese rider Daijiro Katoh in 250cc. Both Honda works riders like himself.

Maybe he said to himself that the Heavens had decided to play it cruel bringing about a spectacular turn of events cynically tripping Honda up in the process. The motorcycle giant had dreamt of glory in its new temple of the twin tracks at Motegi incorporated into an astonishing complex that also houses a huge Honda collection.

Maybe all that was going through his mind just before he closed his visor and turned his attentions to the first problem of the day. "I knew that Biaggi had chosen a tyre that would enable him to spring into action very quickly. And so I knew that I couldn't let him get away and that I had to get a good start and stay on his tail".

The man who the day before had said the best tactics to have were none at all seemed to have changed his tune. Up until the mistake, the third in four GPs by Biaggi. "Max was very fast in the high speed left-hander. Perhaps he was a bit too fast. When he fell, I slowed down to have a think. And I said to myself that my opponent would certainly try and take to the track again. So I had to adapt to the new situation".

The rest is history. A perfect race, the eighth victory of the season, a step closer to a third world title and an added impulse to the general hysteria that surrounds any appearance in Italy. The proof of this came just a few days before his third victory of the season on Japanese soil – including the 8 Hours and the GP at Suzuka – when the switchboard of an Italian daily had been bombarded with calls after printing a scoop in its morning edition: "Rossi quits motorcycle racing!" On the inside pages, a simple phrase attributed

rival Massimiliano Biaggi, Valentino Rossi had taken a definitive step towards his 2001 goal: the 500cc title which would make him the second Mr 875 in history (winner of the three titles: 125, 250 and 500) after Phil Read. And you can rest assured that Rossi will be on the motorcycle track next year attempting to add a new title to his collection: the MotoGP. He will be just 23. And has plenty of time to study this famous contract that will one day take him into the rally championship full time!

250cc
~~GP~~ of the Pacific

7 October
Motegi - 4.801 m

Starting grid

1.	31	T. Harada	MS Aprilia Racing	1'52.789
2.	74	D. Katoh	Telefonica Movistar Honda	1'52.813
3.	5	M. Melandri	MS Aprilia Racing	1'53.115
4.	99	J. McWilliams	Aprilia Grand Prix	1'53.564
5.	7	E. Alzamora	Telefonica Movistar Honda	1'53.834
6.	10	F. Nieto	Valencia Circuit Aspar Team	1'54.158
7.	81	R. De Puniet	Equipe de France - Scrab G	1'54.392
8.	44	R. Rolfo	Safilo Oxydo Race	1'54.501
9.	15	R. Locatelli	MS Eros Ramazzotti Racing	1'54.575
10.	8	N. Matsudo	Petronas Sprinta Yamaha T	1'54.584
11.	6	A. Debon	Valencia Circuit Aspar Team	1'54.859
12.	18	S. Yuzy	Petronas Sprinta Yamaha T	1'54.913
13.	21	F. Battaini	MS Eros Ramazzotti Racing	1'54.932
14.	9	S. Porto	Yamaha Kruz	1'54.947
15.	42	D. Checa	Team Fomma	1'54.976
16.	46	T. Sekiguchi	Edo Racing	1'55.195
17.	88	N. Ohsaki	SP Tadao Racing Team	1'55.214
18.	37	L. Boscoscuro	Campetella Racing	1'55.265
19.	92	H. Aoyama	Team Harc-Pro	1'55.329
20.	89	O. Miyazaki	Motorex Daytona	1'55.385
21.	66	A. Hofmann	Dark Dog Racing Factory	1'55.530
22.	57	L. Lanzi	Campetella Racing	1'55.846
23.	16	D. Tomas	By Queroseno Racing Team	1'55.883
24.	50	S. Guintoli	Equipe de France - Scrab G	1'55.907
25.	22	D. De Gea	Antena 3 Yamaha-d 'Antin	1'55.962
26.	90	D. Sakai	Endurance	1'56.181
27.	91	T. Onodera	Morino Kumazan Miztec RT	1'56.259
28.	20	J. Vidal	PR2 Metrored	1'56.495
29.	24	J. Vincent	QUB Team Optimum	1'56.655
30.	11	R. Chiarello	Aprilia Grand Prix	1'57.675
31.	36	L. Costa	Antena 3 Yamaha-d 'Antin	1'57.970
32.	23	C. Barros	Yamaha Kruz	1'58.543
33.	55	D. Guigovaz	MS Aprilia Racing	1'58.833
34.	45	S. Edwards	FCC-TSR	1'58.864
35.	14	K. Poensgen	Shell Advance Honda	1'59.679

Race: 23 laps = 110.423 km

1. Tetsuya Harada - 23 laps in 43'59.587 (150.600km/h)
2. Emilio Alzamora   at 7.559
3. Jeremy McWilliams   at 8.024
4. Fonsi Nieto   at 11.462
5. Roberto Rolfo   at 11.733
6. Roberto Locatelli   at 13.498
7. Naoki Matsudo   at 24.789
8. Taro Sekiguchi   at 26.671
9. Nobuyuki Ohsaki   at 33.671
10. Randy de Puniet   at 37.114
11. David Checa   at 40.478
12. Osamu Miyazaki   at 41.670
13. David Tomas   at 42.139
14. Lorenzo Lanzi   at 42.568
15. Sylvain Guintoli   at 42.806
16. Alex Hofmann   at 43.379
17. Alex Debon   at 45.790
18. Shahrol Yuzy   at 46.181
19. Daisaku Sakai   at 48.361
20. Hiroshi Aoyama   at 48.507
21. Jay Vincent   at 1'16.106
22. Riccardo Chiarello   at 1'33.167
23. Luis Costa   at 1'53.607
24. Diego Guigovaz   at 1 lap
25. Katja Poensgen   at 1 lap

Retirements

Takayuki Onodera	1st lap not finished
Luca Boscoscuro	at 10 laps
Cesar Barros	at 12 laps
Marco Melandri	at 18 laps (fall)
Daijiro Katoh	at 18 laps (fall)
Stuart Edwards	at 19 laps (fall)
David De Gea	at 20 laps
Sebastian Porto	at 20 laps
Jeronimo Vidal	at 21 laps

Race facts

Pole Position:	Tetsuya Harada	1'52.789
Fastest lap:	Tetsuya Harada	1'53.767
Circuit record lap:	Shinya Nakano	1'52.253 (2000)
Circuit best lap:	Shinya Nakano	1'52.253 (2000)

Championship

1. D. Katoh	247	(8 victories)
2. T. Harada	223	(3 victories)
3. M. Melandri	169	(1 victories)
4. R. Rolfo	147	
5. F. Nieto	127	
6. E. Alzamora	117	(1 victory)
7. J. Mc Williams	106	
8. R. Locatelli	96	
9. N. Matsudo	89	
10. F. Battaini	59	

Tetsuya Harada doesn't miss his chance, once Katoh is out.

As the races go by, Emilio Alzamora gets closer to the best.

Practice:

Harada or Katoh? It's not only a question of a psychological battle between the two main title contenders, but also of honour (remember Nakano's tears twelve months ago when he was beaten by Katoh!) The Aprilia rider dominates the first day of practice but the Honda blue rider sets the fastest time in the last lap of qualifying. But he's only on pole for a few seconds because Harada is still on the track and beats his time by 24 thousandths of a second.

Start:

Katoh gets the best start, but leaves first braking too late and has to run wide. Melandri takes advantage, but Harada even more so, soon diving onto the inside. He finishes the first lap with a lead of 0"202 over Melandri, with Katoh breathing down the young Italian's neck.

6th lap:

Melandri falls, Katoh is unable to avoid running over him. Harada is alone at the front, but that has little importance. Everyone is worried about Melandri's condition (serious concussion, fractured right scaphoid).

12th lap (mid-race):

Harada is all alone. His lead over the McWilliams-Alzamora duo is more than seven seconds. Matsudo (Yamaha) is fourth, but he will soon be overcome by Rolfo, Gonzales-Nieto and Locatelli.

18th lap:

Nothing to report except the distances between the riders. Harada now has a lead of 10"509 over team-mate McWilliams still shadowed by Alzamora.

Finish (23 laps):

Alzamora who suffers from partial facial paralysis – he is unable to close his right eye – mounts an attack on McWilliams at the start of the last lap and resists any ripost from the British rider. It's his best finish in 250cc.

Championship:

Katoh's fall reignites the championship since the rider who has dominated the season now only has 24 points on the day's winner. Whatever happens in Australia in a week's time, we shall have to wait before we know the name of Olivier Jacque's successor.

On the starting grid with Naoki Matsudo. A Japanese postcard.

Youichi Ui begins his autumn campaign.

7 October
Motegi - 4.801 m

STARTING GRID

1. 41	Y. Ui	L & M Derbi Team	1'58.603
2. 54	M. Poggiali	Gilera Racing Team	1'59.288
3. 4	M. Azuma	Liegeois Competition	1'59.546
4. 24	T. Elias	Telefonica Movistar Jr Team	1'59.622
5. 9	L. Cecchinello	MS Aprilia LCR	1'59.625
6. 6	M.Giansanti	Axo Racing Team	2'00.018
7. 26	D. Pedrosa	Telefonica Movistar Jr Team	2'00.124
8. 5	N.Ueda	FCC – TSR	2'00.126
9. 28	G. Talmacsi	Racing Service	2'00.338
10. 11	M. Sabbatani	Bossini Fontana Racing	2'00.356
11. 64	Y. Takahashi	OSL SC & Okegawa School	2'00.415
12. 15	A. de Angelis	Matteoni Racing	2'00.417
13. 8	G. Scalvini	Italjet Racing Team	2'00.519
14. 17	S. Jenkner	LAE – UGT 3000	2'00.523
15. 12	R. Jara	MS Aprilia LCR	2'00.633
16. 20	G. Caffiero	Bossini Fontana Racing	2'00.691
17. 23	G. Borsoi	LAE – UGT 3000	2'00.706
18. 56	Y.Fujioka	Team Plus One	2'00.757
19. 19	A. Branetti	Team Crae	2'00.800
20. 29	A. Nieto jr	Viceroy Team	2'00.983
21. 21	A. Vincent	Team Fomma	2'01.029
22. 18	J. Smrz	Budweiser Budvar Hanusch	2'01.157
23. 16	S. Sanna	Safilo Oxydo Race	2'01.157
24. 7	S. Perugini	Italjet Racing Team	2'01.314
25. 66	S. Aoyama	Showa Denki Team Harc	2'01.462
26. 22	P. Nieto	L & M Derbi Team	2'01.621
27. 31	A. Rodriguez	Valencia Circuit Aspar Team	2'01.738
28. 39	J. Hules	Matteoni Racing	2'01.784
29. 37	W. de Angelis	Racing Service	2'02.104
30. 25	J. Olive	Telefonica Movistar Jr Team	2'02.220
31. 34	E. Bataille	Axo Racing Team	2'02.307
32. 65	T.Kuzuhara	Kumamoto Racing	2'02.586
33. 10	J.Müller	PEV-Spalt-ADAC Sachsen	2'02.748
34. 77	A. Araujo	Liegeois Competition	2'03.081

RACE: 21 LAPS = 100.821

1. Youichi Ui - 21 laps in 42'01.711 (143.932 km/h)
2. Manuel Poggiali — at 1.004
3. Daniel Pedrosa — at 0.129
4. Lucio Cecchinello — at 12.109
5. Masao Azuma — at 23.147
6. Gabor Talmacsi — at 28.345
7. Mirko Giansanti — at 28.387
8. Gino Borsoi — at 29.678
9. Gianluigi Scalvini — at 29.898
10. Alessandro Brannetti — at 30.026
11. Raul Jara — at 30.268
12. Joan Olive — at 35.692
13. Angel Nieto jr — at 35.894
14. Jaroslav Hules — at 36.170
15. Angel Rodriguez — at 45.438
16. Pablo Nieto — at 45.543
17. Gaspare Caffiero — at 45.997
18. Toshihisa Kuzuhara — at 1'10.144
19. Jarno Müller — at 1'14.335
20. William de Angelis — at 1'14.887
21. Adrian Araujo — at 1'29.415

RETIREMENTS

Steve Jenkner	1st lap not finished
Jakub Smrz	1st lap not finished
Shuhei Aoyama	1st lap not finished
Stefano Perugini	1st lap not finished
Simone Sanna	at 8 laps
Eric Bataille	at 10 laps
Yuzo Fujioka	at 15 laps (fall)
Yuki Takahashi	at 16 laps (fall)
Alex de Angelis	at 16 laps (fall)
Toni Elias	at 17 laps (fall)
Noboru Ueda	at 17 laps (fall)
Mark Sabbatani	at 17 tlaps (fall)
Hideyuki Nakajoh	at 19 laps
Arnaud Vincent	at 20 laps (fall)

RACE FACTS

Pole Position:	Youichi Ui	1'58.603
Fastest lap:	Youichi Ui	1'59.010
Circuit record lap:	Roberto Locatelli	1'58.816 (2000)
Circuit best lap:	Youichi Ui	1'58.603

CHAMPIONSHIP

1. M. Poggiali — 190 (4 victories)
2. T. Elias — 178 (2 victories)
3. Y. Ui — 157 (2 victories)
4. L. Cecchinello — 129 (1 victoire)
5. G. Borsoi — 113
6. M. Azuma — 112 (2 victories)
7. S. Sanna — 105 (1 victory)
8. S. Jenkner — 94
9. N. Ueda — 81 (1 victory)
10. D. Pedrosa — 78

PRACTICE:

Like any self-respecting Japanese rider, Youichi Ui is determined to make a mark in front of his home crowd. And even though Toni Elias takes provisional pole on Friday, the Japanese Derbi rider leaves all the competition behind on Saturday. Poggiali, his half-team-mate (he rides a Gilera which is the twin sister of the Derbi) can only assess the damage. Second overall, the resident of San Marino is 0"685 off pole. Azuma and Elias place their two Hondas on the front row. At Italjet, the mood is sombre with Perugini's fall (25th place on the grid) and Gianluigi Scalvini in spite of having a valid contract for next season, learning in Motegi that his services will no longer be required.

START:

Elias gets a perfect start ahead of Ui, Poggiali and Azuma. Smrz makes contact with the Japanese rider Aoyama and Vincent has to run into the sand to avoid them. Jenkner falls a little further on before the end of the first lap..

4TH LAP:

Ui takes control on the second lap and the action is fast and furious. Ueda crashes going onto the front straight, Sabbatani flies over the Japanese rider's bike. At the same time, a few hundred metres further on, Elias finds himself on the floor. Perhaps the championship has just been decided.

10TH LAP (MID-RACE):

Ui has a lead of more than 2" over Poggiali and Pedrosa, with Elias' young team-mate keeping the pressure on the other title contender.

15TH LAP:

Sanna has just stopped with gear selection problems. Ui continues his solitary way with a lead of 5"314 over Poggiali and Pedrosa.

With Toni Elias taking a tumble, Dani Pedrosa appears on the podium.

FINISH (21 LAPS):

Ui protects his advantage. Pedrosa tries a final assault but Poggiali resists in a race that has become boring since Elias crashed out. Cecchinello is happy with fourth place.

CHAMPIONSHIP:

A change at the top with Poggiali taking the lead after Elias' mistake (he's suffering from a sore right heel).

The Japanese fans in their passion colours.

Phillip Islan

Grand Prix of AUSTRALIA

Valentino Rossi going flat out in front of the vast ocean. At Phillip Island the Italian will become the second Mr. 875 in GP history.

Pablo Nieto, the third member of the Derbi-Gilera clan.

Daijiro Katoh: celebrates with champagne.

500cc
GP
of Australia

14 October
Phillip Island – 4.448 m

STARTING GRID

1.	3	M. Biaggi	Marlboro Yamaha Team	1'31.984
2.	46	V. Rossi	Nastro Azzurro Honda	1'32.408
3.	4	A. Barros	West Honda Pons	1'32.421
4.	15	S. Gibernau	Telefonica Movistar Suzuki	1'32.473
5.	19	O. Jacque	Gauloises Yamaha Tech 3	1'32.477
6.	65	L. Capirossi	West Honda Pons	1'32.513
7.	7	C. Checa	Marlboro Yamaha Team	1'32.622
8.	11	T. Ukawa	Repsol YPF Honda Team	1'32.768
9.	56	S. Nakano	Gauloises Yamaha Tech 3	1'32.840
10.	6	N. Abe	Antena 3 Yamaha-d'Antin	1'32.905
11.	41	N. Haga	Red Bull Yamaha WCM	1'32.934
12.	1	K. Roberts	Telefonica Movistar Suzuki	1'32.963
13.	28	A. Crivillé	Repsol YPF Honda Team	1'33.009
14.	5	G. McCoy	Red Bull Yamaha WCM	1'33.049
15.	17	J. vd Goorbergh	Proton TEAM KR	1'33.093
16.	14	A. West	Dee Cee Jeans Racing Team	1'33.714
17.	12	H. Aoki	Arie Molenaar Racing	1'33.731
18.	10	J.L. Cardoso	Antena 3 Yamaha-d'Antin	1'34.039
19.	16	J. Stigefelt	Sabre Sport	1'35.035
20.	9	L. Haslam	Shell Advance Honda	1'35.724
21.	21	B. Veneman	Dee Cee Jeans Racing Team	1'36.043
22.	18	B. Clarke	Shell Advance Honda	1'36.840

RACE: 27 LAPS = 120.096 KM

1.	Valentino Rossi	27 laps in 42'22.383 (170.055 km/h)
2.	Max Biaggi	at 0.013
3.	Loris Capirossi	at 0.581
4.	Alex Barros	at 0.714
5.	Tohru Ukawa	at 1.288
6.	Olivier Jacque	at 2.534
7.	Shinya Nakano	at 2.579
8.	Noriyuki Haga	at 2.582
9.	Sete Gibernau	at 2.832
10.	Jurgen vd Goorbergh	at 19.443
11.	Alex Crivillé	at 20.000
12.	Anthony West	at 20.303
13.	Norick Abe	at 21.043
14.	Haruchika Aoki	at 21.360
15.	Kenny Roberts	at 29.738
16.	Carlos Checa	at 30.023
17.	Johan Stigefelt	at 1'18.349
18.	Barry Veneman	at 1'24.773
19.	Leon Haslam	at 1'24.231
20.	Brendam Clarke	at 1 lap

RETIREMENTS

Garry McCoy	at 9 laps
Jose Luis Cardoso	at 21 laps

RACE FACTS

Pole Position:	Max Biaggi	1'31.984
Fastest lap:	Max Biaggi	1'32.993
Circuit record lap:	Kenny Roberts	1'32.743 (1999)
Circuit best lap:	Max Biaggi	1'31.984 (2001)

CHAMPIONSHIP

1.	V. Rossi	275 (9 victories)
2.	M. Biaggi	203 (3 victories)
3.	L. Capirossi	179
4.	A. Barros	160 (1 victory)
5.	S. Nakano	135
6.	N. Abe	124
7.	C. Checa	111
8.	S. Gibernau	107 (1 victory)
9.	A. Crivillé	101
10.	K. Roberts	97

Biaggi tried all he could this year. But Valentino Rossi was still too strong.

PRACTICE:

On Friday, Rossi has a spectacular crash. And on Saturday, Biaggi strikes with his seventh pole of the season ahead of Rossi, Barros (fall and slight concussion), Gibernau and an on-form Olivier Jacque.

START:

Rossi is quick off the mark ahead of Jacque and Biaggi, who has to run wide. Barros takes advantage and positions himself in the slipstream of bike N° 46. Biaggi is fifth at the end of the first lap.

2ND LAP:

Barros takes the lead. Haga is running a fine race in third place.

7TH LAP:

There are five riders battling for control. Barros still leads ahead of Rossi (36 thousandths behind), Haga, Biaggi and Jacque. Capirossi is making a comeback and is already eighth. Cardoso comes into the pits and collides with a mechanic from the Tech3 team (fortunately without consequence).

10TH LAP:

Haga takes control ahead of Barros, Biaggi and Rossi. The five riders are now only separated by 574 thousandths. On the next lap, Barros touches Rossi's front wheel.

14TH LAP (MID-RACE):

Rossi is aware of the risks of six riders running so closely together – Capirossi has joined the group – and takes the lead. He finishes this decisive lap with a lead of 0"758 over Haga, Barros, Jacque and Biaggi.

16TH LAP:

Biaggi records the fastest race lap and takes the lead.

19TH LAP:

As always at Phillip Island, we hold our breath on every corner. Capirossi now leads by just 146 thousandths from Rossi. Biaggi is three tenths behind but he will go through again. McCoy stops.

24TH LAP:

Rossi seems to have made the break (0"538) over Biaggi, but Max comes back once more to take the lead. Jacque is third.

FINISH (27 LAPS):

It is 15h43 and one second. For thirteen thousandths of a second, Valentino Rossi gets the icing on the cake: he beats Biaggi in this decisive race after a superb attack on the outside..

CHAMPIONSHIP:

It's all over. Following on from Phil Read, Valentino Rossi becomes the second "Mr 875" in history.

What can the two backroom boys be discussing? Roger Van Der Borght, HRC coordinator, and Jacques Hutteau, Mr Elf at the track.

The craziest race of all: Rossi, Barros, Jacque, Haga, Biaggi and the others, positions changing on every corner.

Grand Prix of Australia

"s..t". At this spot we were racing at more than 300 km/h". He had just won the race by just 13 thousandths of a second – more importantly he had just won the 500 World Championship: "The finest, the one that means the most". And what's on his mind?

- To tell his mother to stop talking instead of confiding some childhood secrets to the Italian press.

- To show his famous T-shirt: on the front, a caricature and a huge question mark: "Why did I win the 2001 500 World Championship?"; on the back are 35 very Rossi-like answers, full of fun: "Because I don't have a girlfriend..". "Because I trained in the cellar when I was little..." "Because I would like to marry Angelina Jolie, or Anna Kournikova.." "Because my father will now be forced to cut off his poneytail..." We've missed out some of the best ones.

- To talk about the future. "With the arrival of the four-stroke prototypes, it's a new challenge, a new leap into the unknown. And one thing is sure I will still race with my favourite number 46. It's one of the conditions I made to Honda and they accepted. Can you really see me with the number one plate? For all my fans, I'm number 46".

A number 46 who kept all his promises, who refused to make any calculations during

A weekend of high emotion. Valentino Rossi crashes in practice, but wins in the race by 14 thousandths of a second.

VENNI, VIDI, VINCI

He stopped way over yonder, not far from the clear blue ocean; His yellow bike disappeared for a few moments in a cloud of white smoke. With the smell of burning rubber. His best friends from Tavullia were all there. Some photographers as well who suspected something might happen. A number one plate had quickly been stuck on the front of his fairing while Valentino Rossi was carried aloft in triumph. The T-shirt for the occasion was brought out: "But not a top like all the others, with a huge number 1..." Valentino Rossi would not be the one we all know if he didn't invent something special for the occasion.

He had just won the craziest race of modern times. One where fairings touched more than was healthy. It was entertaining and exciting, but could have ended in drama. "When Barros passed me on the straight and then touched my front wheel, I though

this decisive race. Who reminded everyone in Australia, that he is not your average champion, that he has a raw talent which has been honed over the years, adept at controlling seemingly impossible situations, a titan among the greats. A Titan because, as opposed to Michael Doohan, for example, Valentino Rossi could just as easily leave this milieu as quickly as he arrived, a meteoric rise to fame that surprised everybody, who lives like he rides and who rides like he lives. By entertaining and enjoyment: "Don't talk to me about all these records, Doohan's five titles and so on. When I've had enough, I'll do something else". But for the moment he's enjoying the occasion. He now repeats in English what he has just said in Italian. "I still don't quite realise that I've won the title, because the race was fantastic and crazy and required all my concentration". Valentino Rossi is like that. Talking of his father, Graziano, who stayed home "and who must have been fairly excited in front of his TV". This is how he is and also the reason why his appeal is now phenomenal. And why Rossimania has crossed the frontiers from Tavullia, Italy and Europe.

250cc
GP of Australia

14 October
Phillip Island - 4.448 m

STARTING GRID

1.	31 T. Harada	MS Aprilia Racing	1'33.625
2.	99 J. McWilliams	Aprilia Grand Prix	1'34.195
3.	74 D. Katoh	Telefonica Movistar Honda	1'34.368
4.	15 R. Locatelli	MS Eros Ramazzotti Racing	1'34.405
5.	10 F. Nieto	Valencia Circuit Aspar Team	1'34.624
6.	21 F. Battaini	MS Eros Ramazzotti Racing	1'34.789
7.	66 A. Hofmann	Dark Dog Racing Factory	1'34.862
8.	9 S. Porto	Yamaha Kruz	1'34.887
9.	42 D. Checa	Team Fomma	1'34.950
10.	7 E. Alzamora	Telefonica Movistar Honda	1'35.023
11.	44 R. Rolfo	Safilo Oxydo Race	1'35.045
12.	81 R. de Puniet	Equipe de France - Scrab G	1'35.048
13.	57 L. Lanzi	Campetella Racing	1'35.112
14.	50 S. Guintoli	Equipe de France - Scrab G	1'35.267
15.	8 N. Matsudo	Petronas Sprinta Yamaha T	1'35.428
16.	22 D. De Gea	Antena 3 Yamaha-d 'Antin	1'35.481
17.	37 L. Boscoscuro	Campetella Racing	1'35.564
18.	46 T. Sekiguchi	Edo Racing	1'35.837
19.	18 S. Yuzy	Petronas Sprinta Yamaha T	1'35.851
20.	6 A. Debon	Valencia Circuit Aspar Team	1'36.005
21.	20 J. Vidal	PR2 Metrored	1'36.157
22.	16 D. Tomas	By Queroseno Racing Team	1'36.658
23.	55 D. Guigovaz	MS Aprilia Racing	1'37.251
24.	24 J. Vincent	QUB Team Optimum	1'37.477
25.	23 C. Barros	Yamaha Kruz	1'37.740
26.	11 R. Chiarello	Aprilia Grand Prix	1'37.988
27.	97 J. Brookes	RGV Spares	1'38.290
28.	36 L. Costa	Antena 3 Yamaha-d 'Antin	1'38.671
29.	45 S. Edwards	FCC-TSR	1'39.804
30.	14 K. Poensgen	Shell Advance Honda	1'39.996
31.	96 M. Rowling	Turramurra Cyclery Racing	1'40.026
32.	95 S. Smith	Allect Racing	1'40.035

RACE: 25 LAPS = 111.2 KM

1.	Daijiro Katoh - 25 laps in 39'48.180 (167.625km/h)	
2.	Tetsuya Harada	at 5.644
3.	Roberto Rolfo	at 8.518
4.	Jeremy McWilliams	at 14.303
5.	Fonsi Nieto	at 14.389
6.	Emilio Alzamora	at 14.749
7.	Roberto Locatelli	at 17.546
8.	Luca Boscoscuro	at 37.456
9.	Naoki Matsudo	at 50.872
10.	Shahrol Yuzy	at 53.951
11.	Lorenzo Lanzi	at 1'00.113
12.	Taro Sekiguchi	at 1'10.314
13.	Riccardo Chiarello	at 1'34.981
14.	David Tomas	at 1'39.355
15.	Jeronimo Vidal	at 1 lap
16.	Cesar Barros	at 1 lap
17.	Diego Guigovaz	at 1 lap
18.	Luis Costa	at 1 lap
19.	Katja Poensgen	at 1 lap
20.	Stuart Edwards	at 1 lap

RETIREMENTS

Joshua Brookes	did not start
Franco Battaini	1st lap not finished
David Checa	1st lap not finished
Randy de Puniet	1st lap not finished
Sebastian Porto	1st lap not finished
Alex Debon	at 3 laps
David De Gea	at 7 laps
Marc Rowling	at 8 laps
Alex Hofmann	at 11 laps
Sylvain Guintoli	at 11 laps
Shane Smith	at 13 laps
Jay Vincent	at 24 laps

RACE FACTS

Pole Position:	Tetsuya Harada	1'33.625
Fastest lap:	Daijiro Katoh	1'34.560
Circuit record lap:	Valentino Rossi	1'33.556 (1999)
Circuit best lap:	Valentino Rossi	1'33.521 (1999)

CHAMPIONSHIP

1.	D. Katoh	272 (9 victories)
2.	T. Harada	243 (3 victories)
3.	M. Melandri	169 (1 victory)
4.	R. Rolfo	163
5.	F. Nieto	138
6.	E. Alzamora	127 (1 victory)
7.	J. Mc Williams	119
8.	R. Locatelli	105
9.	N. Matsudo	96
10.	F. Battaini	59

A dominating factor amid the scenery. Daijiro Katoh in the magical surroundings of Phillip Island.

PRACTICE:

Daijiro Katoh arrived in Australia with a slightly injured left hand and Marco Melandri is suffering more serious consequences from his tumble in Motegi. The Italian took to the track on Friday morning and also for qualifying in the afternoon, but he had to withdraw because the pain was too great. But the retirement did not have any effect on the 2001 trends: Katoh up front followed by... Aprilia. Harada claimed pole (in spite of a fall) ahead of McWilliams, Katoh and Locatelli.

START:

Katoh is the fastest of those on the front row, but Gonzales-Nieto takes everyone by surprise on the first corner. At the back things are not going well, with a fall in the middle of the pack: de Puniet, Checa, Battaini and Porto are all taken out.

3RD LAP:

Harada takes the lead but Katoh refuses to sit back and immediately positions himself on his rival's back wheel before passing him on the next lap.

6TH LAP:

Katoh has a lead of 0"932 over Harada. "Fonsi" Nieto is already more than a second adrift battling hard with Rolfo and McWilliams.

13TH LAP (MID-RACE):

Still Katoh with a lead of 2"983 over Harada. Rolfo is now in third place ahead of Gonzales, Locatelli and McWilliams. Once again the 250cc race is a procession.

15TH LAP:

Both Hofmann (fall) and Guintoli (plug problems) have gone after battling for eighth place.

19TH LAP:

Nothing special to report except for the distances between the riders. Katoh now has more than 7 seconds over Harada (who had difficulty lapping Katja Poensgen) just as David De Gea takes a spectacular tumble.

FINISH (25 LAPS):

Katoh again for the ninth time this season. Another podium for Rolfo and cheap points for those behind after the crash on the first lap.

CHAMPIONSHIP:

Katoh now has a 29 point lead over Harada, so the official Honda rider needs to have 25 in a week's time after the Malaysian GP. Rolfo has taken six points back from Melandri with next year's number 3 plate at stake.

"Fonsi" Gonzales-Nieto at the front of a GP: amid Crivillé's misfortunes, Spain is discovering new heroes.

Drama on the first lap: Roberto Rolfo (44) touches the brake lever on Randy de Puniet's Aprilia which flies out of control in the middle of the pack. David Checa, Porto and others will come out of it worst.

Cecchinello (9) with Elias and Pedrosa, it's déjà vu. At Phillip Island, the racing world discovered another young Spaniard, Angel Rodriguez (31) whose efforts were not rewarded.

14 October
Phillip Island - 4.448 m

STARTING GRID

1.	54	M. Poggiali	Gilera Racing Team	1'37.737
2.	9	L. Cecchinello	MS Aprilia LCR	1'37.938
3.	41	Y. Ui	L & M Derbi Team	1'37.975
4.	23	G. Borsoi	LAE – UGT 3000	1'38.770
5.	5	N.Ueda	FCC – TSR	1'38.928
6.	15	A. de Angelis	Matteoni Racing	1'38.936
7.	16	S. Sanna	Safilo Oxydo Race	1'38.989
8.	7	S. Perugini	Italjet Racing Team	1'39.016
9.	21	A. Vincent	Team Fomma	1'39.062
10.	29	A. Nieto jr	Viceroy Team	1'39.102
11.	26	D. Pedrosa	Telefonica Movistar Jr Team	1'39.148
12.	39	J. Hules	Matteoni Racing	1'39.181
13.	31	A. Rodriguez	Valencia Circuit Aspar Team	1'39.187
14.	4	M. Azuma	Liegeois Competition	1'39.295
15.	8	G. Scalvini	Italjet Racing Team	1'39.298
16.	20	G. Caffiero	Bossini Fontana Racing	1'39.313
17.	24	T. Elias	Telefonica Movistar Jr Team	1'39.395
18.	17	S. Jenkner	LAE – UGT 3000	1'39.420
19.	73	C. Stoner	Movistar Team	1'39.449
20.	18	J. Smrz	Budweiser Budvar Hanusch	1'39.459
21.	11	M. Sabbatani	Bossini Fontana Racing	1'39.460
22.	25	J. Olive	Telefonica Movistar Jr Team	1'39.492
23.	34	E. Bataille	Axo Racing Team	1'39.967
24.	12	R. Jara	MS Aprilia LCR	1'40.135
25.	6	M. Giansanti	Axo Racing Team	1'40.166
26.	22	P. Nieto	L & M Derbi Team	1'40.371
27.	28	G. Talmacsi	Racing Service	1'40.391
28.	10	J.Müller	PEV-Spalt-ADAC Sachsen	1'40.397
29.	91	J. Taylor	Taylor Racing	1'40.679
30.	19	A. Branetti	Team Crae	1'41.162
31.	37	W. de Angelis	Racing Service	1'41.670
32.	77	A. Araujo	Liegeois Competition	1'42.059
33.	92	P. Galvin	Tech. M/C Clothing – JBD R	1'42.274
34.	94	C. Thompson	Team eServ	1'44.273

RACE: 23 LAPS = 102.304

1.	Youichi Ui - 21 laps in 38'14.688 (160.498 km/h)	
2.	Manuel Poggiali	at 4.709
3.	Toni Elias	at 4.743
4.	Masao Azuma	at 4.938
5.	Lucio Cecchinello	at 4.974
6.	Alex de Angelis	at 5.053
7.	Daniel Pedrosa	at 5.562
8.	Max Sabbatani	at 5.881
9.	Eric Bataille	at 9.506
10.	Gino Borsoi	at 17.165
11.	Noboru Ueda	at 17.289
12.	Casey Stoner	at 17.372
13.	Angel Nieto jr	at 18.361
14.	Jaroslav Hules	at 18.375
15.	Gaspare Caffiero	at 18.447
16.	Stefano Perugini	at 19.742
17.	Steve Jenker	at 26.857
18.	Gianluigi Scalvini	at 26.892
19.	Jakub Smrz	at 26.916
20.	Pablo Nieto	at 31.486
21.	Arnaud Vincent	at 31.819
22.	Alessandro Brannetti	at 35.783
23.	Angel Rodriguez	at 35.998
24.	Raul Jara	at 42.581
25.	Jarno Müller	at 49.404
26.	Jay Taylor	at 49.494
27.	Joan Olive	at 54.747
28.	Gabor Talmacsi	at 1'13.148
29.	William de Angelis	at 1'13.174

RETIREMENTS

Simone Sanna	at 1 laps (fall)
Peter Galvin	at 9 laps (fall)
Cath Thompson	at 11 laps
Mirko Giansanti	at 12 laps
Adrian Araujo	at 22 laps

RACE FACTS

Pole Position:	Manuel Poggiali	1'37.737
Fastest lap:	Max Sabbatani	1'38.499
Circuit record lap:	Marco Melandri	1'38.118 (1999)
Circuit best lap:	Manuel Poggiali	1'37.737 (2001)

CHAMPIONSHIP

1.	M. Poggiali	210 (4 victories)
2.	T. Elias	194 (2 victories)
3.	Y. Ui	182 (3 victories)
4.	L. Cecchinello	140 (1 victory)
5.	M. Azuma	125 (2 victories)
6.	G. Borsoi	119
7.	S. Sanna	105 (1 victory)
8.	S. Jenkner	94
9.	D. Pedrosa	87
10.	N. Ueda	86 (1 victory)

PRACTICE:

The 125 category is the first on track and the grip conditions are variable, mainly on Friday (Sanna falls on his last lap, while on provisional pole). On Saturday, the conditions have stabilised except for Tony Elias who complains for the first time this season. "The engine isn't working properly." Worse is to come for the Spaniard; the championship leader Manuel Poggiali claims pole ahead of Cecchinello, Ui and Borsoi.

START:

Poggiali gets a perfect start, but the best performance of all comes from Tony Elias who is in second place at the end of the first lap after starting in 17th place on the grid. He takes the lead on the second lap, before succumbing to the power of Ui's Derbi and Poggiali's Gilera.

6TH LAP:

Cecchinello takes control on the preceding lap, leading Ui, an even more promising Rodriguez, Poggiali, Elias and Sabbatani.

10TH LAP:

For the first time in his career, Angel Rodriguez is leading a GP.

Casey Stoner, a young Australian, Mick Doohan's protege has come to see his fortune in Spain.

12TH LAP (MID-RACE):

There are now eleven riders within 1"886. Cecchinello leads ahead of Rodriguez, Elias, Ui, Pedrosa and Poggiali.

18TH LAP:

Ui has taken matters in hand on the 15th lap and immediately increased the rhythm. He now has a lead of 1"326 over Poggiali, with Toni Elias spectacularly clinging to his rival to keep his championship hopes alive.

FINISH (23 LAPS):

Ui has not been troubled, but the show behind is spectacular. Sanna is momentarily in second place before falling on the last lap, and Rodriguez has to go into the grass to avoid him, where his bike ends up on the floor. Poggiali finishes second ahead of Elias who is not able to take the Gilera by surprise even in the slipstream.

CHAMPIONSHIP:

Manuel Poggiali gains four points on Elias with the San Marino resident now 16 points clear. Ui is 28 points behind Poggiali with 50 still to play for.

Giampiero Sacchi is a happy man: the Gilera-Derbi team boss looks after those who will fight for the title in Brazil.

Sepang

Grand Prix of MALAYSIA

The finest grandstand in the world. Big (too big?) for a GP crowd.

Manuel Poggiali is now on the trail that leads to the title.

Rossi, fast and thorough.

500cc
GP
of Malaysia

21 October

Sepang – 5.548 m

STARTING GRID

1.	65	L. Capirossi	West Honda Pons	2'05.637
2.	46	V. Rossi	Nastro Azzurro Honda	2'05.712
3.	3	M. Biaggi	Marlboro Yamaha Team	2'05.842
4.	5	G. McCoy	Red Bull Yamaha WCM	2'05.961
5.	4	A. Barros	West Honda Pons	2'06.465
6.	56	S. Nakano	Gauloises Yamaha Tech 3	2'06.489
7.	19	O. Jacque	Gauloises Yamaha Tech 3	2'06.686
8.	15	S. Gibernau	Telefonica Movistar Suzuki	2'06.736
9.	1	K. Roberts	Telefonica Movistar Suzuki	2'06.755
10.	6	N. Abe	Antena 3 Yamaha-d'Antin	2'06.877
11.	28	A. Crivillé	Repsol YPF Honda Team	2'06.984
12.	11	T. Ukawa	Repsol YPF Honda Team	2'07.055
13.	7	C. Checa	Marlboro Yamaha Team	2'07.751
14.	41	N. Haga	Red Bull Yamaha WCM	2'07.796
15.	12	H. Aoki	Arie Molenaar Racing	2'08.894
16.	10	J.L. Cardoso	Antena 3 Yamaha-d'Antin	2'08.936
17.	1	K. Roberts	Telefonica Movistar Suzuki	2'09.221
18.	14	A. West	Dee Cee Jeans Racing Team	2'09.383
19.	21	B. Veneman	Dee Cee Jeans Racing Team	2'11.695
20.	9	L. Haslam	Shell Advance Honda	2'11.932
21.	16	J. Stigefelt	Sabre Sport	2'11.998
22.	18	B. Clarke	Shell Advance Honda	2'12.903

RACE: 21 LAPS = 116.508 KM

1.	Valentino Rossi - 21 laps in 44'46.652 (156.115 km/h)	
2.	Loris Capirossi	at 3.551
3.	Garry McCoy	at 4.722
4.	Shinya Nakano	at 5.005
5.	Tohru Ukawa	at 8.807
6.	Alex Crivillé	at 12.192
7.	Alex Barros	at 15.682
8.	Sete Gibernau	at 18.772
9.	Noriyuki Haga	at 27.012
10.	Carlos Checa	at 28.829
11.	Jose Luis Cardoso	at 29.007
12.	Anthony West	at 1'02.166
13.	Norick Abe	at 1'20.535
14.	Brendam Clarke	at 2'04.455
15.	Leon Haslam	at 2'04.500

RETIREMENTS

Olivier Jacque	at 9 laps (fall)
Barry Veneman	at 14 laps (fall)
Haruchika Aoki	at 15 laps
Johan Stigefelt	at 16 laps
Kenny Roberts	at 18 laps (fall)
Max Biaggi	at 18 laps (fall)
Kurtis Roberts	at 19 laps (fall)

RACE FACTS

Pole Position:	Loris Capirossi	2'05.637
Fastest lap:	Valentino Rossi	2'06.618
Circuit record lap:	Kenny Roberts	2'06.839 (2000)
Circuit best lap:	Loris Capirossi	2'05.637 (2001)

CHAMPIONSHIP

1.	V. Rossi	300 (10 victories)
2.	M. Biaggi	203 (3 victories)
3.	L. Capirossi	199
4.	A. Barros	169 (1 victory)
5.	S. Nakano	148
6.	N. Abe	127
7.	C. Checa	117
8.	S. Gibernau	115 (1 victory)
9.	A. Crivillé	111
10.	K. Roberts	107

One K Roberts can hide another: Kurtis, Kenny Junior's younger brother, riding daddy's Proton KR3.

PRACTICE:

Capirossi dominates the first day and Rossi the second. The World Champion is finally beaten by just 75 thousandths of a second. A second Proton has been entered, ridden by the boss's younger son, Kurtis Roberts (falls due to mechanical problem during Friday qualifying).

START:

The clouds look more and more menacing, but the daily shower will fall later. Finally there is only one Proton at the start – Kurtis Roberts – since van den Goorbergh withdraws due to the serious concussion he suffered during his fall on Friday. Jacque gets the best start and for the first time in his life, briefly leads a 500 GP. At the end of the first lap, Kenny Roberts leads ahead of Capirossi, Biaggi and Rossi.

3RD LAP:

Kurtis Roberts falls.

4TH LAP:

Max Biaggi mounts an impossible attack on Roberts and touches the former World Champion's wheel. Both riders end up on the ground and walk back together along the side of the track.

The Champion's lap of honour.

6TH LAP:

McCoy leads the top three ahead of Capirossi and Rossi. A second trio follows a little further back made up of Abe, Barros and Nakano.

11TH LAP (MID-RACE):

World Champion Rossi gives himself a scare on the ninth lap. He is still right behind McCoy. Abe and Nakano are back in touch. There are now five within 1"2. Jacque crashes out.

16TH LAP:

Rossi takes control on the 12th lap and gives a demonstration race, increasing the tempo to provide a cushion. Abe goes too far and crashes, and Valentino has the race won. McCoy, Capirossi and Nakano engage in a fine battle behind.

FINISH (21 LAPS):

And it's ten for Rossi. Capirossi is second with a fine braking manœuvre on McCoy on the penultimate lap. Nakano just misses the podium.

CHAMPIONSHIP:

Rossi increases his points tally by 25. Things are more interesting behind him, between Biaggi and Capirossi with second place at stake. With just one race to go, Max has a lead of just four points.

Gibernau: "We're waiting for a reaction from Suzuki for next year, otherwise...".

Concentration before consecration.

KATOH IS ALREADY CAUSING CONCERN

He returned to the pits already dressed in a blue Champion's T-shirt. Then the whole of Fausto Gresini's team enveloped him, picked him up and threw him up into the overcast Sepang sky. For just the few moments he spent in the air, Daijiro Katoh, the Japanese rider we don't know much about, except for his undeniable talent, found himself in another world.

Like Valentino Rossi before him, he totally dominated the start and the end to the 2001 season. Like the 500 cc World Champion, his only "average" point came in bad track conditions. He loves shoes, he hates the rain: Daijiro Katoh made sure of the title in Malaysia racing at the front, forgetting about his opponents and playing around with them. Like Valentino Rossi...

However other points in common are restricted to technical prowess. For where Rossi is extrovert, Katoh keeps himself to himself. With the 250 World Title in the pocket, the Japanese rider will now move into the top category, the MotoGP. And as opposed to Valentino Rossi, next year he will ride an NSR500 two stroke (with Dunlop tyres). And he's already causing some concern: "In Sepang, Katoh took his tenth victory of the season, placing 15 seconds between himself and his closest rivals. Even though this year's 250 Championship was not really of the highest level – Harada was disappointing, Melandri was plagued by bad luck – nothing can take away from the fact that Katoh is talented and that he will be competitive next year. Like all those who move from 250 to 500, he will perhaps have a few problems adapting, but the talent is there. So watch out..."

Who is this talking about the 250 World Champion, this Japanese rider who lives the perfect family life in Italy with the team managed by Fausto Gresini? Of course it's Valentino Rossi who is extremely well placed to speak about his future rival.

And it's a rival who could well cause a few headaches for the elite in the top category: "Daijiro is an extraordinary rider," explains his boss, Fausto Gresini. "His control abilities are phenomenal. He is always calm, never loses control and knows precisely what he wants. One thing is certain, like Rossi and Biaggi before him, Katoh will be a beginner who will get himself noticed in his first 500 season".

But for the moment, he's enjoying the glory. When he was asked at the start of the season if the blue riband category was one of his goals in 2002, he replied in typical Japanese fashion as the excellent Honda employee he is: "You know for the moment, I am in 250cc and my employers will decide. I've already been able to test an NSR500, but today I prefer my 250, the 500 is a bit big for me". He didn't mention that as a multi-talented rider, he was also capable of going very fast with a "big" superbike (he proved it last year at the Eight Hours of Suzuka).

This funny little chap has definitely more surprises in store. And he will only serve to confirm a growing trend: that the new faces setting the blue riband category alight, are those that have cut their teeth in 250cc. There was Biaggi, Rossi and this year we discovered Jacque (in spite of a difficult season after an early injury), Ukawa and especially, Shinya Nakano. So we just have to wait for the first winter tests and the first timed sessions. Shall we make a bet? Daijiro Katoh the World Champion who has become a beginner again could well create a few surprises...

Daijiro Katoh, the 250 World Champion is already worrying his future opponents in the new MotoGP category.

250cc
GP of Malaysia

21 October
Sepang - 5.548 m

STARTING GRID

1.	74	D. Katoh	Telefonica Movistar Honda	2'08.151
2.	10	F. Nieto	Valencia Circuit Aspar Team	2'09.024
3.	7	E. Alzamora	Telefonica Movistar Honda	2'09.358
4.	44	R. Rolfo	Safilo Oxydo Race	2'09.531
5.	81	R. De Puniet	Equipe de France - Scrab G	2'09.697
6.	31	T. Harada	MS Aprilia Racing	2'09.699
7.	15	R. Locatelli	MS Eros Ramazzotti Racing	2'09.813
8.	5	M. Melandri	MS Aprilia Racing	2'09.872
9.	99	J. McWilliams	Aprilia Grand Prix	2'09.901
10.	18	S. Yuzy	Petronas Sprinta Yamaha T	2'10.348
11.	66	A. Hofmann	Dark Dog Racing Factory	2'10.413
12.	8	N. Matsudo	Petronas Sprinta Yamaha T	2'10.634
13.	21	F. Battaini	MS Eros Ramazotti Racing	2'10.719
14.	50	S. Guintoli	Equipe de France - Scrab G	2'11.053
15.	37	L. Boscoscuro	Campetella Racing	2'11.290
16.	11	R. Chiarello	Aprilia Grand Prix	2'11.294
17.	6	A. Debon	Valencia Circuit Aspar Team	2'11.552
18.	42	D. Checa	Team Fomma	2'11.700
19.	57	L. Lanzi	Campetella Racing	2'11.709
20.	9	S. Porto	Yamaha Kruz	2'11.793
21.	22	D. De Gea	Antena 3 Yamaha-d 'Antin	2'12.108
22.	24	J. Vincent	QUB Team Optimum	2'12.629
23.	16	D. Tomas	By Queroseno Racing Team	2'12.688
24.	20	J. Vidal	PR2 Metrored	2'13.445
25.	55	D. Guigovaz	MS Aprilia Racing	2'13.673
26.	36	L. Costa	Antena 3 Yamaha-d 'Antin	2'14.418
27.	14	K. Poensgen	Shell Advance Honda	2'14.568
28.	27	S. Geronimi	Edo Racing	1 tour

RACE: 20 LAPS = 110.96 KM

1. Daijiro Katoh - 20 laps in 43'22.487 (153.490 km/h)
2. Tetsuya Harada — at 14.893
3. Fonsi Nieto — at 15.892
4. Roberto Locatelli — at 19.748
5. Jeremy McWilliams — at 35.867
6. Franco Battaini — at 46.364
7. Naoki Matsudo — at 46.408
8. Alex Hofmann — at 46.731
9. Sylvain Guintolli — at 56.513
10. Roberto Rolfo — at 58.914
11. Marco Melandri — at 1'00.301
12. Randy de Puniet — at 1'00.689
13. Luca Boscoscuro — at 1'09.730
14. Alex Debon — at 1'09.953
15. David Checa — at 1'10.810
16. David Tomas — at 1'10.847
17. Riccardo Chiarello — at 1'12.008
18. Jay Vincent — at 1'26.290
19. Jeronimo Vidal — at 1'30.098
20. David De Gea — at 1'37.261
21. Diego Giugovaz — at 1'37.635
22. Luis Costa — at 1'49.118
23. Shaun Geronimi — at 1 lap

RETIREMENTS

Lorenzo Lanzi	at 9 laps
Katja Poensgen	at 11 laps (fall)
Emilio Alzamora	at 12 laps (fall)
Sebastian Porto	at 14 laps
Shahrol Yuzi	at 18 laps (fall)

RACE FACTS

Pole Position:	Daijiro Katoh	2'08.151
Fastest lap:	Daijiro Katoh	2'08.920
Circuit record lap:	Valentino Rossi	2'09.116 (2000)
Circuit best lap:	Valentino Rossi	2'08.151 (2001)

CHAMPIONSHIP

1. D. Katoh — 297 (10 victories)
2. T. Harada — 263 (3 victories)
3. M. Melandri — 174 (1 victory)
4. R. Rolfo — 169
5. F. Nieto — 154
6. J. Mc Williams — 130
7. E. Alzamora — 127 (1 victory)
8. R. Locatelli — 118
9. N. Matsudo — 105
10. F. Battaini — 69

PRACTICE:

Behind Katoh who has no intention of making any great calculations on this decisive weekend, Frenchman de Puniet gets himself noticed on the first day, setting the second fastest time. On Saturday it's the turn of the other semi-works Aprilia rider, Spaniard Gonzales-Nieto, to grab the attention. Alzamora and Rolfo – who still has hopes of third place in the Championship – make up the front row. Melandri clenches his teeth in eighth place.

START:

38° air temperature and 50° ground temperature, Katoh reminds everyone at the start that just like Rossi a week earlier in Australia, he has no intention of taking any half measures. He gets the best start ahead of Harada, who charges through from the second row, Alzamora and Gonzales-Nieto.

5TH LAP:

With the local rider, Shahrol Yuzy, going a little too far in front of his home crowd and Rolfo who tumbles on the third lap, the opening laps are not lacking in action. Or at least at the back, because Katoh already has a lead of 6"127 over the chasing pack, led by Harada who looks powerless in the face of this fellow countryman.

10TH LAP (MID-RACE):

Alzamora has just fallen while battling for a podium place and Katoh's lead is now 10"513. At the same time, German Katja Poensgen falls.

15TH LAP:

Are we talking imperial? 1st, Katoh, 2nd Harada – 15"683 down! Sometimes the times speak louder than words. Through self-denial Rolfo has come back into the points with third place in the World Championship still at stake against Melandri who is still suffering the after-effects of his tumble in Motegi.

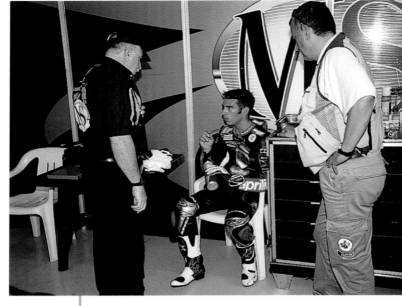

Marco Melandri is still suffering, but the young Italian clings on. Third place in the World Championship is at stake.

FINISH (20 LAPS):

Tenth victory of the season for Katoh, for whom the N° 1 plate fits well. Harada can only concede and Rolfo saves the points from tenth place.

A pensive Tetsuya Harada: in 2001 he had nothing to counter the combination of Katoh and Honda.

CHAMPIONSHIP:

It's all over. One week after Valentino Rossi's title in 500cc, Honda claims its second title of the season thanks to Daijiro Katoh. He has totally dominated the category throughout the season.

Sylvain Guintoli holds on… to finish 9th.

# of Malaysia

21 October
Sepang - 5.548 m

PRACTICE:

Elias stakes a claim from Friday onwards, in practice that proves difficult on a technical level. The 125cc riders are the first to go out on the track in the morning and on both Friday and Saturday are confronted by a wet track for free practice. World Championship leader Poggiali is "only" eighth.

START:

Cecchinello is celebrating his 32nd birthday on this 21st October 2001. When the lights change to green, two of Alberto Puig's protégés Elias and Pedrosa are the fastest off the mark. Poggiali has completely missed the boat and finishes the first lap in eleventh place. Ui has taken the lead with the second Derbi rider, Pablo Nieto, out after crashing.

5TH LAP:

Smrz and Jenkner have both fallen, Ui leads a first group made up of four riders with Borsoi, Elias and Pedrosa. Poggiali is charging back and is already in eighth place.

10TH LAP (MID-RACE):

Ui upped the rhythm on the seventh lap and his rivals are unable to match his pace. The next time they will see him will be on the top step of the podium. The Japanese rider has a lead of 4"544 over Borsoi and Pedrosa. Poggiali is fifth, Elias is further back visibly beaten.

Arnaud Vincent: the return to form for the Frenchman always at ease on the Sepang track.

Elias will not be World Champion. Well, not this year.

Toni Elias and Daniel Pedroso run up front: the two Spaniards will not keep up the illusion for long.

15TH LAP:

Still Ui whose lead has grown to 6"927. Manuel Poggiali is now ensconced in second place ahead of Cecchinello, Azuma (a fine fightback), Pedrosa, Elias and Vincent.

FINISH (19 LAPS):

Ui is definitely unbeatable in this last part of the Championship. Poggiali finishes second and greatly enhances his Championship prospects. Cecchinello celebrates his birthday with third place on the podium.

CHAMPIONSHIP:

Elias has lost all chance of becoming Champion, totally dominated by the "red bullets", Poggiali's Gilera and Ui's Derbi. The Japanese rider is 23 points behind his half-team-mate going into the last GP. "Mathematically, I still have a chance, but don't get carried away: Manuel will be World Champion in Rio", he says.

STARTING GRID

1.	24	T. Elias	Telefonica Movistar Jr Team	2'15.358
2.	41	Y. Ui	L & M Derbi Team	2'15.516
3.	9	L. Cecchinello	MS Aprilia LCR	2'15.615
4.	26	D. Pedrosa	Telefonica Movistar Jr Team	2'15.683
5.	23	G. Borsoi	LAE - UGT 3000	2'15.981
6.	29	A. Nieto jr	Viceroy Team	2'16.054
7.	11	M. Sabbatani	Bossini Fontana Racing	2'16.164
8.	54	M. Poggiali	Gilera Racing Team	2'16.165
9.	16	S. Sanna	Safilo Oxydo Race	2'16.553
10.	4	M. Azuma	Liegeois Competition	2'16.558
11.	21	A. Vincent	Team Fomma	2'16.706
12.	39	J. Hules	Matteoni Racing	2'16.759
13.	5	N. Ueda	FCC - TSR	2'16.793
14.	25	J. Olive	Telefonica Movistar Jr Team	2'17.113
15.	15	A. de Angelis	Matteoni Racing	2'17.213
16.	6	M. Giansanti	Axo Racing Team	2'17.228
17.	18	J. Smrz	Budweiser Budvar Hanusch	2'17.360
18.	22	P. Nieto	L & M Derbi Team	2'17.519
19.	28	G. Talmacsi	Racing Service	2'17.537
20.	10	J.Müller	PEV-Spalt-ADAC Sachsen	2'17.541
21.	8	G. Scalvini	Italjet Racing Team	2'17.576
22.	20	G. Caffiero	Bossini Fontana Racing	2'17.583
23.	31	A. Rodriguez	Valencia Circuit Aspar Team	2'17.928
24.	34	E. Bataille	Axo Racing Team	2'17.983
25.	19	A. Branetti	Team Crae	2'18.008
26.	12	R. Jara	MS Aprilia LCR	2'18.195
27.	7	S. Perugini	Italjet Racing Team	2'18.216
28.	17	S. Jenker	LAE - UGT 3000	2'18.262
29.	37	W. de Angelis	Racing Service	2'18.844
30.	77	A. Araujo	Liegeois Competition	2'18.907

RACE: 19 LAPS = 102.304

1. Youichi Ui - 19 laps in 43'21.269 (145.883 km/h)

2.	Manuel Poggiali	at 2.078
3.	Lucio Cecchinello	at 2.196
4.	Daniel Pedrosa	at 3.161
5.	Gino Borsoi	at 3.987
6.	Toni Elias	at 4.265
7.	Arnaud Vincent	at 4.468
8.	Masao Azuma	at 5.123
9.	Mirko Giansanti	at 30.026
10.	Max Sabbatani	at 30.292
11.	Noboru Ueda	at 30.417
12.	Joan Olive	at 30.684
13.	Stefano Perugini	at 30.860
14.	Alex de Angelis	at 31.433
15.	Jaroslav Hules	at 31.802
16.	Simone Sanna	at 33.406
17.	Angel Rodriguez	at 36.162
18.	Raul Jara	at 36.542
19.	Gaspare Caffiero	at 37.248
20.	Gabor Talmacsi	at 41.564
21.	Jarno Müller	at 41.660
22.	William de Angelis	at 1'11.823
23.	Adrian Araujo	at 1'34.039

RETIREMENTS

Steve Jenker	1st lap not finished
Jakub Smrz	1st lap not finished
Alessandro Brannetti	1st lap not finished
Pablo Nieto	1st lap not finished
Angel Nieto Jr.	at 2 laps
Eric Bataille	at 12 laps
Gianluigi Scalvini	at 12 laps

RACE FACTS

Pole Position:	Toni Elias	2'15.358
Fastest lap:	Youichi Ui	2'14.961
Circuit record lap:	Mirko Giansanti	2'16.138 (2000)
Circuit best lap:	Youichi Ui	2'14.961 (2001)

CHAMPIONSHIP

1.	M. Poggiali	230 (4 victories)
2.	Y. Ui	207 (4 victories)
3.	T. Elias	204 (2 victories)
4.	L. Cecchinello	156 (1 victory)
5.	M. Azuma	133 (2 victories)
6.	G. Borsoi	130
7.	S. Sanna	105 (1 victory)
8.	D. Pedrosa	100
9.	S. Jenker	94
10.	N. Ueda	91 (1 victory)

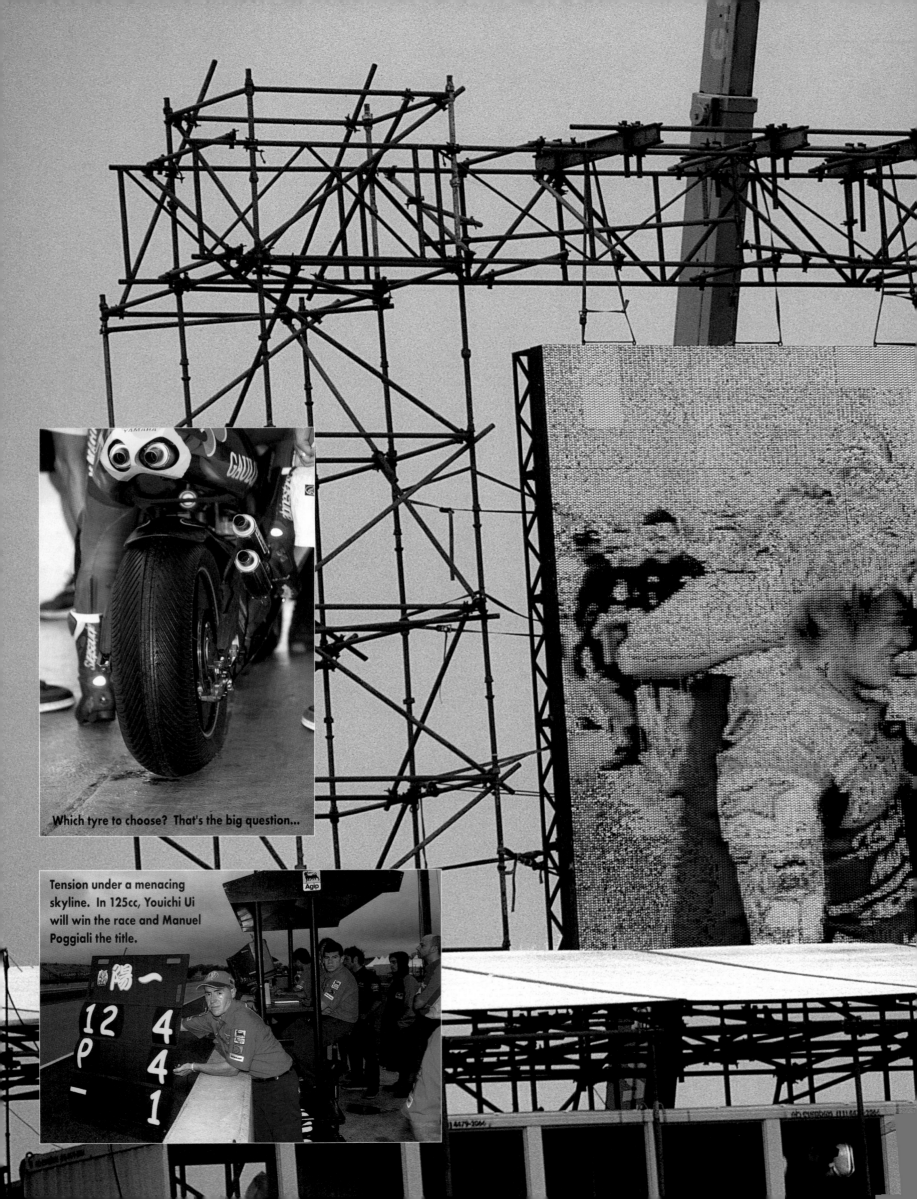

Which tyre to choose? That's the big question...

Tension under a menacing skyline. In 125cc, Youichi Ui will win the race and Manuel Poggiali the title.

Rio
Grand Prix of BRAZIL

Quickly applied dye on the big screen for a World Champion. Daijiro Katoh congratulated by his own in Jacarepagua.

500cc

GP of Brazil

3 November
Rio - 4933 m

Big kisses from Rio...

STARTING GRID

1.	11	T. Ukawa	Repsol YPF Honda Team	1'51.431
2.	65	L. Capirossi	West Honda Pons	1'51.462
3.	1	K. Roberts	Telefonica Movistar Suzuki	1'51.767
4.	56	S. Nakano	Gauloises Yamaha Tech 3	1'51.820
5.	46	V. Rossi	Nastro Azzurro Honda	1'51.863
6.	15	S. Gibernau	Telefonica Movistar Suzuki	1'51.874
7.	7	C. Checa	Marlboro Yamaha Team	1'51.920
8.	19	O. Jacque	Gauloises Yamaha Tech 3	1'51.974
9.	6	N. Abe	Antena 3 Yamaha-d'Antin	1'51.993
10.	3	M. Biaggi	Marlboro Yamaha Team	1'52.011
11.	17	J. vd Goorbergh	Proton Team KR	1'52.109
12.	4	A. Barros	West Honda Pons	1'52.177
13.	5	G. McCoy	Red Bull Yamaha WCM	1'52.324
14.	28	A. Crivillé	Repsol YPF Honda Team	1'52.771
15.	10	J.L. Cardoso	Antena 3 Yamaha-d'Antin	1'53.050
16.	14	A. West	Dee Cee Jeans Racing Team	1'53.764
17.	12	H. Aoki	Arie Molenaar Racing	1'54.319
18.	9	L. Haslam	Shell Advance Honda	1'54.557
19.	18	B. Clarke	Shell Advance Honda	1'56.254
20.	21	B. Veneman	Dee Cee Jeans Racing Team	1'56.776

RACE

1.	Valentino Rossi - 24 laps in 45'57.414 (154.569 km/h)	
2.	Carlos Checa	at 0.143
3.	Max Biaggi	at 6.980
4.	Alex Barros	at 19.503
5.	Loris Capirossi	at 20.655
6.	Norick Abe	at 20.829
7.	Alex Crivillé	at 27.894
8.	Jose Luis Cardoso	at 45.110
9.	Shinya Nakano	at 2'25.532
10.	Garry McCoy	at 1 lap
11.	Leon Haslam	at 1 lap
12.	Sete Gibernau	at 1 lap
13.	Anthony West	at 2 laps
14.	Haruchika Aoki	at 2 laps
15.	Brendan Clarke	at 2 laps
16.	Kenny Roberts	at 2 laps
17.	Barry Veneman	at 2 laps

RETIREMENTS

Olivier Jacque	1st lap not finished
Tohru Ukawa	at 17 laps
Jurgen vd Goorbergh	at 23 laps

RACE FACTS

Pole position	Tohru Ukwa	1'51.431
Fastest lap:	Valentino Rossi	1'53.258
Circuit record lap:	Tadayuki Okada	1'51.928 (1997)
Circuit best lap:	Max Baggi	1'51.058 (2000)

CHAMPIONSHIP

1.	V. Rossi	325 (11 victories)
2.	M. Biaggi	219 (3 victories)
3.	L. Capirossi	210
4.	A. Barros	182 (1 victory)
5.	S. Nakano	155
6.	C. Checa	137
7.	N. Abe	137
8.	A. Crivillé	120
9.	S. Gibernau	119 (1 victory)
10.	T. Ukawa	107

PRACTICE:

We had to wait until the last GP in the history of 500cc racing for the Italian trio of Rossi, Biaggi and Capirossi to be beaten in the battle for pole position. Japanese rider Tohru Ukawa achieved the feat by just 31 thousandths. However, his fellow countryman Noriyuki Haga had to withdraw from the race on the second day of practice following a complicated dental infection.

START:

A few drops of rain are falling and nerves are palpable at the start. Roberts is the fastest off the mark ahead of Jacque who finds himself on the ground in the first corner, taking his team-mate Nakano with him. The disappointed comment from Tech3 team boss, Hervé Poncharal: "It's never been done before, but we managed it!"

6TH LAP:

Gibernau falls on the preceding lap and Ukawa leads from Roberts, Barros (the crowd are going crazy), Rossi and Checa. The rain returns. Arms are raised and the red flag is shown.

SECOND START:

In terms of tyres, there's a bit of everything (the two Suzukis have rain tyres front and back). Checa gets the best start but Rossi leads at the end of the first lap. On aggregate times, Ukawa leads.

12TH LAP (MID-RACE):

Rossi and Barros are racing neck and neck. Behind them, the two red Yamahas, belonging to Biaggi and Checa are also side by side. Ukawa is no longer there (crash).

18TH LAP:

Checa has just taken the lead, on the track and on aggregate times (0"324 ahead of Rossi). The race will be decided by fractions of a second.

FINISH (24 LAPS):

40 thousandths on the 21st lap, then 202 and finally 139 going into the last lap. Checa wins the second leg, but loses out on aggregate times by just 143 thousandths. The Spaniard has fought like crazy and bursts into tears when he hears the result.

CHAMPIONSHIP:

Nothing to report, since the title was decided long ago. Who could rival Valentino Rossi in the long run? The answer is nobody.

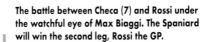
Tohru Ukawa: a tumble during the race after pole position in practice.

The battle between Checa (7) and Rossi under the watchful eye of Max Biaggi. The Spaniard will win the second leg, Rossi the GP.

"I am Emmanuel Poggiali"

There are some who have all the trouble in the world to get themselves known in their own name, such as Angel Nieto's sons – yes, that astonishing racing family. "Fonsi", one of the revelations this year in the 250 World Championship, is actually only 12 + 1's nephew. Some have still been able to succeed, such as Kenny Roberts "the second", who as soon as he became successful, demanded that he no longer be called "Junior". Even though his father had existed before him – and how!

Some fathers would like to see their sons succeed where they have failed, but their offspring have neither the talent nor the inclination. And then there is the one who lost his father at a very early age and who has just lifted the supreme title in Jacarepagua aged just 18 and a few months. A young man who wants everyone to know that "he" is Manuel Poggiali. Why? It's quite simple. Since the most famous inhabitant of San Marino began to shine on the world's circuits, everyone wants to compare him to Valentino Rossi, his elder by three years. "To all those who say I am Rossi Number 2, I simply say they're wrong, that my name is Poggiali and that my first name is not Valentino but Manuel. That..." That? "That I would like to find myself on the track one day against him, even though I know he takes no prisoners".

Whether he likes it or not, Manuel Poggiali will still have to live with this image for some time to come, with the parallel that observers tend to draw, won over by the talent of a young man who is very mature for just 18 years old. Like Valentino Rossi. Comparisons can be misleading, but not always.

People started talking about Manuel Poggiali when he was aged 11 after he finished fifth in the Italian Junior B minibike championship. Statisticians will remember that in 1992 when he was 13, a certain Valentino Rossi took his first title – in endurance, in Italy ... in minibike! And then what? Three years older, Valentino Rossi followed the trail of the 125cc Italian Sport Production Championship, moving on to the European Championship (third place overall) and the Italian Championship (title at aged 16). What did Manuel Poggiali do? He moved straight from minibike into the 125 GP category, with fifth in the European championship and the Italian national title: at just fifteen. Three years later, he has become 125 World Champion, aged 18 and 8 months. Valentino Rossi won his first world title, aged 18... and 8 months! So he has to forgive us, this hero from the Rio GP, for although he isn't Valentino Rossi and he is indeed Manuel Poggiali, the similarities are quite astounding.

Will this continue in the years to come? Valentino Rossi wanted to win the world title in each category before moving on to the next class. Manuel Poggiali sees things differently. He will race for a season with his Number One plate in 125cc before thinking about moving up. Will he automatically go into 250cc? Nothing is certain, because, the Piaggio group and its Gilera make would love to return to the top category (the new MotoGP) in the medium term. So it's quite possible that within two years, a certain Manuel Poggiali at aged just 20, could find himself on the same track as Valentino Rossi. Shall we take bets?

Manuel Poggiali, 18, 125 World Champion who won day dreams of racing against Valentino Rossi.

Poggiali in action. In Rio there was no room for mistakes.

250cc

GP of Brazil

3 November

Rio - 4933m

One Honda and two Aprilias. This time, Katoh will battle with Roberto Locatelli and Marco Melandri.

STARTING GRID

1.	10	F. Nieto	Valencia Circuit Aspar Team	1'53.819
2.	74	D. Katoh	Telefonica Movistar Honda	1'53.860
3.	99	J. McWilliams	Aprilia Grand Prix	1'54.011
4.	15	R. Locatelli	MS Eros Ramazzotti Racing	1'54.376
5.	31	T. Harada	MS Aprilia Racing	1'54.474
6.	8	N. Matsuo	Petronas Sprinta Yamaha T	1'54.511
7.	5	M. Melandri	MS Aprilia Racing	1'54.598
8.	81	R. de Puniet	Equipe de France - Scrab G	1'54.644
9.	21	F. Battaini	MS Eros Ramazzotti Racing	1'54.649
10.	6	A. Debon	Valencia Circuit Aspar Team	1'54.892
11.	7	E. Alzamora	Telefonica Movistar Honda	1'55.123
12.	44	R. Rolfo	Safilo Oxydo Race	1'55.170
13.	66	A. Hofmann	Dark Dog Racing Factory	1'55.343
14.	11	R. Chiarello	Aprilia Grand Prix	1'55.416
15.	37	L. Boscoscuro	Campetella Racing	1'55.482
16.	18	S. Yuzy	Petronas Sprinta Yamaha T	1'55.519
17.	9	S. Porto	Yamaha Kruz	1'55.530
18.	57	L. Lanzi	Campetella Racing	1'55.816
19.	50	S. Guintoli	Equipe de France - Scrab G	1'56.224
20.	42	D. Checa	Team Fomma	1'56.451
21.	22	D. De Gea	Antena 3 Yamaha-d 'Antin	1'56.635
22.	16	D. Tomas	By Queroseno Racing Team	1'57.579
23.	24	J. Vincent	QUB Team Optimum	1'57.696
24.	55	D. Guigovaz	MS Aprilia Racing	1'57.753
25.	27	S. Geronimi	Edo Racing	1'58.425
26.	84	C. Vieira	Vaz Yamaha-d'Antin	1'58.909
27.	23	C. Barros	Dark Dog Yamaha Kurz	1'59.038
28.	36	L. Costa	Antena 3 Yamaha-d 'Antin	1'59.176
29.	45	S. Edwards	Fujitsu Siemens	2'00.192
30.	14	K. Poensgen	Shell Advance Honda	2'00.712
31.	41	D. Nacher	PR2 - Damas	2'01.661

RACE: 22 LAPS = 108.526 KM

1.	Daijiro Katoh	22 laps in 43'38.212 (149.221 km/h)
2.	Marco Melandri	at 0.508
3.	Roberto Locatelli	at 1.382
4.	Fonsi Nieto	at 3.569
5.	Jeremy McWilliams	at 3.846
6.	Tetsuya Harada	at 11.032
7.	Emilio Alzamora	at 14.786
8.	Roberto Rolfo	at 26.769
9.	Naoki Matsudo	at 42.705
10.	Franco Battaini	at 45.602
11.	Sylvain Guintoli	at 46.659
12.	Lorenzo Lanzi	at 55.054
13.	Randy de Puniet	at 1'00.211
14.	Riccardo Chiarello	at 1'04.153
15.	David De Gea	at 1'04.281
16.	Alex Debon	at 1'04.807
17.	Alex Hofmann	at 1'06.148
18.	Luca Boscoscuro	at 1'24.059
19.	Stuart Edwards	at 1 lap
20.	Jay Vincent	at 1 lap
21.	Luis Costa	at 1 lap
22.	David Checa	at 1 lap
23.	Shahrol Yuzy	at 1 lap
24.	Cesar Barros	at 1 lap
25.	Shaun Geronimi	at 2 laps
26.	Katja Poensgen	at 2 laps

RETIREMENTS

Sebastian Porto	at 7 laps
Diego Giugovaz	at 12 laps
Damaso Nacher	at 14 laps
David Tomas	at 19 laps (fall)
Cristiano Vieira	at 19 laps (fall)

RACE FACTS

Pole Position :	Fonsi Nieto	1'53.819
Fastest lap:	Marco Melandri	1'55.315
Circuit record lap:	Valentino Rossi	1'54.320 (1999)
Circuit best lap:	Valentino Rossi	1'53.464 (2000)

CHAMPIONSHIP

1.	D. Katoh	322 (11 victories)
2.	T. Harada	273 (3 victories)
3.	M. Melandri	194 (1 victory)
4.	R. Rolfo	177
5.	F. Nieto	167
6.	J. Mc Williams	141
7.	E. Alzamora	136 (1 victory)
8.	R. Locatelli	134
9.	N. Matsudo	112
10.	F. Battaini	75

PRACTICE:

Second pole position of his career (after "his" GP in Valencia) for "Fonsi" Gonzales-Nieto (Aprilia), who team-mate in Jorge Martinez' team next year will be Toni Elias (the contract was signed just before Rio). Katoh is beaten by 41 thousandths, McWilliams and Locatelli position the habitual Aprilias on the front row.

START:

Intermediates at the front and slicks at the back for almost everyone, but the uncertain conditions do not stop Daijiro Katoh from taking control from the very start ahead of Gonzales-Nieto, McWilliams and Melandri.

6TH LAP:

Things appear less easy than usual for the World Champion. After Gonzales and Melandri, now it's Tetsuya Harada who leads the proceedings taking three other Aprilias with him. Katoh is now "only" fifth.

11TH LAP (MID-RACE):

Melandri, Harada and Katoh, the strong men of the season – or, to be precise the top three in the World Championship in reverse order – are neck and neck.

16TH LAP:

With Harada losing his chance, it's now another black Aprilia that leads the show in the shape of Roberto Locatelli. Katoh doesn't take long to plan his attack and increase the pace.

FINISH (21 LAPS):

He takes the lead on the 20th of 22 laps and crosses the finish with a lead of half a second over Melandri and Locatelli. It's Katoh's 11th victory of the season who is greeted by a team with multi-coloured hair. The World Champion will himself also soon go for a quick-option dye.

CHAMPIONSHIP:

322 points for Katoh, Harada is well and truly beaten. Marco Melandri has successfully defended his third place overall in the face of Roberto Rolfo, the best "privateer" of the season (on a Honda next year). The Aprilia armada that was present in force in 2001, was powerless when confronted by the duo of Katoh and Honda, an explosive combination that we shall see again next year in the new MotoGP category, with a Dunlop shod NSR500.

Daijiro, a number one on a blue background.

Alfonso "Fonsi" Gonzales-Nieto, Jorge Martinez' protege: a second pole position and certain ambitions for next year.

Poggiali battling with Elias: it's a question of honour.

PRACTICE:

From the very first day of qualifying, Ui confirms he is on top form. The Japanese Derbi rider sets a new pole on Friday ahead of Andrea Ballerini. European vice-champion this year, the Italian is replacing Caffiero on the Aprilia at team Fontana. With Ui on pole, emotions are high in the red camp with the crash (without serious consequences) of Poggiali in the last minute of timed practice.

START:

It rained during the morning and it's still drizzling now. The first two rows play safe (rain tyres) but some riders like Borsoi, Sanna and Azuma take the risk of putting slicks at the back. Ballerini has the best reflexes as the lights turn to green, but Ui takes the lead at the end of the first lap.

5TH LAP:

Cecchinello has fallen on the previous lap, and Poggiali is totally ill-at-ease on a track that is gradually drying. Ui is now battling with Perugini (Italjet), with the two men having opened up a gap of more than five seconds. Poggiali is only eighth.

10TH LAP (MID-RACE):

There is carnage on the track. Perugini, Rodriguez and Ballerini are on the floor. Sanna has come back to within 2"147 of Ui. Frenchman Arnaud Vincent occupies a solid third place. At this point in time, Poggiali is ninth and has only five points more than Ui in the Championship.

13TH LAP:

Pedrosa crashes as he was reeling in Vincent.

16TH LAP:

Ui and Sanna are still together (1"413 between the two), Vincent is a lonely third and Olive dominates his team-mate Elias. Azuma, who was coming back strongly with his intermediates goes straight ahead.

FINISH (21 LAPS):

The last two laps of the 2001 season are superb between Ui and Sanna, who is finally beaten by just 112 thousandths. Coming home in fifth place, Poggiali is World Champion.

CHAMPIONSHIP:

Ui was no longer master of his destiny for several weeks. The Japanese rider totally dominated the end of the season and broke down on the top step of the podium.

Arnaud Vincent: "A podium finish is the ideal way to start the winter".

Youichi Ui doesn't know whether to laugh (he's won the GP) or cry (but not the World Championship).

3 November
Rio - 4933 m

STARTING GRID

1.	41	Y. Ui	L & M Derbi Team	1'58.676
2.	50	A. Ballerini	Bossini Fontana Racing	1'59.085
3.	26	D. Pedrosa	Telefonica Movistar Jr Team	1'59.133
4.	24	T. Elias	Telefonica Movistar Jr Team	1'59.187
5.	54	M. Poggiali	Gilera Racing Team	1'59.514
6.	9	L. Cecchinello	MS Aprilia LCR	1'59.244
7.	25	J. Olive	Telefonica Movistar Jr Team	1'59.546
8.	18	J. Smrz	Budweiser Budvar Hanusch	1'59.573
9.	16	S. Sanna	Safilo Oxydo Race	1'59.661
10.	23	G. Borsoi	LAE – UGT 3000	1'59.749
11.	31	A. Rodriguez	Valencia Circuit Aspar Team	1'59.777
12.	17	S. Jenkner	LAE – UGT 3000	1'59.822
13.	11	M. Sabbatani	Bossini Fontana Racing	1'59.903
14.	21	A. Vincent	Team Fomma	1'59.963
15.	39	J. Hules	Matteoni Racing	2'00.017
16.	7	S. Perugini	Italjet Racing Team	2'00.147
17.	5	N. Ueda	FCC – TSR	2'00.213
18.	15	A. de Angelis	Matteoni Racing	2'00.403
19.	28	G. Talmacsi	Racing Service	2'00.453
20.	8	G. Scalvini	Italjet Racing Team	2'00.496
21.	4	M. Azuma	Liegeois Competition	2'00.533
22.	29	A. Nieto jr	Viceroy Team	2'00.548
23.	12	R. Jara	MS Aprilia LCR	2'00.689
24.	10	J. Müller	PEV-Spalt-ADAC Sachsen	2'00.915
25.	6	M. Giansanti	Axo Racing Team	2'01.009
26.	19	A. Branetti	Team Crae	2'01.158
27.	37	W. de Angelis	Racing Service	2'01.175
28.	22	P. Nieto	L & M Derbi Team	2'01.350
29.	34	E. Bataille	Axo Racing Teama	2'02.433
30.	77	A. Araujo	Liegeois Competition	2'02.719
31.	48	L. Panades	Racing Team Panades	2'06.166

RACE

1.	Youichi Ui	21 laps in 46'47.181 (132.850 km/h)
2.	Simone Sanna	at 0.112
3.	Arnaud Vincent	at 27.647
4.	Toni Elias	at 32.325
5.	Manuel Poggiali	at 37.646
6.	Alex de Angelis	at 42.052
7.	Masao Azuma	at 42.563
8.	Jakub Smrz	at 42.642
9.	Gianluigi Scalvini	at 42.867
10.	Jaroslav Hules	at 43.854
11.	Joan Olive	at 1'11.667
12.	Jarno Müller	at 1'11.675
13.	Noboru Ueda	at 1'18.050
14.	Pablo Nieto	at 1'50.142
15.	Alessandro Brannetti	at 1'56.893
16.	Adrian Araujo	at 2'01.428
17.	Steve Jenker	at 2'05.356
18.	Raul Jara	at 2'09.956
19.	Leandro Panades	at 2'10.408
20.	Gino Borsoi	at 1 lap

RETIREMENTS

Angel Nieto	1st lap not finished
Mirko Giansanti	1st lap not finished
Daniel Pedrosa	at 9 laps (fall)
Andrea Ballerini	at 15 aps (fall)
Angel Rodriguez	at 15 aps (fall)
Stefano Perugini	at 16 aps (fall)
Lucio Cecchinello	at 18 aps (fall)
Max Sabbatani	at 18 laps
Eric Bataille	at 20 aps (fall)
William de Angelis	at 20 aps (fall)
Gabor Talmacsi	at 20 laps

RACE FACTS

Pole Position :	Youichi Ui	1'58.676
Fastest lap:	Simone Sanna	2'11.067
Circuit record lap:	Mirko Giansanti	1'59.368 (2000)
Circuit best lap:	Youichi Ui	1'58.676 (2001)

CHAMPIONSHIP

1.	M. Poggiali	241 (4 victories)
2.	Y. Ui	232 (5 victories)
3.	T. Elias	217 (2 victories)
4.	L. Cecchinello	156 (1 victory)
5.	M. Azuma	142 (2 victories)
6.	G. Borsoi	130
7.	S. Sanna	125 (1 victory)
8.	D. Pedrosa	100
9.	N. Ueda	94
10.	A. Vincent	94 (1 victory)

500cc

(1) Rider	Nation	(2)	(3)	(4)	(5)	(6)	(7)	(8)	(9)	(10)
1. ROSSI Valentino	ITA	325	16	4	12	11	13	15	1	1
2. BIAGGI Max	ITA	219	16	7	13	3	9	14	1	2
3. CAPIROSSI Loris	ITA	210	16	4	13	-	9	15	2	1
4. BARROS Alex	BRA	182	16	-	5	1	4	14	1	2
5. NAKANO Shinya	JPN	155	15	-	9	-	1	15	3	-
6. CHECA Carlos	SPA	137	15	-	1	-	3	12	2	2
7. ABE Norick	JPN	137	16	-	1	-	1	13	2	3
8. CRIVILLE Alex	SPA	120	15	-	-	-	2	12	2	3
9. GIBERNAU Sete	SPA	119	16	-	1	1	1	14	1	2
10. UKAWA Tohru	JPN	107	16	1	2	-	1	10	3	5
11. ROBERTS Kenny	USA	97	16	-	3	-	1	11	3	4
12. McCOY Garry	AUS	88	11	-	3	-	3	9	2	2
13. vd GOORBERGH Jurgen	NED	65	15	-	1	-	-	12	7	3
14. HAGA Noriyuki	JPN	59	15	-	-	-	-	9	4	6
15. JACQUE Olivier	FRA	59	13	-	-	-	-	8	5	4
16. CARDOSO Jose Luis	SPA	45	16	-	-	-	-	11	8	4
17. AOKI Haruchika	JPN	33	14	-	-	-	-	9	5	5
18. WEST Anthony	AUS	27	14	-	-	-	-	11	12	3
19. HASLAM Leon	GBR	13	13	-	-	-	-	5	11	3
20. WALKER Chris	GBR	9	7	-	-	-	-	4	12	3
21. KAGAYAMA Yukio	JPN	6	1	-	-	-	-	1	10	-
22. STIGEFELT Johan	SWE	6	15	-	-	-	-	3	13	6
23. CLARKE Brendan	AUS	5	8	-	-	-	-	3	14	3
24. VENEMAN Barry	NED	4	15	-	-	-	-	3	14	6
25. WILLIS Mark	AUS	3	8	-	-	-	-	1	13	2
26. VINCENT Jay	GBR	3	9	-	-	-	-	1	13	5
27. JANSSEN Jarno	NED	1	1	-	-	-	-	1	15	-

FINAL CONSTRUCTORS' WORLD CHAMPIONSHIP CLASSIFICATION

1. HONDA 367 ◆ 2. YAMAHA 295 ◆ 3. SUZUKI 153 ◆ 4. PROTON KR 65 ◆ 5. SABRE V4 6 ◆ 6. PULSE 3

(1)	FINAL CHAMPIONSHIP CLASSIFICATION	(5)	NUMBER OF FRONT ROW STARTS	(9)	BEST RACE FINISH
(2)	NUMBER OF POINTS	(6)	NUMBER OF VICTORIES	(10)	NUMBER OF RETIREMENTS
(3)	NUMBER OF QUALIFICATIONS (OUT OF 16 GP)	(7)	NUMBER OF PODIUMS		
(4)	NUMBER OF POLE POSITIONS	(8)	SCORED POINTS (TOP 15)		

FINAL CONSTRUCTORS' WORLD CHAMPIONSHIP CLASSIFICATION

1. HONDA 361 ◆ **2. APRILIA 345** ◆ **3. YAMAHA 142**

(1) Rider	Nation	(2)	(3)	(4)	(5)	(6)	(7)	(8)	(9)	(10)
1. KATOH Daijiro	JPN	322	16	6	14	11	13	15	1	1
2. HARADA Tetsuya	JPN	273	16	8	12	3	13	14	1	-
3. MELANDRI Marco	ITA	194	15	-	9	1	9	12	1	3
4. ROLFO Roberto	ITA	177	16	-	1	-	4	15	2	1
5. NIETO Fonsi	SPA	167	15	2	7	-	2	15	3	-
6. McWILLIAMS Jeremy	GBR	141	16	-	8	-	2	12	1	4
7. ALZAMORA Emilio	SPA	136	16	-	2	1	2	11	2	4
8. LOCATELLI Roberto	ITA	134	15	-	6	-	2	12	3	2
9. MATSUDO Naoki	JPN	112	16	-	-	-	-	14	4	1
10. BATTAINI Franco	ITA	75	16	-	-	-	-	12	5	2
11. DEBON Alex	SPA	60	16	-	2	-	-	11	6	2
12. HOFMANN Alex	GER	55	16	-	-	-	-	9	7	4
13. DE PUNIET Randy	FRA	50	16	-	1	-	-	8	5	6
14. GUINTOLI Sylvain	FRA	44	16	-	-	-	-	8	4	5
15. YUZY Shahrol	MAL	44	16	-	-	-	-	9	9	4
16. PORTO Sebastian	ARG	39	16	-	-	-	-	9	7	9
17. CHECA David	SPA	35	15	-	-	-	-	9	7	3
18. NÖHLES Klaus	GER	25	11	-	-	-	-	8	11	1
19. DE GEA David	SPA	24	16	-	-	-	1	5	3	6
20. LANZI Lorenzo	ITA	23	16	-	-	-	-	8	11	4
21. BOSCOSCURO Luca	ITA	21	16	-	-	-	-	4	7	7
22. SEKIGUCHI Taro	JPN	20	7	-	-	-	-	4	9	1
23. CHIARELLO Riccardo	ITA	15	15	-	-	-	-	4	8	5
24. LUCCHI Marcellino	ITA	13	2	-	2	-	-	1	4	1
25. VIDAL Jeronimo	SPA	13	15	-	-	-	-	5	9	4
26. TOMAS David	SPA	11	14	-	-	-	-	4	10	1
27. OHSAKI Nobuyuki	JPN	6	1	-	-	-	-	1	10	-
28. AOYAMA Hiroshi	JPN	3	2	-	-	-	-	1	13	-
29. MIYAZAKI Osamu	JPN	3	1	-	-	-	-	1	13	-
30. POENSGEN Katja	GER	2	14	-	-	-	-	1	14	2
31. VINCENT Jay	GBR	2	7	-	-	-	-	1	14	2
32. BOESVELD Jarno	NED	1	1	-	-	-	-	1	15	-

(1) FINAL CHAMPIONSHIP CLASSIFICATION	(5) NUMBER OF FRONT ROW STARTS	(9) BEST RACE FINISH
(2) NUMBER OF POINTS	(6) NUMBER OF VICTORIES	(10) NUMBER OF RETIREMENTS
(3) NUMBER OF QUALIFICATIONS (OUT OF 16 GP)	(7) NUMBER OF PODIUMS	
(4) NUMBER OF POLE POSITIONS	(8) SCORED POINTS (TOP 15)	

125cc

(1) Rider	Nation	(2)	(3)	(4)	(5)	(6)	(7)	(8)	(9)	(10)
1. POGGIALI Manuel	RSM	241	16	2	8	3	11	13	1	3
2. UI Youichi	JPN	232	16	7	14	6	8	12	1	2
3. ELIAS Toni	SPA	217	16	4	5	2	9	13	1	1
4. CECCHINELLO Lucio	ITA	156	16	1	11	1	4	11	1	3
5. AZUMA Masao	JPN	142	16	-	1	2	2	12	1	3
6. BORSOI Gino	ITA	130	16	1	1	-	2	12	2	1
7. SANNA Simone	ITA	125	15	-	3	1	3	11	1	3
8. PEDROSA Daniel	SPA	100	16	-	1	-	2	11	3	2
9. UEDA Noboru	JPN	94	15	-	2	1	2	9	1	5
10. VINCENT Arnaud	FRA	94	15	-	-	-	2	10	2	3
11. JENKNER Steve	GER	94	16	-	-	-	2	10	3	4
12. GIANSANTI Mirko	ITA	75	14	-	-	-	1	10	2	3
13. SABBATANI Max	ITA	72	16	1	1	-	-	12	5	3
14. DE ANGELIS Alex	RSM	63	16	-	-	-	-	11	6	5
15. HULES Jaroslav	CZE	62	16	-	-	-	-	11	6	3
16. NIETO Jr. Angel	SPA	56	15	-	-	-	-	9	5	5
17. SMRZ Jakub	CZE	50	16	-	-	-	-	7	5	4
18. TALMACSI Gabor	HUN	34	16	-	-	-	-	6	6	2
19. OLIVE Joan	SPA	34	16	-	-	-	-	9	8	3
20. RODRIGUEZ Angel	SPA	27	14	-	-	-	-	5	6	6
21. PERUGINI Stefano	ITA	25	16	-	-	-	-	6	11	8
22. SCALVINI Gianluigi	ITA	22	15	-	-	-	-	5	9	6
23. BRANNETTI Alessandro	ITA	22	15	-	-	-	-	5	9	4
24. NIETO Pablo	SPA	21	16	-	-	-	-	5	6	8
25. MÜLLER Jarno	GER	18	11	-	-	-	-	4	9	-
26. JARA Raul	SPA	9	16	-	-	-	-	3	11	3
27. BATAILLE Eric	AND	8	15	-	-	-	-	2	9	6
28. BALLERINI Andrea	ITA	5	2	-	1	-	-	1	11	1
29. STONER Casey	AUS	4	2	-	-	-	-	1	12	-
30. CAFFIERO Gaspare	ITA	4	14	-	-	-	-	1	13	4
31. ARAUJO Adrian	SPA	3	11	-	-	-	-	1	13	2
32. KIKUCHI Hiroyuki	JPN	1	1	-	-	-	-	1	15	-

FINAL CONSTRUCTORS' WORLD CHAMPIONSHIP CLASSIFICATION

1. HONDA 301 ◆ 2. APRILIA 263 ◆ 3. GILERA 241 ◆ 4. DERBI 232 ◆ 5. TSR-HONDA 94 ◆ 6. ITALJET 42

(1)	FINAL CHAMPIONSHIP CLASSIFICATION	(5)	NUMBER OF FRONT ROW STARTS	(9)	BEST RACE FINISH
(2)	NUMBER OF POINTS	(6)	NUMBER OF VICTORIES	(10)	NUMBER OF RETIREMENTS
(3)	NUMBER OF QUALIFICATIONS (OUT OF 16 GP)	(7)	NUMBER OF PODIUMS		
(4)	NUMBER OF POLE POSITIONS	(8)	SCORED POINTS (TOP 15)		

SUZUKA

>> A nice day for the start of the 2001 season which begins in Suzuka, Japan. In the Honda fairground where the Suzuka track is located, the sakuras (Japanese cherry trees) are in blossom and the French bakery is doing a roaring trade. The croissants and other Danish pastries are a delight for the riders and mechanics who have to pass by everyday to get to the track.

>> World Champion Kenny Roberts intends to retain his crown this year. "I will concentrate on scoring points at each Grand Prix", he explains. "That's how you get to be World Champion. A second triumph would be great especially before the four-strokes come in 2002".

>> In order to get over the seven hour jetlag, Marco Melandri and his childhood pal, Tino, had a sleep, took a sauna and traditional Japanese baths, then slept again.

>> In the paddock, there is confirmation that Dunlop is devoting more and more efforts to superbikes in order to be able to develop tyres for the new four-strokes of the future.

WELKOM

>> After the "hot" dispute between Rossi and Biaggi in Japan, FIM President, Francesco Zerbi wrote the two riders an open letter :

"Gentlemen,

It will perhaps seem strange that a President is writing to two riders to reproach them because of certain behaviour that the Race Direction and the Stewards who were present at the scene, did not judge liable for sanction.

In my opinion, it should not be considered strange, but on the contrary, justified.

You are without doubt among the best known riders who give the greatest image to the sport, and for this reason you have not only the responsibility of your own image, but also that of motorcycling in particular and sport in general.

Rules can be subject to different interpretations and applications according to the points of view of the persons who must apply them ; however the impact of the actions of the persons who, like you, are subject to the scrupulous attention of millions of spectators are not unimportant and cannot pass without comment from me in my capacity as the person responsible for the running of our sport.

It is not my role to establish if what happened during the event could have been sanctioned as a sporting offence and what measures could or should have been taken : in this connection, it was the Race Direction at the scene, formed by the four bodies who monitor the races : representatives of the FIM, Dorna, teams and riders. I think that after having verified the events and the (rightly called negative) reactions which materialised in negative judgements in your regard and in the regard of our sport, it is my duty to intervene.

My intervention is two-fold : the first is a reproach to you both, in order to invite you to more attentively and correctly control your actions and reactions, without taking anything away from your fighting instinct and your desire for victory, your skill, your courage and the sporting qualities that a true champion shows to all the world. A real champion must be recognised by his behaviour during the competitions but also by his behaviour in his daily life, by his acts and by the words he uses in his contacts with others around him, including journalists.

The second, much simpler but more direct, aims to avoid repeating situations in the future where the persons who must intervene do not know the manner in which to do so.

For this reason, the Grand Prix Permanent Bureau will request the Race Direction to intervene with the appropriate sanctions according to the gravity of the actions and/or reactions that could happen during an event, or in the area of an event, and which could manifest itself not only as a sporting offence already provided for in the rules, but also more generally as " anti-sporting or censurable behaviour ". I realise that this definition is generic, even if it is precise, but it is not possible to establish a list of cases and actions that would define this behaviour.

We will watch to see that the persons charged with applying the sanctions are, as far as is humanly possible, the most attentive, moderate and conscious of their very important role.

Mistakes can be made, but it is important to do all that is possible to avoid them being made and to avoid them being repeated, and that the persons who make these errors are punished appropriately.

Knowing you, I am sure that you understand the spirit of this letter and the sentiments that inspired it. I hope to see you soon on the circuits, where I am sure that you will again demonstrate your great technical, sporting and human potential, which makes great champions of you both.

Francesco Zerbi

FIM President

patter

by Judith Tomaselli

>> While Europe, especially in the north is in the throes of disastrous weather, it's a pleasure to be in South Africa and enjoy its autumnal sunshine. The little town of Welkom is located around 280 km from the capital, Johannesburg, on a plain littered with gold mines. Since Welkom is not a big city a lot of teams, journalists, etc are staying with the locals enabling us to savour South African hospitality and to spend a few days with them.

>> On Thursday, Harada, Melandri, Ui, Nakano and a few other riders went to visit a reserve not far from the track. After visiting the place by truck followed by the zebra, they were able to play with three-month-old lion cubs for a while – a real childhood dream! Marco Melandri then went to another reserve located 30 minutes from Welkom and the Aprilia rider was able to play with young tigers.

>> Carlos Checa is the big absentee from the South African Grand Prix: two days before leaving as he was training on a small track not far from his home with his brother David, he fell off. After going to hospital doctors detected some bruising on his kidneys and advised him to remain lying down and to rest.

>> The Honda four-stroke has completed its first few laps in the hands of a test rider in Sugo. It's a long way from recording the superbike times, but the noise the V5 makes will certainly arouse some passions and bring back old memories. After the South African Grand Prix, Alex Crivillé is set to test the new bike. Honda also asked for Mick Doohan's advice, but he declined the offer which "does not fit in with his tasks as consultant!"

>> Valentino Rossi arrived tanned and well in Welkom. "I had planned to spend a week's holiday in the Seychelles after Japan because it's a Grand Prix that never suits me and I didn't want to go back to Italy to read it in the papers. This year, Suzuka suited me fine, but I couldn't change my plans. So I didn't see the papers and their comments on our duel (with Biaggi).

>> Mick Doohan is not in Welkom but in Tasmania where he is taking part in the Tarmac car rally driving a Mercedes CLK 55. On Friday he was in 13th place, but on Saturday he crashed, demolishing the fine car but luckily avoiding injury for himself and his co-driver.

>> Valentino Rossi has to wear two sliders for this race because he drags his knee so much that if he only wears one it would wear right through.

The Equipe de France Grand Prix which provides rides for young up and coming French riders, Guintoli and de Puniet have as a godfather one of the most likeable sportsmen around: the skier Luc Alphand.

>> At the start of the 500 race, Valentino Rossi held up a placard which read "Help Africa, provide Aids drugs free of charge and use condoms. The Doctor!"

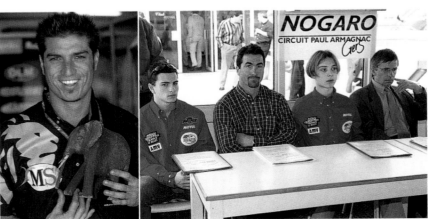

Paddock patter

JEREZ

>> There is definitely no age limit to shining in Grand Prix racing. Aprilia test rider Marcellino Lucchi at 44, put the young kids in their place by setting the second fastest time.

>> During the first free practice session, while breaking in his 500 Yamaha, Olivier Jacque was rammed by Carlos Checa. Still suffering from his scaphoid fracture, the French rider raised his arm to protect it, but hit his head, so now he's suffering from neck muscle strain. On Saturday he complained of pains in his arm and didn't start the race to preserve his chances of competing in Le Mans in two weeks' time. He really is out of luck at the moment.

>> At Jerez the show is guaranteed on race day but also during the preceding nights in the city. Each year, hordes of bikers perform wheelings and other feats in the main street and this year spectators were seated in grandstands separated by a fence from the "track" where the acrobatics take place.

>> Roberto Locatelli attended a flamenco school and took to the dance floor himself. It took less than three minutes for him to understand that the dance was not his cup of tea!

>> Juan-Pablo Montoya and Jarno Trulli, the two Formula 1 drivers, both came to Jerez and spent a long time talking to Mick Doohan. Jarno Trulli was impressed by the relaxed and fun atmosphere in the paddock and the availability of the riders. He promised Valentino Rossi he could try out his F1... and that he would try out the Honda.

>> A fine turn-out once again for the Spanish Grand Prix in Jerez: no less than 200 000 spectators over the weekend and around 80 000 bikes in the fields. As usual this created several traffic jams. It's welcome news to Andalusia that benefits from the influx of pesetas this traffic brings!

>> What a joke. The start of the 250 cc GP had to be delayed when, during the warm up lap, the safety car crashed into one of the low walls that line the circuit... thankfully it was nothing serious !

LE MANS

>> On Thursday, the bus carrying Luis D'Antin's team caught fire in the paddock. Fortunately the fire brigade were on the spot but the fire damaged the luggage compartments and it will not be easy to repair the damage before taking to the road again.

>> There are more and more motorhomes in the paddock every year. This time there were 36 for 47 teams. Even some small teams who don't have the money to buy spare parts or the services of a good rider have a hospitality unit, because the publicity on the tent with some good cooking and a warm welcome is less expensive for sponsors.

>> Jolted by the excellent results achieved by Bridgestone thanks to Erv Kanemoto and Nobuatsu Aoki, Dunlop has come to its senses. "Bridgestone will enter 500, so we must be there too," says Jeremy Ferguson, Dunlop's GP representative. "Nothing has been defined yet, but we want to be in 500 next year with several teams in order to obtain the best information".

>> Always seeking information to help improve rider safety and comfort, Dainese has developed some leathers equipped with 64 sensors to read cardiac rhythms, and body temperatures. Max Biaggi tried out the prototype successfully in Jerez. Dainese is also developing an "air bag" vest which would pump up in the event of excessive deceleration to protect all the vital organs: spinal column, nape of the neck, ribs, etc.

>> Due to the (hypocritical) anti-tobacco and anti-alcohol laws, the teams have to play games to identify the fairings. That's why instead of West on the fairings of Capirossi and Barros, there was Loris and Alex and Valentino Rossi had a huge bar code in the place of Nastro Azzurro. At Aprilia they replaced the cigarette MS with the name of the Superbike RSV. But these laws are not stopping sponsors joining the sport. In 2002 Rossi may run in the colours of Mild Seven.

>> All the old grandstands at Le Mans have been pulled down. There remains just one that is being renovated located at the Dunlop chicane and that's called the "Georges Durand" who was the co-founder of the ACO and secretary general for many years. This grandstand has been classified as an historic monument and was constructed just after the war, opening in 1949 during the first 24 Hour race after the war when Président Vincent Auriol gave the start. It also used to be the grandstand for the press where journalists and speakers could watch the race.

MUGELLO

>> On Saturday, Schwantz, Mamola, Cadalora, Mertens, Cardus and others took part in the BMW race. After practice, Schwantz and Cadalora were slightly doubtful and the American even came into the pits before the end of the race complaining of transmission problems, but it seems he didn't like the selection placed on the other side.

>> Kevin Schwantz has opened a riding school on the Road Atlanta track in the USA. Any interested parties can consult the website on www.schwantzschool.com.

>> On Friday night no-one was allowed into the Honda/Valentino Rossi pits. The mechanics were in the process of transforming his bike which for the Italian Grand Prix was covered in light blue flowers with a pretty vahine on the seat. In the evening Rossi's fan club paraded around the paddock on a pedal car like you see at the seaside also covered in flowers with shells and a picture of Valentino!

>> They are very sporty at Michelin. Coco the technician who takes care of Valentino Rossi's bike, jogs back the 9.5 km to the hotel every evening along the marvellous little road among the fields and woods.

>> Mugello – especially when the weather is warm as it was on Thursday, Friday and Saturday – is always the ideal party location. On Thursday Biaggi's team opened the festivities with a dinner held in a castle built in the Middle Ages. Friday it was the turn of the Aprilia team to organise a table football tournament with a scooter for the winners and then dancing. Saturday, half the hospitality units in the paddock were the centre of entertainment. At team Derbi, they were serving "porchetta" (sucking pig roasted on a spit).

>> At the hospitality unit of the team Italjet, Stefano Saragoni (a journalist from the magazine Motosprint) was the lead singer with his own group. At the Gresini team they were raffling a used pair of Katoh's boots. Around eleven-o-clock in the evening the wind picked up and everyone ran to take shelter before the storm started and the rain began to fall in earnest.

>> Angel Nieto who was crowned World Champion 12 + 1 time (he is very superstitious) is a contender for the title of "Prince of the Asturias" in terms of sport. It's a very high honour in Spain and he has already been a candidate twice missing by just one point.

>> In Le Mans, the gas canister for Valentino Rossi's motorhome was empty. Not finding any replacements in the neighbourhood, Valentino jumped ship and left his friends in it for three days without heat and hot water!

>> A real biker, Ivan Beggio the boss of Aprilia came to Mugello by bike! Since the Italians are very superstitious and Harada won his first race since coming back to 250, Mr Beggio may have to attend all the forthcoming GPs on his bike!

>> On Sunday morning, Randy Mamola took former F1 driver Johnny Herbert out on the two-seater Yamaha. "I'll try and match pole" he announced with a smile.

>> It was so cold during the 500 race, that Tohru Ukawa 's teeth were chattering at the finish and he could hardly speak. After warming up, he admitted that during the last five race laps, he could hardly see anything because of the rain and wondered how he would finish the race, he was so cold and drenched from the driving rain.

CATALUNYA

>> On Thursday, Tetsuya Harada celebrated his 31st birthday! The likeable Japanese rider who always rides with the number 31 is therefore in the right year. "Katoh will be difficult to beat in the dry," he confided. "But I'm starting to find my feet in 250 again and the more I ride, the more I improve. We tested here after Jerez, but the conditions are not the same. I like this track, my back hurts less, but I'm still a bit older!"

>> Who would be the next to announce their four-stroke! After Yamaha's announcement that its prototype would make a lap on Sunday, Honda revealed its V5 on Saturday evening and Suzuki announced its four-stroke investment with a 990cc that will be competitive in 2003.

>> Doctor Costa, the official doctor for the riders now has his own website: You can find it at www.clinicamobile.com

>> There were some famous people in Barcelona. Numerous footballers attended: Marc Overmans (FC Barcelona), Allonson and Luis Enrique who is a friend of Sete Gibernau as well as Sonny Anderson who came to say hello to Alex Barros. Some tennis players also turned out to greet the bikers including Arantxa Sanchez and Juan Carlos Ferrero.

Paddock patter

ASSEN

>> The organisers had organised an exhibition entitled "Roaring Engines and Foaming Beer" retracing the history of the Dutch TT, which is the most famous event on the GP calendar.

>> Assen has been undergoing a face-lift for a few years and in 2002, the final touch will be made to the circuit itself. 8 million Euros have been invested to extend the straight behind the paddock and thus increase its size and to move the corner at the far end of the track to increase the size of the sand trap. The total length of the track will change slightly but the historic connotations will be retained. There will also now be two tunnels to enter and leave the paddock which will avoid having to wait each time at the entrance.

>> Gianpiero Sacchi (Derbi-Gilera team manager), Claudio Verna (Gilera engineer) and Paolo Sesti have announced the arrival in 2002 of a new Italia team that will include two young Italian riders in 125. This is proof of Gilera's (part of the Piaggio group) long-term investment in GP racing.

>> The Red Devil team had a fine attraction in the paddock: a red bull mounted on wheels and powered by a lawn mower engine. On Thursday evening, the mechanics amused themselves by riding round the paddock on its back.

>> Kevin Schwantz still holds the 500 race lap record - since 1991. And since it's raining, it's possible he'll keep it forever since next year the track will have a different layout. Schwantz is also the last rider to have won on a bike other than a Honda. The last Yamaha rider to win the Dutch TT was Wayne Rainey in 1989.

DONINGTON

>> On Thursday evening it was very hot in the paddock and even though a storm threatened some teams still organised a party. At Marlboro Yamaha they organised a darts match that was won by Max Biaggi. The tournament was followed by an excellent curry cooked by an Indian chef and washed down by an English beer. At the other end of the paddock they were celebrating Roberto Locatelli's 27th birthday. His friend Max Biaggi joined him for a drink and gave him some advice on how to brake, how to gain speed in the corners and how to set up his Aprilia 250.

>> On Friday night Daijiro Katoh celebrated his 25th birthday at Fausto Gresini.

>> Locatelli gave himself a new motorhome for his birthday which he bought in the paddock at Donington where it was on display. "I gave myself a nice present", explained the Italian. "But I also thought about Manuela (his girlfriend) and installed a washing machine".

>> All weekend, Max Biaggi had an AC Roma scarf on his wrist to bring him good luck. Marco Melandri spent the week in London looking for a flat. After Valentino Rossi it's now his turn to come and live in England, where Olivier Jacque also resides.

>> Like every year, the Thursday in Donington Park is the traditional "Day of Champions" to raise money for the charity "Riders for Health" which instructs African nurses how to ride and maintain a motorcycle, the only means of transport in the bush. Randy Mamola is the main force behind these days and once again went out of his way to persuade as many people as possible to take part. The activity brought in almost 800 000 FF, 350 000 FF of which just from the auction of helmets, boots and leathers offered by the riders. The highest bid was for Max Biaggi's leathers which were sold for 45,000 FF.

>> Olivier Jacque lives in London and went to watch Nathalie Tauziat in the Wimbledon quarter finals.

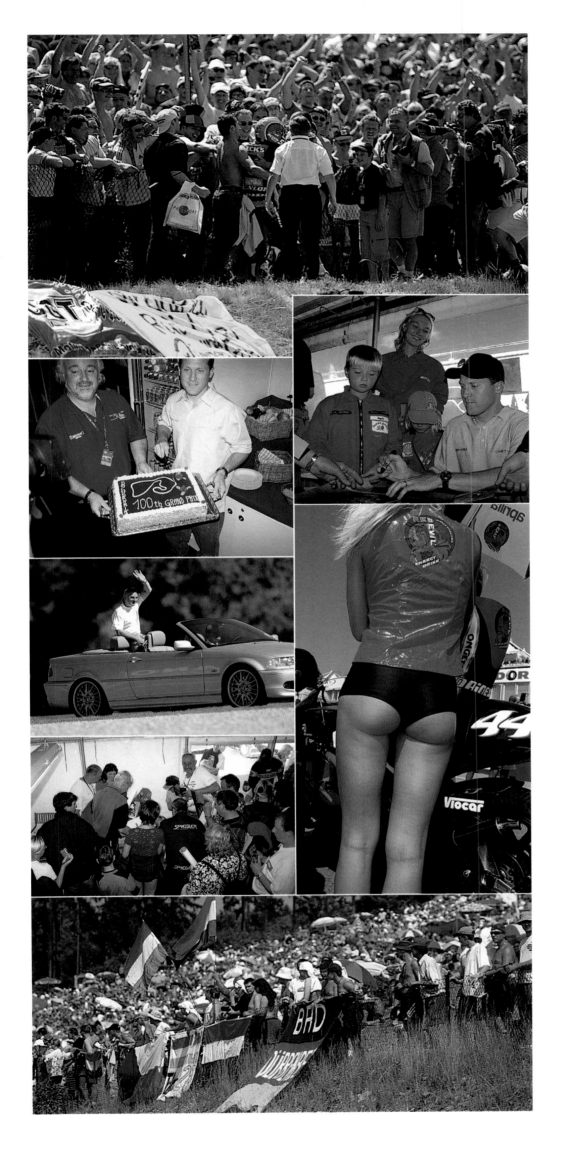

SACHSENRING

>> In spite of its efforts in modernisation, the Sachsenring still remains in pole position in terms of disorganisation! The paddock is kilometres away from the hospitalities that are miles away from the car parks. To cap it all, Dorna had refused access to the paddock for the shuttles, so there was a fair uphill trek on foot to get there.

>> But this is only a problem for the small fry, because others get special treatment such as Alex Crivillé, Kenny Roberts and Mick Doohan who had reserved parking spots in the paddock – with a plaque with their name on it – beside the Dorna trucks. And why them and not others? Because they have all been World Champions? No, because other Champions such as Jacque, Rossi, Biaggi and Locatelli, just to name a few, were "only" World Champions in 125, 250 and here it's the 500 class that counts.

>> On Thursday evening, Marco Melandri exchanged his leathers for a cook's apron and produced some delicious "piadine", a kind of waffle that you cover with ham, cheese, spinach or mushrooms. It's a speciality from the Ravenne region where the Aprilia rider lives.

>> On the eve of practice, a football match was organised to raise funds for Riders for Health. On one side was a team formed from German stars and on the other Grand Prix riders such as Rossi, Biaggi, Barros (the only one to score a goal), Checa, Crivillé, Capirossi, etc. The riders lost 2-1 and there were 6200 spectators!

>> Also on Thursday, an enormous cake was made to celebrate Kenny Roberts' 100th GP. It would have been good if it had degenerated a little like in the good old days, but today's paddock isn't that interested in having fun.

>> On the Sachsenring track, the finish line had been painted like a chess board, with two lines of black and white cheques and it was the first one to cross the chequered line who won.

>> On Friday evening, laughter was to be heard coming from Eros Ramazotti's tent. The meal was prepared by cooks who had travelled specially from Abruzzes (Southern Italy) with home-made pasta, fresh tomato sauce and mutton in their hand luggage! It was an excellent meal washed down with fine local wine. The region of Abruzzes sponsors Roberto Locatelli to publicise the pretty region where the mountains meet the sea and where it's sunny all year long. A must for a visit in terms of climate and cuisine.

>> Graziano Rossi, Valentino's father, follows his son around all the European tracks, but in order to enter into the paddock atmosphere he doesn't go to the hotel, but sleeps in his car. "The best thing," explains Graziano, "would be a motorhome. But it's impossible for me to travel at 100 km/h. So I thought it over and decided that I had everything I needed to shower, sleep and drink in the paddock. I only needed a bed. So I got a BMW hatchback which is fast and spacious. I like to be in the paddock and stay here until the last moment without getting stuck in traffic morning and night".

Paddock patter

BRNO

>> After a four week break, the riders donned their leathers again – in the case of Valentino, made of kangaroo – for the second part of the season on the track at Brno in the Czech Republic. Brno is a nice track with wooded slopes the riders like because it's fast with various changes in direction.

>> On Thursday after a VTT race on BMWs, which was won by Steve Jenkner, it was party time again ... at Aprilia, as usual, where they celebrated the last birthdays in August with much "allegria": Marco Melandri's nineteenth, and Aldo Gandolfo (Aprilia communication manager) - the number of years is a state secret - and Leandro Scomazzon (Aprilia financial director).

>> Olivier Jacque made a dramatic entrance into the paddock driving his new car: a grey Ferrari Modena which he was obliged by IRTA to leave in the car park and not park under his awning.

>> Many Japanese riders went home during the break, but to Tetsuya Harada's great distress it was 46°C! "We stayed inside all holiday, sheltering from the heat and with the air conditioning on full. I have played so much Play Station that my right index finger is really sore. Next year we'll stay in Monaco!"

>> Each year, the Brno Grand Prix takes place in August and each year it is plagued by wasps that sting as many people as possible. It is not very pleasant if you're a mere mortal, but when the riders get one of them in their leathers it's extremely disagreeable! McCoy got one in his leathers and was tearing them off as he rode towards Dr Costa's clinic. Leon Haslam was stung on his lip and his face swelled up to twice the size and Ui was stung in his boot.

>> Thirteen times World Champion, Angel Nieto now has a new challenge: his companion Belinda, gave birth to Hugo on 20 July! Good luck to the parents for if he wants to following in the footsteps of his half-brothers, Gelete and Pablo, Angel Senior will be around the tracks for some time to come!

ESTORIL

>> Daryl Beattie who now works for Channel Ten, an Australian TV Station, was in Estoril with his arm in a sling. "I wanted to take part in the Australian Safari (an off-road rally)", he confessed. "And I broke my collarbone. In November Kevin Schwantz (who took part in the rally last year and broke his foot) is coming back with his father and an American TV channel for a spin in the desert, but this time we'll take it easy, just to have fun and enjoy the scenery".

>> There were some old friends in the paddock at Estoril: Vic Soussan, Mr Fernandez, Patrick's father, and Guy Coulon. Bernie Ecclestone was also there and after discussing with Mick Doohan, visited the pits, the trucks and the hospitalities. He was also bold enough to take a tour behind Randy Mamola on the two-seater as did his wife Slavica! "That's the most expensive cargo I've ever had," said Randy who went slowly to avoid causing the Formula One boss to have a heart attack. "I began my career in motorcycling," joked Ecclestone. "But I'm happy not to have finished it on two wheels! It was a fantastic lap, a great experience and I felt completely at ease with Randy. I haven't done a lap in the latest F1 two-seater but I think the bike is more impressive because your face is just a few inches from the tarmac".

VALENCIA

>> On Thursday and for the second time this season, the riders took part in autograph sessions, interviews and auctions in aid of Riders for Health. At the end of the day, 2000 spectators had visited the paddock and had been able to get the autographs of their favourite riders. The amount raised for Africa currently stands at $32 000.

>> Randy Mamola has been dreaming of testing the BMW Z8 since the beginning of the season. On the occasion of the Bol d'Or that will take place in Magny Cours, BMW has given him a nice surprise: a pink Z8 with a pretty ribbon that he can use for three weeks.

>> The Spanish brought out a Rieju 125, ridden by an Italian, Fabrizio Lai. The Rieju is actually a scooter make but the 125 that competes in the Italian and Spanish championships, is a modified Honda chassis and the team is managed by Italians: Engines Engineering.

>> Luc Alphand came to support the youngsters in the French Grand Prix team – Randy de Puniet and Sylvain Guintoli. The downhill champion is an avid endurance fan and loves watching the Grand Prix trackside. "The mental approach for road racing and for downhill skiers is very similar," he said. "Probably because the risk of falling is about the same".

>> Bridgestone brought a special water tanker from England to spray the track on Tuesday and Wednesday prior to their rain-tyre test. Ironically it was raining cats and dogs on Saturday!

>> Edouard Michelin took a spin on Randy's two-seater. He had come to support the work of his technicians and the 50th consecutive win in 500 for Michelin. "This is a very memorable day for me. It was wonderful because Grand Prix motorcycling is a marvellous show. And my little turn on the two-seater was extraordinary! But I'm not only here to have fun. I'm also here to remind everyone that our investment in motorcycling is 100%!"

MOTEGI

>> Before coming to Motegi which is around a hundred kilometres from Tokyo, Capirossi, Katja, Katoh and Checa attended a tennis match in the capital before taking up a raquet themselves, slightly less easily than the professionals. Japan is traditionally the country for hospitality and this time all the paddock was received with full pomp and ceremony at the "Welcome Party". On this occasion, the riders had a great time trying out all the new Namco electronic games.

>> Carlos Checa spent some time in Paris before flying to Japan. He visited the Two Wheel fair at the Porte de Versailles and took the chance to visit Notre Dame, Saint Germain and other fine quarters in the city of light.

>> Emilio Alzamora had a wisdom teeth operation but unfortunately the surgeon touched a facial nerve which paralysed a part of his face. The Spaniard dedicated his second place in the race to his brother who was injured in a car accident returning from the Valencia race.

>> Some veterans donned their leathers once again to the great delight of the Japanese crowd who came to support the riders at the fine Motegi track. In fact, Mick Doohan and Freddie Spencer all completed around ten laps on the 5 cylinder Honda on Friday. "If I had been in good physical shape", Mick admitted. "I could finish in the top five with this bike on Sunday!"

2001

Paddock patter

PHILLIP ISLAND

>> After Japan and several hours in a plane we reached Australia. But don't think it was tropical sun and blue skies, the Great Barrier Reef is a long way from Phillip Island, where we were heading. Phillip Island is a small island south of Melbourne, an attractive little place … in summer! But don't be mistaken, this is the end of winter in Australia and the more south you go, the colder it is. So the weather is a mixture of big dark clouds, rain and wind. An ideal climate for penguins which every evening put on a show for the tourists. So once they arrived in Phillip Island all the riders got out their padded jackets and the mechanics all made holes in the fairing to ensure that the wind effect would be less acute.

>> To pass the time and to view the scenery, Katja Poensgen and Garry McCoy spent some time with the Air Force aerobatic team while Carlos Checa bravely tried surfing leaving Barros, Gibernau, Abe and others to a quiet visit to the kangaroos and koala bears. Youngsters such as Elias, Poggiali, Haslam, and Pedrosa were taken – forcibly! – back to school where they visited a class the same age as themselves.

>> Wayne Gardner and Barry Sheene were inducted into the galery of the "greats" and received the honours reserved for the "Motorcycle legends": a nice medal presented to them by Mick Doohan, Dorna's ambassador for the occasion.

>> A woman, this time not Katja Poensgen, started the 125 race: Kate Thomson. She is English and managed to qualify in last place but she still qualified for her first Grand Prix. Unfortunately, she was hit by bad luck on the starting grid and had to start from the pits, which was not really a handicap for her. She retired during the race.

>> On Sunday evening all the fan club, team, friends, in fact all the people connected with Valentino Rossi, assembled in an inn to celebrate his magnificent 500 World title. Stefania, his mum, was at his side, while Graziano had stayed at home. "He's really scared to fly," laughed Valentino to excuse his father. And just to prove that they don't take after strangers, Valentino is also afraid of flying!

>> After this GP and before going to Malaysia for the last in the three race back-to-back series, Loris Capirossi and Alex Barros visited Phnom Penh, in Cambodia, where they met the royal family.

>> Valentino complained that in the paddock it was not possible to enjoy yourself like it was in the good old days. To break with the tradition which states that the world champion must dive, fully clothed, into the swimming pool (in any case it was far too cold in Australia), Randy Mamola threw a cream tart into Valentino's face during the press conference.

SEPANG

>> After a muted celebration because his friend Andrea had lost his mother on Friday, Valentino stayed in Australia for two days and took his mother to see the kangaroos and the koalas at Phillip Island. Valentino was sporting a new helmet in Sepang painted by his faithful friend Aldo Drudi.

>> Fonsi Nieto received a fine of 5000 Swiss francs for dangerous riding after he cut across the track and forced Cesar Barros to crash during qualifying on Friday.

>> A new crown was awarded in Sepang, to Daijiro Katoh for winning the 250 cc category after winning the GP with a lead of over 14 seconds over Harada.

RIO

>> The Rio GP was the 580th 500 GP, a category that saw the light of day exactly 52 years and five months earlier. It was on the Isle of Man, June 17 1949. Leslie Graham was the first 500 World Champion and Valentino Rossi will be the last, because next year, the 990cc four-strokes will line up on the starting grid in a category that will be known as MotoGP. The Rio Grand Prix was also the last for Alex Crivillé on a Honda.

>> So Rio hosted the last GP of the season and for once, the weather was fantastic, until Saturday morning! All those who had arrived fairly early were able to take full advantage of the Copacabana and Barra de Tijuca beaches and sample the Caipirinha (local punch) in the small bars alongside the ocean. They could also eat their fill at the churasquerias (restaurants where you can eat as much meat as you can), before sampling the nightlife in the Rio discos.

>> Anna Nogué, Alex Crivillé's fiancé almost didn't see the beaches of Rio at all. She arrived at Brazilian customs at the airport and was rude to a customs officer because he asked her to fill in certain boxes on the immigration forms. This was not to the civil servant's liking and he did all he could to send her back home! Dorna had to intervene at a fairly high level to get her out of her mess, and Anna spent 4h30 at the airport!

>> Michelin also had several misadventures. Some found themselves without their luggage for a few days. And they almost ended up spending some time in jail. In fact, upon their arrival at the airport, they found a smart green minibus waiting for them. After climbing in with all their luggage – at least those that had retrieved it – the driver disappeared. Fed up with waiting, Bernard took the wheel to drive them to their hotel. Fortunately he took some time to find the handbrake, because when the driver came running back, it turned out that this bus was just the shuttle to take them to the car hire zone. So if Bernard had found the brake they would have set off for the hotel in a "stolen" bus without knowing it!

>> On Wednesday riders and other team members played football against the Flamengos. It was a real disaster: 9-1 thanks to a goal from Gibernau. The Flamengo team had a match in the evening, and only three of them took part in the game. The others had been replaced by the basketball team!

>> Against all odds, the grandstands were full for the Rio GP this year. On Thursday and Friday, there were less than 4000 and 6000 spectators, but on Saturday which was race day, 41,374 fans came to the track.

>> On Saturday evening, Honda organised a dinner in a churrascaria at Barra de Tijuca to celebrate the world titles of Daijiro Katoh and Valentino Rossi. It was a fine sporting family atmosphere between the two champions and the young Spaniards in Alberto Puig's junior team: Elias, Olive and Pedrosa. The evening finished in the early hours in a disco hired for the paddock by IRTA, the GP teams association.

A work of art: the inner workings of
the Yamaha YZR500 two-stroke.
Soon to become a museum piece ?

The Yamaha M1: the morning of the Catalunian GP, a test rider
completed two laps with this prototype. This would indicate that the
development is ongoing and that the results are very promising.

The military four-step!

From the 2002 Japanese Grand Prix onwards, and even more so in 2003, it will be a question of the Military Four Step on the Grand Prix circuit. The return of valve techology to the Road Racing World Championship, so desired by the Federation and promoters, should provide the public with real racing prototypes, a myriad of different technological choices and, in theory, new constructors. This revolution which represents the death knell for the 500cc World Championship – from next Spring, it will be known as MotoGP – will take place in several stages.

1) CERTAIN CANDIDATES

- For its RC211V, **Honda** has selected a five cylinder engine. After the first discreet tests – Valentino Rossi could only complete a few laps of the Suzuka track the day after the Eight Hour race, because of the rain - the official presentation which took place during the Pacific GP at Motegi confirmed that the giant constructor was pursuing a permanent project. When invited to test the prototype, both Freddie Spencer and Michael Doohan were enthusiastic: "Even though I no longer have any comparison, there are impressions that cannot deceive, from the very first few yards, I knew that this bike was well-designed", explained Spencer. Doohan went further still. "The RC211V will be competitive from its very first GP, that seems certain". But will it completely dominate the competition, as some observers seem to think taking into account Honda's unrivalled know-how in valve technology? To those who think that the 500 two-strokes will be quickly out-of-date, Valentino Rossi replies with more reticence: "I still wonder if the ideal choice for 2002 would not be a good old NSR". It's important to note that this opinion dates back to end October, before the first serious test session for the World Champion at the Jerez circuit. Two riders will ride the new weapon: Valentino Rossi and Tohru Ukawa.

- At **Yamaha**, the M1 is powered by a four cylinder, which has been installed in a chassis that is very close to the current YZR. The technological challenge would therefore appear less complex than its historical rival. But since history has shown that simplicity can often be an advantage in racing, the M1 should not be too far behind the performances of the RC211V. Its stage of development seems more advanced and both Massimiliano Biaggi and Carlos Checa had the opportunity to make up their own minds in the Czech Republic. Just like Shinya Nakano a few weeks later in Barcelona. A highly excited Checa: "I can hardly wait to ride this bike". Even though the real performance was a closely guarded secret, some leaks are food for thought for the competition: Biaggi supposedly laps as fast round the track at Brno on an M1 as on a YZR, while during a race simulation, Carlos Checa apparently broke all records.

2) THE EUROPEAN CHALLENGE

- **Aprilia** has announced its return to the supreme category. Jan Witteveen, the Italian make's chief engineer has been working on two different paths, three and four cylinder options. More details were unknown as the "Motorcycle Yearbook" went to press. "Rather than talk or publish misleading press releases, I prefer to work", explained the Dutch brains at the end of the season. Will his prototype be ready for the first GP? Will Aprilia begin the MotoGP season with an old two stroke relic? These are just two of the questions that need to be answered in the next few weeks.

- **MZ**, the East German constructor that took par in the World Championship two years ago as a partner to Swissauto (the most powerful two-stroke V4 in the pack, but not the most rider friendly!) has requested two places in 2002 and has received them for one season only. The sticking points in this case are so numerous and

Two Japanese engineers push two RCV211 towards the starting line at the Motegi track.
The new Honda arm, powered by five cylinders, has two impressive godfathers,
Freddie Spencer and Michael Doohan.

complex that no information is forthcoming from Zschoppau. Some say that the only thing that exists is a first cylinder that is working on a test bench in Germany, others confirm that the development of a V4 prototype by a team managed by Mauro Forghieri (ex-Ferrari) has nothing more to do with the German make, who has serious difficulties in meeting its payment schedule.

- The case of **Sauber** is totally different. While we have seen virtually nothing from Aprilia and MZ, the Formula 1 Swiss engineering team of Sauber Petronas have played an open book to such an extent that some questions remain unanswered. During the Japanese GP in Suzuka, the research boss, Osamu Goto (formerly with Honda and Ferrari), presented the first version of a three cylinder engine, a "phase one" that represented a fine study, but whose dimensions – especially in terms of height – seemed to have only a passing interest with possible use in a motorcycle chassis. The phase two – the exact name of the engine is SPX1 – retains the technological philosophy of the first prototype (three cylinders in a row, 12 valves), but has been simplified, since Goto has rejected pneumatic valves. The Swiss went even further in Sepang – the financial partner for the F1 team and the development company is the Malaysian giant Petronas - when they presented the first rolling laboratory, ridden by Niall MacKenzie. With two straights in Sepang and three days of private testing in Shah Alam the following week, the Sauber (with British Harris chassis) charmed observers with its noise, and convinced its test rider "In all my career, I have never felt such a strong impression", said MacKenzie. But we don't know if we shall ever see this high technology jewel in MotoGP, since the leasing costs confirmed by Sauber are quite simply not compatible with motorcycle racing.

3) THE 2003 HORIZON

- From the Spanish GP in Jerez de la Frontera, **Ducati** officially announced its intention to make the move in 2003. The "Reds" are currently working on the in-house twin, in a MotoGP version, which could quite simply become a double twin.

- In Catalunya, **Suzuki** confirmed its intention also to be present in 2003. They are working on a traditional concept – four cylinders – and we still don't know precisely if a partnership agreement in terms of research and development signed with Kawasaki will have a direct consequence on MotoGP for the two makes. For in the autumn at the Two-Wheel show in Paris, Kawaski also confirmed that it had a GP project underway.

4) THE LONG-TERM FUTURE

With purposefully fuelled rumours and closely guarded secrets, the paddock was regularly invaded with possible scenarios. Some are probable others are more unlikely:

- Even though Kenny Roberts will enter the **Proton KR 3** three cylinder in 2002, he has made no secret of his wish to develop a four-stroke prototype.

- **Drysdale**, an Australian technology company, is working on a V8 project.

- **KTM** made official enquiries to world championship promoter Dorna to find out the rules of the game. BMW vehemently denies any desire to enter motorcycle GPs, but many people remain convinced they have a serious project underway.

- Finally at **Gilera**, it is perfectly feasible in terms of image, that after the 125cc triumph thanks to Manuel Poggiali, an ideal next step could be to develop a prototype for MotoGP.

One final thought: even though 2002 will be a transitional year – we should not forget that the arrival of the 1000cc four-stroke prototypes will not automatically mean the disappearance of the 500cc two-strokes – it will only be in 2003 or even 2004 that we shall see if the revolution has the hoped-for effect on enlarging the grid. Not in terms of the number of riders, but in terms of the quantity of makes present.

Although we know nothing about the Aprilia and even less of the MZ – the two European makes have obtained places for the first MotoGP Championship in history; a Sauber prototype made its first outing on the track at Sepang, Malaysia.

Niall MacKensie, the test rider for the Swiss Prototype. The three cylinder engine has already been installed. Harris appears convinced as do all those who have heard the amazing noise this machine generates.

Peter Sauber, founder and team owner of the Sauber Formula 1 team, which had some excellent results in 2001, was the first to take a close look at this new category.

Mother hen and her astonishing chickens

They listen to Alberto Puig like attentive students during a university lecture. Dani Pedrosa (with his back to the camera), Toni Elias (partially hidden from view) and Joan Olive are the first jewels of the Spanish training school for racing.

The image is superb. It certainly rapidly spread around the paddock. Nobody really knows at which track it actually came about. And yet: a man with a limp comes out of the pits followed by three little men all dressed in blue. "Hey, they look like a mother hen and her chickens," someone said. The mother hen is Alberto Puig, the boss of the Movistar Junior team. And the three chickens that at that stage were not familiar to us were Antonio Elias, Daniel Pedrosa and Joan Olive. A few months later, as the curtain came down on the 2001 World Championship, everyone was applauding: Elias finished third in the 125cc World Championship in just his second season and Pedrosa (8th) and Olive (19th) made an astounding debut. There is an intelligent training programme behind these performances: a Honda single-make trophy in Spain, more than a hundred young hopefuls at the start, then regular selection processes for Alberto Puig and his partners to sort out the wheat from the chaff. Then they have to be trained and shaped. And the gates to Paradise are opened up to them: GP. To bring this activity to a successful conclusion, it needed someone demanding. From his days as a rider Alberto Puig always was with regards to himself. He never cheated, always gritted his teeth, in spite of the disadvantages of his chosen profession of which he had more than his fair share, in particular a very serious injury after a dreadful accident at Le Mans.

THE BIG BROTHER

The success of the Spanish subsidiary, easy to explain in theory – as wide a base as possible, quality technical back-up – is the subject of some envy. It remains to be seen if all the other countries who intend to launch a similar project will be able to find a "big brother" like Alberto Puig, capable of raising his voice when necessary, of giving precious advice and of protecting his charges in a world where no-one takes any prisoners. "It's mostly for that reason that rather than sleep in a motorhome in the paddock, we go back to the hotel each night," explains Puig. "My guys can then see something else, and avoid all the demands of the racing world, which is closed in on itself". The surprising proof of how well this works is Toni Elias, who as long as he could avoid all the paddock gossip was untouchable. But as soon as his name began to circulate in different teams for the future, and as soon as serious or less serious offers were made to him via the media, the Young Spaniard became less focused. It will be interesting to follow the next episode of this adventure, when he moves into 250cc in 2002 with Jorge Martinez. Far away from his mother hen.

And it also remains to be seen whether it's a good idea to apply the same concept in other countries: France, Germany (the "Darg Dog Challenge", under auspices of Ralf Waldmann) and in Italy where, with the support of the national Federation, Gilera is offering a vast training system.

The mother hen has most definitely inspired envy.

Effective the Puig method ? Until Motegi, Toni Elias was nothing more than a tough adversary for the future World Champion, Manuel Poggiali. Here in Spain however, he takes the lead.

Katja, the beauty among the beasts

On this particular day, she was being interviewed by two journalists from "Bild am Sonntag". A few weeks earlier, it was the popular German magazines and TV stations. The regular paddock photographers are astounded: they get orders from the United States, from Figaro Magazine and numerous women's magazines. Thanks to her, motorcycling has found coverage in the German media, coverage that had become minimal over two decades. And her popularity has had a direct effect on her season, since on the eve of the German GP, her split with the Racing Factory team was made official. And the reason? "The Poensgen clan has not honoured its financial commitments", according to team boss Dieter Theis. "Not at all. Dieter could not abide the fact that people only talked about Katja", according to the other side. And who is she? Katja Poensgen of course, long blond hair, a cheeky look and the straight talking of a 24-year-old. Katja Poensgen, motorcycle rider, or better, GP rider since the start of the 2001 season. A season that began with an Aprilia and finished with the team Shell Advance Honda. A season marked by the astonishing result at the Italian GP: fourteenth place and two championship points in the rain, the only points scored by a woman in 250cc world championship history.

Even though a proportion of the paddock were fairly scornful, not convinced that this special world was particularly suitable for women, her appearance has opened up a whole new audience for motorcycling that would never have been interested before.

The new hard look: Katja Poensgen finds a new bike and a new team in Portugal after leaving the Racing Factory team.

- How do you react to your direct opponents?
- In the Japanese GP, those that were behind me ended up pulling into the pits and invented mechanical problems. In South Africa, it was the same thing again and this scenario has been repeated several times during the season. On the first day of practice, when I was lagging behind, some people started to snigger. But on Saturday, when I began to react, these same opponents were immediately calmer.

- There is enormous interest in you. Do you feel endowed with some kind of mission?
- No way do I want to become the German flag bearer in the World Championship. I appreciate the interest, but I'm not at the helm. I'm in racing firstly for myself, not for the others.

- Do you enjoy the huge media interest or is it an additional stress?
- In the last few weeks leading up to the season, I had only one dream: to find myself on the plane for Suzuka and get some peace. During the winter, there were daily requests from 7 until 22h00. Katja here, Katja there. Katja in the kitchen, Katja working out, Katja out for a walk, etc. I even got some TV crews who made nasty remarks because sometimes we had to reshoot scenes. But it's all part of the game. Modern sport must not only be the exponent of its art, it must also be a vehicle of communication.

- In terms of sport, your previous experience has been in smaller categories. Now it's GP racing, a new world and a totally different bike.
- Yes. During the winter when I was offered a GP 250 ride, I asked myself if I was up to the challenge. After a sleepless night, I finally said yes. Every rider starting out in racing has the words GP etched in his dreams. I had always raced in four-stroke categories, and so I saw myself more in world supersport or superbike. But here I am among the 30 best riders in the category. And I have no regrets.

"FROM NOW ON, MY OPPONENTS HAVE TWO GOALS"

Woman or rider? Katja Poensgen is living what seems to be a strange double life. What's more she is totally aware that once the race has started, her beautiful eyes make no difference whatsoever.

- Woman and rider – is it an advantage or a disadvantage?
- During the race when I pass a rider, I have the impression they try three times harder to get back their place than if I were a man. From now on in 250cc, there are two clearly defined goals: firstly, to win the race; then do all you can to beat the woman.

"I CAN'T STAND TO FAIL"

- Which is the real Katja Poensgen: a young girl who goes out to the disco or a rider who can be aggressive?
- In everyday life, I'm a real layabout. But when it comes to my sport, I'll do everything to succeed. At those times, even the most intense efforts are fun. You know, I hate failure. When I was little and I used to play board games with my father and sister, I would sometimes tip everything over if I lost. Sports soon became a therapy for me, an ideal solution for my character.

Identity Card

NAME: POENSGEN

FIRST NAME: KATJA

BORN ON 23 SEPTEMBER 1976 AT MINDELHEIM (GERMANY)

FIRST RACE: 1993.

FIRST GP: JAPAN 2001 (250).

CAREER

1993: ADAC 125 JUNIOR RACES IN GERMANY (SUZUKI)

1994: ADAC 125 JUNIOR RACES IN GERMANY (SUZUKI)

1995: WINNER OF THE ADAC 125 JUNIOR CUP IN GERMANY (SUZUKI)

1996: 10TH IN THE GERMAN 125 CHAMPIONSHIP (YAMAHA)

1997: GERMAN SUPERSPORT CHAMPIONSHIP (SUZUKI)

1998: EUROPE SUPERMONO CUP WINER, 63RD IN THE EUROPEAN SUPERSPORT CHAMPIONSHIP (SUZUKI)

1999: 68TH IN EUROPEAN SUPERSPORT CHAMPIONSHIP, 15TH IN THE EUROPEAN SUPERSTOCK CHAMPIONSHIP (SUZUKI)

2000: 6TH IN THE EUROPEAN SUPERSTOCK CHAMPIONSHIP (SUZUKI)

2001: 30TH IN THE 250 WORLD CHAMPIONSHIP (APRILIA/HONDA).

A rider and a woman: "When I climb aboard my racing bike I am 'a rider' full stop. However, when I put on my civilian clothes...."

- In theory, what are the disadvantages for a woman as opposed to a man in racing a motorcycle?

  - There are no major ones. However, I soon learned that I had to do some exercises to give me more strength in my forearms. Those muscles are not generally useful for a woman, but come naturally for a man.

- Your father is the Suzuki importer in Germany. What has been his influence?

  - Since I have been doing this, he is the only person never to have stood in my way. When I got the chance to come into GP riding a make he doesn't represent, he didn't hesitate. On the other hand, he's less happy with me posing in my underwear for certain magazines...

- What is your personal goal?

  - For the moment I am first and foremost a rider and secondly a woman. I have some sporting ambitions. If after three years I keep finding myself in 20th place with no sign of progress, I'll stop. But for the moment, there is no question of giving myself precise goals; it would be stupid after just one season in GP, to say: in four years' time I will be seventh in the World Championship.

The "Equipe de France": the right calculation

Randy de Puniet and Sylvain Guintoli in
Suzuka: the French are well represented in
250 cc GP racing.

An interesting concept and a well known
godfather: Luc Alphand on the starting grid.

It can be very tough starting out in GP racing
can it not Mr. Guintoli ?

Randy de Puniet, 13th in the World Championship in his debut 250 season, one qualifying place on the front row, regular success in timed practice. Sylvain Guintoli, 15th in the World Championship in the same category, for a beginner who was racing at the majority of tracks for the first time and who achieved a fine result in the tyre lottery that was the Dutch GP. A fine technical team is behind these unexpectedly regular performances – Jean-Claude Besse's Scrab team who has been joined this year by two talented technicians, Didier Langouët and former rider Christian Boudinot. There is also the concept, devised by Claude Michy, organiser of the French GP.

"The "Equipe de France" was created to enable French riders and French teams in the World Championship. The structure mounted by Jean-Claude Bresse with competent and efficient collaborators proved very satisfactory. Sylvain and Randy had fine machines throughout the season: Aprilias prepared and set up by Scrab Competition. Each member of the team always gave his best, which enabled Randy and Sylvain finish respectively 13th and 14th in the 250 World Championship. Both our riders also achieved some personal feats this season", explains Claude Michy.

- Claude, tell us about the basic idea behind this "Equipe de France" GP team.
  - *My company has a contract with Dorna to organise the French GP until 2006. Last October I tried to envisage a long-term plan. What did we have to offer the fans? A World Champion, Olivier Jacque, who had moved into 500 and one team - Tech3. At that stage of the close-season that was it. Which meant that OJ just needed to have an injury – which unfortunately happened during winter testing in Malaysia – and we'd have no-one else. And remember the French GP was undergoing a revival exactly because we had tried to attract a different kind of clientele who needed to be able to relate to the show.*

- So the next step was the agreement with the Scrab team, the technical structure managed by Jean-Claude Besse?
  - *The Federation was continuing its training programme with its "Equipe de France", but it was lacking the last piece in the puzzle which was a GP team. Scrab existed but didn't have the funding, so we had to join forces. This is what we did with a three-year deal between the Federation, the team and my company. We invested 300,000 dollars, the FFM contributed 80,000 dollars and we set off* to look for partners. *It was a simple calculation for me: as the organiser of the French GP, if I can expect to lose 2000 spectators because there are no French riders, then over eight years, I will have recouped the investment in the "Equipe de France".*

"Natural Choice"

- Why the choice of riders, Randy de Puniet and Sylvain Guintoli?
  - *It was a natural selection. Randy had made his GP debut with Scrab and Guintoli had come through the "Equipe de France". Since Jean-Claude Besse had good contacts with Aprilia, the puzzle was soon complete with the whole team soon based in Nogaro.*

- You are obviously aware that some of your riders were fairly critical during the season?
  - *It's a little bit of a reflection of today's youth who want results immediately. Everyone should remember that the greatest champions are those who work the most. I don't know much about riding and technical matters, but I do know that our bikes have often featured among the fastest in the category ... and that our riders were among the recordmen in terms of number of falls.*

- And what if you lose these two riders?
  - *Let's be clear: if next year one of our guys joins the Tech3 Team with Hervé Poncharal and the other finds himself on a better bike than this year, I'll say "Bingo". That would indicate that the two French riders have established themselves in GP and that there will be room for other young hopefuls. Today, a rider's job is like mountain climbing. You can't overcome the difficulty until you get to the top. If you stay in the middle that means you have lost.*

- Can we talk about the future?
  - *In 2002 Sylvain Guintoli will join a renowned 500cc team. Randy de Puniet will continue in 250 in the Safilo Oxydo team which this year entered the revelation of the season Roberto Rolfo. In 2002, The "Equipe de France" will bring in new riders. The decision concerning the choice of riders belongs to the FFM, Jean-Claude Besse and myself. A certain number of riders can hope to gain a place.*

A ray of sunshine for road racing in France: Sylvain Guintoli takes to the track in Brno.

Teams

HONDA DIGEST

Honda Nastro Azzuro

TEAM BASE: Via della Cecchignola 5/7, 00143 Rome (Italy)

TEAM MANAGER: Carlo Fiorani

RIDER

Valentino Rossi (16.2.1979)
- First GP: Malaysia, 1996 (125)
- 125 World Champion (1997)
- 250 World Champion (1999)
- 500 World Champion (2001)
- Number of GP victories: 39 (12/125; 14/250; 13/500)
- First GP victory: Czech Republic, 1996 (125)

ORGANIGRAMME

Consultant: Michael Doohan

Technical chief: Jeremy Burgess

Repsol YPF Honda

TEAM BASE: Wijngaardveld 1, 9300 Aalst (Belgium)

TEAM MANAGER: Shoji Tachikawa

RIDERS

Tohru Ukawa (18.5.1973)
- First GP: Japan, 1994 (250)
- Number of GP victories: 4 (250).
- First GP victory: France, 1999 (250)

Alex Crivillé (4.3.1970)
- First GP: Spain, 1987 (80)
- 125 World Champion (1989)
- 500 World Champion (1999)
- Number of GP victories: 20 (5/125; 15/500).
- First GP victory: Australia, 1989 (125)

ORGANIGRAMME

Consultant: Michael Doohan

Technical chiefs: Gilles Bigot (Alex Crivillé) and Trevor Morris (Tohru Ukawa).

West Honda Pons

TEAM BASE: : Poligono Industrial Sta. Rita, C/Acustica 16, 08755 Castellbisbali, Barcelona (Spain)

TEAM MANAGER: Sito Pons

RIDERS

Alexandre Barros (18.10.1970)
- First GP: Spain, 1986 (80)
- Number of GP victories: 4 (500)
- First GP victory: FIM (Jarama), 1993 (500)

Loris Capirossi (4.4.1973)
- First GP: Japan, 1990 (125)
- 125 World Champion (1990 and 1991)
- 250 World Champion (1998)
- Number of GP victories: 22 (8/125; 12/250; 2/500)
- First GP victory: Great Britain, 1990 (125)

ORGANIGRAMME

Racing director: Manuel Burillo

Technical chief: Antonio Cobas

Shell Advance Honda

TEAM BASE: Hardwick Racing LLC, Edifici Font 2-2, La Cortinada (Andorra)

TEAM MANAGER: Jeff Hardwick

RIDERS

Chris Walker (25.4.1972)
- First GP: Great Britain, 1995 (250 and 500)

Leon Haslam (31.5.1983)
- First GP: Great Britain, 1998 (125)

ORGANIGRAMME

Racing Director: Clyde Wolfenden.

Technical chiefs: Simon Bleasdale (Chris Walker) and Michael Shanley (Leon Haslam).

Two 100% Honda works teams had the 2001 NSR500. These were Honda Nastro Azzurro (Valentino Rossi) and Repsol YPF Honda (Alex Crivillé and Tohru Ukawa). From the Czech Republic GP onwards following loud complaints from Loris Capirossi's camp, the team West Honda Pons received supplementary help from the factory. At Shell Advance, Chris Walker began the season riding an NSR 4 cylinder, but the Briton never really settled and was shown the door. His young team-mate Leon Haslam inherited the V4, but he too soon decided to return to a far less complex V2.

9 Leon Haslam

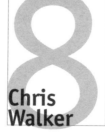

8 Chris Walker

46 Valentino Rossi

28 Alex Crivillé

11 Tohru Ukawa

65 Loris Capirossi

4 Alexandre Barros

Nastro Azzuro Honda

Repsol YPF Honda

West Honda Pons

Shell Advance Honda

HONDA DIGEST

14 Anthony West

12 Haruchika Aoki

21 Barry Veneman

ARIE MOLENAAR RACING

TEAM BASE: Panoven 20, 3401 RA Ijsselstein
(Netherlands)

TEAM MANAGER: Arie Molenaar

RIDERS

Haruchika Aoki (28.3.1976)
First GP: Australia, 1993 (125)
125 World Champion (1995 and 1996)
Number of GP victories: 9 (125)
First GP victory: Australia, 1995 (125)

ORGANIGRAMME

Research and development: Hans Spaan.

DEE CEE RACING TEAM

TEAM BASE: Westlandseweg 12, 2291 PG Wateringen
(Netherlands)

TEAM MANAGER: Jan Huberts.

RIDERS

Anthony West (17.7.1981)
First GP: Australia, 1998 (125)

Barry Veneman (22.3.1977)
First GP: Japon, 2001 (500)

ORGANIGRAMME

Chief executive: Martin Van Genderen.

Technical chief: Mar Schouten.

SABRE DIGEST

16 Johann Stigefelt

SABRE SPORT

TEAM BASE: Dunmow Road (A120), Felsted, Essex, CM6
3LF (Great Britain)

TEAM MANAGER: Keith Newnham.

RIDER

Johan Stigefelt (17.3.1976)
First GP: Rio, 1997 (250)

ORGANIGRAMME

Technical Chief: Stuart Nicholls.

Sabre Sport was formed in 1995 for the British
Superbike Championship. In 1999, the English
team made its debut in 250cc GP before moving
to 500 in 2000, firstly with the South African
Shane Norval. In 2001 Sabre entered an
evolved 1996 Yamaha engine mounted on a
ROC chassis.

PULSE DIGEST

24 Jason Vincent

68 Mark Willis

PULSE GP

TEAM BASE: 840, Chemin des Berles, Z.I. Perrusier,
83230 Bormes-les-Mimosas (France)

TEAM MANAGER: Dave Stewart.

RIDERS

Jason Vincent (20.2.1972)
First GP: Great Britain, 1996 (250)

Mark Willis (3.5.1976)
First GP: Australia, 1998 (500)

ORGANIGRAMME

Technical chiefs: Murray Aitken (Jason Vincent) and
Graeme Irvine (Mark Willis).

Dave Stewart who managed the New Zealand BSL
project, was taking a risk trying to convince potential
backers. His idea was to establish himself in the
category and then sell his place on when the
championship becomes MotoGP to a big make. On a
technical level, the team was based in France at Bormes-
les-Mimosas and had purchased the V4 MZ-Swissautos.
But with inadequate financing – no winter testing, a
very limited stock of spare parts – the Pulses never
worked properly. The project ground to a halt and even
disappeared before the end of the season.

Arie Molenaar Racing

Dee Cee Racing Team

Sabre Sport

Pulse GP

YAMAHA DIGEST

MARLBORO YAMAHA TEAM

TEAM BASE: Koolhovenlaan 101, 1119 NC Schipol-Rijk (Netherlands)

TEAM MANAGER: Geoff Crust

RIDERS

Massimiliano Biaggi (26.6.1971)

First GP: Europe, 1991 (250)

250 World Champion (1994, 1995, 1996 and 1997)

Number of GP victories: 37 (29/250; 8/500)

First GP victory: South Africa, 1992 (250)

Carlos Checa (15.10.1972)

First GP: Europe, 1993 (125)

Number of GP victories: 2 (500)

First GP victory: Catalunya, 1996 (500)

ORGANIGRAMME

Director: Hiroya Atsumi.

Technical chiefs: Fiorenzo Fanali (Massimiliano Biaggi) and Mike Webb (Carlos Checa).

GAULOISES YAMAHA TECH 3

TEAM BASE: 635, Chemin du Niel, 83230 Bormes-les-Mimosas (France)

TEAM MANAGER: Hervé Poncharal

RIDERS

Olivier Jacque (29.8.1973)

First GP: Australia, 1995 (250)

250 World Champion (2000)

Number of GP victories: 7 (250)

First GP victory: Brazil, 1996 (250)

Shinya Nakano (10.10.1977)

First GP: Japan, 1998 (250)

Number of GP victories: 6 (250)

First GP victory: Japan, 1999 (250)

ORGANIGRAMME

Technical chiefs: Guy Coulon (Olivier Jacque) and Bernard Martignac (Shinya Nakano).

Yamaha had increased the works YZRs in 2001 with the arrival in 500 of the 250 World Champion team (Tech3 with Olivier Jacque and Shinya Nakano) and the appointment of a second rider at Luis D'Antin. The 100% works Marlboro team was given priority (and in some cases exclusivity) for all the development parts. The factory placed its favourite rider, Norijuki Haga at Red Bull WCM.

3 Massimiliano Biaggi

7 Carlos Checa

19 Olivier Jacque

56 Shinya Nakano

YAMAHA DIGEST

Red Bull Yamaha WCM

TEAM BASE: Feldstrasse 8, 5204 Strasswalchen (Austria)

TEAM MANAGER: Bob Maclean

RIDERS

Garry McCoy (81.4.1972)

First GP: Australia, 1992 (125)

Number of GP victories: 5 (2/125; 3/500)

First GP victory: Malaysia, 1995 (125)

Noriyuki Haga (2.3.1975)

First GP : Japan, 1998 (500)

ORGANIGRAMME

Racing Director: Peter Clifford.

Technical chiefs: Hamish Jamieson (Garry McCoy) and Colin Davies (Noriyuki Haga).

Antena 3 Yamaha-D'Antin

TEAM BASE: Ramon y Cajal 25 (Pol. Ind. Gitesa), 28814 Daganzo/Madrid (Spain)

TEAM MANAGER: Luis D'Antin.

RIDERS

Norifumi Abe (7.9.1975)

First GP: Japan, 1994 (500)

Number of GP victories: 3 (500)

First GP victory: Japan, 1996 (500)

Jose Luis Cardoso (2.2.1975)

First GP: Spain, 1993 (125)

ORGANIGRAMME

Director: Joaquin Contreras

Technical chiefs: Kaneko Naoya (Norifumi Abe) and George Vukmanovich (who would not finish the season for Jose Luis Cardoso)

5
Garry McCoy

41
Noriyuki Haga

6
Norifumi Abe

10
Jose Luis Cardoso

Red Bull Yamaha WCM

Antena 3 Yamaha-D'Antin

MOTO

SUZUKI DIGEST

TELEFONICA MOVISTAR SUZUKI

TEAM BASE: Enterprise Way, Edenbridge, Kent, TN8 6EW

(Great Britain)

TEAM MANAGER: Garry Taylor

RIDERS

Kenny Roberts (25.7.1973)

First GP: United States, 1993 (250)

500 World Champion (2000)

Number of GP victories: 8 (500)

First GP victory: Malaysia, 1999 (500)

Manuel "Sete" Gibernau (15.12.1972)

First GP: Spain, 1992 (250)

Number of GP victories: 1

First GP victory: Valencia, 2001 (500)

ORGANIGRAMME

Racing Director: Sadayuki Inobe.

Technical Director: Warren Willing

Crew chiefs: Bob Toomey (Kenny Roberts) and Stuart Shenton (Manuel Gibernau).

The World Champion RGV 500 did not evolve much throughout the winter and from the very first pre-season testing, and even more so in the first GPs, Kenny Roberts had a tough job on his hands. The scenario became repetitive: the number 1 would spend the first few laps at the front before falling back in the closing stages. A demotivated Roberts was regularly beaten by his new team-mate, the Spaniard Manuel "Sete" Gibernau, who gave the team managed by Garry Taylor is one and only victory of the season in Valencia.

TELEFONICA MOVISTAR SUZUKI

1 Kenny Roberts

15 Manuel "Sete" Gibernau

PROTON DIGEST

PROTON TEAM KR

TEAM BASE: 419 Medina Road, Medina, Ohio 44256

(United States)

TEAM MANAGER: Chuck Aksland

RIDER

Jurgen van den Goorbergh (29.12.1969)

First GP: France, 1991 (250)

ORGANIGRAMME

Owner: Kenny Roberts

Technical chief: Nick Davis

The KR3 constructed in the workshops at Banbury has been renamed after Kenny Roberts' major partner, Proton Cars. Nothing revolutionary came about, but the KR3 continued to be a development laboratory and several new ideas were tried out during the season. Thanks to the talent of the new rider, Jurgen Van Den Goorbergh, the only 3 cylinder in the championship would go on to beat its previous times at all the circuits on the calendar and in some cases by a long margin.

17

Jurgen van den Goorbergh

PATON DIGEST

PATON GRAND PRIX-SLOVNAFT

TEAM BASE: Via Fratelli Lumiere 16/18, 20019 Settimo Milanese (Italy)

TEAM MANAGER: Roberto Pattoni

RIDER

Vladimir Castka (6.10.1975)

First GP: Czech Republic, 1995 (125)

ORGANIGRAMME

President: Alessandro Fassi

Technical chief: Andrea Realini

The PG500R entered by Roberto Pattoni who took up the family business upon the death of his father, received a brand new chassis from the Castiglioni brothers, the owners of Cagiva. The European 500 did not have a fixed contract with Dorna, and appeared on some occasions punctuated by numerous tumbles from a rider whose international experience was limited to the European 250 championship.

26

Vladimir Castka

25

Shaun Geronimi

HONDA DIGEST

TELEFONICA MOVISTAR HONDA

TEAM BASE: Gresini Racing SRL, Via Fra Domenico Paganelli 8, 48018 Faenza (Italy)

TEAM MANAGER: Fausto Gresini.

RIDERS

Daijiro Katoh (4.7.1976)

First GP: Japan, 1996 (250)

250 World Champion (2001)

Number of GP victories: 17 (250)

First GP victory: Japan, 1997 (250)

Emilio Alzamora (22.5.1973)

First GP: Malaysia, 1994 (125)

125 World Champion (1999)

Number of GP victories: 4 (125)

First GP victory: Argentina, 1995 (125)

ORGANIGRAMME

General Manager: Angel Nieto.

Technical Director: Fabrizio Cecchini.

FOMMA

TEAM BASE: CE BA Corse Srl, Via Brodolini 55/2, 61025 Montelabbate, Pesaro (Italy)

TEAM MANAGER: Cirano Mularoni.

RIDER

David Checa (20.4.1980)

First GP: South Africa, 2000 (250)

ORGANIGRAMME

Technical director: Giancarlo Cecchini.

SHELL ADVANCE TEAM

TEAM BASE: Team Hardwick Racing LLC, Edifici Font 2-2, La Cortinada (Andorra)

TEAM MANAGER: Jeff Hardwick

RIDER

Katja Poensgen (23.9.1976)

First GP: Japan, 2001 (250)

Fausto Gresini's team had the exclusivity for the NSR250s. Alongside Daijiro Katoh was Spaniard Emilio Alzamora, who was making another attempt in 250 after his disastrous 1997 season. Katoh dominated the season while Alzamora's performances improved. David Checa (at Fomma) then Katja Poensgen after her transfer at the end of the Summer (to Shell Advance), had kit 250 RSs with a TSR chassis.

74 Daijiro Katoh

7 Emilio Alzamora

42 David Checa

14 Katja Poensgen

TELEFONICA MOVISTAR HONDA

FOMMA

SHELL ADVANCE TEAM

APRILIA DIGEST

MS Aprilia Racing

TEAM BASE: Racing Service Competition, Strada la Ciarulla 72, 47899 Serravalle (San Marino).

TEAM MANAGER: Jan Witteveen

RIDERS

Marco Melandri (7.8.1982)
First GP: Czech Republic, 1997 (125)
Number of GP victories: 8 (7/125; 1/250)
First GP victory: Netherlands, 1998 (125)

Tetsuya Harada (14.6.1970)
First GP: Japan, 1990 (250)
250 World Champion (1993)
Number of GP victories: 17 (250)
First GP victory: Australia, 1993 (250)

ORGANIGRAMME

President: Ivano Beggio.

Crew chiefs: Rossano Brazzi (Marco Melandri) et Giovanni Sandi (Tetsuya Harada).

5 Marco Melandri

Safilo Oxydo Race

TEAM BASE: Worldwide Communication Sàrl, Via Borrohini 3, 6900 Lugano (Switzerland)

TEAM MANAGER: Fiorenzo Caponera.

RIDER

Roberto Rolfo (23.3.1980)
First GP: Italy, 1996 (250)

ORGANIGRAMME

President: Fiorenzo Caponera

Crew chief: Tommaso Quadrini

Aprilia Grand Prix

TEAM BASE: Racing Service Competition, Strada la Ciarulla 72, 47899 Serravalle (San Marino).

TEAM MANAGER: Jan Witteveen

RIDERS

Riccardo Chiarello (4.5.1982)
First GP: Imola, 1998 (125)

Jeremy McWilliams (4.4.1964)
First GP: Australia, 1993 (500)
Number of GP victories: 1
First GP victory: Netherlands, 2001 (250)

Klaus Nöhles (12.12.1976)
First GP: Germany, 1997 (125)

Aprilia played the numbers game. 100% works RSWs were entered by the in-house team for Marco Melandri and Tetsuya Harada, while Klaus Nöhles had the status of works rider but in a German structure managed by Dieter Stappert. Locatelli was riding in the colours of Eros Ramazzotti. With financial problems weighing down on Jeremy McWilliams, the Briton was soon welcomed into Stappert's team to take the pressure off Nöhles. But it was in vain: in Valencia, the young German was shown the door. From the start of the season, semi-works riders such as Alfonso "Fonsi" Gonzales-Nieto at Jorge Martinez, Randy de Puniet at Scrab and Roberto Rolfo at Safilo filled the role of rank outsiders.

11 Riccardo Chiarello

12 Klaus Nöhles

44 Roberto Rolfo

34 Tetsuya Harada

99 Jeremy McWilliams

MS Aprilia Racing

Safilo Oxydo Race

Aprilia Grand Prix

Valencia Circuit-Aspar Team

TEAM BASE: Team Aspar, Poligono Industrial No 1, Avenida de los Deportes Travesia, 46600 Alzira/Valencia (Spain)

TEAM MANAGER: Jorge "Aspar" Martinez

RIDERS

Alex Debon (1.3.1976)
First GP: Madrid, 1998 (250)

Alfonso "Fonsi" Gonzales-Nieto (2.12.1978)
First GP : Spain, 1997 (125)

ORGANIGRAMME

Technical Director: Sergio Bonaldo.

MS Eros Ramazzotti Racing

TEAM BASE: Team Battaini, Via Alfieri 102, 50013 Campi Bisenzio (Italie).

TEAM MANAGER: Omar Nicola

RIDERS

Roberto Locatelli (5.7.1974)
First GP: Italy, 1994 (125)
125 World Champion (2000)
Number of GP victories: 7 (125)
First GP victory: France, 1999 (125)

Franco Battaini (22.7.1972)
First GP: Italy, 1996 (250)

ORGANIGRAMME

Technical Director: Mauro Noccioli.
Crew chief: Massimo Branchini.

Equipe de France-Scrab GP

TEAM BASE: Scrab Compétition, Avenue des Sports, 32110 Nogaro (France)

TEAM MANAGER: Jean-Claude Besse

RIDERS

Sylvain Guintoli (24.6.1982)
First GP: France, 2000 (250)

Randy de Puniet (14.2.1981)
First GP: France, 1998 (125)

ORGANIGRAMME

Technical Director: Bernard Foures.
Crew chiefs: Didier Langouët (Sylvain Guintoli) and Christian Boudinot (Randy de Puniet).

50 Sylvain Guintoli

6 Alex Debon

81 Randy de Puniet

15 Roberto Locatelli

10 Alfonso Gonzales-Nieto

21 Franco Battaini

MS Eros Ramazzotti Racing

Valencia Circuit-Aspar Team

Equipe de France-Scrab GP

APRILIA DIGEST

Campetella Racing

TEAM BASE: Via De Gasperi 74, 62010 Montecassiano (Italy)

TEAM MANAGER: Eros Braconi.

RIDERS

Luca Boscoscuro (27.12.1971)
First GP: Italy, 1995 (250)

Lorenzo Lanzi (26.10.1981)
First GP: Italy, 1999 (125)

ORGANIGRAMME

President: Caterina Dezi.

Crew chiefs: Aligi Deganello (Luca Boscoscuro) and Gianluca Montanari (Lorenzo Lanzi).

Racing Factory

TEAM BASE: Racing Factory GmbH, Un der Mark 99, 44869 Bochum Eppendorf (Germany)

TEAM MANAGER: Dieter Theis

RIDER

Alexander Hofmann (25.5.1980)
First GP: Germany, 1997 (125)

ORGANIGRAMME

Technical Director: Lucas Schmidt.

37 Luca Boscoscuro

57 Lorenzo Lanzi

66 Alexander Hofmann

RACING FACTORY

CAMPETELLA RACING

YAMAHA DIGEST

PETRONAS SPRINTA YAMAHA TVK

TEAM BASE: TVK Motorsports SL, Solicrup s/n Nave 6-c, 08800 Vilanova i la Geltru (Spain)

TEAM MANAGER: Janey Looi.

RIDERS

Naoki Matsudo (25.7.1973)
First GP: Japan, 1997 (250)

Shahrol Yuzy (23.1.1976)
First GP : Malaysia, 1996 (250)

ORGANIGRAMME

President: Tong Yew Kuan

Technical chiefs: Emanuele Martinelli (Naoki Matsudo) and Gabrielle Fontanelli (Shahrol Yuzy).

ANTENA 3 YAMAHA-D'ANTIN

TEAM BASE: Ramon y Cajal 25, Poligono Ind. Gitesa, 28814 Daganzo/Madrid (Spain)

TEAM MANAGER: Luis D'Antin

RIDERS

David De Gea (9.12.1977)
First GP: Catalunya, 1995 (125)

Julien Allemand (23.3.1977)
First GP: France, 1998 (250)

YAMAHA KURZ

TEAM BASE: Geiselroter Heidle 1, 73494 Rosenberg (Germany)

TEAM MANAGER: Hermann Kurz

RIDERS

Sebastian Porto (12.9.1978)
First GP: Argentina, 1994 (125)

Cesar Barros (1.5.1973)
First GP: Rio, 1997 (125)

ORGANIGRAMME

Racing Director: Manfred Geissler.

Technical Director: Konrad Hefele.

The Petronas team had inherited the YZR250s which totally dominated the 2000 season in the hands of Olivier Jacque and Shinya Nakano. The German Kurz and the Spaniard D'Antin had bikes in kit form. Frenchman Julien Allemand began the season but didn't finish because of a financial misunderstanding with Luis D'Antin.

9 Sebastian Porto

8 Naoki Matsudo

23 Cesar Barros

19 Julien Allemand

18 Shahrol Yuzy

22 David De Gea

PETRONAS SPRINTA YAMAHA TVK

ANTENA 3 YAMAHA-D'ANTIN

YAMAHA KURZ

motogrand

125cc

prix.com

GILERA DIGEST

GILERA RACING

TEAM BASE: Corso Sempione 43, 20145 Milano (Italy)

TEAM MANAGER: Giampiero Sacchi

RIDER

Manuel Poggiali (14.2.1983)

First GP: Imola 1998 (125)

125 World Champion (2001)

Number of GP victories: 3 (125)

First GP victory: France, 2001 (125)

ORGANIGRAMME

President: Claudio Verna

Technical Director: Harald Bartol

The Piaggio group which owns the mythical Gilera make also purchased the Spanish constructor Derbi just before the season started. So it was a good occasion to make a grand appearance in racing with Poggiali's Gilera and the Derbis ridden by Ui and Pablo Niando as twin sisters. The bike was built by Austrian Harald Bartol and soon became the reference in the category.

Manuel Poggiali

DERBI DIGEST

DERBI LM

TEAM BASE: La Barca 5-7, 08107 Martorelles (Spain)

TEAM MANAGER: Giampiero Sacchi

RIDERS

Pablo Nieto (4.6.1980)

First GP: Catalunya, 1998 (125)

Youichi Ui (27.11.1972)

First GP: Japan, 1995 (125)

Number of GP victories: 11 (125)

First GP victory: Japan, 2000 (125)

ORGANIGRAMME

President: Emilio Diaz-Caneja

Team manager: Giampiero Sacchi

Technical Director: Harald Bartol

Technical crew chief: Mario Galeotti

Youichi Ui

Pablo Nieto

Queen of the small cylinders twenty years ago, the Derbi make was back in business last year (second place overall for Youichi Ui). In 2001, the " little red bullands " as they are known in Spain would once again be at the forefront with the Japanese Ui who won six of the sixteen grand prix, including the last four in a row. But Ui was still beaten to the title by his semi-team-mate, Manuel Poggiali.

GILERA RACING

DERBI LM

TELEFONICA MOVISTAR JUNIOR

TEAM BASE: Josep Trueta 4-2, 08970 Sant Joan
Despi/Barcelone (Spain)

TEAM MANAGER: Alberto Puig

RIDERS

Antonio "Toni" Elias (26.3.1983)
First GP: Spain, 1999 (125)
Number of GP victories: 2 (125)
First GP Victory : Netherlands, 2001 (125)

Joan Olive (22.11.1984)
First GP: Japan, 2001 (125)

Daniel Pedrosa (29.9.1985)
First GP: Japan, 2001 (125)

ORGANIGRAMME

Technical Director: Paolo Cordioli.

Chief mechanics: Francesco Nicosia (Antonio Elias),
Daniele Morellato (Joan Olive) and Fabrizio Brutti
(Daniel Pedrosa).

LIÉGEOIS COMPÉTITION

TEAM BASE: 30, rue de la Tour, 4458 Fexhe-Slins
(Belgium)

TEAM MANAGER: Olivier Liégeois

PILOTES

Masao Azuma (24.3.1971)
First GP: Japan, 1996 (125)
Number of GP victories: 9 (125)
First GP Victory: Australia, 1998 (125)

Philipp Hafenegger (21.6.1983)
First GP: Germany, 1999 (125)

ORGANIGRAMME

Administrative Director: Marie Paule Willems.

Chief mechanic: Gérard Petit.

TECHNICAL SPORTS RACING

TEAM BASE: Unit 3, Avant Business Centre, 24 First
Avenue, Denbigh West, Milton Keynes,
Bucks MK1 1DL (Great Britain)

TEAM MANAGER: Dieter Toru Furuyama

RIDER

Noboru Ueda (23.7.1967)
First GP: Japan, 1991 (125)
Number of GP victories: 13 (125)
First GP Victory: Japan, 1991 (125)

ORGANIGRAMME

President: Masakazu Fujii.

Chief mechanic: Hideki Omori.

There are no real works Hondas in 125cc
anymore, but several teams have A kits at their
disposal. The most renowned tuners are still
in evidence, such as Belgian Olivier Liégeois
and Italian Massimo Matteoni. There was a
remarkable randurn by Noboru Ueda to FCC,
who thus joined a totally Japanese team.

4 Masao Azuma

14 Phillip Hafenegger

5 Noboru Ueda

24 Antonio "Toni" Elias

25 Joan Olive

26 Daniel Pedrosa

Telefonica Movistar Junior

Liégeois Compétition

Technical Sport Racing

FOMMA

TEAM BASE: CE BA Corse Srl, Via Brodolini 55/2, 61025

Montelabbate/Pesaro (Italy)

TEAM MANAGER: Cirano Mularoni

RIDER

Arnaud Vincent (30.11.1974)

First GP: France, 1996 (125)

Number of GP victories: 2 (125)

First GP Victory : Catalunya, 1999 (125)

ORGANIGRAMME

Technical Director: Giancarlo Cecchini

AXO RACING TEAM

TEAM BASE: Team Semprucci Srl, Via Villagrande 224,

61024 Mombaroccio/Pesaro (Italy)

TEAM MANAGER: Giorgio Semprucci.

RIDERS

Mirko Giansanti (14.9.1976)

First GP: Italy, 1996 (125)

Eric Bataille (18.4.1981)

First GP: Catalunya, 2000 (125)

ORGANIGRAMME

President: Stefano Colalelli

Technical Director: Daniele Romagnoli

Chief mechanics: Angeli Angelo (Mirko Giansanti)
and Maurizio Massimiani (Eric Bataille).

MATTEONI RACING

TEAM BASE: Via Larga 22, Zona artigianale, 47843

Misano Adriatico (Italy)

TEAM MANAGER: Massimo Matteoni

RIDERS

Alex de Angelis (26.2.1984)

First GP: Imola, 1999 (125)

Jaroslav Hules (2.7.1974)

First GP: Czech Republic, 1993 (125)

ORGANIGRAMME

Chief mechanics: Roberto Bava (Alex de Angelis)
and Massimo Matteoni (Jaroslav Hules).

6 Mirko Giansanti

15 Alex de Angelis

21 Arnaud Vincent

34 Eric Bataille

39 Jaroslav Hules

Fomma

AXO Racing Team

Matteoni Racing

Team Viceroy

TEAM BASE: Dr. Esquerdo 165, 28007 Madrid (Spain)

TEAM MANAGER: Cirano Mularoni

RIDER

Angel Nieto Junior (19.11.76)

First GP: Czech Republic, 1995 (125)

ORGANIGRAMME

Technical Director: Giancarlo Cecchini.

Budweiser Budvar Hanusch

TEAM BASE: J. Hanus, Ricarda-Huchstrasse 44a, 90471
Nürnberg (Germany)

TEAM MANAGER: Jaroslav Hanus

RIDER

Jakub Smrz (7.4.1983)

First GP: Czech Republic, 1998 (125)

ORGANIGRAMME

Technical Director: Manfred Wittenborn

Racing Service

TEAM BASE: Via Statale 467, 42013 Casalgrande (Italy)

TEAM MANAGER: Gabriele Debbia

RIDERS

Marco Petrini (2.12.1981)

First GP: Italy, 1999 (125)

Gabor Talmacsi (28.5.1981)

First GP: Czech Republic, 1997 (125)

ORGANIGRAMME

Technical Director: Tiziano Altabella

Chief mechanics: Massimo Corti (Marco Petrini) and
Alberto Iotti (Gabor Talmacsi).

PEV-Spalt-Moto ADA C Sachsen

TEAM BASE: Striesener Strasse 37, 01307 Dresden
(Germany)

TEAM MANAGER: Thomas Reister

RIDER

Jarno Müller (6.1.1978)

First GP: Germany, 1999 (125)

ORGANIGRAMME

Presidents: Rolf et Lutz Uhlig

Technical chief: Stefan Kurfiss

10 Jarno Müller

18 Jakub Smrz

27 Marco Petrini

28 Gabor Talmacsi

29 Angel Nieto Junior

APRILIA DIGEST

MS Aprilia LCR

TEAM BASE: Gildo Pastor Centre, 7 rue du Gabian, 98000 Monaco

TEAM MANAGER: Lucio Cecchinello

RIDERS

Lucio Cecchinello (21.10.1969)

Lucio Cecchinello (21.10.1969)

First GP: Australia, 1993 (125)

Number of GP victories: 2 (125)

First GP Victory: Madrid, 1998 (125)

Raul Jara (17.4.1980)

First GP: Japan, 2001 (125)

ORGANIGRAMME

Technical Director: Sergio Bonaldo.

LAE-UGT 3000

TEAM BASE: SYN Srl, Via del Consorzio 10, 60015 Falconara/Ancona (Italy)

TEAM MANAGER: Giordano Ceigioni

RIDERS

Steve Jenkner (31.5.1976)

First GP: Germany, 1996 (125)

Gino Borsoi (11.3.1974)

First GP: Italy, 1996 (125)

ORGANIGRAMME

Technical Director: Andrea Orlandi

Chief mechanics: Rolando Zanni (Steve Jenkner) and Marco Agostini (Gino Borsoi).

Aprilia had achieved " the " coup of the year in enticing Lucio Cecchinello, rider and team manager rolled into one, away from the Honda fold to join the Noale make. A second team based in Italy is made up of Steve Jenkner and Gino Borsoi – who would even lead the World Championship for a few days -, the team Fontana (with Massimiliano Sabbatani, the jockey) remained faithful to Aprilia. Simone Sanna had a kit at Safilo.

9 Lucio Cecchinello

17 Steve Jenkner

12 Raul Jara

23 Gino Borsoi

MS APRILIA LCR

LAE-UGT 3000

APRILIA DIGEST

SAFILO OXYDO RACE

TEAM BASE: Worldwide Communication Sàrl, Via Borromini 3, 6900 Lugano (Switzerland)

TEAM MANAGER: Fiorenzo Caponera

RIDER

Simone Sanna (16.3.1978)

First GP: Italy, 1997

Number of GP victories: 3 (125)

First GP Victory: Catalunya, 2000 (125)

ORGANIGRAMME

Technical Director: Pietro Caprara

Chief mechanic: Giancarlo Noe

BOSSINI FONTANA RACING

TEAM BASE: Fontana Racing, Via Cavour 33, 46043 Castglione delle Stiviere/Mantova (Italy)

TEAM MANAGER: Italo Fontana

RIDERS

Massimiliano Sabbatani (4.8.1975)

First GP: Imola, 1998 (125)

Gaspare Caffiero (23.5.1976)

First GP: Italy, 1999 (125)

ORGANIGRAMME

Chief mechanics: Claudio Maciotta (Massimiliano Sabbatani) and Guglielmo Pieretto (Gaspare Caffiero).

VALENCIA CIRCUIT – ASPAR TEAM

TEAM BASE: Poligono Industrial no 2, Avenida de los Deportes Travesia, 46600 Alzira/Valencia (Spain)

TEAM MANAGER: Jorge Martinez

RIDER

Angel Rodriguez (20.5.1985)

First GP: Catalunya, 2000 (125)

ORGANIGRAMME

Technical Director: Sergio Bonaldo.

11 Massimiliano Sabbatani

16 Simone Sanna

20 Gaspare Caffiero

30 Angel Rodriguez

SAFILO OXYDO RACE

BOSSINI FONTANA RACING

ITALJET  DIGEST

ITALJET RACING TEAM

TEAM BASE: 4th Floor, 50 Hans Crescent, Knightbridge, London SW1X 0NB (Great Britain)

TEAM MANAGER: Massimo Broccoli

RIDERS

Stefano Perugini (10.9.1974)

First GP: Italy, 1993 (125)

Number of GP victories: 3 (125)

First GP Victory: Malaysia, 1996 (125)

Gianluigi Scalvini (10.4.1971)

First GP: Italy, 1993 (125)

Number of GP victories: 2 (125)

First GP Victory: Valencia, 1999 (125)

ORGANIGRAMME

Administrative Director: Marco Tresoldi

Research and Development: Jörg Möller.

After a first GP season of discovery, the Italynne Italjand make came back in force with two renowned riders, former GP winners, including Stefano Perugini who had taken a sabbatical in 2000. The engine was still developed by Jörg Möller and Massimo Broccoli was managed the team which had some ups (at the start of the season) and then some downs.

ITALJET RACING TEAM

7 Stefano Perugini

8 Gianluigi Scalvini

...and the other

championships...

Superbike World Championship

March 11th - Spain - Valencia

Race I:

1. T. Corser (AUS, Aprilia), 37'17"253 (148.224 km/h); 2. T. Bayliss (AUS, Ducati), 3"609; 3. B. Bostrom (USA, Ducati), 3"695; 4. R. Laconi (F, Aprilia), 6"680; 5. G. Lavilla (E, Ducati), 11"570; 6. C. Edwards (USA, Honda), 22"708; 7. P. Chili (I, Suzuki), 25"319; 8. A. Yanagawa (J, Kawasaki), 25"554; 9. H. Izutsu (J, Kawasaki), 29"739; 10. S. Chambon (F, Suzuki), 53"040; 11. S. Martin (AUS, Ducati), 56"667; 12. L. Pedercini (I, Ducati), 1'00"769; 13. M. Borciani (I, Ducati), 1'00"771; 14. J.-B. Borja (E, Yamaha), 1'01"797; 15. J. Rodriguez (E, Honda), 1'21"897. 20 finishers.

Fastest lap:

Corser (AUS, Aprilia), 1'36"128 (149.988 km/h).

Race II:

1. T. Corser (AUS, Aprilia), 37'15"171 (148.362 km/h); 2. T. Bayliss (AUS, Ducati), 5"122; 3. G. Lavilla (E, Ducati), 9"307; 4. C. Edwards (USA, Honda), 19"271; 5. N. Hodgson (GB, Ducati), 23"513; 6. A. Yanagawa (J, Kawasaki), 24"543; 7. P. Chili (I, Suzuki), 31"243; 8. R. Xaus (E, Ducati), 36"284; 9. J. Toseland (GB, Ducati), 46"004; 10. S. Chambon (F, Suzuki), 47"521; 11. M. Borciani (I, Ducati), 48"116; 12. R. Ulm (A, Ducati), 50"226; 13. B. Parkes (AUS, Ducati), 51"699; 14. J.-B. Borja (E, Yamaha), 57"828; 15. L. Pedercini (I, Ducati), 1'13"812. 22 finishers.

Fastest lap:

Corser (AUS, Aprilia), 1'36"424 (149.365 km/h).

April 1st - South Africa - Kyalami

Race I:

1. C. Edwards (USA, Honda), 43'17"222 (147.723 km/h); 2. T. Bayliss (AUS, Ducati), 1"848; 3. T. Corser (AUS, Aprilia), 4"156; 4. B. Bostrom (USA, Ducati), 9"768; 5. A. Yanagawa (J, Kawasaki), 13"506; 6. P. Chili (I, Suzuki), 32"699; 7. G. Lavilla (E, Kawasaki), 35"252; 8. R. Laconi (F, Aprilia), 35"513; 9. R. Xaus (E, Ducati), 41"956; 10. S. Chambon (F, Suzuki), 49"721; 11. G. Bussei (I, Ducati), 51"503; 12. B. Parkes (AUS, Ducati), 53"418; 13. R. Ulm (A, Ducati), 1'04"241; 14. J. Toseland (GB, Ducati), 1'17"800; 15. M. Borciani (I, Ducati), 1'18"148. 24 finishers.

Fastest lap:

C. Edwards (USA, Honda), 1'43"101 (148.852 km/h).

Race II:

1. B. Bostrom (USA, Ducati), 43'13"513 (147.934 km/h); 2. T. Bayliss (AUS, Ducati), 4"305; 3. T. Corser (AUS, Aprilia), 12"551; 4. N. Hodgson (GB, Ducati), 17"340; 5. R. Xaus (E, Ducati), 18"234; 6. R. Laconi (F, Aprilia), 18"832; 7. G. Lavilla (E, Kawasaki), 32"113; 8. P. Chili (I, Suzuki), 38"828; 9. G. Bussei (I, Ducati), 43"682; 10. S. Chambon (F, Suzuki), 48"876; 11. B. Parkes (AUS, Ducati), 1'02"689; 12. R. Ulm (A, Ducati), 1'10"353; 13. M. Malatesta (I, Kawasaki), 1'14"585; 14. L. Pedercini (I, Ducati), 1'16"396; 15. B. Stey (F, Honda), 1'19"116. 17 finishers.

Fastest lap:

B. Bostrom (USA, Ducati), 1'42"928 (149.102 km/h).

April 22nd - Australia - Phillip Island

Race I:

1. C. Edwards (USA, Honda), 39'58"665 (146.767 km/h); 2. T. Okada (J, Honda), 4"455; 3. T. Bayliss (AUS, Ducati), 22"884; 4. A. Yanagawa (J, Kawasaki), 49"731; 5. B. Parkes (AUS, Ducati), 1'17"183; 6. T. Corser (AUS, Aprilia), 1'17"998; 7. P. Chili (I, Suzuki), 1'38"610; 8. S. Chambon (F, Suzuki), 1'39"639; 9. R. Ulm (A, Ducati), 1 lap; 10. M. Craggill (AUS, Ducati); 11. N. Hodgson (GB, Ducati); 12. S. Martin (AUS, Ducati); 13. A. Maxwell (AUS, Kawasaki); 14. J. Toseland (GB, Ducati); 15. J. Mrkyvka (CZ, Ducati). 15 finishers.

Fastest lap:

R. Xaus (E, Ducati), 1'46"456 (150.316 km/h).

Race II:

Cancelled.

April 29th - Japan - Sugo

Race I:

1. M. Tamada (J, Honda), 37'45"090 (148.484 km/h); 2. T. Corser (AUS, Aprilia), 4"090; 3. H. Izutsu (J, Kawasaki), 7"668; 4. S. Itoh (J, Honda), 12"117; 5. A. Ryo (J, Suzuki), 12"431; 6. G. Lavilla (E, Kawasaki), 18"679; 7. N. Hodgson (GB, Ducati), 19"091; 8. P. Chili (I, Suzuki), 19"244; 9. B. Bostrom (USA, Ducati), 25"008; 10. W. Yoshikawa (J, Yamaha), 25"307; 11. J. Toseland (GB, Ducati), 36"006; 12. C. Edwards (USA, Honda), 38"281; 13. T. Bayliss (AUS, Ducati), 39"485; 14. R. Laconi (F, Aprilia), 40"355; 15. S. Chambon (F, Suzuki), 42"331. 27 finishers.

Fastest lap:

M. Tamada (J, Honda), 1'29"624 (150.107 km/h).

Race II:

1. M. Tamada (J, Honda), 37'43"033 (148.619 km/h); 2. H. Izutsu (J, Kawasaki), 3"122; 3. T. Serizawa (J, Kawasaki), 4"303; 4. B. Bostrom (USA, Ducati), 5"988; 5. N. Hodgson (GB, Ducati), 9"022; 6. T. Corser (AUS, Aprilia), 11"788; 7. A. Ryo (J, Suzuki), 17"504; 8. P. Chili (I, Suzuki), 17"810; 9. S. Itoh (J, Honda), 19"088; 10. Y. Kagayama (J, Suzuki), 19"234; 11. A. Yanagawa (J, Kawasaki), 23"662; 12. T. Okada (J, Honda), 34"147; 13. C. Edwards (USA, Honda), 34"768; 14. R. Laconi (F, Aprilia), 35"043; 15. T. Bayliss (AUS, Ducati), 39"648. 28 finishers.

Fastest lap:

M. Tamada (J, Honda), 1'29"522 (150.278 km/h).

May 13th - Italy - Monza

Race I:

1. T. Bayliss (AUS, Ducati), 32'55"293 (190.041 km/h); 2. C. Edwards (USA, Honda), 0'066; 3. A. Yanagawa (J, Kawasaki), 16"559; 4. G. Lavilla (E, Kawasaki), 16"623; 5. R. Laconi (F, Aprilia), 16"800; 6. S. Chambon (F, Suzuki), 33"870; 7. L. Pedercini (I, Ducati), 45"666; 8. G. Bussei (I, Ducati), 49"191; 9. M. Sanchini (I, Ducati), 49"252; 10. M. Borciani (I, Ducati), 52"204; 11. B. Stey (F, Honda), 53"590; 12. A. Gramigni (I, Yamaha), 1'01"097; 13. J.-B. Borja (E, Yamaha), 1'06"563; 14. P. Chili (I, Suzuki), 1'07"595; 15. L. Holon (F, Kawasaki), 1'28"200. 16 finishers.

Fastest lap:

C. Edwards (USA, Honda), 1'48"913 (191.481 km/h).

Race II:

1. T. Bayliss (AUS, Ducati), 32'57"108 (189.969 km/h); 2. C. Edwards (USA, Honda), 3"310; 3. A. Yanagawa (J, Kawasaki), 8"374; 4. T. Okada (J, Honda), 8"597; 5. P. Chili (I, Suzuki), 9"186; 6. R. Xaus (E, Ducati), 18"322; 7. N. Hodgson (GB, Ducati), 19"590; 8. R. Laconi (F, Aprilia), 20"331; 9. S. Chambon (F, Suzuki), 34"515; 10. A. Gramigni (I, Yamaha), 43"389; 11. G. Bussei (I, Ducati), 46"833; 12. R. Ulm (A, Ducati), 49"212; 13. L. Pedercini (I, Ducati), 52"838; 14. S. Martin (AUS, Ducati), 55"190; 15. M. Sanchini (I, Ducati), 55"544. 18 finishers.

Fastest lap:

T. Bayliss (AUS, Ducati), 1'48"942 (191.426 km/h).

May 27th - Great Britain - Donington

Race I:

1. N. Hodgson (GB, Ducati), 39'46"490 (151.717 km/h); 2. P. Chili (I, Suzuki), 2"692; 3. S. Hislop (GB, Ducati), 2"830; 4. T. Okada (J, Honda), 4"018; 5. C. Edwards (USA, Honda), 4"641; 6. B. Bostrom (USA, Ducati), 5"393; 7. R. Xaus (E, Ducati), 12"070; 8. J. Toseland (GB, Ducati), 20"773; 9. S. Chambon (F, Suzuki), 20"975; 10. G. Lavilla (E, Kawasaki), 24"616; 11. T. Corser (AUS, Aprilia), 24"951; 12. R. Laconi (F, Aprilia), 25"170; 13. T. Bayliss (AUS, Ducati), 27"600; 14. A. Yanagawa (J, Kawasaki), 40"585; 15. M. Craggill (AUS, Ducati), 45"330. 22 finishers.

Fastest lap:

S. Hislop (GB, Ducati), 1'34"336 (153.524 km/h).

Race II:

1. P. Chili (I, Suzuki), 39'30"374 (152.748 km/h); 2. N. Hodgson (GB, Ducati), 0"125; 3. T. Corser (AUS, Aprilia), 0"556; 4. B. Bostrom (USA, Ducati), 7"414; 5. J. Reynolds (GB, Ducati), 9"368; 6. C. Edwards (USA, Honda), 11"718; 7. T. Okada (J, Honda), 11"872; 8. A. Yanagawa (J, Kawasaki), 13"053; 9. T. Bayliss (AUS, Ducati), 16"536; 10. R. Xaus (E, Ducati), 18"237; 11. R. Laconi (F, Aprilia), 18"617; 12. S. Chambon (F, Suzuki), 19"467; 13. Lavilla (E, Kawasaki), 19"653; 14. B. Parkes (AUS, Ducati), 40"619; 15. G. Bussei (I, Ducati), 48"451. 23 finishers.

Fastest lap:

P. Chili (I, Suzuki), 1'34"055 (153.982 km/h).

June 10th - Germany - Lausitz

Race I:

1. C. Edwards (USA, Honda), 38'47"683 (151.714 km/h); 2. T. Bayliss (AUS, Ducati), 0"663; 3. T. Okada (J, Honda), 2"810; 4. P. Chili (I, Suzuki), 19"777; 5. T. Corser (AUS, Aprilia), 20"618; 6. G. Lavilla (E, Kawasaki), 22"821; 7. R. Laconi (F, Aprilia), 26"277; 8. N. Hodgson (GB, Ducati), 28"008; 9. H. Izutsu (J, Kawasaki), 30"684; 10. S. Chambon (F, Suzuki), 31"029; 11. B. Bostrom (USA, Ducati), 31"653; 12. A. Yanagawa (J, Kawasaki), 42"547; 13. M. Craggill (AUS, Ducati), 52"542; 14. B. Parkes (AUS, Ducati), 52"744; 15. S. Martin (AUS, Ducati), 54"040. 23 finishers.

Fastest lap:

T. Bayliss (AUS, Ducati), 1'40"599 (152.626 km/h).

Race II:

1. T. Bayliss (AUS, Ducati), 45'57"655 (133.627 km/h); 2. N. Hodgson (GB, Ducati), 0"229; 3. C. Edwards (USA, Honda), 22"922; 4. H. Izutsu (J, Kawasaki), 24"326; 5. P. Chili (I, Suzuki), 32"584; 6. R. Xaus (E, Ducati), 34"798; 7. T. Corser (AUS, Aprilia), 37"623; 8. S. Chambon (F, Suzuki), 38"601; 9. T. Okada (J, Honda), 40"295; 10. A. Yanagawa (J, Kawasaki), 46"178; 11. R. Ulm (A, Ducati), 53"801; 12. M. Sanchini (I, Ducati), 56"019; 13. R. Laconi (F, Aprilia), 1'06"037; 14. S. Martin (AUS, Ducati), 1'16"714; 15. B. Stey (F, Honda), 1'26"934. 22 finishers.

Fastest lap:

M. Sanchini (I, Ducati), 1'52"672 (136.272 km/h).

June 24th - San Marino - Misano

Race I:

1. T. Bayliss (AUS, Ducati), 40'23"410 (150.779 km/h); 2. B. Bostrom (USA, Ducati), 0"482; 3. C. Edwards (USA, Honda), 11"386; 4. G. Lavilla (E, Kawasaki)(*), 13"372; 5. A. Yanagawa (E, Kawasaki), 16"203; 6. N. Hodgson (GB, Ducati), 16"334; 7. T. Corser (AUS, Aprilia), 16"337; 8. A. Antonello (I, Aprilia), 20"745; 9. T. Okada (J, Honda), 26"049; 10. R. Xaus (E, Ducati), 34"104; 11. J. Toseland (GB, Ducati), 34"412; 12. P. Chili (I, Suzuki), 34"505; 13. S. Martin (AUS, Ducati), 50"022; 14. S. Chambon (F, Suzuki), 55"651; 15. A. Gramigni (I, Yamaha), 57"206. 23 finishers.

Fastest lap:

T. Bayliss (AUS, Ducati), 1'36"090 (152.107 km/h).

(*): Gregorio Lavilla (E, Kawasaki) who crossed the finish line in third place was penalised 5 seconds for overtaking under the yellow flag

Race II:

1. B. Bostrom (USA, Ducati), 40'20"677 (150.950 km/h); 2. T. Bayliss (AUS, Ducati), 7"547; 3. G. Lavilla (E, Kawasaki), 12"483; 4. A. Antonello (I, Aprilia), 15"069; 5. T. Okada (J, Honda), 18"050; 6. R. Xaus (E, Ducati), 26"912; 7. B. Parkes (AUS, Ducati), 29"588; 8. J. Toseland (GB, Ducati), 30"862; 9. T. Corser (AUS, Aprilia), 33"192; 10. P. Chili (I, Suzuki), 38"494; 11. C. Edwards (USA, Honda), 47"174; 12. A. Gramigni (I, Yamaha), 52"147; 13. S. Chambon (F, Suzuki), 56"119; 14. G. Bussei (I, Ducati), 57"719; 15. M. Sanchini (I, Ducati), 59"291. 20 finishers.

Fastest lap:

N. Hodgson (GB, Ducati), 1'35"403 (153.203 km/h).

July 8th - United States - Laguna Seca

Race I:

1. B. Bostrom (USA, Ducati), 40'32"161 (149.615 km/h); 2. N. Hodgson (GB, Ducati), 1"337; 3. T. Corser (AUS, Aprilia), 2"923; 4. T. Bayliss (AUS, Ducati), 16"729; 5. E. Bostrom (USA, Kawasaki), 18"425; 6. C. Edwards (USA, Honda), 30"762; 7. R. Xaus (E, Ducati), 33"449; 8. T. Okada (J, Honda), 34"371; 9. D. Chandler (USA, Kawasaki), 35"638; 10. J. Toseland (GB, Ducati), 37"617; 11. R. Laconi (F, Aprilia), 37"960; 12. G. Lavilla (E, Kawasaki), 44"361; 13. B. Parkes (AUS, Ducati), 47"356; 14. S. Martin (AUS, Ducati), 49"117; 15. G. Bussei (I, Ducati), 56"070. 21 finishers.

Fastest lap:

T. Corser (AUS, Aprilia), 1'26"144 (150.864 km/h).

Race II:

1. B. Bostrom (USA, Ducati), 40'31"320 (149.667 km/h); 2. T. Corser (AUS, Aprilia), 2"360; 3. N. Hodgson (GB, Ducati), 15"310; 4. T . Bayliss (AUS, Ducati), 18"128; 5. E. Bostrom (USA, Kawasaki), 18"584; 6. C. Edwards (USA, Honda), 18"806; 7. J. Toseland (GB, Ducati), 19"079; 8. A. Yanagawa (J, Kawasaki), 19"397; 9. R. Laconi (F, Aprilia), 30"747; 10. R. Xaus (E, Ducati), 34"099; 11. T. Okada (J, Honda), 34"796; 12. S. Chambon (F, Suzuki), 44"423; 13. S. Martin (AUS, Ducati), 48"303; 14. B. Parkes (AUS, Ducati), 1'00"068; 15. P. Goddard (AUS, Benelli), 1'01"003. 23 finishers.

Fastest lap:

B. Bostrom (USA, Ducati), 1'26"210 (150.748 km/h).

July 29th - Europe - Brands Hatch

Race I:

1. B. Bostrom (USA, Ducati), 36'41"759 (172.539 km/h); 2. N. Hodgson (GB, Ducati), 1"508; 3. C. Edwards (USA, Honda), 9"202; 4. P. Chili (I, Suzuki), 10"016; 5. T. Bayliss (AUS, Ducati), 14"634; 6. R. Xaus (E, Ducati), 21"882; 7. S. Chambon (F, Suzuki), 24"246; 8. T. Corser (AUS, Aprilia), 25"236; 9. S. Emmett (GB, Ducati), 25"810; 10. A. Yanagawa (J, Kawasaki), 26"552; 11. J. Toseland (GB, Ducati), 26"720; 12. T. Okada (J, Honda), 43"970; 13. P. Goddard (AUS, Benelli), 47"177; 14. S. Martin (AUS, Ducati), 52"671; 15. M. Borciani (I, Ducati), 53"072. 22 finishers.

Fastest lap:

P. Chili (I, Suzuki), 1'27"194 (174.273 km/h).

Race II:

1. B. Bostrom (USA, Ducati), 36'28"522 (173.583 km/h); 2. N. Hodgson

(GB, Ducati), 2"581; 3. T. Bayliss (AUS, Ducati), 10"907; 4. P. Chili (I, Suzuki), 10"942; 5. C. Edwards (USA, Honda), 11"485; 6. J. Toseland (GB, Ducati), 17"234; 7. J. Reynolds (GB, Ducati), 17"236; 8. A. Yanagawa (J, Kawasaki), 23"920; 9. S. Chambon (F, Suzuki), 24"169; 10. S. Emmett (GB, Ducati), 29"332; 11. R. Laconi (F, Aprilia), 31"874; 12. R. Xaus (E, Ducati), 32"034; 13. T. Corser (AUS, Aprilia), 32"568; 14. G. Lavilla (E, Kawasaki), 32"928; 15. T. Okada (J, Honda), 33"200. 21 finishers.

Fastest lap:
B. Bostrom (USA, Ducati), 1'26"884 (174.895 km/h).

September 2nd - Germany - Oschersleben
Race I:
1. C. Edwards (USA, Honda), 41'23"687 (148.825 km/h); 2. R. Xaus (E, Ducati), 3"355; 3. B. Bostrom (USA, Ducati), 15"312; 4. A. Yanagawa (J, Kawasaki), 17"715; 5. T. Okada (J, Honda), 21"418; 6. P. Chili (I, Suzuki), 21"693; 7. N. Hodgson (GB, Ducati), 23"071; 8. R. Laconi (F, Aprilia), 24"734; 9. T. Corser (AUS, Aprilia), 28"618; 10. J. Toseland (GB, Ducati), 30"064; 11. G. Lavilla (E, Kawasaki), 38"195; 12. S. Chambon (F, Suzuki), 59"160; 13. J.-B. Borja (E, Yamaha), 1'10"117; 14. G. Bussei (I, Ducati), 1'11"182; 15. B. Stey (F, Honda), 1'11"271. 19 finishers.

Fastest lap:
C. Edwards (USA, Honda), 1'27"988 (150.034 km/h).

Race II:
1. R. Xaus (E, Ducati), 41'17"957 (149.169 km/h); 2. C. Edwards (USA, Honda), 9"938; 3. T. Bayliss (AUS, Ducati), 14"907; 4. B. Bostrom (USA, Ducati), 17"570; 5. R. Laconi (F, Aprilia), 29"311; 6. P. Chili (I, Suzuki), 29"392; 7. G. Lavilla (E, Kawasaki), 29"607; 8. T. Okada (J, Honda), 29"741; 9. A. Yanagawa (J, Kawasaki), 30"047; 10. N. Hodgson (GB, Ducati), 32"621; 11. T. Corser (AUS, Aprilia), 32"947; 12. J. Toseland (GB, Ducati), 33"121; 13. S. Chambon (F, Suzuki), 45"098; 14. S. Martin (AUS, Ducati), 51"486; 15. R. Ulm (A, Ducati), 53"782. 16 finishers.

Fastest lap:
R. Xaus (E, Ducati), 1'27"669 (150.580 km/h).

September 9th - The Netherlands - Assen
Race I:
1. T. Bayliss (AUS, Ducati), 27'08"793 (173.806 km/h); 2. R. Xaus (E, Ducati), 0"166; 3. C. Edwards (USA, Honda), 1"082; 4. P. Chili (I, Suzuki), 5"067; 5. N. Hodgson (GB, Ducati), 12"751; 6. T. Corser (AUS, Aprilia), 13"338; 7. T. Okada (J, Honda), 15"258; 8. A. Yanagawa (J, Kawasaki), 15"606; 9. R. Laconi (F, Aprilia), 15"811; 10. J. Toseland (GB, Ducati), 20"582; 11. B. Bostrom (USA, Ducati), 21"011; 12. G. Lavilla (E, Kawasaki), 25"607; 13. S. Chambon (F, Suzuki), 33"383; 14. J.-B. Borja (E, Yamaha), 46"135; 15. L. Pedercini (I, Ducati), 53"682. 24 finishers.

Fastest lap:
R. Xaus (E, Ducati), 2'04"165 (175.383 km/h).

Race II:
1. T. Bayliss (AUS, Ducati), 33'31"896 (173.181 km/h); 2. R. Xaus (E, Ducati), 0"221; 3. T. Corser (AUS, Aprilia), 4"575; 4. P. Chili (I, Suzuki), 4"776; 5. N. Hodgson (GB, Ducati), 6"711; 6. A. Yanagawa (J, Kawasaki), 6"821; 7. R. Laconi (F, Aprilia), 12"510; 8. J. Toseland (GB, Ducati), 13"849; 9. G. Lavilla (E, Kawasaki), 14"026; 10. C. Edwards (USA, Honda), 21"065; 11. B. Bostrom (USA, Ducati), 21"627; 12. S. Chambon (F, Suzuki), 21"639; 13. T. Okada (J, Honda), 22"337; 14. G. Bussei (I, Ducati), 45"388; 15. L. Pedercini (I, Ducati), 54"778. 22 finishers.

Fastest lap:
R. Xaus (E, Ducati), 2'04"744 (174.569 km/h).

September 30th - Italy - Imola
Race I:
1. R. Xaus (E, Ducati), 38'42"598 (160.558 km/h); 2. T. Corser (AUS, Aprilia), 3"601; 3. C. Edwards (USA, Honda), 4"079; 4. B. Bostrom (USA, Ducati), 6"340; 5. T. Okada (J, Honda), 13"737; 6. S. Martin (AUS, Ducati), 21"421; 7. G. Lavilla (E, Kawasaki), 24"100; 8. S. Chambon (F, Suzuki), 24"280; 9. L. Pedercini (I, Ducati), 46"537; 10. N. Hodgson (GB, Ducati), 49"078; 11. G. Bussei (I, Ducati), 49"581; 12. M. Craggill (AUS, Ducati), 1'06"503; 13. M. Sanchini (I, Ducati), 1'21"356; 14. P. Blora (I, Ducati), 1'29"430; 15. A. Gramigni (I, Yamaha), 1'50"371. 16 finishers.

Fastest lap:
C. Edwards (USA, Honda), 1'49"708 (161.873 km/h).

Race II:
1. R. Laconi (F, Aprilia), 38'33"264 (161.216 km/h); 2. R. Xaus (E, Ducati), 0"021; 3. T. Okada (J, Honda), 0"844; 4. B. Bostrom (USA, Ducati), 15"975; 5. S. Martin (AUS, Ducati), 32"895; 6. G. Lavilla (E, Kawasaki), 37"450; 7. N. Hodgson (GB, Ducati), 38"727; 8. B. Parkes (AUS, Ducati), 38"890; 9. P. Chili (I, Suzuki), 39"935; 10. G. Bussei (I, Ducati), 1'00"646; 11. A. Gramigni (I, Yamaha), 1'01"170; 12. L. Pedercini (I, Ducati), 1'01"276; 13. P. Goddard (AUS, Benelli), 1'04"505; 14. M. Craggill (AUS, Ducati), 1'06"090; 15. M. Borciani (I, Ducati), 1'15"583. 19 finishers.

Fastest lap:
T. Corser (AUS, Aprilia), 1'49"398 (162.332 km/h).

Final Classification
1. Troy Bayliss (AUS, Ducati), 369
2. Colin Edwards (USA, Honda), 333
3. Ben Bostrom (USA, Ducati), 312
4. T. Corser (AUS, Aprilia), 284; 5. N. Hodgson (GB, Ducati), 269; 6. R. Xaus (E, Ducati), 236; 7. P. Chili (I, Suzuki), 232; 8. T. Okada (J, Honda), 176; 9. A. Yanagawa (J, Kawasaki), 170; 10. G. Lavilla (E, Kawasaki), 166; 11. R. Laconi (F, Aprilia), 152; 12. S. Chambon (F, Suzuki), 122; 13. J. Toseland (GB, Ducati), 91; 14. H. Izutsu (J, Kawasaki), 63; 15. M. Tamada (J, Honda), 50.

Manufacturers
1. Ducati, 553
2. Honda, 401
3. Aprilia, 343
4. Kawasaki, 289
5. Suzuki, 256
6. Yamaha, 36
7. Benelli, 7

SUPERSPORT WORLD CHAMPIONSHIP

March 11th - Spain - Valencia
1. P. Riba Cabana (E, Honda), 38'40"558 (142.903 km/h); 2. P. Bontempi (I, Yamaha), 3"410; 3. C. Kellner (D, Yamaha), 3"643; 4. K. Fujiwara (J, Suzuki), 3"976; 5. K. Curtain (AUS, Honda), 14"357; 6. K. Muggeridge (AUS, Suzuki), 19"039; 7. C. Cogan (F, Yamaha), 19"913; 8. V. Guareschi (I, Ducati), 20"416; 9. F. Pirovano (I, Suzuki), 20"679; 10. W. Daemen (B, Yamaha), 21"895; 11. A. Pitt (AUS, Kawasaki), 21"950; 12. P. Casoli (I, Yamaha), 23"030; 13. C. Lindholm (S, Yamaha), 23"613; 14. J. Hanson (S, Yamaha), 23"709; 15. F. Foret (F, Honda), 25"697. 25 finishers.

Fastest lap:
P. Riba Cabana (E, Honda), 1'40"047 (144.112 km/h).

April 22nd - Australia - Phillip Island
1. K. Curtain (AUS, Honda), 39'32"490 (141.641 km/h); 2. A. Fergusson (AUS, Honda), 2"220; 3. A. Pitt (AUS, Kawasaki), 12"674; 4. V. Guareschi (I, Ducati), 17"615; 5. P. Riba Cabana (E, Honda), 20"163; 6. D. Thomas (AUS, Ducati), 23"899; 7. P. Casoli (I, Yamaha), 31"744; 8. J. Teuchert (D, Yamaha), 53"661; 9. I. Goi (I, Honda), 56"197; 10. C. Cogan (F, Yamaha), 59"971; 11. C. Lindholm (S, Yamaha), 1'11"971; 12. R. Baird (AUS, Yamaha), 1'16"559; 13. M. Barth (D, Honda), 1'35"536; 14. P. Bontempi (I, Yamaha), 1'40"861; 15. V. Iannuzzo (I, Suzuki), 1'50"333. 23 finishers.

Fastest lap:
I. MacPherson (GB, Kawasaki), 1'50"610 (144.670 km/h).

April 29th - Japan - Sugo
1. P. Casoli (I, Yamaha), 39'29"124 (141.964 km/h); 2. J. Teuchert (D, Yamaha), 5"374; 3. A. Pitt (AUS, Kawasaki), 12"878; 4. P. Riba Cabana (E, Honda), 13"874; 5. K. Muggeridge (AUS, Suzuki), 14"101; 6. K. Curtain (AUS, Honda), 15"866; 7. F. Pirovano (I, Honda), 16"535; 8. F. Foret (F, Honda), 16"690; 9. C. Kellner (D, Yamaha), 17"059; 10. I. MacPherson (GB, Kawasaki), 30"589; 11. J. Hanson (S, Yamaha), 37"925; 12. V. Iannuzzo (I, Suzuki), 38"884; 13. C. Cogan (F, Yamaha), 40"131; 14. C. Vermeulen (AUS, Honda), 42"787; 15. S. Legrelle (B, Honda), 48"837. 21 finishers.

Fastest lap:
J. Whitham (GB, Yamaha), 1'33"516 (143.706 km/h).

May 13th - Italy - Monza
1. J. Whitham (GB, Yamaha), 30'45"850 (180.771 km/h); 2. P. Casoli (I, Yamaha), 0"278; 3. K. Muggeridge (AUS, Suzuki), 0"579; 4. A. Pitt (AUS, Kawasaki), 0"644; 5. I. MacPherson (GB, Kawasaki), 0"780; 6. J. Teuchert (D, Yamaha), 0"842; 7. V. Guareschi (I, Ducati), 1"604; 8. F. Pirovano (I, Suzuki), 2"807; 9. P. Bontempi (I, Yamaha), 7"696; 10. A. Corradi (I, Yamaha), 8"150; 11. C. Migliorati (I, Honda), 13"700; 12. C. Cogan (F, Yamaha), 15"322; 13. K. Fujiwara (J, Suzuki), 15"850; 14. K. Curtain (AUS, Honda), 23"462; 15. S. Le Grelle (B, Honda), 23"642. 23 finishers.

Fastest lap :
A. Pitt (AUS, Kawasaki), 1'54"271 (182.503 km/h).

May 27th - Great Britain - Donington
1. P. Casoli (I, Yamaha), 37'30"193 (148.034 km/h); 2. K. Muggeridge (AUS, Suzuki), 8"585; 3. J. Teuchert (D, Yamaha), 8"730; 4. J. Whitham (GB, Yamaha), 8"808; 5. K. Fujiwara (J, Suzuki), 9"066; 6. P. Bontempi (I, Yamaha), 10"096; 7. K. Harris (GB, Suzuki), 13"413; 8. K. Curtain (AUS, Honda), 13"673; 9. F. Pirovano (I, Suzuki), 14"406; 10. A. Pitt (AUS, Kawasaki), 14"831; 11. F. Foret (F, Honda), 15"636; 12. P. Riba Cabana (E, Honda), 15"886; 13. C. Cogan (F, Yamaha), 20"807; 14. I. MacPherson (GB, Kawasaki), 23"804; 15. S. Smart (GB, Suzuki), 32"000. 25 finishers.

Fastest lap:
P. Casoli (I, Yamaha), 1'36"753 (149.688 km/h).

June 10th - Germany - Lausitz
1. K. Curtain (AUS, Honda), 45'56"744 (128.101 km/h); 2. A. Fergusson (AUS, Honda), 8"225; 3. A. Pitt (AUS, Kawasaki), 14"576; 4. V. Guareschi (I, Ducati), 20"477; 5. C. Cogan (F, Yamaha), 26"603; 6. I. MacPherson (GB, Kawasaki), 42"174; 7. J. Teuchert (D, Yamaha), 57"493; 8. C. Vermeulen (AUS, Honda), 1'00"454; 9. C. Kellner (D, Yamaha), 1'02"035; 10. W. Daemen (B, Yamaha), 1'17"333; 11. C. Migliorati (I, Honda), 1'19"338; 12. C. Lindholm (S, Yamaha), 1'23"157; 13. J. Oelschläger (D, Suzuki), 1'23"254; 14. M. Barth (D, Honda), 1'23"822; 15. P. Casoli (I, Yamaha), 1'23"952. 19 finishers.

Fastest lap:
F. Foret (F, Honda), 1'43"974 (147.672 km/h).

June 24th - San Marino - Misano
1. J. Teuchert (D, Yamaha), 38'26"298 (145.761 km/h); 2. I. MacPherson (GB, Kawasaki), 0"084; 3. P. Casoli (I, Yamaha), 0"419; 4. F. Foret (F, Honda), 2"460; 5. C. Vermeulen (AUS, Honda), 3"633; 6. K. Fujiwara (J, Suzuki), 4"064; 7. J. Whitham (GB, Yamaha), 8"055; 8. A. Pitt (AUS, Kawasaki), 18"531; 9. K. Muggeridge (AUS, Suzuki), 18"638; 10. P. Bontempi (I, Yamaha), 18"999; 11. N. Russo (I, Yamaha), 19"125; 12. C. Cogan (F, Yamaha), 19"245; 13. A. Corradi (I, Yamaha), 32"490; 14. C. Mariottini (I, Ducati), 35"685; 15. W. Daemen (B, Yamaha), 35"841. 22 finishers.

Fastest lap:
I. MacPherson (GB, Kawasaki), 1'39"253 (147.260 km/h).

July 29th - Europe - Brands Hatch
1. J. Teuchert (D, Yamaha), 34'53"995 (166.905 km/h); 2. A. Pitt (AUS, Kawasaki), 0"011; 3. J. Whitham (GB, Yamaha), 1"497; 4. K. Fujiwara (J, Suzuki), 1"497; 5. F. Pirovano (I, Suzuki), 4"676; 6. P. Riba Cabana (E, Honda), 5"197; 7. P. Casoli (I, Yamaha), 5"480; 8. K. Harris (GB, Suzuki), 9"979; 9. F. Foret (F, Honda), 10"042; 10. C. Kellner (D, Yamaha), 10"670; 11. K. Curtain (AUS, Honda), 13"711; 12. C. Migliorati (I, Honda), 36"433; 13. W. Daemen (B, Yamaha), 36"546; 14. V. Ianuzzo (I, Suzuki), 36"909; 15. A. Fergusson (AUS, Honda), 37"270. 22 finishers.

Fastest lap:
K. Muggeridge (AUS, Suzuki), 1'30"395 (168.102 km/h).

September 2nd - Germany - Oschersleben
1. F. Foret (F, Honda), 43'00"008 (143.268 km/h); 2. P. Riba Cabana (E, Honda), 0"442; 3. A. Pitt (AUS, Kawasaki), 0"539; 4. P. Casoli (I, Yamaha), 0"982; 5. J. Whitham (GB, Yamaha), 1"288; 6. C. Kellner (D, Yamaha), 2"218; 7. F. Pirovano (I, Suzuki), 2"353; 8. K. Muggeridge (AUS, Suzuki), 2"723; 9. C. Cogan (F, Yamaha), 8"103; 10. A. Fergusson (AUS, Honda), 12"086; 11. D. Thomas (AUS, Ducati), 12"448; 12. K. Curtain (AUS, Honda), 11"004; 13. M. Schulten (D, Yamaha), 25"883; 14. P. Bontempi (I, Yamaha), 34"096; 15. S. Cruciani (I, Yamaha), 47"694. 20 finishers.

Fastest lap:
J. Whitham (GB, Yamaha), 1'30"806 (145.378 km/h).

September 9th - The Netherlands - Assen

1. P. Casoli (I, Yamaha), 34'58"965 (165.997 km/h); 2. A. Pitt (AUS, Kawasaki), 2'457; 3. J. Whitham (GB, Yamaha), 3"648; 4. J. Teuchert (D, Yamaha), 5"847; 5. F. Pirovano (I, Suzuki), 7"209; 6. K. Curtain (AUS, Honda), 9"239; 7. V. Iannuzzo (I, Suzuki), 15"988; 8. I. MacPherson (GB, Kawasaki), 17"462; 9. C. Cogan (F, Yamaha), 17"679; 10. F. Foret (F, Honda), 20"175; 11. C. Kellner (D, Yamaha), 21"117; 12. P. Bontempi (I, Yamaha), 25"360; 13. W. Daemen (B, Yamaha), 30"267; 14. A. Fergusson (AUS, Honda), 31"982; 15. C. Migliorati (I, Honda), 39"601. 25 finishers.

Fastest lap:
J. Whitham (GB, Yamaha), 2'08"748 (169.140 km/h).

September 30th - Italy - Imola

1. F. Foret (F, Honda), 40'09"883 (154.752 km/h); 2. K. Muggeridge (AUS, Suzuki), 0"191; 3. J. Whitham (GB, Yamaha), 2"251; 4. A. Pitt (AUS, Kawasaki), 8"022; 5. P. Riba Cabana (E, Honda), 12"810; 6. I. MacPherson (GB, Kawasaki), 12"966; 7. J. Teuchert (D, Yamaha), 13"093; 8. K. Fujiwara (J, Suzuki), 16"532; 9. P. Bontempi (I, Yamaha), 22"537; 10. C. Vermeulen (AUS, Honda), 23"889; 11. F. Pirovano (I, Suzuki), 24"704; 12. V. Iannuzzo (I, Suzuki), 37"754; 13. C. Migliorati (I, Suzuki), 38"743; 14. K. Curtain (AUS, Honda), 46"963; 15. R. Frost (GB, Yamaha), 49"437. 22 finishers.

Fastest lap:
F. Foret (F, Honda), 1'53"954 (155.842 km/h).

Final Classification
1. Andrew Pitt (AUS, Kawasaki), 149
2. Paolo Casoli (I, Yamaha), 147
3. Jörg Teuchert (D, Yamaha), 135
4. J. Whitham (GB, Yamaha), 106; 5. K. Curtain (AUS, Honda), 102; 6. P. Riba Cabana (E, Honda), 94; 7. K. Muggeridge (AUS, Suzuki), 92; 8. F. Foret (F, Honda), 90; 9. I. MacPherson (GB, Kawasaki), 67; 10. F. Pirovano (I, Suzuki), 67; 11. P. Bontempi (I, Yamaha), 58; 12. K. Fujiwara (J, Suzuki), 58; 13. C. Cogan (F, Yamaha), 54; 14. C. Kellner (D, Yamaha), 51; 15. A. Fergusson (AUS, Honda), 49.

Manufacturers
1. Yamaha, 219 ;
2. Honda, 184 ;
3. Kawasaki, 161 ;
4. Suzuki, 127 ;
5. Ducati, 50.

ENDURANCE WORLD CHAMPIONSHIP

April 14th-15th - Le Mans 24 Hours - France

1. Guyot/Scarnato/Dussauge (F, Suzuki), 759 laps;
2. Charpentier/Foret/Gimbert (F, Honda), 1 lap; 3. Lavieille/Morisson/Van Den Bossche (F/GB/F, Suzuki), 4 laps; 4. Mizera/Fernandez/Lagrive (F, Yamaha), 12 laps; 5. Giabbani/Roche/Kishida (F/F/J, Kawasaki), laps; 6. Haquin/Waldmeier/Michel (F, Kawasaki), 33 laps; 7. Jolivet/Moisan/Millochau (F, Suzuki), 41 laps; 8. Rulfo/Jaulneau/Albertini (F, Yamaha), 42 laps; 9. Morillas/Gomez/Ulmann (F, Suzuki), 43 laps; 10. Cuzin/Donischal/Kempener (F/F/B, Yamaha), 45 laps; 11. Robert/Lentaigne/Diss (F, Yamaha), 46 laps; 12. Boutin/Loustalet/Briere (F, Yamaha), 47 laps; 13. Desmaris/Leblanc/Veille (F, Kawasaki), 50 laps; 14. Naveau/Aerts/Platacis (B/B/AUS, Honda), 55 laps; 15. Pscherer/Guinant/Vintaer (F, Yamaha), 57 laps. 37 finishers.

May 6th - Brno 6 Hours - Czech Republic

1. Lavieille/Morrisson/Brian (F/GB/F, Suzuki), 162 laps;
2. Mertens/Nowland/Hinterreiter (B/AUS/A, Suzuki), 1 lap;
3. Jennings/Edwards (GB, Suzuki), 2 laps; 4. Naveau/Aerts/Platacis (B/B/D, Honda), 4 laps; 5. F. Jond/Four/Lerat-Vanstaen (F, Suzuki); 6. Paillot/Giabbani/Roche (F, Kawasaki); 7. Truchsess/Bursa (A/CZ, Kawasaki), 5 laps; 8. Graf/Kellenberger/Heiler (CH/CH/D, Kawasaki); 9. Guyot/Scarnato/Dussauge (F, Suzuki); 10. Linden/Jerman/Coutelle (S/SLO/F, Suzuki); 11. Gallis/Chenais (F, Honda), 6 laps; 12. Barnes/Van Achter (USA/B, Suzuki); 13. Blug/Herber (D, Suzuki), 7 laps; 14. Seefeldt/Josch (D, Suzuki), 8 laps; 15. Saiger/Kainz (A, Yamaha). 31 finishers.

June 9th - Brands Hatch 6 Hours - Great Britain

1. Lavieille/Morrisson/Brian (F/GB/F, Suzuki), 225 laps;
2. Mertens/Nowland (B/AUS, Suzuki), 1'06"226; 3. Jerman/Van Den Bossche (SLO/F, Suzuki), 3 laps; 4. F. Jond/Four/Lerat-Vanstaen (F, Suzuki), 4 laps; 5. Guyot/Scarnato/Dussauge (F, Suzuki), 6 laps; 6. Cuzin/S. Jond/Haquin (F, Yamaha), 7 laps; 7. Kellenberger/Heiler (CH/D, Kawasaki), 8 laps; 8. Blug/Palmer (D/GB, Suzuki), 10 laps; 9. Naveau/Aerts/Platacis (B/B/AUS, Honda); 10. Casaer/Scheers (B, MV-Agusta), 12 laps; 11. Williams/Martin/Norris (GB, Honda); 12. Pscherer/Guinand/Vinaer (F, Yamaha), 16 laps; 13. Gabriel/Wehrli/Bosonnet (CH, Yamaha), 17 laps; 14. Watts/Smith-Halvorsen/Piggott (GB, Yamaha), 21 laps; 15. Barnes/Cicotto (GB/USA, Suzuki).

July 1st - Nürburgring 6 Hours - Germany

1. Guyot/Scarnato/Dussauge (F, Suzuki), 199 laps;
2. Bonhuil/Chow/Hinterreiter (F/CHI/A, Suzuki), 1 lap; 3. Kaufmann/Ehrenberger (D, Suzuki); 4. F. Jond/Four/Lerat-Vanstaen (F, Suzuki), 3 laps; 5. Mertens/Nowland (B/AUS, Suzuki), 4 laps; 6. Naveau/Aerts/Platacis (B/B/D, Honda); 7. Lavieille/Morrisson/Brian (F/GB/F, Suzuki), 5 laps; 8. Gallis/Di Giovanni (F, Honda), 6 laps; 9. Schmidt/Schüller/Jost (D, Suzuki), 7 laps; 10. Giabbani/Roche (F, Kawasaki), 9 laps; 11. Ripault/Salvaia (F, Ducati); 12. Delling/Heidger (D, Aprilia); 13. Jaggi/Coulon/Briguet (CH, Suzuki), 10 laps; 14. Strauch/Roethig/Borkowski (F, Suzuki); 15. G.-P. Meyer/S. Meyer/Warmke (D, Yamaha).

July 14th-15th - Spa-Francorchamps 24 Hours - Belgium

1. Lavieille/Morrisson/Brian (F/GB/F, Suzuki), 498 laps;
2. Guyot/Scarnato/Dussauge (F, Suzuki), 4 laps;
3. Mizera/Sebileau/Lagrive (F, Yamaha); 4. Linden/Jerman/Ulmann (S/SLO/F, Suzuki), 5 laps; 5. Naveau/Aerts/Platacis (B/B/D, Honda), 17 laps; 6. Jennings/Ellison/Baker (GB, Suzuki), 19 laps; 7. Pister/Schildermans/Buylinckx (B/B/L, Aprilia), 28 laps; 8. Vanlandschoot/De Maegt/Roelens (B, Suzuki), 32 laps; 9. Graf/Blug/Wacker (CH/D/D, Suzuki); 10. Strauch/Röthig/Borkowski (D, Suzuki); 11. Rulfo/Jaulneau/Herriberry (F, Yamaha), 33 laps; 12. Fabra/Bonvicini/Granie (F, Suzuki); 13. Ripault/Salvaia/Dequesne (F/F/B, Ducati), 34 laps; 14. Giabbani/Roche/Gebelin (F, Kawasaki); 15. Schulz/Schmidt/Schüller (D, Suzuki), 37 laps.

August 5th - Suzuka 8 Hours - Japan

1. Rossi/Edwards (I/USA, Honda), 217 laps; 2. Okada/Barros (J/BR, Honda), 14"286; 3. Ryo/Kagayama/Watanabe (J, Suzuki), 1'13"229; 4. Ukawa/Katoh (J, Honda), 1'23"918; 5. Kitagawa/Arakaki/Toda (J, Suzuki), 4 laps; 6. Takeda/Yamaguchi (J, Honda), 5 laps; 7. Fujiwara/Numata (J, Yamaha), 6 laps; 8. Sakai/Noda (J, Honda), 8 laps; 9. Mertens/Nowland (B/AUS, Suzuki), 9 laps; 10. Senmyo/Nakamura (J, Honda); 11. Takahashi/Nakai (J, Kawasaki), 11 laps; 12. Saitoh/Fukami (J, Yamaha); 13. H. Aoki/Maeda (J, Honda), 12 laps; 14. Hasegawa/Maruyama (J, Honda); 15. Yamashita/Hotta (J, Kawasaki), 14 laps.

August 11th-12th - Oschersleben 24 Hours - Germany

1. Linden/Jerman/Ulmann (S/SLO/F, Suzuki), 887 laps;
2. Mertens/Nowland/Cristobal (B/AUS/E, Suzuki), 9 laps; 3. Donischal/Jond/Cuzin (F, Yamaha), 11 laps; 4. Naveau/Aerts/Platacis (B/B/AUS, Honda), 15 laps; 5. Giabbani/Roche/Gebelin (F, Kawasaki), 24 laps; 6. Schmidt/Süller/Seefeldt (D, Suzuki), 29 laps; 7. Kellenberger/Heidger/Galinski (CH/D/D, Suzuki), 32 laps; 8. Lavieille/Morrison/Brian (F/GB/F, Suzuki); 9. Carrard/Rollier/Jaggi (CH, Suzuki), 33 laps; 10. Penzkofer/Maher/Ludwig (D/IRL/D, Yamaha), 40 laps; 11. Strauch/Röthig/Borkowski (D, Suzuki), 46 laps; 12. P. Meyer/S. Meyer/Klett (D, Yamaha), 48 laps; 13. K. Schulz/Martensen/F. Schulz (D, Suzuki), 51 laps; 14. Schönfelder/Freiberger/Franzreb (D, Suzuki), 53 laps; 15. Carlberg/Baker/Nyström (S/GB/SF, Yamaha), 55 laps.

September 15th-16th - Bol d'Or 24 Hours (Magny-Cours) - France

1. Lavieille/Morrison/Brian (F/GB/F, Suzuki), 799 laps;
2. Costes/Foret/Gimbert (F, Honda), 8 laps; 3. Jerman/Ulmann/Ellison (SLO/F/GB, Suzuki), 8 laps; 4. Lagrive/Sebileau/Fernandez (F, Yamaha), 9 laps; 5. Delétang/Willis/Paillot (F/AUS/F, Yamaha), 16 laps; 6. Haquin/Amalric/Le Glatin (F, Kawasaki), 20 laps; 7. F. Jond/Four/Lerat-Vanstaen (F, Kawasaki), 20 laps; 8. Hinterreiter/Bonhuil/Bennett (D/F/GB, Suzuki), 21 laps; 9. Scarnato/Van Den Bossche/Protat (F, Suzuki), 24 laps; 10. Giabbani/Roche/Gebelin (F, Kawasaki), 31 laps; 11. Mertens/Nowland/Cristobal (B/AUS/E, Suzuki), 34 laps; 12. Neff/Foggia/Tauziede (F, Honda), 36 laps; 13. Nystrom/Gaillard/Dubus (F, Suzuki), 39 laps; 14. Jaggi/Rollier/Carrard (CH, Suzuki), 43 laps; 15. Rulfo/Jaulnau/Waldmeier (F, Yamaha), 45 laps.

Endurance World Championship
1. Wim Motors Racing (Honda), 182
2. Free Bike Performance (Yamaha), 130
3. Honda Elf (Honda), 100
4. Ducateam (Ducati), 92; 5. Herman Verboven Racing (Suzuki), 91; 6. Bolliger Team (Kawasaki), 65; 7. Moto Shop (Kawasaki), 58; 8. Empp Endurance (Suzuki), 58; 9. Team Dap Moto (Honda), 52; 10. K & W Racing Team (Suzuki), 39; 11. Yamaha Motor France (Yamaha), 32; 12. Motorsport Gerhard Wacker (Honda), 32; 13. Ardouin Motos (Kawasaki), 26; 14. Team Cabin Honda (Honda), 25; 15. Chomat Moto (Honda), 22.

Endurance World Cup
1. Suzuki Castrol Team (Suzuki), 222
2. GMT 94 (Suzuki), 177
3. Zongshen Team 2 (Suzuki), 150
4. Phase One (Suzuki), 132; 5. Endurance Moto (Yamaha), 90; 6. Junior Team LMS (Suzuki), 87; 7. Bergmann und Söhne Racing (Suzuki), 75; 8. Motomax-Derbi (Suzuki), 67; 9. Schäfer Mo Devil Racing Team (Suzuki), 60; 10. Zongshen Team 3 (Suzki), 52; 11. Stehl Endurance (Suzuki), 50; 12. Cottard Moto-Axe (Suzuki), 32; 13. Motorsport Mabbe (Suzuki), 22; 14. GB Moto (Yamaha), 21; 15. Team 22 Police Nationale (Kawasaki), 20.

Endurance FIM Cup (Stocksport)
1. Team 22 Police Nationale (Kawasaki), 192
2. Jet Endurance Team 23 (Suzuki), 124
3. Bridgestone Bikers Profi-Thunderbike (Suzuki), 108;
4. Chalon Motos (Yamaha), 104;
5. PS-Schlesinger Endurance (Yamaha), 90;
5. Infini Team Endurance (Suzuki), 86;
7. Octopus (Yamaha), 54; 8. Team JLC Moto & Co (Yamaha), 50; 9. Stand Bike Endurance (Kawasaki), 42; 10. Team Top Moto 61 (Yamaha), 41; 11. Team Motorep Nantes (Suzuki), 40; 12. Yamaha Obi Shel Bike Promo (Yamaha), 32; 13. Jet Endurance Team 24 (Suzuki), 31; 14. Team Yamaha Oslo (Yamaha), 26; 15. Motostart Racing (Yamaha), 26.

Side-Cars World Championship

March 11th - Spain - Valencia
1. Klaffenböck/Parzer (A, Suzuki), 37'53"877 (139.496 km/h);
2. Webster/Woodhead (D/GB, Suzuki), 4"646; 3. Steinhausen/Hetherington (D/GB, Suzuki), 14"926; 4. Abbott/Biggs (GB, Yamaha), 15"366;
5. Hanks/Biggs (GB, Suzuki), 52"615; 6. Muldoon/Crone (GB, Yamaha), 1 lap; 7. Hauzenberger/Hänni (A/CH, Suzuki); 8. Hemmerling/Kolloch (D, Suzuki); 9. Liechti/Locher (CH, Kawasaki); 10. Schröder/Wäfler (CH, Suzuki); 11. Guy/Peach (GB, Suzuki); 12. Eilers/Engelmann (D, Suzuki); 13. Steenbergen/Steenbergen (NL, Suzuki);
14. Hayakawa/Kobe (J, Suzuki), 2 laps. 14 finishers.

April 22nd - Australia - Phillip Island
Race cancelled.

May 13th - Italy - Monza
1. Klaffenböck/Parzer (A, Suzuki), 31'37"201 (175.876 km/h);
2. Abbott/Biggs (GB, Yamaha), 8"307; 3. Van Gils/Van Gils (NL, Suzuki), 48"380; 4. Hauzenberger/Hänni (A/CH), Suzuki, 1'08"219;
5. Liechti/Locher (CH, Kawasaki), 1'36"169; 6. Schröder/Wäfler (CH, Suzuki), 1'41"837; 7. Roscher/Neubert (D, Suzuki), 1'44"198;
8. Eilers/Kolloch (D, Suzuki), 1'52"479; 9. Hall/Wood (GB, Suzuki), 1 lap; 10. Morrisey/Cox (GB, Yamaha); 11. Reuter/Langschädel (D, Suzuki); 12. Veltjens/Hildebrand (D, Suzuki); 13. Delannoy/Vannier (F, Suzuki), 2 laps. 13 finishers.

May 27th - Great Britain - Donington
1. Klaffenböck/Parzer (A, Suzuki), 38'21"628 (144.726 km/h);
2. Abbott/Biggs (GB, Yamaha), 22"750; 3. Steinhausen/Hopkinson (D/GB, Suzuki), 24"249; 4. Hanks/Biggs (GB, Yamaha), 48"176;
5. Van Gils/Van Gils (NL, Suzuki), 1'05"218; 6. Guy/Peach (GB, Suzuki), 1'10"014; 7. Hauzenberger/Hänni (A/CH, Suzuki), 1'30"659;
8. Fleury/Birchall (AUS/GB, Suzuki), 1 lap; 9. Roscher/Neubert (D, Suzuki); 10. Liechti/Locher (CH, Kawasaki); 11. Biggs/Biggs (GB, Yamaha); 12. Founds/Founds (GB, Suzuki); 13. Schröder/Wäfler (CH, Suzuki); 14. Eilers/Kolloch (D, Suzuki); 15. Delannoy/Vannier (F, Suzuki), 2 laps. 17 finishers.

June 10th - Germany - Lausitz (*)
1. Webster/Woodhead (GB, Suzuki), 48'20"040 (121.771 km/h);
2. Muldoon/Crone (GB, Yamaha), 2'12"566; 3. Roscher/Neubert (D, Suzuki), 1 lap; 4. Göttlich/Helbig (D, Suzuki); 5. Liechti/Locher

(CH, Kawasaki); 6. Eilers/Kolloch (D, Suzuki); 7. Guy/Peach (GB, Suzuki);
8. Hanks/Biggs (GB, Yamaha); 9. Steinhausen/Hopkinson (D/GB, Suzuki);
10. Hayakawa/Kobe (J, Suzuki); 11. Schröder/Wäfler (CH, Suzuki), 2 laps;
12. Steenbergen/Steenbergen (NL, Suzuki); 13. Veltjens/Hildebrand (D, Suzuki), 3 laps; 14. Cameron/Harper (GB, Suzuki); 15. Becker/Nils (D, Kawasaki), 4 laps. 15 finishers.

June 24th - San Marino - Misano
1. Webster/Woodhead (GB, Suzuki), 38'50"739 (144.232 km/h);
2. Klaffenböck/Parzer (A, Suzuki), 14"945; 3. Steinhausen/Hopkinson (D/GB, Suzuki), 1'11"513; 4. Hanks/Biggs (GB, Yamaha), 1'15"979;
5. Muldoon/Crone (GB, Yamaha), 1 lap; 6. Schröder/Wäfler (CH, Suzuki);
7. Cameron/Harper (GB, Suzuki); 8. Liechti/Locher (CH, Kawasaki);
9. Eilers/Engelmann (D, Suzuki); 10. Hayakawa/Kobe (J, Suzuki);
11. Founds/Founds (GB, Yamaha); 12. Mattoni/Tonelli (I, Suzuki), 2 laps;
13. Morrisey/Gusman (GB, Yamaha); 14. Steenbergen/Steenbergen (NL, Suzuki); 15. Delannoy/Vannier (F, Suzuki). 15 finishers.

July 29th - Europe - Brands Hatch
1. Webster/Woodhead (GB, Suzuki), 24'57"466 (146.169 km/h);
2. Steinhausen/Hopkinson (D/GB, Suzuki), 0"871; 3. Guy/Peach (GB, Suzuki), 33"578; 4. Hauzenberger/Simmons (A/GB, Suzuki), 40"889; 5. Van Gils/Van Gils (NL, Suzuki), 42"958; 6. Muldoon/Crone (GB, Yamaha), 44"371; 7. Stafford/Wright (GB, Yamaha), 1'05"532;
8. Liechti/Locher (CH, Kawasaki), 1'08"977; 9. Schröder/Wäfler (CH, Suzuki), 1'09"488; 10. Steenbergen/Steenbergen (NL, Suzuki), 1'09"900; 11. Hanquet/Rodrigue (B, Suzuki), 1'11"911; 12. Biggs/Biggs (GB, Yamaha), 1'18"944; 13. Founds/Founds (GB, Suzuki), 1'29"381;
14. Lambert/Murray (GB, Yamaha), 1'45"881; 15. Hayakawa/Kobe (J, Suzuki), 1 lap. 17 finishers.

September 2nd - Germany - Oschersleben
1. Klaffenböck/Parzer (A, Suzuki), 44'14"005 (139.274 km/h);
2. Abbott/Biggs (GB, Yamaha), 0"360; 3. Hanks/Biggs (GB, Yamaha), 44"823; 4. Guy/Peach (GB, Suzuki), 1'25"738; 5. Van Gils/Van Gils (NL, Suzuki), 1 lap; 6. Founds/Founds (GB, Yamaha); 7. Göttlich/Helbig (D, Suzuki); 8. Roscher/Neubert (D, Suzuki); 9. Steenbergen/Buyze

(NL, Suzuki); 10. Eilers/Kolloch (D, Suzuki), 2 laps; 11. Hayakawa/Kobe (J, Suzuki); 12. Morrisey/Cox (GB, Yamaha); 13. Reuter/Langschädel (D, Suzuki); 14. Fleury/Pointer (NZ, Suzuki); 15. Delannoy/Vannier (F, Suzuki). 15 finishers.

September 9th - The Netherlands - Assen
1. Abbott/Biggs (GB, Yamaha), 35'51"459 (161.947 km/h);
2. Klaffenböck/Parzer (A, Suzuki), 17"898; 3. Van Gils/Van Gils (NL, Suzuki), 33"075; 4. Cameron/Darby (GB, Suzuki), 2'11"963;
5. Steenbergen/Buyze (NL, Suzuki), 2'12"193; 6. Guy/Peach (GB, Suzuki), 2'14"942; 7. Muldoon/Crone (GB, Yamaha), 2'30"425; 8. Hayakawa/Kobe (J, Suzuki), 1 lap; 9. Eilers/Kolloch (D, Suzuki); 10. Lambert/Murray (GB, Yamaha); 11. Founds/Founds (GB, Yamaha); 12. Morrisey/Cox (GB, Suzuki); 13. Bevers/Bevers (NL, Suzuki); 14. Delannoy/Vannier (F, Suzuki). 14 finishers.

September 30th - Italy - Imola
1. Webster/Woodhead (GB, Suzuki), 41'45"455 (148.849 km/h);
2. Klaffenböck/Parzer (A, Suzuki), 9"424; 3. Steinhausen/Hopkinson (D/GB, Suzuki), 19"185; 4. Abbott/Biggs (GB, Yamaha), 22"172;
5. Hanks/Biggs (GB, Suzuki), 1'05"866; 6. Van Gils/Van Gils (NL, Suzuki), 1'25"365; 7. Guy/Peach (GB, Suzuki), 1'25"927;
8. Fisher/Long (GB, Suzuki), 1'58"285; 9. Schröder/Wäfler (CH, Suzuki), 1 lap; 10. Eilers/Kolloch (D, Suzuki); 11. Liechti/Locher (CH, Kawasaki); 12. Steenbergen/Steenbergen (NL, Suzuki); 13. Biggs/Biggs (GB, Yamaha); 14. Fleury/Pointer (NZ, Suzuki); 15. Hayakawa/Ohzeki (J, Suzuki). 15 finishers.

Final Classification
1. Klaus Klaffenböck (A, Suzuki), 160
2. Steve Webster (GB, Suzuki), 120
3. Steve Abbott (GB, Yamaha), 111
4. Steinhausen (D, Suzuki), 91; 5. Hanks (GB, Yamaha), 72; 6. Guy (GB, Suzuki), 72;
7. Van Gils (NL, Suzuki), 64; 8. Muldoon (GB, Yamaha), 61; 9. Liechti (CH, Kawasaki), 57; 10. Eilers (D, Suzuki), 51; 11. Schröder (CH, Suzuki), 49; 12. Hauzenberger (A, Suzuki), 44; 13. Roscher (D, Suzuki), 40;
14. Steenbergen (NL, Suzuki), 38;
15. Hayakawa (J, Suzuki), 30.

European Championship

125 CC

April 29th - Italy - Vallelunga
1. Ballerini (I, Aprilia), 27'16"335 (134.598 km/h); 2. Dovizioso (I, Aprilia), 3"483; 3. Kallio (SF, Honda), 18"797; 4. Badolini (I, Aprilia), 18"915; 5. W. De Angelis (RSM, Honda), 19"031; 6. Angeloni (I, Honda), 19"310; 7. E. Leardini (I, Honda), 20"338; 8. Bianco (I, Honda), 20"459;
9. Beno (SLO, Aprilia), 20"579; 10. Biaocco (I, Aprilia), 24"442;
11. Tresoldi (CH, Honda), 25"316; 12. Pellino (I, Honda), 28"743;
13. Manna (I, Aprilia), 32"851; 14. Nedog (SLO, Aprilia), 41"983;
15. Pagnoni (I, Honda), 42"091.

May 27th - Hungary - Hungaroring
1. Dovizioso (I, Aprilia), 28'45"19 (132.609 km/h); 2. Ballerini (I, Aprilia), 0"19; 3. Kallio (SF, Honda), 12"67; 4. Bianco (I, Honda), 16"37; 5. Baldolini (I, Aprilia), 19"04; 6. E. Leardini (I, Honda), 27"02;
7. Romboli (I, Honda), 29"00; 8. Martin (GB, Honda), 29"16; 9. Angeloni (I, Honda), 35"75; 10. Miksovsky (CZ, Honda), 36"10; 11. Beno (SLO, Aprilia), 36"25; 12. Tallevi (I, Aprilia), 36"47; 13. Pagnoni (I, Honda), 36"67; 14. Bittman (CZ, Honda), 37"75; 15. Reissmann (D, Honda), 39"77.

June 10th - Croatia - Grobnik
1. Ballerini (I, Aprilia), 25'24"431 (157.500 km/h); 2. Baldolini (I, Aprilia), 14"785; 3. Kallio (SF, Honda), 14"824; 4. Conti (I, Honda), 14"868; 5. Angeloni (I, Honda), 28"221; 6. Romboli (I, Honda), 28"279;
7. Bianco (I, Honda), 28"509; 8. Manna (I, Aprilia), 28"528; 9. Bruschi (I, Honda), 28"750; 10. Tallevi (I, Aprilia), 29"112; 11. W. De Angelis (RSM, Honda), 29"207; 12. Stern (SLO, Aprilia), 33"396; 13. Harms (DK, Honda), 34"160; 14. Kalab (CZ, Honda), 34"536; 15. Danese (I, Aprilia), 37"469.

June 29th - The Netherlands - Assen
1. Ballerini (I, Aprilia), 27'16"019 (159.727 km/h); 2. Bianco (I, Honda), 13"069; 3. Dovizioso (I, Aprilia), 16"307; 4. Baldolini (I, Aprilia), 18"723; 5. Lorenzo (E, Honda), 22"103; 6. Kallio (SF, Honda), 22"392; 7. Martin (GB, Honda), 22"574; 8. Tresoldi (CH, Honda), 30"901; 9. Pellino (I, Honda), 31"171; 10. Pistoni (I, Rumi), 31"383; 11. Conti (I, Honda), 35"278; 12. Aldrovandi (I, Honda), 38"014; 13. Tallevi (I, Aprilia), 39"645; 14. Kalab (CZ, Honda), 45"425; 15. Lefort (F, Honda), 47"631.

July 8th - Hungary - Pannoniaring
1. Dovizioso (I, Aprilia), 32'12"463 (141.283 km/h); 2. Ballerini (I, Aprilia), 0"009; 3. Pellino (I, Honda), 17"115; 4. Baldolini (I, Aprilia), 1 lap; 5. Angeloni (I, Honda); 6. E. Leardini (I, Honda);
7. Aldrovandi (I, Honda); 8. Stern (SLO, Aprilia); 9. Conti (I, Honda);
10. Pistoni (I, Rumi); 11. Manna (I, Aprilia); 12. W. De Angelis (RSM, Honda); 13. Van Ginhoven (NL, Aprilia); 14. Kalab (CZ, Honda);
15. Bittman (CZ, Honda).

July 29th - Czech Republic - Most
1. Dovizioso (I, Aprilia), 28'52"985 (156.152 km/h); 2. Lorenzo (E, Honda), 0"124; 3. Baldolini (I, Aprilia), 11"480; 4. Bianco (I, Honda), 11"667; 5. Ballerini (I, Aprilia), 12"813; 6. Klein (D, Honda), 15"097; 7. Angeloni (I, Honda), 22"410; 8. Bruschi (I, Honda), 22"491;
9. R. Harms (DK, Honda), 23"313; 10. Kirmeier (D, Honda), 23"445;
11. E. Leardini (I, Honda), 23"750; 12. Conti (I, Honda), 36"358;
13. Saltarelli (I, Aprilia), 37"349; 14. W. De Angelis (RSM, Honda), 37"601; 15. Danese (I, Aprilia), 37"918.

September 30th - Portugal - Braga
1. Lorenzo (E, Honda), 29'02"708 (131.010 km/h); 2. Bianco (I, Honda), 0"534; 3. Dovizioso (I, Aprilia), 1'680; 4. Ballerini (I, Aprilia), 11"928;
5. Klein (D, Honda), 15"315; 6. M. Kallio (SF, Honda), 23"764; 7. Lenart

(H, Honda), 24"955; 8. Tallevi (I, Aprilia), 30"264; 9. Baldolini (I, Aprilia), 33"397; 10. Stern (SLO, Aprilia), 35"393; 11. Martin (GB, Honda), 36"167; 12. Van Ginhoven (NL, Aprilia), 39"146;
13. Kalab (CZ, Honda), 39"528; 14. Aldrovandi (I, Honda), 45"053;
15. H. Lauslehto (SF, Honda), 49"531.

October 7th - Spain - Cartagena
1. Pellino (I, Honda), 36'56"197 (126.300 km/h); 2. Bianco (I, Honda), 2"087; 3. Nöhles(*) (D, Honda), 21"256; 4. Dovizioso (I, Aprilia), 23"564; 5. Bonache (E, Aprilia), 23"705; 6. Baldolini (I, Aprilia), 33"679; 7. Klein (D, Honda), 34"956; 8. Tallevi (I, Aprilia), 43"686;
9. Fabricio (I, Aprilia), 43"701; 10. Lenar (H, Honda), 43"844;
11. Aldrovandi (I, Honda), 55"070; 12. Kalab (CZ, Honda), 56"704;
13. Ortega (E, Honda), 1'01"286; 14. H. Lauslehto (SF, Honda), 1'01"663;
15. Martin (GB, Honda), 1'02"690.

Final Classification
1. Andrea Dovizioso (I, Aprilia), 140
2. Andrea Ballerini (I, Aprilia), 139
3. Stefano Bianco (I, Honda), 103
4. Baldolini (I, Aprilia), 103; 5. M. Kallio (SF, Honda), 68; 6. Lorenzo (E, Honda), 56;
7. Pellino (I, Honda), 52; 8. Angeloni (I, Honda), 48; 9. E. Leardini (I, Honda), 34;
10. Klein (D, Honda), 31; 11. Stern (SLO, Aprilia), 30; 12. Tallevi (I, Aprilia), 29;
13. Conti (I, Honda), 29; 14. Martin (GB, Honda), 23; 15. W. De Angelis (RSM, Honda), 22.

250CC

March 18th - France - Le Mans

1. Guintoli (F, Aprilia), 31'25"576 (147.946 km/h); 2. Oliver (E, Honda), 44"767; 3. Mizera (F, Yamaha), 44"937; 4. Garcia (F, Honda), 45"212; 5. Janssen (NL, Honda), 58"531; 6. Barton (GB, Honda), 58"582; 7. Heidolf (D, Yamaha), 1'00"342; 8. Philippe (F, Honda), 1'01"106; 9. Van De Lagemaat (NL, Honda), 1'02"640; 10. Mora (F, Honda), 1'09"956; 11. Coates (IRL, Honda), 1'12"144; 12. Fouloi (F, Yamaha), 1'14"571; 13. Gemmel (D, Honda), 1'26"608; 14. Rebuttini (F, Honda), 1'27"140; 15. Dietrich (F, Honda), 1'27"291.

April 29th - Italy - Vallelunga

1. Coates (IRL, Honda), 31'26"761 (135.164 km/h); 2. Janssen (NL, Honda), 5"310; 3. Rous (CZ, Honda), 6"023; 4. Neukirchen (D, Yamaha), 6"123; 5. Heidolf (D, Yamaha), 9"129; 6. Bartolini (I, Honda), 9"418; 7. Tunstall (GB, Honda), 9"539; 8. Selmar (DK, Yamaha), 11"005; 9. Gemmel (D, Honda), 11"590; 10. Ribalta (E, Honda), 16"564; 11. Van De Lagemaat (NL, Aprilia), 21"507; 12. Boccolini (I, Aprilia), 30"883; 13. Visscher (NL, Aprilia), 31"184; 14. Filart (NL, Honda), 33"176; 15. Ramponi (I, Honda), 44"233.

May 27th - Hungary - Hungaroring

1. Garcia (E, Honda), 32'05"62 (133.657 km/h); 2. Coates (IRL, Honda), 1"21; 3. Rizmayer (H, TSR-Honda), 3"55; 4. Janssen (NL, Honda), 3"76; 5. Heidolf (D, Yamaha), 6"12; 6. Van De Lagemaat (NL, Aprilia), 14"40; 7. Gemmel (D, Honda), 20"10; 8. Rous (CZ, Honda), 20"31; 9. Tunstall (GB, Honda), 34"40; 10. Boccolini (I, Aprilia), 36"82; 11. Rank (D, Honda), 47"89; 12. Di Salvo (USA, Honda), 48"03; 13. Visscher (NL, Aprilia), 1'24"70; 14. Heierli (CH, Honda), 1 lap; 15. Westra (B, Honda).

June 10th - Croatia - Grobnik

1. Janssen (NL, Honda), 27'59"465 (160.800 km/h); 2. Garcia (E, Honda), 0"367; 3. Coates (IRL, Honda), 0"391; 4. Oliver (E, Honda), 7"915; 5. Rizmayer (H, TSR-Honda), 8"329; 6. Van De Lagemaat (NL, Aprilia), 8"575; 7. Heidolf (D, Yamaha), 10"091; 8. Gemmel (D, Honda), 20"052; 9. Sorensen (DK, Yamaha), 20"357; 10. Di Salvo (USA, Honda), 26"769; 11. Boccolini (I, Aprilia), 27"423; 12. Dietrich (F, Honda), 27"586; 13. Vincent (F, Honda), 28"204; 14. Marchand (F, Honda), 28"347; 15. Neukirchen (D, Yamaha), 28"784.

June 30th - The Netherlands - Assen

1. Coates (IRL, Honda), 30'30"076 (166.588 km/h); 2. Janssen (NL, Honda), 8"202; 3. Van De Lagemaat (NL, Aprilia), 25"660; 4. Philippe (F, Honda), 29"068; 5. Oliver (E, Honda), 31"176; 6. Gemmel (D, Honda), 40"772; 7. Rizmayer (H, TSR-Honda), 40"854; 8. V. Kallio (SF, Yamaha), 46"085; 9. Neukirchner (D, Honda), 47"140; 10. Marchand (F, Honda), 55"863; 11. Filart (NL, Honda), 59"713; 12. Rous (CZ, TSR-Honda), 59"832; 13. Selmar (DK, Yamaha), 1'07"665; 14. Hoogeveen (NL, Yamaha), 1'08"216; 15. Blok (NL, Honda), 1'08"303.

July 29th - Czech Republic - Most

1. Garcia (E, Honda), 31'12"347 (159.509 km/h); 2. Rizmayer (H, TSR-Honda), 0"217; 3. Oliver (E, Honda), 2"146; 4. Di Salvo (USA, Honda), 24"032; 5. Gemmel (D, Honda), 24"222; 6. Hafenegger (D, Aprilia), 24"400; 7. Coates (IRL, Honda), 25"837; 8. Heidolf (D, Yamaha), 26"336; 9. Selmar (DK, Yamaha), 43"547; 10. Lucchetti (I, Aprilia), 50"766; 11. Van De Lagemaat (NL, Aprilia), 51"271; 12. Dietrich (F, Honda), 51"682; 13. Sorensen (DK, Yamaha), 51"905; 14. Polzer (A, TSR-Honda), 1'03"596; 15. Litjens (NL, Honda), 1'12"474.

September 30th - Portugal - Braga

1. Rizmayer (H, TSR-Honda), 32'29"831 (133.821 km/h); 2. Oliver (E, Honda), 3"979; 3. Garcia (E, Honda), 13"835; 4. Janssen (NL, Honda), 22"882; 5. Gemmel (D, Honda), 36"516; 6. Di Salvo (USA, Honda), 36"707; 7. Dietrich (F, Honda), 37"192; 8. V. Kallio (SF, Yamaha), 45"852; 9. T. Lauslehto (SF, Yamaha), 1'05"151; 10. Hafenegger (D, Aprilia), 1'12"986; 11. Aubry (F, Honda), 1 lap; 12. Heierli (CH, Honda), 2 laps. 12 finishers.

October 7th - Spain - Cartagena

1. Molina (E, Yamaha), 37'50"269 (129,100 km/h); 2. Oliver (E, Honda), 0"103; 3. Garcia (E, Honda), 5"720; 4. Coates (IRL, Honda), 8"541; 5. Rizmayer (H, TSR-Honda), 19"321; 6. Gemmel (D, Honda), 20"065; 7. Philippe (F, Honda), 24"612; 8. Sörensen (DK, Yamaha), 24"886; 9. Heidolf (D, Yamaha), 28"856; 10. Hafenegger (D, Aprilia), 29"918; 11. V. Kallio (SF, Yamaha), 35"272; 12. Neukirchner (D, Honda), 48"751; 13. Dietrich (F, Honda), 1'11"890; 14. T. Lauslehto (SF, Honda), 1 lap; 15. Heierli (CH, Honda).

Final Classification

1. David Garcia (E, Honda), 118
2. Adrian Coates (IRL, Honda), 114
3. Lucas Oliver (E, Honda), 105
4. Janssen (NL, Honda), 104; 5. Rizmayer (H, TSR-Honda), 92; 6. Gemmel (D, Honda), 70; 7. Heidolf (D, Yamaha), 56; 8. Van De Lagemaat (NL, Aprilia), 54; 9. Philippe (F, Honda), 34; 10. Di Salvo (USA, Honda), 33; 11. Rous (CZ, Honda), 28; 12. Molina (E, Yamaha), 25; 13. Hafenegger (D, Aprilia), 22; 14. Dietrich (F, Honda), 22; 15. V. Kallio (SF, Yamaha), 21.

SUPERSPORT

March 18th - France - Le Mans

1. Corradi (I, Yamaha), 33'48"764 (131.121 km/h); 2. Lagrive (F, Yamaha), 8"791; 3. Schulten (D, Yamaha), 8"839; 4. Gomez (F, Suzuki), 10"617; 5. Hartelman (NL, Honda), 13"675; 6. Soren-Nielsen (DK, Yamaha), 14"611; 7. Rodriguez (E, Ducati), 16"717; 8. Penzkofer (D, Yamaha), 21"887; 9. Moreira (F, Kawasaki), 22"971; 10. Van Beek (NL, Yamaha), 29"957; 11. Bisconti (I, Yamaha), 35"023; 12. Zaiser (A, Honda), 35"835; 13. Folkesson (S, Ducati), 36"483; 14. Bulega (I, Yamaha), 36"888; 15. Marangon (I, Yamaha), 43"767.

April 29th - Italy - Vallelunga

1. Corradi (I, Yamaha), 35'52"400 (134.640 km/h); 2. Russo (I, Yamaha), 5"893; 3. Nannelli (I, Ducati), 10"729; 4. Schulten (D, Yamaha), 12"512; 5. Pennese (I, Yamaha), 32"784; 6. Penzkofer (D, Ducati), 32"975; 7. Melone (I, Yamaha), 37"297; 8. Camparno (I, Yamaha), 39"738; 9. Bisconti (I, Yamaha), 41"566; 10. Tocca (I, Yamaha), 41"938; 11. Hartelman (NL, Honda), 42"189; 12. Folkesson (S, Ducati), 55'016; 13. Morreale (I, Yamaha), 55'413; 14. Conti (I, Yamaha), 55"692; 15. Cavalloni (I, Suzuki), 55"838.

May 27th - Hungary - Hungaroring

1. Corradi (I, Yamaha), 39'21"82 (133.188 km/h); 2. Schulten (D, Yamaha), 2"63; 3. Zaiser (A, Honda), 27"37; 4. Tarizzo (I, Yamaha), 49"29; 5. Nannelli (I, Ducati), 56"76; 6. Bisconti (I, Yamaha), 1'04"94; 7. Szabo (H, Yamaha), 1'11"50; 8. Maher (IRL, Yamaha), 1'13"92; 9. Prager (CZ, Suzuki), 1'34"20; 10. Bican (CZ, Suzuki), 1'38"64; 11. Marangon (I, Yamaha), 1'47"66; 12. Ouda (CZ, Honda), 1'54"39; 13. Balaz (SK, Honda), 1 lap; 14. Tchoi (GB, Suzuki); 15. Ludwig (D, Suzuki).

June 10th - Croatia - Grobnik

1. Schulten (D, Yamaha), 31'27"165 (159.000 km/h); 2. Corradi (I, Yamaha), 13"055; 3. Zaiser (A, Honda), 19"537; 4. Magnadi (I, Yamaha), 35"514; 5. Tarizzo (I, Yamaha), 35"533; 6. Lagrive (F, Yamaha), 36"071; 7. Nannelli (I, Ducati), 40"772; 8. Folkesson (S, Ducati), 43"911; 9. Bisconti (I, Yamaha), 54"652; 10. Furlan (I, Yamaha), 54"948; 11. Marangon (I, Yamaha), 1'02"039; 12. Ferrini (I, Yamaha), 1'05"043; 13. Mayrhofer (A, Honda), 1'05"332; 14. Camparno (I, Yamaha), 1'05"451; 15. Maher (IRL, Yamaha), 1'06"437.

June 30th - The Netherlands - Assen

1. Corradi (I, Yamaha), 35'14"636 (164.767 km/h); 2. Schulten (D, Yamaha), 0"452; 3. Lagrive (F, Yamaha), 12"280; 4. Verstraeten (NL, Honda), 15"237; 5. Zaiser (A, Honda), 17"117; 6. Hartelmann (NL, Honda), 24"636; 7. Nannelli (I, Ducati), 25"521; 8. Van Beek (NL, Yamaha), 28"485; 9. Tarizzo (I, Yamaha), 30"619; 10. Pajic (NL, Kawasaki), 37"265; 11. Steinmetz (D, Yamaha), 48"303; 12. Theunissen (NL, Honda), 57"264; 13. Wanninger (D, Kawasaki), 1'01"836; 14. Ekerold (SA, Suzuki), 1'03"035; 15. Greven (NL, Yamaha), 1'03"398.

July 29th - Czech Republic - Most

1. Schulten (D, Yamaha), 23'36"112 (158.174 km/h); 2. Corradi (I, Yamaha), 3"972; 3. Nannelli (I, Ducati), 4"139; 4. Zaiser (A, Honda), 4"388; 5. Lagrive (F, Yamaha), 4"895; 6. Penzkofer (D, Ducati), 16"379; 7. Soren-Nielsen (DK, Yamaha), 26"234; 8. Fritzsche (D, Suzuki), 35"902; 9. Stief (D, Yamaha), 37"734; 10. Folkesson (S, Ducati), 39"614; 11. Tarizzo (I, Yamaha), 44"573; 12. Maher (IRL, Yamaha), 44"798; 13. Patek (SLO, Yamaha), 45"339; 14. Ouda (CZ, Honda), 56"955; 15. Prager (CZ, Suzuki), 1'09"346.

September 30th - Portugal - Braga

1. Corradi (I, Yamaha), 37'00"726 (132.164 km/h); 2. Zaiser (A, Honda), 23"237; 3. Soren-Nielsen (DK, Yamaha), 1'07"953; 4. Bisconti (I, Yamaha), 1'09"649; 5. Folkesson (S, Ducati), 1'23"178; 6. Rasmussen (DK, Kawasaki), 1'23"528; 7. Carreira (P, Honda), 1 lap; 8. Prager (CZ, Suzuki); 9. Andersson (S, Kawasaki); 10. Silva (P, Honda); 11. Livi (I, Ducati), 2 laps. 11 finishers.

October 7th - Spain - Cartagena

1. Corradi (I, Yamaha), 40'16"041 (126,100 km/h); 2. Schulten (D, Yamaha), 5"086; 3. Lagrive (F, Yamaha), 15"115; 4. Martinez (E, Yamaha), 18"987; 5. Lindström (S, Suzuki), 21"059; 6. Hervas (E, Yamaha), 23"262; 7. Folkesson (S, Ducati), 35"397; 8. Soren-Nielsen (DK, Yamaha), 47"682; 9. Devahive (E, Yamaha), 57"927; 10. Rasmussen (DK, Kawasaki), 1'07"902; 11. Pandilla (E, Kawasaki), 1'10"087; 12. Velini (I, Yamaha), 1'10"837; 13. Oliver (E, Yamaha), 1'13"034; 14. Neukirchen (D, Yamaha), 1'13"247; 15. Moraga (E, Yamaha), 1'13"589.

Final Classification

1. Alessio Corradi (I, Yamaha), 195
2. Michael Schulten (D, Yamaha), 114
3. Christian Zaiser (A, Honda), 84
4. Lagrive (F, Yamaha), 74; 5. Nanelli (I, Ducati), 62; 6. Soren-Nielsen (DK, Yamaha), 43; 7. Bisconti (I, Yamaha), 43; 8. Folkesson (S, Ducati), 42; 9. Tarizzo (I, Yamaha), 38; 10. Penzkofer (D, Ducati), 28; 11. Hartelman (NL, Honda), 26; 12. Russo (I, Yamaha), 20; 13. Rasmussen (DK, Kawasaki), 16; 14. Prager (CZ, Suzuki), 16; 15. Magnani (I, Yamaha), 16.

SUPERSTOCK

March 11th - Spain - Valencia

1. Ellison (GB, Suzuki), 22'01"991 (152.065 km/h); 2. Tortoroglio (I, Suzuki), 1"770; 3. Alfonsi (I, Ducati), 6"118; 4. Johnson (GB, Honda), 6"425; 5. Oliver-Bulto (E, Aprilia), 15"168; 6. Heckles (GB, Honda), 16"221; 7. Jerzenbeck (D, Suzuki), 17"167; 8. Wegscheider (I, Suzuki), 17"994; 9. Vankeymeulen (B, Honda), 19"570; 10. Nutt (GB, Suzuki), 23"709; 11. Tosolini (I, Ducati), 24"017; 12. Romanelli (I, Suzuki), 25"285; 13. Vizziolo (I, Yamaha), 28"367; 14. Four (F, Honda), 32"692; 15. Fourreau (F, Suzuki), 41"619.

May 13th - Italy - Monza

1. Tortoroglio (I, Suzuki), 20'57"373 (182.446 km/h); 2. Ellison (GB, Suzuki), 3"424; 3. Nutt (GB, Suzuki), 18"488; 4. Jerzenbeck (D, Suzuki), 20"376; 5. Tosolini (I, Ducati), 20"469; 6. Alfonsi (I, Ducati), 26"970; 7. Nabert (D, Suzuki), 28"360; 8. Oliver (E, Aprilia), 28"846; 9. Vizziello (I, Yamaha), 29"626; 10. Fourreau (F, Suzuki), 46"013; 11. Knobloch (A, Yamaha), 46"074; 12. Four (F, Honda), 46"773; 13. Ricci (I, Suzuki), 47"047; 14. Weynand (B, Yamaha), 47"507; 15. Mooijman (NL, Yamaha), 54"518.

May 27th - Great Britain - Donington

1. Ellison (GB, Suzuki), 24'52"807 (145.526 km/h); 2. Tortoroglio (I, Suzuki), 0"426; 3. Heckles (GB, Honda), 8"582; 4. Wegscheider (I, Suzuki), 13"305; 5. Tosolini (I, Ducati), 15"602; 6. Mason (GB, Honda), 18"888; 7. Nutt (GB, Suzuki), 20"625; 8. Jerzenbeck (D, Suzuki), 21"117; 9. Murphy (GB, Suzuki), 23"571; 10. Four (F, Honda), 25"741; 11. Brogan (GB, Aprilia), 26"525; 12. Miller (GB, Suzuki), 33"730; 13. Mauri (I, Ducati), 46"057; 14. Tibble (GB, Honda), 53"521; 15. Mooijman (NL, Yamaha), 58"512.

June 10th - Germany - Lausitz

1. Ellison (GB, Suzuki), 24'40"943 (145.148 km/h); 2. Tortoroglio (I, Suzuki), 6"650; 3. Heckles (GB, Honda), 12"209; 4. Jerzenbeck (D, Suzuki), 16"605; 5. Romanelli (I, Suzuki), 21"439; 6. Vizziello (I, Yamaha), 25"533; 7. Tosolini (I, Ducati), 26"068; 8. Alfonsi (I, Ducati), 26"146; 9. Notman (GB, Suzuki), 28"353; 10. Wegscheider (I, Suzuki), 33"273; 11. Mauri (I, Ducati), 34"851; 12. Knobloch (A, Yamaha), 43"650; 13. Fourreau (F, Suzuki), 52"113; 14. Mooijman (NL, Yamaha), 1'04"483; 15. Vleugels (B, Yamaha), 1'04"536.

June 24th - San Marino - Misano

1. Oliver-Bulto (E, Aprilia), 20'19"359 (143.840 km/h); 2. Heckles (GB, Honda), 0"674; 3. Romanelli (I, Suzuki), 4"343; 4. Jerzenbeck (D, Suzuki), 12"391; 5. Tosolini (I, Ducati), 14"258; 6. Battisti (I, Suzuki), 30"181; 7. Fabbroni (I, Honda), 33"970; 8. Weynand (B, Yamaha), 34"284; 9. Ricci (I, Suzuki), 34"663; 10. Nabert (B, Suzuki), 34"977; 11. Fourreau (F, Suzuki), 39"910; 12. Mauri (I, Ducati), 42"038; 13. Gyger (CH, Honda), 43"252; 14. Bakker (NL, Ducati), 44"366; 15. Martinez (E, Aprilia), 45"792.

July 29th - Europe - Brands Hatch

1. Heckles (GB, Honda), 22'59"554 (165.223 km/h); 2. Tortoroglio (I, Suzuki), 2"327; 3. Ellison (GB, Suzuki), 3"460; 4. Murphy (GB, Suzuki), 4"254; 5. Burns (GB, Suzuki), 5"047; 6. Nutt (GB, Suzuki), 6"737; 7. Four (F, Suzuki), 7"398; 8. Vizziello (I, Yamaha), 13"656; 9. Romanelli (I, Suzuki), 13"884; 10. Notman (GB, Suzuki), 20"723; 11. Johnson (GB, Suzuki), 21"049; 12. Jerzenbeck (D, Suzuki), 22"714; 13. Vanckeymeulen (B, Suzuki), 28"650; 14. Vleugels (B, Yamaha), 29"056; 15. Nabert (D, Suzuki), 32"992.

September 2nd - Germany - Oschersleben

1. Ellison (GB, Suzuki), 23'22"173 (141.222 km/h); 2. Nutt (GB, Suzuki), 3"112; 3. Tortoroglio (I, Suzuki), 4"198; 4. Notman (GB, Suzuki), 5"390; 5. Jerzenbeck (D, Suzuki), 5"713; 6. Wegscheider (I, Suzuki), 6"977; 7. Four (F, Suzuki), 9"291; 8. Vizziello (I, Yamaha), 9"748; 9. Romanelli (I, Suzuki), 12"539; 10. Heckles (GB, Honda), 17"752; 11. Mauri (I, Ducati), 18"032; 12. Fourreau (F, Suzuki), 18"868;

13. Alfonsi (I, Ducati), 21"118; 14. Knobloch (A, Yamaha), 26"520;
15. Vanckeymeulen (B, Suzuki), 27"528.

September 9th - The Netherlands - Assen
1. Mauri (I, Ducati), 29'58"127 (145.327 km/h); 2. Bakker (NL, Ducati), 3"969; 3. Withag (NL, Honda), 34"898; 4. Vizziello (I, Yamaha), 36"656; 5. Tortoroglio (I, Suzuki), 48"684; 6. Ellison (GB, Suzuki), 48"698; 7. Martinez (E, Aprilia), 54"782; 8. Oliver (E, Aprilia), 1'12"701; 9. Tosolini (I, Ducati), 1'15"802; 10. Alfonsi (I, Ducati) 1'27"358; 11. Vleugels (B, Yamaha), 1'57"320; 12. Nutt (GB, Suzuki), 2'02"716; 13. Gyger (CH, Honda), 2'17"723; 14. Murphy (GB, Suzuki), 1 lap; 15. Jerzenbeck (D, Suzuki).

September 30th - Italy - Imola
1. Tortoroglio (I, Suzuki), 25'18"608 (152.024 km/h); 2. Wegscheider (I, Suzuki), 3"009; 3. Ellison (GB, Suzuki), 4"805; 4. Nutt (GB, Suzuki), 6"045; 5. Heckles (GB, Honda), 6"315; 6. Vizziello (I, Yamaha), 11"699; 7. Four (F, Suzuki), 19"265; 8. Mauri (I, Ducati), 27"469; 9. Notman (GB, Suzuki), 27"520; 10. Fourreau (F, Suzuki), 29"727; 11. Romanelli (I, Suzuki), 30"842; 12. Pellizzon (I, Aprilia), 30"967; 13. Alfonsi (I, Ducati), 37"455; 14. Ricci (I, Suzuki), 38"275; 15. Tosolini (I, Ducati), 39"392.

Final Classification
1. James Ellison   (GB, Suzuki),   162
2. Walter Tortoroglio (I, Suzuki),   157

3. Mark Heckles   (GB, Honda),   104
4. Nutt (GB, Suzuki), 78; 5. Jerzenbeck (D, Suzuki), 72; 6. Vizziello (I, Yamaha), 59; 7. Wegscheider (I, Suzuki), 57; 8. Tosolini (I, Ducati), 55; 9. Oliver-Bulto (E, Aprilia), 52; 10. Romanelli (I, Suzuki), 50; 11. Mauri (I, Ducati), 49; 12. Alfonsi (I, Ducati), 46; 13. Four (F, Suzuki), 39; 14. Notman (GB, Suzuki), 33; 15. Fourreau (F, Suzuki), 25.

FRANCE CHAMPIONSHIP

125 CC

March 18th - Le Mans
1. Lefort (Aprilia); 2. Nigon (Yamaha); 3. Enjolras (Honda); 4. Tiberio (Honda); 5. Lougassi (Honda); 6. Sueur (Honda); 7. Petit (Honda); 8. A. Lagrive (Honda); 9. Perdriat (Yamaha); 10. Baudot (BR).

April 1st - Magny-Cours
1. Lefort (Aprilia); 2. Petit (Honda); 3. Nigon (Yamaha); 4. Chêne (Honda); 5. Tiberio (Honda); 6. De Rosa (Yamaha); 7. Lougassi (Honda); 8. Herouin (Honda); 9. Sicard (Honda); 10. Marsac (Honda).

April 8th - Albi
1. Petit (Honda); 2. Nigon (Yamaha); 3. Tiberio (Honda); 4. Enjolras (Honda); 5. Herouin (Honda); 6. Sicard (Honda); 7. A. Lagrive (Honda); 8. Burdin (Honda); 9. Lougassi (Honda); 10. Roma (Honda).

April 29th - Carole
1. Petit (Honda); 2. Nigon (Yamaha); 3. Chêne (Honda); 4. Sicard (Honda); 5. Enjolras (Honda); 6. Herouin (Honda); 7. Lougassi (Honda); 8. Gregoire (Honda); 9. Tiberio (Honda); 10. Goudet (Honda).

May 13th - Nogaro
1. Petit (Honda); 2. Nigon (Yamaha); 3. Tiberio (Honda); 4. Enjolras (Honda); 5. Gregoire (Honda); 6. Sueur (Honda); 7. Marsac (Honda); 8. Chêne (Honda); 9. Lougassi (Honda); 10. Goudet (Honda).

May 27th - Le Vigeant
1. Nigon (Yamaha); 2. Gregoire (Honda); 3. Noailly (Honda); 4. Lougassi (Honda); 5. De Rosa (Yamaha); 6. Sicard (Honda); 7. Roma (Honda); 8. Enjolras (Honda); 9. Goudet (Honda); 10. A. Lagrive (Honda).

June 24th - Lédenon
1. Nigon (Yamaha); 2. Petit (Honda); 3. Sicard (Honda); 4. Tiberio (Honda); 5. De Rosa (Yamaha); 6. Lougassi (Honda); 7. Grégoire (Honda); 8. Leblanc (Honda); 9. Lagrive (Honda); 10. Baudot (BR).

Final Classification
1. Erwan Nigon   (Yamaha), 146
2. Jimmy Petit   (Honda), 124
3. Yoann Tiberio (Honda), 76
4. Lougassi (Honda), 66; 5. Sicard (Honda), 56; 6. Gregoire (Honda), 55; 7. Enjolras (Honda), 53; 8. Lefort (Aprilia), 50; 9. Chêne (Honda), 41; 10. De Rosa (Yamaha), 37; 11. Hérouin (Honda), 34; 12. A. Lagrive (Honda), 30; 13. Goudet (Honda), 22; 14. Sueur (Honda), 20; 15. Roma (Honda), 20 .

250CC

March 18th - Le Mans
1. Mizera (Yamaha); 2. Philippe (Honda); 3. De Puniet (Aprilia); 4. Marchand (Honda); 5. K. Rebuttini (Honda); 6. Ouvrard (Yamaha); 7. Louatron (Honda); 8. Fouloi (Yamaha); 9. Raffeau (Yamaha); 10. B. Rebuttini (Yamaha).

April 1st - Magny-Cours
1. Philippe (Honda); 2. Mizera (Yamaha); 3. Mora (Honda); 4. Marchand (Honda); 5. Dietrich (Honda); 6. Ouvrard (Yamaha); 7. Chauchot (Yamaha); 8. Lussiana (Honda); 9. Fouloi (Yamaha); 10. Lecomte (Aprilia).

April 8th - Albi
1. Mizera (Yamaha); 2. Marchand (Honda); 3. Dietrich (Honda); 4. Metro (Aprilia); 5. Lussiana (Honda); 6. Louatron (Honda); 7. Ouvrard (Yamaha); 8. K. Rebuttini (Honda); 9. B. Rebuttini (Yamaha); 10. Aubry (Honda).

April 29th - Carole
1. Mora (Honda); 2. Dietrich (Honda); 3. Fouloi (Yamaha); 4. K. Rebuttini (Honda); 5. Mizera (Yamaha); 6. Aubry (Honda); 7. Lussiana (Honda); 8. Vecchioni (Yamaha); 9. B. Rebuttini (Yamaha); 10. Ouvrard (Yamaha).

May 13th - Nogaro
1. Mizera (Yamaha); 2. Mora (Honda); 3. Metro (Aprilia); 4. Marchand (Honda); 5. Fouloi (Yamaha); 6. K. Rebuttini (Honda); 7. B. Rebuttini (Yamaha); 8. Ouvrard (Yamaha); 9. Lecomte (Aprilia); 10. Aubry (Honda).

May 27th - Le Vigeant
1. Mora (Honda); 2. Dietrich (Honda); 3. K. Rebuttini (Honda); 4. Ouvrard (Yamaha); 5. Aubry (Honda); 6. Poulle (Honda) ; 7. Boutin (Honda) ; 8. Fouloi (Yamaha); 9. Lussiana (Honda); 10. Lecomte (Aprilia).

June 24th - Lédenon
1. Mora (Honda); 2. Marchand (Honda); 3. Dietrich (Honda); 4. Mizera (Yamaha); 5. K. Rebuttini (Honda); 6. Poulle (Honda); 7. Aubry (Honda); 8. Lussiana (Honda); 9. B. Rebuttini (Yamaha); 10. Palacios (Honda).

Final Classification
1. Eric Mizera   (Yamaha), 119
2. Hervé Mora   (Honda), 116
3. Guillaume Dietrich (Honda),   83
4. Marchand (Honda), 79; 5. K. Rebuttini (Honda), 62; 6. Ouvrard (Yamaha), 56; 7. Fouloi (Yamaha), 50; 8. Lussiana (Honda), 48; 9. Aubry (Honda), 47; 10. Philippe (Honda), 45; 11. B. Rebuttini (Yamaha), 45; 12. Metro (Aprilia), 32; 13. Poulle (Honda), 24; 14. Louatron (Honda), 24; 15. Lecomte (Aprilia), 23.

SUPERSPORT

March 18th - Le Mans
1. Muscat (Ducati); 2. Devoyon (Yamaha); 3. Costes (Honda); 4. Gimbert (Honda); 5. M. Lagrive (Yamaha); 6. Muteau (Yamaha); 7. Guezennec (Yamaha); 8. Moreira (Kawasaki); 9. Mounier (Yamaha); 10. Rousseau (Kawasaki).

April 1st - Magny-Cours
1. Muscat (Ducati); 2. M. Lagrive (Yamaha); 3. Muteau (Yamaha); 4. Gomez (Suzuki); 5. Cortinovis (Suzuki); 6. Costes (Honda); 7. Morillon (Yamaha); 8. Gimbert (Honda); 9. Mounier (Yamaha); 10. Giabbani (Suzuki).

April 8th - Albi
1. Muscat (Ducati); 2. Muteau (Yamaha); 3. M. Lagrive (Yamaha); 4. Moreira (Kawasaki); 5. Diss (Ducati); 6. Cortinovis (Suzuki); 7. Mounier (Yamaha); 8. Rousseau (Kawasaki); 9. Morillon (Yamaha); 10. Giabbani (Suzuki).

April 29th - Carole
1. Muscat (Ducati); 2. Mounier (Yamaha); 3. M. Lagrive (Yamaha); 4. Giabbani (Suzuki); 5. Muteau (Yamaha); 6. Moreira (Kawasaki); 7. Cortinovis (Suzuki); 8. Diss (Ducati); 9. Rousseau (Kawasaki); 10. Capela (Yamaha).

May 13th - Nogaro
1. Costes (Honda); 2. Gimbert (Honda); 3. Giabbani (Suzuki); 4. Mounier (Yamaha); 5. M. Lagrive (Yamaha); 6. Moreira (Kawasaki); 7. Morillon (Yamaha); 8. Diss (Ducati); 9. Rousseau (Kawasaki); 10. Cortinovis (Suzuki).

May 27th - Le Vigeant
1. Muscat (Ducati); 2. M. Lagrive (Yamaha); 3. Costes (Honda); 4. Giabbani (Suzuki); 5. Morillon (Yamaha); 6. Muteau (Yamaha); 7. Morillas (Yamaha) ; 8. Gimbert (Honda); 9. Mounier (Yamaha); 10. Da Costa (Yamaha).

June 24th - Lédenon
1. Da Costa (Yamaha); 2. Morillon (Yamaha); 3. Diss (Ducati); 4. Rogier (Yamaha); 5. Guezennec (Yamaha); 6. Cortinovis (Suzuki); 7. Devoyon (Yamaha); 8. Fremy (Yamaha); 9. Gomez (Suzuki); 10. Palesso (Yamaha).

Final Classification
1. David Muscat   (Ducati),   125
2. Matthieu Lagrive (Yamaha),   94
3. William Costes   (Honda),   67
4. Muteau (Yamaha), 67; 5. Morillon (Yamaha), 65; 6. Mounier (Yamaha), 63; 7. Giabbani (Suzuki), 57; 8. Cortinovis (Suzuki), 56; 9. Gimbert (Honda), 50; 10. Diss (Ducati), 46; 11. Moreira (Kawasaki), 45; 12. Devoyon (Yamaha), 41; 13. Da Costa (Yamaha), 40; 14. Guezennec (Yamaha), 36; 15. Rousseau (Kawasaki), 29.

STOCKSPORT

March 18th - Le Mans
1. Dobe (Suzuki); 2. Moreira (Kawasaki); 3. Nogueira (Suzuki); 4. Bonhuil (Suzuki); 5. Rulfo (Suzuki); 6. Lerat-Vanstaen (Suzuki); 7. Di Foggia (Suzuki); 8. Neff (Yamaha); 9. Four (Suzuki); 10. Gabrieli (Suzuki).

April 1st - Magny-Cours
1. Dobe (Suzuki); 2. Moreira (Kawasaki); 3. Lerat-Vanstaen (Suzuki); 4. Nogueira (Suzuki); 5. Le Glatin (Suzuki); 6. Bonhuil (Suzuki); 7. Fernandez (Yamaha); 8. F. Jond (Suzuki); 9. S. Jond (Suzuki); 10. Donischal (Suzuki).

April 8th - Albi
1. Moreira (Kawasaki); 2. Dobe (Suzuki); 3. Bonhuil (Suzuki); 4. Le Glatin (Suzuki); 5. Lerat-Vanstaen (Suzuki); 6. Nogueira (Suzuki); 7. Neff (Yamaha); 8. Ulmann (Suzuki); 9. Donischal (Suzuki); 10. Di Foggia (Suzuki).

April 29th - Carole
1. Moreira (Kawasaki); 2. Nogueira (Suzuki); 3. Le Glatin (Suzuki); 4. Di Foggia (Suzuki); 5. Lerat-Vanstaen (Suzuki); 6. Laurent (Suzuki); 7. Ulmann (Suzuki); 8. Notte (Suzuki) ; 9. Roche (Yamaha) 10. Duterne (Yamaha).

May 13th - Nogaro

1. Duterne (Yamaha); 2. Lerat-Vanstaen (Suzuki); 3. Ulmann (Suzuki); 4. Nogueira (Suzuki); 5. Bonhuil (Suzuki); 6. Moreira (Kawasaki); 7. F. Jond (Suzuki); 8. Donischal (Suzuki); 9. Donzel (Suzuki); 10. Moisan (Suzuki).

May 27th - Le Vigeant

1. Le Glatin (Suzuki); 2. Lerat-Vanstaen (Suzuki); 3. F. Jond (Suzuki); 4. Ulmann (Suzuki); 5. Di Foggia (Suzuki); 6. Bonhuil (Suzuki); 7. Moreira (Kawasaki); 8. Moisan (Suzuki); 9. Jolivet (Suzuki); 10. Donzel (Suzuki).

June 24th - Lédenon

1. Le Glatin (Suzuki); 2. Moreira (Kawasaki); 3. F. Jond (Suzuki); 4. Bonhuil (Suzuki); 5. Di Foggia (Suzuki); 6. Lerat-Vanstaen (Suzuki); 7. Donischal (Suzuki); 8. Nogueira (Suzuki); 9. Roche (Yamaha); 10. Duterne (Yamaha).

Final Classification

1. **Frédéric Moreira** (Kawasaki), 129
2. **Pierrot Lerat-Vanstaen** (Suzuki), 98
3. **Jean-François Le Glatin** (Suzuki), 90
4. Nogueira (Suzuki), 80; 5. Bonhuil (Suzuki), 73; 6. Dobe (Suzuki), 70; 7. Ulmann (Suzuki), 55; 8. Di Foggia (Suzuki), 52; 9. F. Jond (Suzuki), 49; 10. Duterne (Yamaha), 47; 11. Donischal (Suzuki), 34; 12. Moisan (Suzuki), 22; 13. Roche (Yamaha), 21; 14. Neff (Yamaha), 17; 15. Fernandez (Yamaha), 15.

SUPERBIKE

March 18th - Le Mans

1. Delétang (Yamaha); 2. Sebileau (Kawasaki); 3. Protat (Ducati); 4. Cazade (Yamaha); 5. Dobe (Suzuki STK); 6. Moreira (Kawasaki STK); 7. Nogueira (Suzuki STK); 8. Bonhuil (Suzuki STK); 9. Rulfo (Suzuki STK); 10. Mulot (Ducati).

April 1st - Magny-Cours

1. Protat (Ducati); 2. Sebileau (Kawasaki); 3. Cazade (Yamaha); 4. Mulot (Ducati); 5. Dobe (Suzuki STK); 6. Moreira (Kawasaki STK); 7. Lerat-Vanstaen (Suzuki STK); 8. Nogueira (Suzuki STK); 9. Le Glatin (Suzuki STK); 10. Bonhuil (Suzuki STK).

April 8th - Albi

1. Sebileau (Kawasaki); 2. Protat (Ducati); 3. Cazade (Yamaha); 4. Moreira (Kawasaki STK); 5. Dobe (Suzuki STK); 6. Bonhuil (Suzuki STK); 7. Le Glatin (Suzuki STK); 8. Lerat-Vanstaen (Suzuki STK); 9. Nogueira (Suzuki STK); 10. Neff (Yamaha STK).

April 29th - Carole

1. Protat (Ducati); 2. Sebileau (Kawasaki); 3. Moreira (Kawasaki STK); 4. Cazade (Yamaha); 5. Nogueira (Suzuki STK); 6. Le Glatin (Suzuki STK); 7. Di Foggia (Suzuki STK); 8. Lerat-Vanstaen (Suzuki STK); 9. Laurent (Suzuki); 10. Ulmann (Suzuki STK).

May 13th - Nogaro

1. Protat (Ducati); 2. Cazade (Yamaha); 3. Sebileau (Kawasaki); 4. Duterne (Yamaha STK); 5. Lerat-Vanstaen (Suzuki STK); 6. Ulmann (Suzuki STK); 7. Nogueira (Suzuki STK); 8. Bonhuil (Suzuki STK); 9. Moreira (Kawasaki STK); 10. F. Jond (Suzuki STK).

May 27th - Le Vigeant

1. Protat (Ducati); 2. Delétang (Yamaha); 3. Sebileau (Kawasaki); 4. Le Glatin (Suzuki STK); 5. Lerat-Vanstaen (Suzuki STK); 6. F. Jond (Suzuki STK); 7. Ulmann (Suzuki STK); 8. Di Foggia (Suzuki STK); 9. Bonhuil (Suzuki STK); 10. Moreira (Kawasaki STK).

June 24th - Lédenon

1. Protat (Ducati); 2. Cazade (Yamaha); 3. Le Glatin (Suzuki STK); 4. Sebileau (Kawasaki); 5. Moreira (Kawasaki STK); 6. F. Jond (Suzuki STK); 7. Bonhuil (Suzuki STK); 8. Di Foggia (Suzuki STK); 9. Lerat-Vanstaen (Suzuki STK); 10. Donischal (Suzuki STK).

Final Classification

1. **Frédéric Protat** (Ducati), 161
2. **Bertrand Sebileau** (Kawasaki), 130
3. **Bernard Cazade** (Yamaha), 98
4. Moreira (Kawasaki), 73; 5. Lerat-Vanstaen (Suzuki), 59; 6. Le Glatin (Suzuki), 55; 7. Nogueira (Suzuki), 49; 8. Bonhuil (Suzuki), 48; 9. Delétang (Yamaha), 45; 10. Dobe (Suzuki), 33; 11. Ulmann (Suzuki), 32; 12. Di Foggia (Suzuki), 32; 13. F. Jond (Suzuki), 30; 14. Duterne (Yamaha), 20; 15. Mulot (Ducati), 19.

SIDE-CARS

March 18th - Le Mans

1. Hansen/Gougaud (Suzuki); 2. Joron/Virey (Suzuki); 3. Niogret/Goncalves (Suzuki); 4. Huet/Nicolas (Schelbourne); 5. Gautier/Gruel (Yamaha); 6. Marzloff/Marzloff (Suzuki); 7. Dernoncourt/Alterro (Suzuki); 8. Minguet/Voilque (Suzuki); 9. Bessy/Bessy (Suzuki); 10. Michon/Chaigneau (Suzuki).

April 1st - Magny-Cours

1. Joron/Virey (Suzuki); 2. Minguet/Voilque (Suzuki); 3. Michon/Chaigneau (Suzuki); 4. Piroutet/Greffet (Suzuki); 5. Mercier/Vincendeau (Suzuki); 6. Marzloff/Marzloff (Suzuki); 7. Cluze/Cluze (Stelec); 8. Niogret/Goncalves (Suzuki); 9. Morio/Jehanno (ALSA); 10. Hachet/Alzina (Senig).

April 8th - Albi

1. Minguet/Voilque (Suzuki); 2. Michon/Chaigneau (Suzuki); 3. Marzloff/Marzloff (Suzuki); 4. Hachet/Alzina (Senig); 5. Cluze/Cluze (Stelec); 6. Huet/Nicolas (Schelbourne); 7. Niogret/Goncalves (Suzuki); 8. Montagnier/Midrouet (Kawasaki); 9. Morio/Jehanno (ALSA); 10. Leblond/Leblond (Honda).

April 29th - Carole

1. Joron/Virey (Suzuki); 2. Minguet/Voilque (Suzuki); 3. Niogret/Goncalves (Suzuki); 4. Marzloff/Marzloff (Suzuki); 5. Michon/Chaigneau (Suzuki); 6. Hachet/Alzina (Senig); 7. Gautier/Gruel (Yamaha); 8. Huet/Nicolas (Schelbourne); 9. Pilault/Prigent (Honda); 10. Dureau/Roux (Suzuki).

May 13th - Nogaro

1. Minguet/Voilque (Suzuki); 2. Joron/Virey (Suzuki); 3. Michon/Chaigneau (Suzuki); 4. Dernoncourt/Alterro (Suzuki); 5. Niogret/Goncalves (Suzuki); 6. Marzloff/Marzloff (Suzuki); 7. Cluze/Cluze (Stelec); 8. Hachet/Alzina (Senig); 9. Gautier/Gruel (Yamaha); 10. Bessy/Bessy (Suzuki).

May 27th - Le Vigeant

1. Minguet/Voilque (Suzuki); 2. Dernoncourt/Alterro (Suzuki); 3. Marzloff/Marzloff (Suzuki); 4. Cluze/Cluze (Stelec); 5. Mercier/Vincendeau (Suzuki); 6. Pincon/Guillotin (Suzuki); 7. Huet/Nicolas (Schelbourne); 8. Gautier/Gruel (Yamaha); 9. Michon/Chaigneau (Suzuki); 10. Dureau/Roux (Suzuki).

June 24th - Lédenon

1. Dernoncourt/Alterro (Suzuki); 2. Minguet/Voilque (Suzuki); 3. Michon/Chaigneau (Suzuki); 4. Niogret/Goncalves (Suzuki); 5. Marzloff/Marzloff (Suzuki); 6. Montagnier/Midrouet (Kawasaki); 7. Gautier/Gruel (Yamaha); 8. Baumier/Deydier (Yamaha); 9. Pilault/Prigent (Honda); 10. Mercier/Vincendeau (Suzuki).

FINAL CLASSIFICATION

1. **Minguet/Voilque** (Suzuki), 143
2. **Michon/Chaigneau** (Suzuki), 92
3. **Joron/Virey** (Suzuki), 90
4. Marzloff/Marzloff (Suzuki), 86; 5. Niogret/Goncalves (Suzuki), 73; 6. Dernoncourt/Alterro/Lailheugui (Suzuki), 67; 7. Gautier/Gruel (Yamaha), 49; 8. Cluze/Cluze (Stelec), 42; 9. Huet/Nicolas (Schelbourne), 40; 10. Hachet/Alzina (Senig), 37; 11. Montagnier/Midrouet (Kawasaki), 34; 12. Mercier/Vincendeau/Mercier (Suzuki), 31; 13. Hansen/Gougaud (Suzuki), 25; 14. Leblond/Leblond (Honda), 23; 15. Morio/Jehanno (ALSA), 19.

ITALIAN CHAMPIONSHIP

125 CC

April 8th - Misano

1. Ballerini (Aprilia); 2. Dovizioso (Aprilia); 3. Pellino (Honda); 4. Angeloni (Honda); 5. W. De Angelis (Honda); 6. Orioli (Honda); 7. Aldrovandi (Honda); 8. Bruschi (Honda); 9. Baiocco (Aprilia); 10. Gronchi (Aprilia).

June 17th - Monza

1. Ballerini (Aprilia); 2. Dovizioso (Aprilia); 3. Talevi (Aprilia); 4. Angeloni (Honda); 5. Pellino (Honda); 6. Lai (Honda); 7. Conti (Honda); 8. Manna (Aprilia); 9. Aldrovandi (Honda); 10. Castellani (Aprilia).

September 16th - Vallelunga

1. Pellino (Honda); 2. Talevi (Aprilia); 3. Ballerini (Aprilia); 4. Angeloni (Honda); 5. Aldrovandi (Honda); 6. Lai (Honda); 7. Baldolini (Aprilia); 8. Saltarelli (Aprilia); 9. Bruschi (Honda); 10. Manna (Aprilia).

October 14th - Misano

1. Angeloni (Honda); 2. Pellino (Honda); 3. Baldolini (Aprilia); 4. Aldrovandi (Honda); 5. Talevi (Aprilia); 6. Saltarelli (Aprilia); 7. Gronchi (Aprilia); 8. Simoncelli (Honda); 9. Lai (Honda); 10. Fabrizio (Aprilia).

October 28th - Misano

1. Angeloni (Honda); 2. Lai (Honda); 3. Pellino (Honda); 4. Simoncelli (Honda); 5. Aldrovandi (Honda); 6. Dovizioso (Aprilia); 7. Bruschi (Honda); 8. Baldolini (Aprilia); 9. Fabrizio (Aprilia); 10. Corsi (Honda).

FINAL CLASSIFICATION

1. **Gioele Pellino** (Honda), 77
2. **Mattia Angeloni** (Honda), 76
3. **Andrea Ballerini** (Aprilia), 66
4. Dovizioso (Aprilia), 50; 5. Lai (Honda), 47; 6. Tallevi (Aprilia), 47; 7. Aldrovandi (Honda), 44; 8. Baldolini (Aprilia), 38; 9. Simoncelli (Honda), 25; 10. Bruschi (Honda), 24.

250CC

April 8th - Misano

1. Boccolini (Aprilia); 2. Ramponi (Honda); 3. Stella (Honda); 4. Berta (Honda); 5. Funiciello (Aprilia); 6. Sabbatucci (Yamaha); 7. Anghetti (Honda); 8. Pigliacelli (Honda); 9. Tomba (Yamaha); 10. Pistone (Honda).

June 17th - Monza

1. Bartolini (Honda); 2. Boccia (Aprilia); 3. Anghetti (Honda); 4. Berta (Honda); 5. Ramponi (Honda); 6. Funiciello (Aprilia); 7. Ronzoni (Yamaha); 8. Tomba (Yamaha); 9. Isola (Yamaha); 10. Sabbatucci (Yamaha).

September 16th - Vallelunga

1. Boccolini (Aprilia); 2. Bartolini (Honda); 3. Ramponi (Honda); 4. Ronzoni (Yamaha); 5. Tomba (Yamaha); 6. Menghi (Honda); 7. Sabbatucci (Yamaha); 8. Mengoni (Honda); 9. Isola (Yamaha); 10. Pistone (Honda).

October 14th - Misano

1. Bartolini (Honda); 2. Anghetti (Honda); 3. Ramponi (Honda);

4. Menghi (Honda); 5. Ronzoni (Yamaha); 6. Villa (Yamaha); 7. Tomba (Yamaha); 8. Pigliacelli (Honda); 9. Sabbatucci (Yamaha); 10. Tonini (Honda).

October 28th - Misano
1. Boccolini (Aprilia); 2. Bartolini (Honda); 3. Anghetti (Honda); 4. Ramponi (Honda); 5. Berta (Honda); 6. Ronzoni (Yamaha); 7. Menghi (Honda); 8. Tomba (Yamaha); 9. Pigliacelli (Honda); 10. Pierucci (Honda).

FINAL CLASSIFICATION
1. Alter Bartolini (Honda), 90
2. Gilles Boccolini (Aprilia), 80
3. Stefano Ramponi (Honda), 65
4. Anghetti (Honda), 61; 5. Ronzoni (Yamaha), 43; 6. Berta (Honda), 37; 7. Menghi (Honda), 36; 8. Tomba (Yamaha), 36; 9. Sabbatucci (Yamaha), 32; 10. Pigliacelli (Honda), 26.

SUPERSPORT

April 8th - Misano
1. Cruciani (Yamaha); 2. Russo (Yamaha); 3. Guareschi (Suzuki); 4. Corradi (Yamaha); 5. Tondini (Yamaha); 6. Velini (Yamaha); 7. Colombo (Ducati); 8. Brugnara (Yamaha); 9. Pratichizzo (Yamaha); 10. Proietto (Honda).

June 17th - Monza
1. Corradi (Yamaha); 2. Cruciani (Yamaha); 3. Russo (Yamaha); 4. Pratichizzo (Yamaha); 5. Clementi (Yamaha); 6. Meregalli (Yamaha); 7. Conforti (Suzuki); 8. Nannelli (Ducati); 9. Brugnara (Yamaha); 10. Cipriani (Yamaha).

September 16th - Vallelunga
1. De Marco (Yamaha); 2. Cruciani (Yamaha); 3. Brugnara (Yamaha); 4. Corradi (Yamaha); 5. Proietto (Honda); 6. Nannelli (Ducati); 7. Galiè (Yamaha); 8. Pratichizzo (Yamaha); 9. Grandi (Yamaha); 10. Camparmò (Yamaha).

October 14th - Misano
1. Cruciani (Yamaha); 2. Nannelli (Ducati); 3. Valia (Ducati); 4. Russo (Yamaha); 5. De Marco (Yamaha); 6. Brugnara (Yamaha); 7. Cipriani (Yamaha); 8. Corradi (Yamaha); 9. Magnani (Yamaha); 10. Mariottini (Suzuki).

October 28th - Misano
1. Cruciani (Yamaha); 2. Tortoroglio (Suzuki); 3. Russo (Yamaha); 4. Carlacci (Yamaha); 5. Nannelli (Ducati); 6. Valia (Ducati); 7. Bisconti (Yamaha); 8. Brignola (Suzuki); 9. Cipriani (Yamaha); 10. Proietto (Honda).

FINAL CLASSIFICATION
1. Stefano Cruciani (Yamaha), 95
2. Nello Russo (Yamaha), 63
3. Alessio Corradi (Yamaha), 59
4. Nannelli (Ducati), 49; 5. Brugnara (Yamaha), 41; 6. De Marco (Yamaha), 46; 7. Pratichizzo (Yamaha), 31; 8. Cipriani (Yamaha), 26; 9. Valia (Ducati), 26; 10. Proietto (Honda), 25.

SUPERSTOCK

April 8th - Misano
1. Antonello (Suzuki); 2. Heckles (Honda); 3. Battisti (Suzuki); 4. Romanelli (Suzuki); 5. Tosolini (Ducati); 6. Mauri (Ducati); 7. Temporali (Suzuki); 8. Ricci (Suzuki); 9. Dionisi (Aprilia); 10. Pontini (Suzuki).

June 17th - Monza
1. Romanelli (Suzuki); 2. Vizziello (Yamaha); 3. Tosolini (Ducati); 4. Mauri (Ducati); 5. Tessarolo (Suzuki); 6. Paradiso (Suzuki); 7. Alfonsi (Ducati); 8. Pasini (Ducati); 9. Andaloro (Honda); 10. Rossi (Yamaha).

September 16th - Vallelunga
1. Antonello (Suzuki); 2. Vizziello (Yamaha); 3. Messori (Aprilia); 4. Temporali (Suzuki); 5. Mauri (Ducati); 6. Capriotti (Suzuki); 7. Pontini (Suzuki); 8. Andaloro (Honda); 9. Fabbroni (Honda); 10. Rossi (Yamaha).

October 14th - Misano
1. Antonello (Suzuki); 2. Vizziello (Yamaha); 3. Romanelli (Suzuki); 4. Temporali (Suzuki); 5. Tosolini (Suzuki); 6. Mauri (Ducati); 7. Battisti (Suzuki); 8. Andaloro (Honda); 9. Ricci (Suzuki); 10. Pellizon (Aprilia).

October 28th - Misano
1. Vizziello (Yamaha); 2. Antonello (Suzuki); 3. Romanelli (Suzuki); 4. Temporali (Suzuki); 5. Alfonsi (Ducati); 6. Ricci (Suzuki); 7. Pellizzon (Aprilia); 8. Tosolini (Aprilia); 9. Capriotti (Suzuki); 10. Tessarolo (Suzuki).

FINAL CLASSIFICATION
1. Roberto Antonello (Suzuki), 95

2. Gianluca Vizziello (Yamaha), 85
3. Giacomo Romanelli (Suzuki), 73
4. Temporali (Suzuki), 52; 5. Tosolini (Aprilia), 48; 6. Mauri (Ducati), 45; 7. Battisti (Suzuki), 32; 8. Ricci (Suzuki), 26; 9. Alfonsi (Ducati), 25; 10. Tessarolo (Suzuki), 25.

SUPERBIKE

April 8th - Misano
1. Pedercini (Ducati); 2. Blora (Ducati); 3. Foti (Ducati); 4. Pasini (Ducati); 5. Assirelli (Yamaha); 6. Boccelli (Ducati); 7. Di Maso (Suzuki); 8. Villa (Suzuki); 9. Cantalupo (Suzuki); 10. Capriotti (Yamaha).

June 17th - Monza
1. Pedercini (Ducati); 2. Blora (Ducati); 3. Pedersoli (Kawasaki); 4. Assirelli (Yamaha); 5. Pasini (Ducati); 6. Foti (Ducati); 7. Panichi (Suzuki); 8. Tomassoni (Suzuki); 9. Calasso (Suzuki); 10. Villa (Suzuki).

September 16th - Vallelunga
1. Pedercini (Ducati); 2. Gramigni (Yamaha); 3. Blora (Suzuki); 4. Pasini (Ducati); 5. Assirelli (Yamaha); 6. Di Maso (Kawasaki); 7. Villa (Suzuki); 8. Tomassoni (Suzuki); 9. Cantalupo (Ducati); 10. Oliver (E, Aprilia).

October 14th - Misano
1. Pedercini (Ducati); 2. Blora (Ducati); 3. Foti (Ducati); 4. Assirelli (Yamaha); 5. Di Maso (Kawasaki); 6. Morigi (Ducati); 7. Pedersoli (Kawasaki); 8. Villa (Suzuki); 9. Tomassoni (Suzuki); 10. Calasso (Suzuki).

October 28th - Misano
1. Pasini (Ducati); 2. Foti (Ducati); 3. Di Maso (Kawasaki); 4. Pedersoli (Kawasaki); 5. Assirelli (Yamaha); 6. Tomassoni (Suzuki); 7. Calasso (Suzuki); 8. Cantalupo (Ducati); 9. Mazzali (MV Agusta); 10. Scatola (Suzuki).

FINAL CLASSIFICATION
1. Lucio Pedercini (Ducati), 100
2. Paolo Blora (Ducati), 76
3. Serafino Foti (Ducati), 62
4. Pasini (Ducati), 62; 5. Assirelli (Yamaha), 48; 6. Di Maso (Kawasaki), 46; 7. Pedersoli (Kawasaki), 38; 8. Tomassoni (Suzuki), 33; 9. Villa (Suzuki), 31; 10. Cantalupo (Ducati), 27.

BRITISH CHAMPIONSHIP

125 CC

April 1st - Donington Park
1. Stoner (AUS, Honda); 2. P. Robinson (Honda); 3. Camier (Honda); 4. Pearson (Honda); 5. Owens (Honda); 6. Green (Honda); 7. Patrickson (Honda); 8. Cahill (Honda); 9. Jennings (Honda); 10. Wilcox (Honda).

April 16th - Silverstone
1. Stoner (AUS, Honda); 2. Camier (Honda); 3. P. Robinson (Honda); 4. Pearson (Honda); 5. Owens (Honda); 6. Patrickson (Honda); 7. Jennings (Honda); 8. Mateer (Honda); 9. Wilcox (Honda); 10. Davies (Honda).

May 7th - Snetterton
1. Stoner (AUS, Honda); 2. Patrickson (Honda); 3. Owens (Honda); 4. Wilcox (Honda); 5. P. Robinson (Honda); 6. Camier (Honda); 7. Mateer (Honda); 8. Green (Honda); 9. Cahill (Honda); 10. Jennings (Honda).

May 13th - Oulton Park
1. Green (Honda); 2. Owens (Honda); 3. P. Robinson (Honda); 4. Patrickson (Honda); 5. Laverty (Honda); 6. Pearson (Honda); 7. Mainwaring (Honda); 8. Wilcox (Honda); 9. R. Hodgson (Honda); 10. Pearson (Honda).

June 17th - Brands Hatch
1. Stoner (AUS, Honda); 2. Green (Honda); 3. Pearson (Honda); 4. Patrickson (Honda); 5. Owens (Honda); 6. P. Robinson (Honda); 7. Davies (Honda); 8. Wilcox (Honda); 9. R. Hodgson (Honda); 10. Mainwaring (Honda).

July 1st - Thruxton
1. Davies (Honda); 2. Camier (Honda); 3. P. Robinson (Honda); 4. Patrickson (Honda); 5. R. Hodgson (Honda); 6. Weston (Honda); 7. Mainwaring (Honda); 8. Farbrother (Honda); 9. Jennings (Honda); 10. A. Walker (Honda).

July 22nd - Oulton Park
1. Stoner (AUS, Honda); 2. Camier (Honda); 3. Green (Honda); 4. P. Robinson (Honda); 5. Laverty (Honda); 6. Davies (Honda); 7. Patrickson (Honda); 8. Pearson (Honda); 9. Wilcox (Honda); 10. Elkin (Honda).

August 12th - Knockhill
1. Stoner (AUS, Honda); 2. Pearson (Honda); 3. Camier (Honda); 4. Owens (Honda); 5. Davies (Honda); 6. P. Robinson (Honda); 7. Sproston (Honda); 8. Lindsay (Honda); 9. Jennings (Honda); 10. Laverty (Honda).

August 27th - Cadwell Park
1. Stoner (AUS, Honda); 2. Davies (Honda); 3. Owens (Honda); 4. Camier (Honda); 5. Pearson (Honda); 6. R. Hodgson (Honda); 7. Laverty (Honda); 8. Patrickson (Honda); 9. Sykes (Honda); 10. Clark (Honda).

September 2nd - Brands Hatch
1. Camier (Honda); 2. Owens (Honda); 3. Green (Honda); 4. P. Robinson (Honda); 5. A. Walker (Honda); 6. Farbrother (Honda); 7. Patrickson (Honda); 8. Mainwaring (Honda); 9. R. Hodgson (Honda); 10. Sproston (Honda).

September 16th - Mallory Park
1. Camier (Honda); 2. Pearson (Honda); 3. Patrickson (Honda); 4. A. Walker (Honda); 5. R. Hodgson (Honda); 6. Jennings (Honda); 7. Wilcox (Honda); 8. Green (Honda); 9. Mainwaring (Honda); 10. Cahill (Honda).

September 30th - Rockingham
1. P. Robinson (Honda); 2. Green (Honda); 3. A. Walker (Honda); 4. Farbrother (Honda); 5. Sproston (Honda); 6. Mainwaring (Honda); 7. Wilcox (Honda); 8. Clark (Honda); 9. R. Hodgson (Honda); 10. Weston (Honda).

October 14th - Donington Park
1. Davies (Honda); 2. P. Robinson (Honda); 3. Laverty (Honda); 4. Camier (Honda); 5. A. Walker (Honda); 6. Wilcox (Honda); 7. Green (Honda); 8. Cahill (Honda); 9. Farbrother (Honda); 10. Patrickson (Honda).

FINAL CLASSIFICATION
1. Leon Camier (Honda), 178
2. Casey Stoner (AUS, Honda), 175
3. Paul Robinson (Honda), 170
4. Green (Honda), 132; 5. Patrickson (Honda), 131; 6. Owens (Honda), 118; 7. Davies (Honda) and Pearson (Honda), 111; 9. Wilcox (Honda), 81; 10. R. Hodgson (Honda), 67.

250CC

April 1st - Donington Park
1. Norval (SA, Honda); 2. Coates (Honda); 3. Barton (Honda); 4. Sawford (Yamaha); 5. Tunstall (Honda); 6. G. Haslam (Honda); 7. Dickinson (Honda); 8. Herzberg (Yamaha); 9. G. Jackson (Honda); 10. Hincks (Honda).

April 16th - Silverstone
1. Coates (Honda); 2. Norval (SA, Honda); 3. G. Haslam (Honda); 4. Tunstall (Honda); 5. Di Salvo (USA, Honda); 6. Dickinson (Yamaha); 7. Sawford (Yamaha); 8. G. Jackson (Honda); 9. Herzberg (Yamaha); 10. Easton (Honda).

May 7th - Snetterton
1. Coates (Honda); 2. Barton (Honda); 3. Norval (SA, Honda); 4. Easton (Honda); 5. Sawford (Yamaha); 6. Herzberg (Yamaha); 7. G. Haslam (Honda); 8. G. Jackson (Honda); 9. Dickinson (Yamaha); 10. Tunstall (Honda).

May 13th - Oulton Park
1. Barton (Honda); 2. Coates (Honda); 3. Norval (SA, Honda); 4. Easton (Honda); 5. G. Jackson (Honda); 6. G. Haslam (Honda); 7. Dickinson (Yamaha); 8. Thompson (Yamaha); 9. Hincks (Honda); 10. Levy (Honda).

June 17th - Brands Hatch
1. Barton (Honda); 2. Norval (SA, Honda); 3. Coates (Honda); 4. Easton (Honda); 5. G. Haslam (Honda); 6. Sawford (Yamaha); 7. Tunstall (Honda); 8. Thompson (Yamaha); 9. G. Jackson (Honda); 10. Bennett (Yamaha).

July 1st - Thruxton
1. Easton (Honda); 2. Barton (Honda); 3. Coates (Honda); 4. Thompson (Yamaha); 5. G. Haslam (Honda); 6. Sawford (Yamaha); 7. Tunstall (Honda); 8. P. Robinson (Honda); 9. Bishop (Yamaha); 10. Hutchinson (Yamaha).

July 22nd - Oulton Park
1. Barton (Honda); 2. Norval (SA, Honda); 3. Easton (Honda); 4. Coates (Honda); 5. Dickinson (Yamaha); 6. Jackson (Honda); 7. Herzberg (Yamaha); 8. Tunstall (Honda); 9. Grinling (Yamaha); 10. Thompson (Yamaha).

August 12th - Knockhill
1. Coates (Honda); 2. Norval (SA, Honda); 3. Easton (Honda); 4. G. Jackson (Honda); 5. G. Haslam (Honda); 6. Dickinson (Yamaha); 7. Tunstall (Honda); 8. Herzberg (Yamaha); 9. Thompson (Yamaha); 10. Sawford (Yamaha).

August 27th - Cadwell Park
Race cancelled.

September 2nd - Brands Hatch
1. Norval (SA, Honda); 2. Coates (Honda); 3. Easton (Honda); 4. G. Haslam (Honda); 5. Bennett (Honda); 6. Jackson (Honda); 7. Thompson (Yamaha); 8. Barton (Honda); 9. Bishop (Yamaha); 10. Tunstall (Honda).

September 16th - Mallory Park
1. Coates (Honda); 2. Norval (SA, Honda); 3. G. Haslam (Honda); 4. Jackson (Honda); 5. Barton (Honda); 6. Easton (Honda); 7. Thompson (Yamaha); 8. Tunstall (Honda); 9. Bennett (Yamaha); 10. Grinling (Yamaha).

September 30th - Rockingham
1. G. Haslam (Honda); 2. Barton (Honda); 3. Tunstall (Honda); 4. Bishop (Yamaha); 5. Zanotti (Honda); 6. Bennett (Yamaha); 7. Jackson (Honda); 8. Sawford (Yamaha); 9. Thompson (Yamaha); 10. Easton (Honda).

October 14th - Donington Park
Race I:
1. Coates (Honda); 2. Easton (Honda); 3. Norval (SA, Honda); 4. Tunstall (Honda); 5. Jackson (Honda); 6. Dickinson (Yamaha); 7. Bennett (Honda); 8. Thompson (Yamaha); 9. Sawford (Yamaha); 10. Bishop (Yamaha).

Race II:
1. Coates (Honda); 2. Easton (Honda); 3. Norval (SA, Honda); 4. Barton (Honda); 5. Tunstall (Honda); 6. Sawford (Yamaha); 7. Dickinson (Yamaha); 8. Thompson (Yamaha); 9. Bennett (Yamaha); 10. Grinling (Yamaha).

FINAL CLASSIFICATION
1. Adrian Coates (Honda), 255
2. Shane Norval (SA, Honda), 214
3. Derek Barton (Honda), 188
4. Easton (Honda), 174; 5. G. Haslam (Honda), 137; 6. Tunstall (Honda), 119; 7. Jackson (Honda), 112; 8. Sawford (Yamaha), 91; 9. Thompson (Yamaha), 88; 10. Dickinson (Yamaha), 75.

SUPERSPORT

April 1st - Donington Park
1. Vermeulen (AUS, Honda); 2. McCarthy (NZ, Honda); 3. Llewellyn (Yamaha); 6. Coulter (Suzuki); 5. McGuiness (Honda); 6. Smart (Suzuki); 7. Richards (Honda); 8. Young (Suzuki); 9. Sherring (Yamaha); 10. Andrews (Honda).

April 16th - Silverstone
1. McCarthy (NZ, Honda); 2. McGuiness (Honda); 3. Harris (Suzuki); 4. Llewellyn (Yamaha); 5. Smart (Suzuki); 6. Frost (Yamaha); 7. Richards (Honda); 8. Quigley (Suzuki); 9. Mason (Honda); 10. Beaumont (Yamaha).

May 7th - Snetterton
1. Llewellyn (Yamaha); 2. McCarthy (AUS, Honda); 3. Frost (Yamaha); 4. McGuiness (Honda); 5. Young (Suzuki); 6. Harris (Suzuki); 7. Smart (Suzuki); 8. Mason (Honda); 9. Quigley (Suzuki); 10. Hobbs (Yamaha).

May 13th - Oulton Park
1. Young (Suzuki); 2. McCarthy (NZ, Honda); 3. Harris (Suzuki); 4. Smart (Suzuki); 5. Frost (Yamaha); 6. McGuiness (Honda); 7. Llewellyn (Yamaha); 8. Mason (Honda); 9. Quigley (Suzuki); 10. Norris (Yamaha).

June 17th - Brands Hatch
1. McGuiness (Honda); 2. Coulter (Suzuki); 3. McCarthy (NZ, Honda); 4. Beaumont (Yamaha); 5. Andrews (Honda); 6. May (Yamaha); 7. Davies (Honda); 8. Llewellyn (Yamaha); 9. Cowie (Kawasaki); 10. Turner (Yamaha).

July 1st - Thruxton
1. Harris (Suzuki); 2. Llewellyn (Yamaha); 3. Richards (Honda); 4. Young (Suzuki); 5. McGuiness (Honda); 6. McCarthy (NZ, Honda); 7. Smart (Suzuki); 8. Coulter (Suzuki); 9. May (Yamaha); 10. Andrews (Honda).

July 22nd - Oulton Park
1. Young (Suzuki); 2. Harris (Suzuki); 3. Llewellyn (Yamaha); 4. Mason (Honda); 5. McCarthy (AUS, Honda); 6. Frost (Yamaha); 7. Richards (Honda); 8. Smart (Suzuki); 9. Ashkenazi (J, Kawasaki); 10. May (Yamaha).

August 12th - Knockhill
1. Harris (Suzuki); 2. McCarthy (NZ, Honda); 3. Young (Suzuki); 4. McGuiness (Honda); 5. Llewellyn (Yamaha); 6. Mason (Honda); 7. Shand (Honda); 8. McCulloch (Yamaha); 9. May (Yamaha); 10. Ramsay (Suzuki).

August 27th - Cadwell Park
1. Harris (Suzuki); 2. McGuiness (Honda); 3. Frost (Yamaha); 4. Llewellyn (Yamaha); 5. Richards (Honda); 6. Ashkenazi (J, Kawasaki); 7. McCulloch (Yamaha); 8. Quigley (Suzuki); 9. Beaumont (Yamaha); 10. Norris (Yamaha).

September 2nd - Brands Hatch
1. McGuiness (Honda); 2. Harris (Suzuki); 3. Llewellyn (Yamaha); 4. Young (Suzuki); 5. Quigley (Suzuki); 6. McCarthy (NZ, Honda); 7. Smart (Suzuki); 8. Mason (Honda); 9. Ashkenazi (J, Kawasaki); 10. Redding (Kawasaki).

September 16th - Mallory Park
1. Harris (Suzuki); 2. McGuiness (Honda); 3. McCarthy (NZ, Honda); 4. Llewellyn (Yamaha); 5. McCulloch (Yamaha); 6. Ashkenazi (J, Kawasaki); 7. Young (Suzuki); 8. Mason (Honda); 9. Laverty (Suzuki); 10. Burgess (Yamaha).

September 30th - Rockingham
1. Harris (Yamaha); 2. McGuiness (Honda); 3. Smart (Suzuki); 4. Young (Suzuki); 5. McCarthy (NZ, Honda); 6. Richards (Honda); 7. Ashkenazi (J, Kawasaki); 8. Mason (Honda); 9. Quigley (Suzuki); 10. Swanton (Yamaha).

October 14th - Donington Park
1. Harris (Suzuki); 2. Smart (Suzuki); 3. McCarthy (NZ, Honda); 4. Frost (Yamaha); 5. Young (Suzuki); 6. Mason (Honda); 7. McCulloch (Yamaha); 8. Richards (Honda); 9. Ashkenazi (J, Kawasaki); 10. Andrews (Honda).

FINAL CLASSIFICATION
1. Karl Harris (Suzuki), 235
2. Kirk McCarthy (NZ, Honda), 200
3. John McGuiness (Honda), 190
4. Llewellyn (Yamaha), 164; 5. Young (Suzuki), 145; 6. Smart (Suzuki), 106; 7. Mason (Honda), 80; 8. Frost (Yamaha), 77; 9. Richards (Honda), 73; 10. Ashkenazi (J, Kawasaki), 56.

SUPERSTOCK

April 1st - Donington Park
1. Young (Suzuki); 2. Mason (Honda); 3. Coulter (Suzuki); 4. Jefferies (Yamaha); 5. Crockford (Suzuki); 6. Morley (Suzuki); 7. Burns (Suzuki); 8. Jennings (Yamaha); 9. Ashkenazi (J, Suzuki); 10. Duffus (Yamaha).

April 16th - Silverstone
1. Young (Suzuki); 2. Richards (AUS, Honda); 3. Morley (Suzuki); 4. Burns (Suzuki); 5. Ashkenazi (J, Suzuki); 6. Mason (Honda); 7. Jefferies (Yamaha); 8. Murphy (Suzuki); 9. Palmer (Yamaha); 10. Duffus (Yamaha).

May 7th - Snetterton
1. Young (Suzuki); 2. Morley (Suzuki); 3. Scott (Suzuki); 4. Ashkenazi (J, Suzuki); 5. Burns (Suzuki); 6. Smith (Suzuki); 7. Whitby (Suzuki); 8. Mason (Honda); 9. Palmer (Yamaha); 10. Miller (Yamaha).

May 13th - Oulton Park
1. Young (Suzuki); 2. Jefferies (Yamaha); 3. Whitby (Suzuki); 4. Burns (Suzuki); 5. Heal (Suzuki); 6. Smith (Suzuki); 7. Crockford (Suzuki); 8. Allan (Suzuki); 9. Scott (Suzuki); 10. Miller (Yamaha).

June 17th - Brands Hatch
1. Young (Suzuki); 2. Crockford (Suzuki); 3. Morley (Suzuki); 4. Mason (Honda); 5. Richards (AUS, Honda); 6. Jefferies (Yamaha); 7. Jennings (Yamaha); 8. Tinsley (Suzuki); 9. Burns (Suzuki); 10. Miller (Suzuki).

July 1st - Thruxton
1. Crockford (Suzuki); 2. Jefferies (Yamaha); 3. Young (Suzuki); 4. Richards (AUS, Honda); 5. Heal (Suzuki); 6. Chapman (Yamaha); 7. Johnson (Suzuki); 8. Murphy (Suzuki); 9. Burns (Suzuki); 10. Morley (Suzuki).

July 22nd - Oulton Park
1. Jefferies (Yamaha); 2. Mason (Honda); 3. Richards (AUS, Honda); 4. Crockford (Suzuki); 5. Mitchell (Suzuki); 6. Jennings (Suzuki); 7. Scott (Suzuki); 8. Giles (Suzuki); 9. Miller (Suzuki); 10. Tinsley (Suzuki).

August 12th - Knockhill
1. Crockford (Suzuki); 2. Richards (AUS, Honda); 3. Young (Suzuki); 4. Jennings (Suzuki); 5. Jefferies (Yamaha); 6. Morley (Suzuki); 7. Mason (Honda); 8. Nutt (Suzuki); 9. Giles (Suzuki); 10. Allan (Suzuki).

August 27th - Cadwell Park
1. Jefferies (Yamaha); 2. Young (Suzuki); 3. Morley (Suzuki); 4. Johnson (Suzuki); 5. Quigley (Suzuki); 6. Mason (Honda); 7. Scott (Suzuki); 8. Burns (Suzuki); 9. Mitchell (Suzuki); 10. Allan (Suzuki).

September 2nd - Brands Hatch
1. Young (Suzuki); 2. Crockford (Suzuki); 3. Richards (AUS, Honda); 4. Mason (Honda); 5. Jefferies (Yamaha); 6. Giles (Suzuki); 7. Jennings (Suzuki); 8. Burns (Suzuki); 9. Morley (Suzuki); 10. Murphy (Suzuki).

September 16th - Mallory Park
1. Crockford (Suzuki); 2. Morley (Suzuki); 3. Jefferies (Yamaha); 4. Richards (AUS, Honda); 5. Whitby (Suzuki); 6. Giles (Suzuki); 7. Scott (Suzuki); 8. Burns (Suzuki); 9. Tinsley (Suzuki); 10. Mitchell (Suzuki).

September 30th - Rockingham
1. Morley (Suzuki); 2. Jennings (Suzuki); 3. Giles (Suzuki); 4. Crockford (Suzuki); 5. Burns (Suzuki); 6. Jefferies (Yamaha); 7. Young (Suzuki); 8. Brogan (Aprilia); 9. Tinsley (Suzuki); 10. McMillan (Suzuki).

October 14th - Donington Park
1. Young (Suzuki); 2. Richards (AUS, Honda); 3. Jennings (Suzuki); 4. Burns (Suzuki); 5. Mason (Honda); 6. Morley (Suzuki); 7. Jefferies (Yamaha); 8. Giles (Suzuki); 9. Whitby (Suzuki); 10. Morrison (Suzuki).

FINAL CLASSIFICATION
1. Paul Young   (Suzuki),   236
2. David Jefferies (Yamaha),   183
3. John Crockford (Suzuki),   169
4. Morley (Suzuki), 156; 5. Richards (AUS, Honda), 129; 6. Mason (Honda), 119; 7. Burns (Suzuki), 108; 8. Jennings (Suzuki), 85; 9. Giles (Suzuki), 65; 10. Scott (Suzuki), 64.

SUPERBIKE

April 1st - Donington Park
Race I:
1. Reynolds (Ducati); 2. Hislop (Ducati); 3. Crawford (Suzuki); 4. Plater (Kawasaki); 5. Rutter (Kawasaki); 6. Brown (Ducati); 7. Byrne (Suzuki); 8. Haydon (Yamaha); 9. Ellison (Honda); 10. Williamson (Yamaha).
Race II:
1. Reynolds (Ducati); 2. Haydon (Yamaha); 3. Crawford (Suzuki); 4. Hislop (Ducati); 5. Rutter (Kawasaki); 6. Emmett (Ducati); 7. Brown (Ducati); 8. Byrne (Suzuki); 9. J. Robinson (Yamaha); 10. Williamson (Yamaha).

April 16th - Silverstone
Race I:
1. Reynolds (Ducati); 2. Hislop (Ducati); 3. Crawford (Suzuki); 4. Haydon (Yamaha); 5. Emmett (Ducati); 6. Rutter (Kawasaki); 7. Brown (Ducati); 8. J. Robinson (Yamaha); 9. Byrne (Suzuki); 10. Blackley (Kawasaki).
Race II:
1. Hislop (Ducati); 2. Reynolds (Ducati); 3. Haydon (Yamaha); 4. Emmett (Ducati); 5. Crawford (Suzuki); 6. Rutter (Kawasaki); 7. J. Robinson (Yamaha); 8. Brown (Ducati); 9. Byrne (Suzuki); 10. Ellison (Honda).

May 7th - Snetterton
Race I:
1. Reynolds (Ducati); 2. Hislop (Ducati); 3. Haydon (Yamaha); 4. Emmett (Ducati); 5. Brown (Ducati); 6. Byrne (Suzuki); 7. Crawford (Suzuki); 8. Jones (Honda); 9. Jackson (Yamaha); 10. Wood (Kawasaki).
Race II:
1. Reynolds (Ducati); 2. Hislop (Ducati); 3. Haydon (Yamaha); 4. Emmett (Ducati); 5. Brown (Ducati); 6. Byrne (Suzuki); 7. Crawford (Suzuki); 8. J. Robinson (Yamaha); 9. Jones (Honda); 10. Jackson (Yamaha).

May 13th - Oulton Park
Race I:
1. Hislop (Ducati); 2. Reynolds (Ducati); 3. Emmett (Ducati); 4. Byrne (Suzuki); 5. Brown (Ducati); 6. Rutter (Kawasaki); 7. Morley (Kawasaki); 8. Robinson (Yamaha); 9. Wood (Kawasaki); 10. Nottingham (Yamaha).
Race II:
1. Hislop (Ducati); 2. Reynolds (Ducati); 3. Haydon (Yamaha); 4. Crawford (Suzuki); 5. Rutter (Kawasaki); 6. Emmett (Ducati); 7. Brown (Ducati); 8. Byrne (Suzuki); 9. Jackson (Yamaha); 10. Jones (Honda).

June 17th - Brands Hatch
Race I:
1. Hislop (Ducati); 2. Reynolds (Ducati); 3. Plater (Kawasaki); 4. Rutter (Kawasaki); 5. Byrne (Suzuki); 6. J. Robinson (Yamaha); 7. Wood (Kawasaki); 8. Jackson (Yamaha); 9. Davis (Honda); 10. Ellison (Honda).
Race II:
1. Hislop (Ducati); 2. Rutter (Kawasaki); 3. Haydon (Yamaha); 4. Byrne (Suzuki); 5. Plater (Kawasaki); 6. Crawford (Suzuki); 7. Brown (Ducati); 8. Jackson (Yamaha); 9. Nottingham (Yamaha); 10. Davis (Honda).

July 1st - Thruxton
Race I:
1. Hislop (Ducati); 2. Plater (Kawasaki); 3. Emmett (Ducati); 4. Reynolds (Ducati); 5. Haydon (Yamaha); 6. Brown (Ducati); 7. Rutter (Kawasaki); 8. Byrne (Suzuki); 9. Crawford (Suzuki); 10. Jackson (Yamaha).
Race II:
1. Reynolds (Ducati); 2. Haydon (Yamaha); 3. Rutter (Kawasaki); 4. Emmett (Ducati); 5. Byrne (Suzuki); 6. Hislop (Ducati); 7. Brown (Ducati); 8. Crawford (Suzuki); 9. J. Robinson (Yamaha); 10. Jackson (Yamaha).

July 22nd - Oulton Park
Race I:
1. Hislop (Ducati); 2. Reynolds (Ducati); 3. Haydon (Yamaha); 4. Emmett (Ducati); 5. Crawford (Suzuki); 6. Brown (Ducati); 7. J. Robinson (Yamaha); 8. Ellison (Honda); 9. Wood (Kawasaki); 10. Jackson (Yamaha).
Race II:
1. Hislop (Ducati); 2. Reynolds (Ducati); 3. Haydon (Yamaha); 4. Emmett (Ducati); 5. Brown (Ducati); 6. Rutter (Kawasaki); 7. J. Robinson (Yamaha); 8. Byrne (Suzuki); 9. Wood (Kawasaki); 10. Ellison (Honda).

August 12th - Knockhill
Race I:
1. Reynolds (Ducati); 2. Emmett (Ducati); 3. Hislop (Ducati); 4. Haydon (Yamaha); 5. MacKenzie (Suzuki); 6. Crawford (Suzuki); 7. Brown (Ducati); 8. Byrne (Suzuki); 9. J. Robinson (Yamaha); 10. Ellison (Honda).
Race II:
1. Reynolds (Ducati); 2. Hislop (Ducati); 3. Emmett (Ducati); 4. MacKenzie (Suzuki); 5. Rutter (Kawasaki); 6. Byrne (Suzuki); 7. Brown (Ducati); 8. J. Robinson (Yamaha); 9. Burr (Kawasaki); 10. Blackley (Kawasaki).

August 27th - Cadwell Park
Race I:
1. Hislop (Ducati); 2. Haydon (Yamaha); 3. Reynolds (Ducati); 4. Emmett (Ducati); 5. Crawford (Suzuki); 6. Rutter (Kawasaki); 7. Byrne (Suzuki); 8. Plater (Yamaha); 9. Jackson (Yamaha); 10. Wood (Kawasaki).
Race II:
1. Hislop (Ducati); 2. Reynolds (Ducati); 3. Emmett (Ducati); 4. Haydon (Yamaha); 5. Rutter (Kawasaki); 6. Brown (Ducati); 7. Jackson (Yamaha); 8. Plater (Yamaha); 9. Davis (Honda); 10. Ellison (Honda).

September 2nd - Brands Hatch
Race I:
1. Hislop (Ducati); 2. Reynolds (Ducati); 3. Emmett (Ducati); 4. Haydon (Yamaha); 5. Brown (Ducati); 6. Crawford (Suzuki); 7. Rutter (Kawasaki); 8. Byrne (Suzuki); 9. J. Robinson (Yamaha); 10. Ellison (Honda).
Race II:
1. Reynolds (Ducati); 2. Hislop (Ducati); 3. Emmett (Ducati); 4. Haydon (Yamaha); 5. Brown (Ducati); 6. Rutter (Kawasaki); 7. Crawford (Suzuki); 8. Byrne (Suzuki); 9. J. Robinson (Yamaha); 10. Jackson (Yamaha).

September 16th - Mallory Park
Race I:
1. Reynolds (Ducati); 2. Emmett (Ducati); 3. Hislop (Ducati); 4. Crawford (Suzuki); 5. Brown (Ducati); 6. Plater (Yamaha); 7. J. Robinson (Yamaha); 8. Jackson (Yamaha); 9. Burr (Kawasaki); 10. Blackley (Kawasaki).
Race II:
1. Hislop (Ducati); 2. Brown (Ducati); 3. Haydon (Yamaha); 4. Crawford (Suzuki); 5. Reynolds (Ducati); 6. Plater (Yamaha); 7. Byrne (Suzuki); 8. Emmett (Ducati); 9. J. Robinson (Yamaha); 10. Jackson (Yamaha).

September 30th - Rockingham
Race I:
1. Emmett (Ducati); 2. Rutter (Kawasaki); 3. Reynolds (Ducati); 4. Brown (Ducati); 5. Haydon (Yamaha); 6. Jackson (Yamaha); 7. Wood (Kawasaki); 8. Nottingham (Yamaha); 9. Ellison (Honda); 10. Marks (Yamaha).
Race II:
1. Rutter (Kawasaki); 2. Reynolds (Ducati); 3. Emmett (Ducati); 4. Haydon (Yamaha); 5. Byrne (Suzuki); 6. Brown (Ducati); 7. Jackson (Yamaha); 8. Blackley (Kawasaki); 9. Ellison (Honda); 10. Burr (Kawasaki).

October 14th - Donington Park
Race I:
1. Reynolds (Ducati); 2. Brown (Ducati); 3. Plater (Yamaha); 4. Emmett (Ducati); 5. Crawford (Suzuki); 6. Rutter (Kawasaki); 7. Byrne (Suzuki); 8. J. Robinson (Yamaha); 9. Jackson (Yamaha); 10. Ellison (Honda).
Race II:
1. Reynolds (Ducati); 2. Haydon (Yamaha); 3. Rutter (Kawasaki); 4. Brown (Ducati); 5. Plater (Yamaha); 6. Crawford (Suzuki); 7. Byrne (Suzuki); 8. Ellison (Honda); 9. J. Robinson (Yamaha); 10. Emmett (Ducati).

FINAL CLASSIFICATION
1. John Reynolds (Ducati),   536
2. Steve Hislop   (Ducati),   475
3. Sean Emmett   (Ducati),   326
4. Haydon (Yamaha), 316; 5. Brown (Ducati), 264; 6. Rutter (Kawasaki), 256; 7. Crawford (Suzuki), 222; 8. Byrne (Suzuki), 204; 9. J. Robinson (Yamaha), 144; 10. Jackson (Yamaha), 138; 11. Plater (Yamaha), 123; 12. Ellison (Honda), 100; 13. Nottingham (Yamaha), 82; 14. Wood (Kawasaki), 81; 15. Blackley (Kawasaki), 77.

SPANISH CHAMPIONSHIP

125 CC

May 13th - Jarama
1. Rodriguez (Aprilia); 2. Faubel (Aprilia); 3. Stoner (AUS, Honda); 4. Simon (Honda); 5. Pinera (Honda); 6. Bonache (Aprilia); 7. Fores (Aprilia); 8. Martin (Honda); 9. Lai (I, Honda); 10. Lorenzo (Honda).

June 10th - Albacete
1. Stoner (AUS, Honda); 2. Rodriguez (Aprilia); 3. Simon (Honda); 4. Fores (Aprilia); 5. Faubel (Aprilia); 6. Bataille (AND, Honda); 7. Lorenzo (Honda); 8. Barbera (Aprilia); 9. Castillejo (Aprilia); 10. Lai (I, Honda).

July 15th - Valencia
1. Rodriguez (Aprilia); 2. Faubel (Aprilia); 3. Lorenzo (Honda); 4. Zappa (I, Aprilia); 5. Carrasco (Honda); 6. Buch (D, Honda); 7. Pinera (Honda); 8. Ballesteros (Aprilia); 9. Perera (Honda); 10. Perez (Aprilia).

September 2nd - Albacete
1. Rodriguez (Aprilia); 2. Lorenzo (Honda); 3. Bataille (AND, Honda); 4. Faubel (Aprilia); 5. Zappa (I, Aprilia); 6. Stoner (AUS, Honda); 7. Fores (Aprilia); 8. Lai (I, Rieju); 9. Pinera (Honda); 10. Castillejo (Aprilia).

September 16th - Jarama
1. Stoner (AUS, Honda); 2. Faubel (Aprilia); 3. Rodriguez (Aprilia); 4. Simon (Honda); 5. Lorenzo (Honda); 6. Zappa (I, Aprilia); 7. Davies (GB, Honda); 8. Bautista (Honda); 9. Salom (Honda); 10. Castillejo (Aprilia).

2 races to go :
November 18th - Valencia
November 25th - Jerez de la Frontera

250CC

May 13th - Jarama
1. Debon (Aprilia); 2. De Gea (Yamaha); 3. Garcia (Honda); 4. Tomas (Honda); 5. Vidal (Aprilia); 6. Oliver (Honda); 7. Bonilla (Honda); 8. Molina (Yamaha); 9. Costa (Yamaha); 10. Ribalta (Honda).

June 10th - Albacete
1. Debon (Aprilia); 2. De Gea (Yamaha); 3. Bonilla (Honda); 4. Molina (Yamaha); 5. Tomas (Honda); 6. Ribalta (Honda); 7. Ortega (Honda); 8. Costa (Yamaha); 9. Guardiola (Honda); 10. Lozano (Honda).

July 15th - Valencia
1. Debon (Aprilia); 2. De Gea (Yamaha); 3. Tomas (Honda); 4. Vidal (Aprilia); 5. Oliver (Honda); 6. Garcia (Honda); 7. Bonilla (Honda); 8. Molina (Yamaha); 9. Ribalta (Honda); 10. Costa (Yamaha).

September 2nd - Albacete
1. De Gea (Yamaha); 2. Debon (Aprilia); 3. Tomas (Honda); 4. Garcia (Honda); 5. Vidal (Aprilia); 6. Bonilla (Honda); 7. Oliver (Honda); 8. Costa (Yamaha); 9. Molina (Yamaha); 10. Marchand (F, Honda).

September 16th - Jarama
1. Debon (Aprilia); 2. Garcia (Honda); 3. De Gea (Yamaha); 4. Tomas (Honda); 5. Oliver (Honda); 6. Costa (Yamaha); 7. Bonilla (Honda); 8. Molina (Yamaha); 9. Janssen (NL, Honda); 10. Ribalta (Honda).

2 races to go :
November 18th - Valencia
November 25th - Jerez de la Frontera

SUPERSPORT

May 13th - Jarama
1. Fernandez (Yamaha); 2. Rodriguez (Ducati); 3. Paillot (F, Yamaha); 4. Roda (Honda); 5. Ullastres (Yamaha); 6. Sarda (Suzuki); 7. Del Amor (Yamaha); 8. Hervas (Yamaha); 9. Maturana (Yamaha); 10. Martinez (Yamaha).

June 10th - Albacete
1. Fernandez (Yamaha); 2. Rodriguez (Ducati); 3. Ullastres (Yamaha); 4. E. Gavira (Yamaha); 5. Roda (Honda); 6. Sarda (Suzuki); 7. Martinez (Yamaha); 8. Maturana (Yamaha); 9. Del Amor (Yamaha); 10. Sanchez (Suzuki).

July 15th - Valencia
1. Ullastres (Honda); 2. Gavira (Yamaha); 3. Rodriguez (Ducati); 4. Martinez (Yamaha); 5. Buffa (Yamaha); 6. Hervas (Yamaha); 7. Sarda (Suzuki); 8. Roda (Honda); 9. Sanchez (Suzuki); 10. Maturana (Yamaha).

September 2nd - Albacete
1. Fernandez (Yamaha); 2. Gavira (Yamaha); 3. Rodriguez (Ducati); 4. Sarda (Suzuki); 5. Maturana (Yamaha); 6. Ullastres (Honda); 7. Vazquez (Yamaha); 8. Martinez (Yamaha); 9. Cabana (Yamaha); 10. Sanchez (Suzuki).

September 16th - Jarama
1. Fernandez (Yamaha); 2. Gavira (Yamaha); 3. Rodriguez (Ducati); 4. Sarda (Suzuki); 5. Maturana (Yamaha); 6. Ullastres (Honda); 7. Vazquez (Yamaha); 8. Martinez (Yamaha); 9. Cabana (Yamaha); 10. Sanchez (Suzuki).

2 races to go :
November 18th - Valencia
November 25th - Jerez de la Frontera

GERMAN CHAMPIONSHIP

125 CC

May 6th - Lausitz
1. R. Harms (DK, Honda); 2. Walther (Honda); 3. Hahn (Honda); 4. Knoefler (Yamaha); 5. Kiiveri (SF, Honda); 6. Gersunde (Honda); 7. M. Kallio (SF, Honda); 8. Maerz (Honda); 9. Lenart (H, Honda); 10. Schwing (Honda).

May 20th - Hockenheim
1. R. Harms (DK, Honda); 2. Klein (Honda); 3. M. Kallio (SF, Honda); 4. Treutlein (Honda); 5. Kirmeier (Honda); 6. Unger (Honda); 7. Gersunde (Honda); 8. Knoefler (Yamaha); 9. Reissmann (Honda); 10. Lauer (Honda).

June 3rd - Oschersleben
1. M. Kallio (SF, Honda); 2. Klein (Honda); 3. R. Harms (DK, Honda); 4. Reissmann (Honda); 5. Kirmeier (Honda); 6. Knoefler (Yamaha); 7. Unger (Honda); 8. Hahn (Honda); 9. Toth (H, Honda); 10. Walther (Honda).

July 15th - Augsburg
1. Kirmeier (Honda); 2. Hahn (Honda); 3. Klein (Honda); 4. Unger (Honda); 5. R. Harms (DK, Honda); 6. Reissmann (Honda); 7. Schwing (Honda); 8. Maerz (Honda); 9. Reif (Honda); 10. Treutlein (Honda).

August 5th - Schleiz
1. Kirmeier (Honda); 2. Klein (Honda); 3. Lenart (H, Honda); 4. Knoefler (Honda); 5. Schwing (Honda); 6. Lougher (GB, Honda); 7. Maerz (Honda); 8. Walther (Honda); 9. Treutlein (Honda); 10. Reif (Honda).

August 19th - Nürburgring
1. Unger (Honda); 2. Klein (Honda); 3. Knoefler (Honda); 4. Lenart (H, Honda); 5. R. Harms (DK, Honda); 6. Treutlein (Honda); 7. Knoefler (Yamaha); 8. Walther (Honda); 9. Schwing (Honda); 10. Reif (Honda).

September 16th - Oschersleben
1. M. Kallio (SF, Honda); 2. R. Harms (DK, Honda); 3. Klein (Honda); 4. Hahn (Honda); 5. Unger (Honda); 6. Lenart (H, Honda); 7. Treutlein (Honda); 8. Kiiveri (SF, Honda); 9. Knoefler (Yamaha); 10. Gersunde (Honda).

September 23rd - Hockenheim
1. Klein (Honda); 2. R. Harms (DK, Honda); 3. Lenart (H, Honda); 4. Hahn (Honda); 5. Treutlein (Honda); 6. Walther (Honda); 7. Unger (Honda); 8. Gersunde (Honda); 9. Reif (Honda); 10. Schwing (Honda).

Final Classification
1. Claudius Klein (Honda), 141
2. Robin Harms (DK, Honda), 128
3. Andreas Hahn (Honda), 86
4. Unger (Honda), 78; 5. M. Kallio (SF, Honda), 75; 6. Kirmeier (Honda), 72; 7. Lenart (H, Honda), 62; 8. Knoefler (Yamaha), 60; 9. Walther (Honda), 58; 10. Treutlein (Honda), 57; 11. Schwing (Honda), 43; 12. Gersunde (Honda), 37; 13. Reif (Honda), 36;
14. Reissmann (Honda), 30; 15. Kiiveri (SF, Honda), 27.

250CC

May 6th - Lausitz
1. Neukirchen (Yamaha); 2. S. Harms (DK, TSR-Honda); 3. Heidolf (Yamaha); 4. Neukirchner (Honda); 5. Palander (S, Honda); 6. Gemmel (Honda); 7. Schneider (Honda); 8. Hartmann (Honda); 9. Josephowitz (Yamaha); 10. Ziegler (Honda).

May 20th - Hockenheim
1. Neukirchen (Yamaha); 2. Heidolf (Yamaha); 3. Gemmel (Honda); 4. Palander (S, Honda); 5. Goebel (Honda); 6. Neukirchner (Honda); 7. Polzer (A, Honda); 8. Schneider (Honda); 9. Lehmann (Honda); 10. Andersson (S, Honda).

June 3rd - Oschersleben
1. Heidolf (Yamaha); 2. Gemmel (Honda); 3. Neukirchen (Yamaha); 4. Palander (S, Honda); 5. Neukirchner (Honda); 6. Schneider (Honda); 7. Polzer (A, Honda); 8. Lehmann (Honda); 9. Litjens (NL, Honda); 10. S. Harms (DK, TSR-Honda).

July 15th - Augsburg
1. Gemmel (Honda); 2. Heidolf (Yamaha); 3. Palander (S, Honda); 4. Neukirchner (Honda); 5. Polzer (A, Honda); 6. Schneider (Honda); 7. S. Harms (DK, Honda); 8. Lehmann (Honda); 9. Koegler (Honda); 10. Kehrer (Honda).

August 5th - Schleiz
1. Heidolf (Yamaha); 2. Neukirchen (Yamaha); 3. Neukirchner (Honda); 4. Gemmel (Honda); 5. Hafenegger (Aprilia); 6. Rank (Honda); 7. Welch (GB, Yamaha); 8. S. Harms (DK, Honda); 9. Brown (GB, Honda); 10. Polzer (A, Honda).

August 19th - Nürburgring
1. Gemmel (Honda); 2. Neukirchen (Yamaha); 3. Palander (S, Honda); 4. Lehmann (Honda); 5. Goebel (Honda); 6. Andersson (Honda); 7. S. Harms (DK, Honda); 8. Koegler (Honda); 9. Kehrer (Honda); 10. Huber (Honda).

September 16th - Oschersleben
1. Neukirchen (Yamaha); 2. Heidolf (Yamaha); 3. Hafenegger (Aprilia); 4. Schneider (Honda); 5. Polzer (A, Honda); 6. Goebel (Honda); 7. Lehmann (Honda); 8. Palander (S, Honda); 9. Josephowitz (Yamaha); 10. S. Harms (DK, Honda).

September 23rd - Hockenheim
1. Gemmel (Honda); 2. Palander (S, Honda); 3. Heidolf (Yamaha); 4. Goebel (Honda); 5. Schneider (Honda); 6. V. Kallio (SF, Yamaha); 7. Lauslehto (SF, Honda); 8. Watz (S, Yamaha); 9. Neukirchen (Yamaha); 10. Josephowitz (Yamaha).

Final Classification
1. Matthias Neukirchen (Yamaha), 145
2. Dirk Heidolf (Yamaha), 142
3. Christian Gemmel (Honda), 134
4. Palander (S, Honda), 97; 5. Neukirchner (Honda), 63; 6. S. Harms (DK, Honda), 61; 7. Schneider (Honda), 61; 8. Lehmann (Honda), 61; 9. Goebel (Honda), 54; 10. Polzer (A, Honda), 49; 11. Kehrer (Honda), 41; 12. Kögler (Honda), 32; 13. Josephowitz (Yamaha), 30; 14. Hafenegger (Aprilia), 27; 15. Huber (Honda), 25.

SUPERSPORT

May 6th - Lausitz
Cancelled

May 20th - Hockenheim
1. Schulten (Yamaha); 2. Oelschläger (Suzuki); 3. Kaufmann (Suzuki); 4. Ekerold (SA, Suzuki); 5. Kuttruf (Honda); 6. Schading (Kawasaki); 7. Penzkofer (Ducati); 8. Maher (IRL, Yamaha); 9. Sluka (Yamaha); 10. Goetz (Yamaha).

June 3rd - Oschersleben
Race I (replace Lausitz):
1. Schulten (Yamaha); 2. Kaufmann (Suzuki); 3. Penzkofer (Ducati); 4. Witzeneder (A, Suzuki); 5. Stamm (CH, Kawasaki); 6. Ekerold (SA, Suzuki); 7. Maher (IRL, Yamaha); 8. Bauer (A, Kawasaki); 9. Ludwig (Yamaha); 10. Schading (Kawasaki).
Race II:
1. Penzkofer (Ducati); 2. Schulten (Yamaha); 3. Kaufmann (Suzuki); 4. Oelschläger (Suzuki); 5. Nebel (Suzuki); 6. Scheschowitsch (Suzuki); 7. Ekerold (SA, Suzuki); 8. Steinmetz (Yamaha); 9. Kuttruf (Honda); 10. Schading (Kawasaki).

July 15th - Augsburg
1. Penzkofer (Ducati); 2. Schulten (Yamaha); 3. Kaufmann (Suzuki); 4. Nebel (Suzuki); 5. Galinski (Yamaha); 6. Oelschläger (Suzuki); 7. Ekerold (SA, Suzuki); 8. Maher (IRL, Yamaha); 9. Ludwig (Yamaha); 10. Joerg (Honda).

August 5th - Schleiz
1. Schulten (Yamaha); 2. Kaufmann (Suzuki); 3. Scheschowitsch (Suzuki); 4. Nebel (Suzuki); 5. Ekerold (SA, Suzuki); 6. Steinmetz (Yamaha); 7. Lougher (GB, Suzuki); 8. Witzeneder (A, Suzuki); 9. Maher (IRL, Yamaha); 10. Bauer (A, Kawasaki).

August 19th - Nürburgring
1. Kellner (Yamaha); 2. Schulten (Yamaha); 3. Kaufmann (Suzuki); 4. Oelschläger (Suzuki); 5. Maher (IRL, Yamaha); 6. Nebel (Suzuki); 7. Bauer (A, Kawasaki); 8. Penzkofer (Ducati); 9. Steinmetz (Yamaha); 10. Schading (Kawasaki).

September 16th - Oschersleben
1. Kaufmann (Suzuki); 2. Penzkofer (Ducati); 3. Schulten (Yamaha); 4. Zaiser (A, Honda); 5. Scheschowitsch (Suzuki); 6. Oelschläger (Suzuki); 7. Bauer (Kawasaki); 8. Steinmetz (Yamaha); 9. Nebel (Suzuki); 10. Galinski (Yamaha).

September 23rd - Hockenheim
1. Penzkofer (Ducati); 2. Kaufmann (Suzuki); 3. Oelschläger (Suzuki); 4. Bauer (A, Kawasaki); 5. Scheschowitsch (Suzuki); 6. Ekerold (SA, Suzuki); 7. Steinmetz (Yamaha); 8. Nebel (Suzuki); 9. Schading (Kawasaki); 10. Kuttruf (Honda).

Final Classification
1. Michael Schulten   (Yamaha),   156
2. Herbert Kaufmann   (Suzuki),   153
3. Rico Penzkofer   (Ducati),   129
4. Oelschläger (Suzuki), 86; 5. Ekerold (SA, Suzuki), 68; 6. Nebel (Suzuki), 67; 7. Bauer (Kawasaki), 53; 8. Scheschowitsch (Suzuki), 50; 9. Maher (IRL, Yamaha), 46; 10. Steinmetz (Yamaha), 44; 11. Witzeneder (A, Suzuki), 42; 12. Schading (Kawasaki), 40; 13. Galinski (Yamaha), 33; 14. Kuttruf (Honda), 30; 15. Stamm (CH, Kawasaki), 28.

SUPERSTOCK

May 6th - Lausitz
1. Wegscheider (I, Suzuki); 2. Bähr (Yamaha); 3. Ehrenberger (Suzuki); 4. Sebrich (Suzuki); 5. Kraft (Suzuki); 6. Knobloch (Yamaha); 7. Fritz (Kawasaki); 8. Heidger (Suzuki); 9. Geiger (Suzuki); 10. Hecker (Suzuki).

May 20th - Hockenheim
1. Bähr (Yamaha); 2. Ehrenberger (Suzuki); 3. Sebrich (Suzuki); 4. Heidger (Suzuki); 5. Geiger (Suzuki); 6. Fritz (Kawasaki); 7. Stather (Suzuki); 8. Nabert (Suzuki); 9. Leuthard (CH, Yamaha); 10. Schulz (Suzuki).

June 3rd - Oschersleben
1. Jerzenbeck (Suzuki); 2. Geiger (Suzuki); 3. Ehrenberger (Suzuki); 4. Baehr (Yamaha); 5. Stather (Suzuki); 6. Sebrich (Suzuki); 7. Heidger (Suzuki); 8. Schmidt (Suzuki); 9. Fritz (Kawasaki); 10. Sessler (Yamaha).

July 15th - Augsburg
1. Wegscheider (I, Suzuki); 2. Jerzenbeck (Suzuki); 3. Klein (Suzuki); 4. Ehrenberger (Suzuki); 5. Baehr (Yamaha); 6. Heidger (Suzuki); 7. Sebrich (Suzuki); 8. Scheschowitsch (Suzuki); 9. Schmidt (Suzuki); 10. Nau (Suzuki).

August 5th - Schleiz
1. Bauer (A, Kawasaki); 2. Jerzenbeck (Suzuki); 3. Baehr (Yamaha); 4. Sebrich (Suzuki); 5. Ehrenberger (Suzuki); 6. Klass (Suzuki); 7. Sessler (Yamaha); 8. Lederer (Kawasaki); 9. Leuthard (CH, Yamaha); 10. Heidger (Suzuki).

August 19th - Nürburgring
1. Ehrenberger (Suzuki); 2. Wegscheider (I, Suzuki); 3. Bauer (A, Kawasaki); 4. Sebrich (Suzuki); 5. Klein (Suzuki); 6. Geiger (Suzuki); 7. Sessler (Yamaha); 8. Nabert (Suzuki); 9. Heydt (Suzuki); 10. Stather (Suzuki).

September 16th - Oschersleben
1. Kaufmann (Suzuki); 2. Wegscheider (I, Suzuki); 3. Bauer (A, Kawasaki); 4. Jerzenbeck (Suzuki); 5. Geiger (Suzuki); 6. Ehrenberger (Suzuki); 7. Sebrich (Suzuki); 8. Heidger (Suzuki); 9. Jensen (DK, Suzuki); 10. Duchene (Suzuki).

September 23rd - Hockenheim
1. Kaufmann (Suzuki); 2. Wegscheider (I, Suzuki); 3. Baehr (Yamaha); 4. Sebrich (Suzuki); 5. Jerzenbeck (Suzuki); 6. Bauer (A, Kawasaki); 7. Heidger (Suzuki); 8. Ehrenberger (Suzuki); 9. Geiger (Suzuki); 10. Duchene (Suzuki).

Final Classification
1. Claus Ehrenberger   (Suzuki),   123
2. Volker Baehr   (Yamaha),   106
3. Stefan Sebrich   (Suzuki),   99
4. Bauer (A, Kawasaki), 92; 5. Wegscheider (I, Suzuki), 85; 6. Jerzenbeck (Suzuki), 84; 7. Geiger (Suzuki), 65; 8. Heidger (Suzuki), 65; 9. Kaufmann (Suzuki), 50; 10. Sessler (Yamaha), 36; 11. Stather (Suzuki), 35; 12. Fritz (Kawasaki), 34; 13. Nabert (Suzuki), 27; 14. Schmidt (Suzuki), 26; 15. Leuthard (CH, Yamaha), 23.

PRO SUPERBIKE

April 16th - Assen - The Netherlands
Race I:
1. Vleugels (B, Yamaha); 2. Heidger (D, Suzuki); 3. Van Keymeulen (B, Honda); 4. Malec (SLO, Kawasaki);

5. Manz (Kawasaki); 6. Coopman (B, Yamaha); 7. Pollheide (Suzuki); 8. Versteeg (NL, Suzuki); 9. Badziak (POL, Kawasaki); 10. Nolden (Suzuki).
Race II:
1. Vleugels (B, Yamaha); 2. Heidger (Suzuki); 3. Van Keymeulen (B, Honda); 4. Dimperl (Ducati); 5. Malec (SLO, Kawasaki); 6. Manz (Kawasaki); 7. Weynand (B, Yamaha); 8. Nolden (Suzuki); 9. Coopman (B, Yamaha); 10. Badziak (POL, Kawasaki).

May 6th - Magny-Cours - France
Race I:
1. Kedzior (POL, Kawasaki); 2. Badziak (POL, Kawasaki); 3. Bruner (CH, Suzuki); 4. Dimperl (Ducati); 5. Furrer (CH, Kawasaki); 6. Truninger (CH, Kawasaki); 7. Malec (SLO, Ducati); 8. Jud (CH, Kawasaki); 9. Manz (Kawasaki); 10. De Feyter (B, Yamaha).
Race II:
1. Malec (SLO, Ducati); 2. Truninger (CH, Kawasaki); 3. Richter (Suzuki); 4. Kedzior (POL, Kawasaki); 5. Jud (CH, Kawasaki); 6. Manz (Kawasaki); 7. Badziak (POL, Kawasaki); 8. Versteeg (NL, Suzuki); 9. Van Bogaert (B, Yamaha); 10. De Feyter (B, Yamaha).

May 20th - Rijeka - Croatia
Race I:
1. Camlek (SLO, Yamaha); 2. Malec (SLO, Ducati); 3. Etzthaler (I, Yamaha); 4. Tuden (CRO, Ducati); 5. Kedzior (POL, Kawasaki); 6. Manz (Kawasaki); 7. Badziak (POL, Kawasaki); 8. Trunninger (CH, Kawasaki); 9. Kemenovic (CRO, Yamaha); 10. Zrinic (CRO, Yamaha).
Race II:
1. Camlek (SLO, Yamaha); 2. Campana (I, Ducati); 3. Malec (SLO, Ducati); 4. Sala (I, Suzuki); 5. Etzthaler (I, Yamaha); 6. Vegh (H, Yamaha); 7. Kedzior (POL, Kawasaki); 8. Manz (Kawasaki); 9. Badziak (POL, Kawasaki); 10. Ancilotti (I, Yamaha).

June 24th - Brno - Czech Republic
Race I:
1. Weder (CH, Yamaha); 2. Truninger (CH, Kawasaki); 3. Kedzior (POL, Kawasaki); 4. Steidel (Ducati); 5. Badziak (POL, Kawasaki); 6. Weinmüller (Suzuki); 7. Fischer (Suzuki); 8. Manz (Kawasaki); 9. Geulen (Suzuki); 10. Jud (CH, Kawasaki).
Race II:
1. Weder (CH, Yamaha); 2. Malec (SLO, Ducati); 3. Truninger (CH, Kawasaki); 4. Kedzior (POL, Kawasaki); 5. Steidel (Ducati) Badziak (POL, Kawasaki); 7. Manz (Kawasaki); 8. Flohrer (Suzuki); 9. Jud (CH, Kawasaki); 10. Geulen (Suzuki).

July 8th - Pannoniaring - Hungary
Race I:
1. Vegh (H, Yamaha); 2. Borgelt (Kawasaki); 3. Weder (CH, Yamaha); 4. Malec (SLO, Ducati); 5. Manz (Kawasaki); 6. Müller (Ducati); 7. Caspon (I, Ducati); 8. Truninger (CH, Kawasaki); 9. Kedzior (POL, Kawasaki); 10. Badziak (POL, Kawasaki).
Race II:
1. Weder (CH, Yamaha); 2. Borgelt (Kawasaki); 3. Manz (Kawasaki); 4. Strasser (A, Honda); 5. Malec (SLO, Ducati); 6. Truninger (CH, Kawasaki); 7. Schleindlhuber (A, Suzuki); 8. Kedzior (POL, Kawasaki); 9. Blümel (A, Honda); 10. Geulen (Suzuki).

July 22nd - Most - Czech Republic
Race I:
1. Mrkyvka (CZ, Ducati); 2. Malec (SLO, Ducati); 3. Manz (Kawasaki); 4. Foukal (CZ, Yamaha); 5. Myszkovski (POL, Yamaha); 6. Müller (Ducati); 7. Badziak (POL, Kawasaki); 8. Weder (CH, Yamaha); 9. Holz (Ducati); 10. Drazdak (CZ, Kawasaki).
Race II:
1. Malec (SLO, Ducati); 2. Weder (CH, Yamaha); 3. Truninger (CH, Kawasaki); 4. Manz (Kawasaki); 5. Luger (Suzuki); 6. Badziak (POL, Kawasaki); 7. Kuba (CZ, Suzuki); 8. Dobrovolski (POL, Yamaha); 9. Holz (Yamaha); 10. Geulen (Suzuki).

August 19th - Brno - Czech Republic
Race I:
1. Malec (SLO, Ducati); 2. Truninger (CH, Kawasaki); 3. Mrkyvka (CZ, Ducati); 4. Badziak (POL, Kawasaki); 5. Wolfsteiner (A, Suzuki); 6. Kedzior (POL, Kawasaki); 7. Manz (Kawasaki); 8. Marcheti (I, Ducati); 9. Vograndl (A, Yamaha); 10. Geulen (Suzuki).
Race II:
1. Weder (CH, Yamaha); 2. Luger (Suzuki); 3. Malec (SLO, Ducati); 4. Manz (Kawasaki); 5. Kuba (POL, Suzuki); 6. Badziak (POL, Kawasaki); 7. Bursa (CZ, Honda); 8. Kedzior (POL, Kawasaki); 9. Dobrovolski (POL, Yamaha); 10. Geulen (Suzuki).

September 30th - Mugello - Italy
Race I:
1. Weder (CH, Yamaha); 2. Janssen (CH, Kawasaki); 3. Brunner (CH, Suzuki); 4. Wüthrich (CH, Yamaha); 5. Malec (SLO, Ducati); 6. Furrer (CH, Kawasaki); 7. Badziak (POL, Kawasaki); 8. Janetzko (Yamaha); 9. Manz (Kawasaki); 10. Erkert (Suzuki).
Race II:
1. Malec (SLO, Ducati); 2. Brunner (CH, Suzuki); 3. Manz (Kawasaki); 4. Badziak (POL, Kawasaki); 5. Furrer (CH, Kawasaki); 6. Wüthrich (CH, Yamaha); 7. Schmitter (CH, Yamaha); 8. Jud (CH, Kawasaki); 9. Erkert (Suzuki); 10. Janetzko (Yamaha).

Final Classification
1. Marjan Malec   (SLO, Ducati),   472
2. Norman Manz   (Kawasaki),   364
3. Adam Badziak   (POL, Kawasaki),   315
4. Weder (CH, Yamaha), 284; 5. Truninger (CH, Kawasaki), 273; 6. Kedzior (POL, Kawasaki), 240; 7. Geulen (Suzuki), 166; 8. Brunner (CH, Suzuki), 97; 9. Jud (CH, Kawasaki), 92; 10. Camlek (SLO, Yamaha), 80; 11. Vleugels (B, Yamaha), 80; 12. Dimperl (Ducati), 79; 13. Mrkyvka (CZ, Ducati), 71; 14. Borgelt (Kawasaki), 70; 15. Heidger (Suzuki), 70.

SIDE-CARS

May 6th - Lausitz
Cancelled.

May 20th - Hockenheim
1. Steinhausen/Hetherington (D/GB, Suzuki); 2. Roscher/Neubert (Suzuki); 3. Goettlich/Helbig (Suzuki); 4. Becker/Abel (Kawasaki); 5. Hock/Kasel (Kawasaki); 6. Häberli/Sanapo (CH, LCR); 7. Hug/Roth (CH, Suzuki); 8. Kutschke/Kolloch (Honda); 9. Zimmermann/Backmann (Suzuki); 10. Steiner/Koloska (CH, Suzuki).

June 3rd - Oschersleben
1. Steinhausen/Gries (Suzuki); 2. Hemmerling/Kölsch (Suzuki); 3. Goettlich/Helbig (Suzuki); 4. Roscher/Neubert (Suzuki); 5. Eilers/Kolloch (Suzuki); 6. Becker/Abel (Kawasaki); 7. Kohlmann/Anderle (Honda); 8. Centner/Langschädel (Suzuki); 9. Neumayer/Höss (LCR-Krauser); 10. Häberli/Sanapo (CH, Suzuki).

June 17th - Augsburg
1. Steinhausen/Gries (Suzuki); 2. Roscher/Neubert (Suzuki); 3. Häberli/Sanapo (CH, Suzuki); 4. Hock/Kasel (Kawasaki); 5. Hug/Roth (CH, Suzuki); 6. Kohlmann/Baptist (Honda); 7. Reuter/Auer (Suzuki); 8. Neumayer/Höss (LCR-Krauser); 9. Baert/Langschädel (B/D, Suzuki) ; 10. Zimmermann/Kolloch (Suzuki).

August 5th - Schleiz
1. Vermeijmeren/Kruip (NL, Suzuki); 2. Goettlich/Helbig (Suzuki); 3. Roscher/Neubert (Suzuki); 4. Hug/Roth (CH, Suzuki); 5. Doppler/Wagner (A, Yamaha); 6. Centner/Rodler (Suzuki); 7. Veltjens/Hildebrand (Suzuki); 8. Hainbucher/Wörner (A, Suzuki); 9. Kohlmann/Anderle (Honda); 10. Häberli/Sanapo (CH, Suzuki).

August 19th - Nürburgring
1. Steinhausen/Kölsch (Suzuki); 2. Van Gils/Van Gils (NL, Suzuki); 3. Goettlich/Helbig (Suzuki); 4. Hock/Kasel (Kawasaki); 5. Centner/Rodler (Suzuki); 6. Eilers/Engelmann (Suzuki); 7. Hayakawa/Kobe (J, Suzuki); 8. Doppler/Wagner (A, Yamaha); 9. Kohlmann/Anderle (Honda); 10. Häberli/Sanapo (CH, Suzuki).

September 16th - Oschersleben
1. Steinhausen/Kölsch (Suzuki); 2. Kohlmann/Anderle (Honda); 3. Goettlich/Rodler (Suzuki); 4. Hock/Kasel (Kawasaki); 5. Becker/Kolloch (Kawasaki); 6. Roscher/Neubert (Suzuki); 7. Doppler/Wagner (A, Yamaha); 8. Veltjens/Hildebrand (Suzuki); 9. Kiser/Buhrer (CH, Kawasaki); 10. Hug/Roth (CH, Suzuki).

September 23rd - Hockenheim
Race I (replace Lausitz):
1. Steinhausen/Kölsch (Suzuki); 2. Centner/Helbig (Suzuki); 3. Roscher/Neubert (Suzuki); 4. Göttlich/Rodler (Suzuki); 5. Hock/Kasel (Kawasaki); 6. Becker/Kolloch (Suzuki); 7. Doppler/Wagner (A, Yamaha); 8. Zimmermann/Backmann (Suzuki); 9. Reuter/Langschädel (Suzuki); 10. Kohlmann/Anderle (Honda).
Race II:
1. Steinhausen/Kölsch (Suzuki); 2. Centner/Helbig (Suzuki); 3. Roscher/Neubert (Suzuki); 4. Hock/Kasel (Kawasaki); 5. Göttlich/Rodler (Suzuki); 6. Doppler/Wagner (A, Yamaha); 7. Zimmermann/Backmann (Suzuki); 8. Kohlmann/Anderle (Honda); 9. Kiser/Bührer (CH, Kawasaki); 10. Veltjens/Hildebrand (Suzuki).

Final Classification
1. Jörg Steinhausen   (Suzuki),   175
2. Uwe Goettlich   (Suzuki),   117
3. Mike Roscher   (Suzuki),   115
4. Hock (Kawasaki), 82; 5. Centner (Suzuki), 73; 6. Kohlmann (Honda), 72; 7. Doppler (A, Yamaha), 57; 8. Hug (CH, Suzuki), 55; 9. Häberli (CH, Suzuki), 55; 10. Becker (Kawasaki), 45; 11. Veltjens (Suzuki), 37; 12. Reuter (Suzuki), 34; 13. Zimmermann (Suzuki), 33; 14. Neumayer (LCR-Krauser), 27; 15. Kiser (CH, Kawasaki), 26.

US Championship

250 CC

March 11th - Daytona
1. Oliver (Yamaha); 2. Sands (Yamaha); 3. Renfrow (Honda); 4. Filice (Yamaha); 5. Di Salvo (Honda); 6. Palander (Honda); 7. Melneciuc (Yamaha); 8. Hannas (Yamaha); 9. Turner (IRL, Yamaha); 10. Wood (Yamaha).

May 6th - Sears Point
1. Sands (Yamaha); 2. Filice (Yamaha); 3. Hannas (Yamaha); 4. Turner (IRL, Yamaha); 5. Marchini (Yamaha); 6. Melneciuc (Yamaha); 7. Castanos (Honda); 8. Leggitt (Yamaha); 9. Sorensen (Yamaha); 10. West (Yamaha).

May 20th - Road Atlanta
1. Oliver (Yamaha); 2. Sorensen (Yamaha); 3. Filice (Yamaha); 4. Turner (IRL, Yamaha); 5. Marchini (Yamaha); 6. Hannas (Yamaha); 7. W. Himmelsbach (Yamaha); 8. Pyles (Yamaha); 9. Sorbo (Yamaha); 10. Walters (Yamaha).

June 10th - Road America
1. Oliver (Yamaha); 2. Filice (Yamaha); 3. Melneciuc (Yamaha); 4. Hannas (Yamaha); 5. Stephens (Honda); 6. Pyles (Yamaha); 7. W. Himmelsbach (Yamaha); 8. West (Yamaha); 9. De Groot (Yamaha); 10. Sorensen (Yamaha).

17th - Loudon
1. Filice (Yamaha); 2. Sorensen (Yamaha); 3. Wood (Yamaha); 4. Hannas (Yamaha); 5. Melneciuc (Yamaha); 6. Turner (IRL, Yamaha); 7. King (TSR-Honda); 8. Marchini (Yamaha); 9. Scott (Yamaha); 10. Pyles (Yamaha).

July 8th - Laguna Seca
1. Oliver (Yamaha); 2. Filice (Yamaha); 3. Turner (IRL, Yamaha); 4. Melneciuc (Yamaha); 5. Hannas (Yamaha); 6. Leggitt (Honda); 7. Ienatsch (Yamaha); 8. Jensen (Aprilia); 9. Ellsworth (Yamaha); 10. Webb (Yamaha).

July 22nd - Lexington
1. Filice (Yamaha); 2. Oliver (Yamaha); 3. Sorensen (Yamaha); 4. Melneciuc (Yamaha); 5. Hannas (Yamaha); 6. Renfrow (Honda); 7. M. Himmelsbach (Aprilia); 8. Turner (IRL, Yamaha); 9. W. Himmelsbach (Yamaha); 10. Pyles (Yamaha).

July 29th - Brainerd
1. Oliver (Yamaha); 2. Sorensen (Yamaha); 3. Filice (Yamaha); 4. Renfrow (Honda); 5. Turner (IRL, Yamaha); 6. Melneciuc (Yamaha); 7. Piz (Yamaha); 8. Sorbo (Yamaha); 9. West (Yamaha); 10. France (Honda).

August 26th - Fountain
1. Oliver (Yamaha); 2. Sands (Yamaha); 3. Filice (Yamaha); 4. Hannas (Yamaha); 5. Hough (Yamaha); 6. Piz (Yamaha); 7. Esser (Honda); 8. Leggitt (Honda); 9. Jensen (Aprilia); 10. Sorbo (Yamaha).

September 16th - Willow Springs
Race cancelled.

September 30th - Alton
1. Oliver (Yamaha); 2. Sorensen (Yamaha); 3. Renfrow (Honda); 4. M. Himmelsbach (Aprilia); 5. Turner (IRL, Yamaha); 6. Filice (Yamaha); 7. Hannas (Yamaha); 8. Melneciuc (Yamaha); 9. Sorbo (Yamaha); 10. West (Yamaha).

Final Classification
1. Jim Filice   (Yamaha),   309
2. Richard Oliver   (Yamaha),   308
3. Michael Hannas   Yamaha,   249
4. Melneciuc (Yamaha), 224; 5. Turner (IRL, Yamaha), 221; 6. Sorensen (Yamaha), 211; 7. Sorbo (Yamaha), 176; 8. Esser (Honda), 169; 9. Piz (Yamaha), 163; 10. West (Yamaha), 153; 11. France (Honda), 147; 12. Pyles (Yamaha), 124; 13. Renfrow (Honda), 110; 14. W. Himmelsbach (Yamaha), 106; 15. Sands (Yamaha), 105.

Supersport 600

March 11th - Daytona
1. Mi. Duhamel (CAN, Honda); 2. N. Hayden (Honda); 3. An. Gobert (AUS, Yamaha); 4. Ku. Roberts (Honda); 5. E. Bostrom (Kawasaki); 6. Hacking (Suzuki); 7. T. Hayden (Yamaha); 8. Yates (Suzuki); 9. Zemke (Honda); 10. Hayes (Honda).

May 6th - Sears Point
1. An. Gobert (AUS, Yamaha); 2. E. Bostrom (Kawasaki); 3. Mi. Duhamel (CAN, Honda); 4. Hayes (Honda); 5. T. Hayden (Yamaha); 6. Hopkins (Suzuki); 7. Zemke (Honda); 8. Parriott (Suzuki); 9. Lopez (Suzuki); 10. Weichel (CAN, Kawasaki).

May 20th - Road Atlanta
1. E. Bostrom (Kawasaki); 2. Yates (Suzuki); 3. Hacking (Suzuki); 4. An. Gobert (AUS, Yamaha); 5. Hayes (Honda); 6. T. Hayden (Yamaha); 7. Hopkins (Suzuki); 8. Ku. Roberts (Honda); 9. Aa. Gobert (Yamaha); 10. Mi. Duhamel (CAN, Honda).

June 10th - Road America
1. Yates (Suzuki); 2. Hacking (Suzuki); 3. E. Bostrom (Kawasaki); 4. Hopkins (Suzuki); 5. T. Hayden (Yamaha); 6. Ku. Roberts (Honda); 7. An. Gobert (AUS, Yamaha); 8. Aa. Gobert (AUS, Yamaha); 9. Hayes (Honda); 10. Mi. Duhamel (CAN, Honda).

June 17th - Loudon
1. Greenwood (Suzuki); 2. Silva (Kawasaki); 3. Hopkins (Yamaha); 4. Salemi (Honda); 5. Williams (Suzuki); 6. Niksa (Suzuki); 7. Martire (Kawasaki); 8. Blake (Honda); 9. Seaton (Yamaha); 10. Richey (Yamaha).

July 8th - Laguna Seca
1. E. Bostrom (Kawasaki); 2. Yates (Suzuki); 3. Hacking (Suzuki); 4. T. Hayden (Yamaha); 5. N. Hayden (Honda); 6. Hopkins (Suzuki); 7. An. Gobert (AUS, Yamaha); 8. Hayes (Honda); 9. Mi. Duhamel (CAN, Honda); 10. R.-L. Hayden (Honda).

July 22nd - Lexington
1. Mi. Duhamel (CAN, Honda); 2. T. Hayden (Yamaha); 3. E. Bostrom (Kawasaki); 4. Ku. Roberts (Honda); 5. An. Gobert (AUS, Yamaha); 6. Hayes (Honda); 7. Hopkins (Suzuki); 8. Zemke (Honda); 9. Lopez (Suzuki); 10. Aa. Gobert (AUS, Yamaha).

July 29th - Brainerd
1. Mi. Duhamel (CAN, Honda); 2. E. Bostrom (Kawasaki); 3. An. Gobert (AUS, Yamaha); 4. Hopkins (Suzuki); 5. Ku. Roberts (Honda); 6. T. Hayden (Yamaha); 7. Hayes (Honda); 8. Aa. Gobert (AUS, Yamaha); 9. Zemke (Honda); 10. Lopez (Suzuki).

August 26th - Fountain
1. E. Bostrom (Kawasaki); 2. An. Gobert (AUS, Yamaha); 3. Yates (Suzuki); 4. T. Hayden (Yamaha); 5. Hacking (Suzuki); 6. Mi. Duhamel (CAN, Honda); 7. Zemke (Honda); 8. Hayes (Honda); 9. Aa. Gobert (Yamaha); 10. R.-L. Hayden (Honda).

September 16th - Willow Springs
Race cancelled.

September 30th - Alton
1. An. Gobert (AUS, Yamaha); 2. Yates (Suzuki); 3. Mi. Duhamel (CAN, Honda); 4. Hopkins (Suzuki); 5. Ku. Roberts (Honda); 6. T. Hayden (Yamaha); 7. E. Bostrom (Kawasaki); 8. Zemke (Honda); 9. Hayes (Honda); 10. Lopez (Suzuki).

FINAL CLASSIFICATION
1. Eric Bostrom   (Kawasaki),   285
2. Anthony Gobert   (AUS, Yamaha)   265
3. Miguel Duhamel   (CAN, Honda),   259
4. T. Hayden (Yamaha), 239; 5. Hayes (Honda), 213; 6. Zemke (Honda), 195; 7. Yates (Suzuki), 188; 8. Hopkins (Suzuki), 179; 9. Hacking (Suzuki), 159; 10. Aa. Gobert (AUS, Yamaha), 158; 11. Ku. Roberts (Honda), 156; 12. R.-L. Hayden (Honda), 122; 13. Moore (Suzuki), 120; 14. Lopez (Suzuki), 115; 15. Ortega (MEX, Suzuki), 109.

Supersport 750

March 11th - Daytona
1. Pridmore (Suzuki); 2. Spies (Suzuki); 3. Alexander (Suzuki); 4. Moore (Suzuki); 5. Gibbs (Suzuki); 6. Schmidt (CAN, Suzuki); 7. Ashmead (Suzuki); 8. Jacobi (Suzuki); 9. Haskovec (CZ, Suzuki); 10. Chouinard (Suzuki).

May 6th - Sears Point
1. Parriott (Suzuki); 2. Moore (Suzuki); 3. Alexander (Suzuki); 4. Ulrich (Suzuki); 5. Acree (Suzuki); 6. Haskovec (CZ, Suzuki); 7. Randolph (Suzuki); 8. Spies (Suzuki); 9. Lupo (Suzuki); 10. Meiring (Suzuki).

May 20th - Road Atlanta
1. Ciccotto (Suzuki); 2. Parriott (Suzuki); 3. Spies (Suzuki); 4. Moore (Suzuki); 5. Ulrich (Suzuki); 6. Alexander (Suzuki); 7. Haskovec (CZ, Suzuki); 8. Conicelli (Suzuki); 9. Ashmead (Suzuki); 10. Suzuki (J, Suzuki).

June 10th - Road America
1. Moore (Suzuki); 2. Spies (Suzuki); 3. Ulrich (Suzuki); 4. Junge (Suzuki); 5. Haskovec (CZ, Suzuki); 6. Meiring (Suzuki); 7. Conicelli (Suzuki); 8. Ortega (MEX, Suzuki); 9. Alexander (Suzuki); 10. Lupo (Suzuki).

June 17th - Loudon
1. Cicotto (Suzuki); 2. Alexander (Suzuki); 3. Hayes (Honda); 4. Haskovec (CZ, Suzuki); 5. Moore (Suzuki); 6. Suzuki (J, Suzuki); 7. Silva (Suzuki); 8. Meiring (Suzuki); 9. Ortega (MEX, Suzuki); 10. Ashmead (Suzuki).

July 8th - Laguna Seca
1. Ulrich (Suzuki); 2. Suzuki (J, Suzuki); 3. Meiring (Suzuki); 4. Alexander (Suzuki); 5. Isaacs (SA, Honda); 6. Schmidt (CAN, Suzuki); 7. Deatherage (Suzuki); 8. Lupo (Suzuki); 9. Conicelli (Suzuki); 10. Kishida (J, Kawasaki).

July 22nd - Lexington
1. Moore (Suzuki); 2. Ulrich (Suzuki); 3. Spies (Suzuki); 4. Hayes (Honda); 5. Haskovec (CZ, Suzuki); 6. Suzuki (J, Suzuki); 7. Lupo (Suzuki); 8. Schmidt (CAN, Suzuki); 9. King (Suzuki); 10. Meiring (Suzuki).

July 29th - Brainerd
1. Moore (Suzuki); 2. Alexander (Suzuki); 3. Meiring (Suzuki); 4. Jensen (Suzuki); 5. Spies (Suzuki); 6. Haskovec (CZ, Suzuki); 7. Lupo (Suzuki); 8. Ortega (MEX, Suzuki); 9. Mennenga (Suzuki); 10. Schmidt (CAN, Suzuki).

August 26th - Fountain
1. Spies (Suzuki); 2. Moore (Suzuki); 3. Ulrich (Suzuki); 4. Haskovec (CZ, Suzuki); 5. Lupo (Suzuki); 6. Dugan (Suzuki); 7. Ortega (MEX, Suzuki); 8. Schmidt (CAN, Suzuki); 9. Schnackenberg (Suzuki); 10. Jensen (Suzuki).

September 16th - Willow Springs
Race cancelled.

September 30th - Alton
1. Acree (Suzuki); 2. Moore (Suzuki); 3. Jensen (Suzuki); 4. Ciccotto (Suzuki); 5. Harwell (Suzuki); 6. Conicelli (Suzuki); 7. Haskovec (CZ, Suzuki); 8. Caldwell (Suzuki); 9. Lupo (Suzuki); 10. Ortega (MEX, Suzuki).

Final Classification
1. Jimmy Moore   (Suzuki),   310
2. Vincent Haskovec   (CZ, Suzuki)   229
3. Ben Spies   (Suzuki),   226
4. Alexander (Suzuki), 210; 5. Ulrich (Suzuki), 208; 6. Meiring (Suzuki), 208; 7. Ortega (MEX, Suzuki), 187; 8. Lupo (Suzuki), 179; 9. Schmidt (CAN, Suzuki), 152; 10. Conicelli (Suzuki), 149; 11. Suzuki (JAP, Suzuki), 133; 12. Cicotto (Suzuki), 103; 13. Blake (Suzuki), 77; 14. Parriott (Suzuki), 70; 15. Acree (Suzuki), 63.

Superbike

March 11th - Daytona
1. Mladin (AUS, Suzuki); 2. E. Bostrom (Kawasaki); 3. Ku. Roberts (Honda); 4. Chandler (Kawasaki); 5. T. Hayden (Yamaha); 6. Pegram (Ducati); 7. Smith (Harley-Davidson); 8. Moore (Suzuki); 9. Cereda (Suzuki); 10. N. Hayden (Honda).

May 6th - Sears Point
1. An. Gobert (AUS, Yamaha); 2. N. Hayden (Honda); 3. Yates (Suzuki); 4. Mladin (AUS, Suzuki); 5. Mi. Duhamel (CAN, Honda); 6. E. Bostrom (Kawasaki); 7. Chandler (Kawasaki); 8. Rapp (Ducati); 9. Pegram (Ducati); 10. Ku. Roberts (Honda).

May 20th - Road Atlanta
Race I: 1. Hacking (Suzuki); 2. Mladin (AUS, Suzuki); 3. Yates (Suzuki); 4. N. Hayden (Honda); 5. E. Bostrom (Kawasaki); 6. Chandler (Kawasaki); 7. Picotte (CAN, Harley-Davidson); 8. Pegram (Ducati); 9. T. Hayden (Yamaha); 10. Rapp (Ducati).
Race II: 1. Mladin (AUS, Suzuki); 2. Yates (Suzuki); 3. Hacking (Suzuki); 4. E. Bostrom (Kawasaki); 5. Ku. Roberts (Honda); 6. Mi. Duhamel (CAN, Honda); 7. Rapp (Ducati); 8. T. Hayden (Yamaha); 9. Pegram (Ducati); 10. An. Gobert (AUS, Yamaha).

June 10th - Road America
Race I: 1. Mladin (AUS, Suzuki); 2. An. Gobert (Yamaha); 3. Hacking (Suzuki); 4. E. Bostrom (Kawasaki); 5. N. Hayden (Honda); 6. Yates (Suzuki); 7. T. Hayden (Yamaha); 8. Mi. Duhamel (CAN, Honda); 9. Meklau

(A, Ducati); 10. Chandler (Kawasaki).
Race II: 1. An. Gobert (AUS, Yamaha); 2. Mi. Duhamel (CAN, Honda); 3. N. Hayden (Honda); 4. Meklau (A, Ducati); 5. E. Bostrom (Kawasaki); 6. T. Hayden (Yamaha); 7. Mladin (AUS, Suzuki); 8. Szoke (CAN, Harley-Davidson); 9. Chandler (Kawasaki); 10. Jacobi (Suzuki).

June 17th - Loudon
1. E. Bostrom (Kawasaki); 2. Mladin (AUS, Suzuki); 3. Yates (Suzuki); 4. N. Hayden (Honda); 5. Hacking (Suzuki); 6. Chandler (Kawasaki); 7. Rapp (Ducati); 8. Mi. Duhamel (CAN, Honda); 9. T. Hayden (Yamaha); 10. Pegram (Ducati).

July 8th - Laguna Seca
1. E. Bostrom (Kawasaki); 2. Mi. Duhamel (CAN, Honda); 3. Mladin (AUS, Suzuki); 4. Hacking (Suzuki); 5. Chandler (Kawasaki); 6. Meklau (A, Ducati); 7. Rapp (Ducati); 8. T. Hayden (Yamaha); 9. Picotte (CAN, Harley-Davidson); 10. Smith (Harley-Davidson).

July 22nd - Lexington
Race I: 1. Mladin (AUS, Suzuki); 2. E. Bostrom (Kawasaki); 3. N. Hayden (Honda); 4. Hacking (Suzuki); 5. Ku. Roberts (Honda); 6. Mi. Duhamel (CAN, Honda); 7. Chandler (Kawasaki); 8. Rapp (Ducati); 9. T. Hayden (Yamaha); 10. Meklau (A, Ducati).
Race II: 1. N. Hayden (Honda); 2. Mladin (AUS, Suzuki); 3. Mi. Duhamel (CAN, Honda); 4. Ku. Roberts (Honda); 5. Chandler (Kawasaki); 6. Hacking (Suzuki); 7. Rapp (Ducati); 8. Pegram (Ducati); 9. T. Hayden (Yamaha); 10. Meklau (A, Ducati).

July 29th - Brainerd
1. N. Hayden (Honda); 2. Ku. Roberts (Honda); 3. Mi. Duhamel (CAN, Honda); 4. Hacking (Suzuki); 5. E. Bostrom (Kawasaki); 6. Rapp (Ducati); 7. Chandler (Kawasaki); 8. Meklau (A, Ducati); 9. Pegram (Ducati); 10. T. Hayden (Yamaha).

August 26th - Fountain
1. N. Hayden (Honda); 2. E. Bostrom (Kawasaki); 3. Chandler (Kawasaki); 4. Mladin (AUS, Suzuki); 5. Rapp (Ducati); 6. Ku. Roberts (Honda); 7. Hacking (Suzuki); 8. Mi. Duhamel (CAN, Honda); 9. Yates (Suzuki); 10. T. Hayden (Yamaha).

September 16th - Willow Springs
Race cancelled.

September 30th - Alton
1. N. Hayden (Honda); 2. An. Gobert (AUS, Yamaha); 3. Ku. Roberts (Honda); 4. Chandler (Kawasaki); 5. Mi. Duhamel (CAN, Honda); 6. Yates (Suzuki); 7. Meklau (A, Ducati); 8. T. Hayden (Yamaha); 9. Rapp (Ducati); 10. E. Bostrom (Kawasaki).

Final Classification
1. Mladin   (AUS, Suzuki), 380
2. E. Bostrom   (Kawasaki),   365
3. N. Hayden   (Honda),   340
4. Chandler (Kawasaki), 319; 5. Mi. Duhamel (CAN, Honda), 300; 6. T. Hayden (Yamaha), 293; 7. Rapp (Ducati), 268; 8. Hacking (Suzuki), 267; 9. Ku. Roberts (Honda), 253; 10. Meklau (A, Ducati), 235; 11. Pegram (Ducati), 219; 12. Smith (Harley-Davidson), 205; 13. Yates (Suzuki), 202; 14. Szoke (CAN, Harley-Davidson), 187; 15. Picotte (CAN, Harley-Davidson), 171.

Switzerland Championship

Supersport

April 15th - Lédenon - France
Race I: 1. Stamm (Kawasaki); 2. Portmann (Yamaha); 3. Keist (Yamaha); 4. Leibundgut (Honda); 5. Schmid (Yamaha); 6. Häfeli (Yamaha); 7. Krummenacher (Honda); 8. Lang (Suzuki); 9. Hagmann (Yamaha); 10. Bantle (Yamaha).
Race II: 1. Stamm (Kawasaki); 2. Portmann (Yamaha); 3. Hagmann (Yamaha); 4. Leibundgut (Honda); 5. Keist (Yamaha); 6. Schmid (Yamaha); 7. Häfeli (Yamaha); 8. Alma (Yamaha); 9. Krummenacher (Honda); 10. Meier (Kawasaki).

May 26th - Oschersleben - Germany
Race I: 1. Portmann (Yamaha); 2. Leibundgut (Honda); 3. Keist (Yamaha); 4. Schmid (Yamaha); 5. Hagmann (Yamaha); 6. Lang (Suzuki); 7. Femmer (Kawasaki); 8. Häfeli (Yamaha); 9. Bantle (Yamaha); 10. Hoare (Yamaha).
Race II: 1. Leibundgut (Honda); 2. Portmann (Yamaha); 3. Keist (Yamaha); 4. Hagmann (Yamaha); 5. Schmid (Yamaha); 6. Lang (Suzuki); 7. Bantle (Yamaha); 8. Alma (Yamaha); 9. Hoare (Yamaha); 10. Ritter (Yamaha).

June 17th - Magny-Cours - France
Race I: 1. Hagmann (Yamaha); 2. Stamm (Kawasaki); 3. Häfeli (Yamaha); 4. Alma (Yamaha); 5. Meier (Kawasaki); 6. Portmann (Yamaha); 7. Lang (Suzuki); 8. Leibundgut (Honda); 9. Ritter (Yamaha). 9 finishers.
Race II: 1. Stamm (Kawasaki); 2. Häfeli (Yamaha); 3. Leibundgut (Honda); 4. Bantle (Yamaha); 5. Hagmann (Yamaha); 6. Lang (Suzuki). 6 finishers.

July 1st - Boécourt - La Caquerelle
Race I: 1. Krummenacher (Honda); 2. Leibundgut (Honda); 3. Stamm (Kawasaki); 4. Meier (Kawasaki); 5. Häfeli (Yamaha). 5 finishers.
Race II: 1. Krummenacher (Honda); 2. Stamm (Kawasaki); 3. Leibundgut (Honda); 4. Häfeli (Yamaha); 5. Meier (Kawasaki). 5 finishers.

July 15th - Châtel-Saint-Denis - Les Paccots
1. Krummenacher (Honda); 2. Leibundgut (Honda); 3. Häfeli (Yamaha). 3 finishers.

August 12th - Magione - Italy
Race I: 1. Stamm (Kawasaki); 2. Leibundgut (Honda); 3. Häfeli (Yamaha); 4. Keist (Yamaha); 5. Schmid (Yamaha); 6. Alma (Yamaha); 7. Bantle (Yamaha); 8. Ritter (Yamaha); 9. Schlachter (Ducati). 9 finishers.
Race II: 1. Leibundgut (Honda); 2. Stamm (Kawasaki); 3. Häfeli (Yamaha); 4. Schmid (Yamaha); 5. Hagmann (Yamaha); 6. Lang (Suzuki); 7. Bantle (Yamaha); 8. Alma (Yamaha); 9. Ritter (Yamaha). 9 finishers.

August 26th - Zetzwil - Leutwil
1. Lang (Suzuki); 2. Krummenacher (Honda); 3. Stamm (Kawasaki); 4. Keist (Yamaha); 5. Hagmann (Yamaha); 6. Haefeli (Yamaha); 7. Meier (Kawasaki); 8. Streuli (Yamaha); 9. Landolt (Yamaha). 9 finishers.

October 22nd - Lausitz - Germany
Race I: 1. Linke (D, Suzuki); 2. Stamm (Kawasaki); 3. Leibundgut (Honda); 4. Hagmann (Yamaha); 5. Kopp (D, Yamaha); 6. Häfeli (Yamaha); 7. Schmid (Yamaha); 8. Wehran (D, Kawasaki); 9. Keist (Yamaha); 10. Alma (Yamaha).
Race II: 1. Linke (D, Suzuki); 2. Stamm (Kawasaki); 3. Leibundgut (Honda); 4. Hagmann (Yamaha); 5. Häfeli (Yamaha); 6. Wehran (D, Kawasaki); 7. Lang (Suzuki); 8. Kopp (D, Yamaha); 9. Schmid (Yamaha); 10. Keist (Yamaha).

October 29th - Lédenon - France
Race I: 1. Stamm (Kawasaki); 2. Hagmann (Yamaha); 3. Devoyon (F, Yamaha); 4. Leibundgut (Honda); 5. Jenny (Yamaha); 6. Lang (Suzuki); 7. Keist (Yamaha); 8. Kopp (D, Yamaha); 9. Schmid (Yamaha); 10. Häfeli (Yamaha).
Race II: 1. Hagmann (Yamaha); 2. Stamm (Kawasaki); 3. Leibundgut (Honda); 4. Jenny (Yamaha); 5. Keist (Yamaha); 6. Lang (Suzuki); 7. Devoyon (F, Yamaha); 8. Häfeli (Yamaha); 9. Schmid (Yamaha); 10. Kopp (D, Yamaha).

FINAL CLASSIFICATION
1. Roman Stamm   (Kawasaki),   225
2. Daniel Leibundgut   (Honda),   201
3. Rolf Hagmann   (Yamaha),   165
4. Häfeli (Yamaha), 132; 5. Keist (Yamaha), 108; 6. Schmid (Yamaha), 101; 7. Portmann (Yamaha), 95; 8. Lang (Suzuki), 88; 9. Bantle (Yamaha), 77; 10. Alma (Yamaha), 68.

FINAL CLASSIFICATION MIXT CHAMPIONSHIP
1. Peter Krummenacher   (Honda),   111
2. Roman Stamm   (Kawasaki),   102
3. Daniel Leibundgut   (Honda),   82
4. Haefeli (Yamaha), 69; 5. Meier (Kawasaki), 44; 6. Portmann (Yamaha) and Keist (Yamaha), 40; 8. Hagmann (Yamaha), 34; 9. Lang (Suzuki), 33; 10. Schmid (Yamaha), 10.

Promosport

April 15th - Lédenon - France
Race I: 1. Keiser (Yamaha); 2. Demonsant (Yamaha); 3. Jantz (Suzuki); 4. Da. Maillard (Ducati); 5. Cosson (Yamaha); 6. Raschle (Kawasaki); 7. Zimmermann (Yamaha); 8. Egli (Kawasaki); 9. Hauser (Yamaha); 10. Grosjean (Suzuki).
Race II: 1. Jantz (Suzuki); 2. Keiser (Yamaha); 3. Da. Maillard (Ducati); 4. Demonsant (Yamaha); 5. Cosson (Yamaha); 6. Grosjean (Suzuki); 7. Egli (Kawasaki); 8. Raschle (Kawasaki); 9. Leemann (Kawasaki); 10. Hauser (Yamaha).

May 26th - Oschersleben - Germany
Race I: 1. Jantz (Suzuki); 2. Keiser (Yamaha); 3. Chevallier (Yamaha); 4. Grosjean (Suzuki); 5. Demonsant (Yamaha); 6. Zimmermann (Yamaha); 7. Gentile (Yamaha); 8. Erdin (Yamaha); 9. Dupraz (Honda); 10. Da. Maillard (Ducati).
Race II: 1. Keiser (Yamaha); 2. Jantz (Suzuki); 3. Demonsant (Yamaha); 4. Zimmermann (Yamaha); 5. Chevallier (Yamaha); 6. Raschle (Kawasaki); 7. Gentile (Yamaha); 8. Grosjean (Suzuki); 9. Erdin (Yamaha); 10. Ammann (Honda).

June 17th - Magny-Cours - France
Race I: 1. Jantz (Suzuki); 2. Raschle (Kawasaki); 3. Chevallier (Yamaha); 4. Zimmermann (Yamaha); 5. Demonsant (Yamaha); 6. Erdin (Yamaha); 7. Cosson (Suzuki); 8. Villiger (Yamaha); 9. Lehmann (Yamaha); 10. Egli (Kawasaki).
Race II: 1. Leemann (Kawasaki); 2. Grosjean (Suzuki); 3. Raschle (Kawasaki); 4. Chevallier (Yamaha); 5. Jantz (Suzuki); 6. Villiger (Yamaha); 7. Zimmermann (Yamaha); 8. Di. Maillard (Kawasaki); 9. Keiser (Yamaha); 10. Demonsant (Yamaha).

July 1st - Boécourt - La Caquerelle
Race I: 1. Da. Maillard (Ducati); 2. Hauser (Yamaha); 3. Curchod (Yamaha); 4. L. Papaux (Honda); 5. Mettraux (Ducati); 6. Di. Maillard (Kawasaki). 6 finishers.
Race II: 1. Da. Maillard (Ducati); 2. Hauser (Yamaha); 3. Mettraux (Ducati); 4. Kroug (Suzuki); 5. Curchod (Yamaha); 6. Di. Maillard (Kawasaki); 7. L. Papaux (Honda). 7 finishers.

July 15th - Châtel-Saint-Denis - Les Paccots
1. Da. Maillard (Ducati); 2. Hauser (Yamaha); 3. Di. Maillard (Kawasaki); 4. Kroug (Suzuki); 5. Dupraz (Honda); 6. L. Papaux (Honda); 7. Mettraux (Ducati); 8. Argand (Yamaha); 9. Lambercy (Suzuki); 10. Esposito (Yamaha).

August 12th - Magione - Italy
Race I: 1. Jantz (Suzuki); 2. Keiser (Yamaha); 3. Da. Maillard (Ducati); 4. Raschle (Kawasaki); 5. Grosjean (Suzuki); 6. Leemann (Kawasaki); 7. Dupraz (Honda); 8. Cosson (Suzuki); 9. Bürgi (Yamaha); 10. Erdin (Yamaha).
Race II: 1. Jantz (Suzuki); 2. Keiser (Yamaha); 3. Demonsant (Yamaha); 4. Raschle (Kawasaki); 5. Grosjean (Suzuki); 6. Villiger (Yamaha); 7. Lehmann (Yamaha); 8. Erdin (Yamaha); 9. Kroug (Suzuki); 10. Egli (Kawasaki).

August 26th - Zetzwil - Leutwil
1. Hauser (Yamaha); 2. Keiser (Yamaha); 3. Lehmann (Yamaha); 4. Bürgi (Yamaha); 5. Da. Maillard (Ducati); 6. Di. Maillard (Kawasaki); 7. Villiger (Yamaha); 8. Kroug (Suzuki); 9. D. Bigler (Honda); 10. R. Bigler (Suzuki).

October 22nd - Lausitz - Germany
Race I: 1. Jantz (Suzuki); 2. Keiser (Yamaha); 3. Demonsant (Yamaha); 4. Raschle (Kawasaki); 5. Leemann (Kawasaki); 6. Grosjean (Suzuki); 7. Cosson (Suzuki); 8. Villiger (Yamaha); 9. Da. Maillard (Ducati); 10. Brönnimann (Yamaha).
Race II: 1. Jantz (Suzuki); 2. Keiser (Yamaha); 3. Raschle (Kawasaki); 4. Demonsant (Yamaha); 5. Grosjean (Suzuki); 6. Cosson (Yamaha); 7. Villiger (Yamaha); 8. Lehmann (Yamaha); 9. Da. Maillard (Ducati); 10. Egli (Kawasaki).

October 29th - Lédenon - France
Race I: 1. Keiser (Yamaha); 2. Demonsant (Yamaha); 3. Raschle (Kawasaki); 4. Cosson (Yamaha); 5. Da. Maillard (Ducati); 6. Jantz (Suzuki); 7. Villiger (Yamaha); 8. Bantli (Suzuki); 9. Egli (Kawasaki); 10. Leemann (Kawasaki).
Race II: 1. Da. Maillard (Ducati); 2. Raschle (Kawasaki); 3. Cosson (Suzuki); 4. Keiser (Yamaha); 5. Jantz (Suzuki); 6. Villiger (Yamaha); 7. Bantli (Suzuki); 8. Kroug (Suzuki); 9. Egli (Kawasaki); 10. Lehmann (Yamaha).

FINAL CLASSIFICATION
1. Roger Jantz (Suzuki), 243
2. Ruedi Keiser (Yamaha), 215
3. Roman Raschle (Kawasaki), 155
4. Demonsant (Yamaha); 5. Grosjean (Suzuki), 106; 6. Da. Maillard (Ducati), 104; 7. Cosson (Suzuki), 91; 8. Villiger (Yamaha), 75; 9. Leemann (Kawasaki), 68; 10. Egli (Kawasaki), 62.

FINAL CLASSIFICATION MIXT CHAMPIONSHIP
1. Daniel Maillard (Ducati), 115
2. Andreas Hauser (Yamaha), 98
3. Ruedi Keiser (Yamaha), 65
4. Di. Maillard (Kawasaki), 46; 5. Jantz (Suzuki), 41; 6. Kroug (Suzuki), 39; 7. Metraux (Ducati), 36; 8. Demonsant (Yamaha), 33; 9. L. Papaux (Honda), 32; 10. Curchod (Yamaha), 27.